THE
NATURE OF
REMEMBERING

THE
NATURE OF
REMEMBERING

ESSAYS IN HONOR OF ROBERT G. CROWDER

EDITED BY HENRY L. ROEDIGER III, JAMES S. NAIRNE,
IAN NEATH, AND AIMÉE M. SURPRENANT

AMERICAN PSYCHOLOGICAL ASSOCIATION
WASHINGTON, DC

Published by
American Psychological Association
750 First Street, NE
Washington, DC 20002

Copies may be ordered from
APA Order Department
P.O. Box 92984
Washington, DC 20090-2984

In the U.K., Europe, Africa, and the Middle East, copies may be ordered from
American Psychological Association
3 Henrietta Street
Covent Garden, London
WC2E 8LU England

Typeset in Berkeley Book by AGS, White Plains, MD

Printer: Edwards Brothers, Ann Arbor, MI
Dust jacket designer: NiDesign, Baltimore, MD
Technical/Production Editor: Amy J. Clarke

The opinions and statements published are the responsibility of the authors, and such opinions and statements do not necessarily represent the policies of the American Psychological Association.

Library of Congress Cataloging-in-Publication Data
The nature of remembering : essays in honor of Robert G. Crowder / edited by Henry L. Roediger, III . . . [et al.].—1st ed.
    p. cm. — (Science conference series)
    Proceedings of a conference held June 11–12, 1999, at Yale University, New Haven, CT.
    Includes bibliographical references and index.
    ISBN 1-55798-750-5 (cb : acid-free paper).
    1. Memory—Congresses.   I. Crowder, Robert G. II. Roediger, Henry L. III. Series
    BF371.N375   2001
    153.1'2—dc21   00-060599

British Library Cataloguing-in-Publication Data
A CIP record is available from the British Library.

Printed in the United States of America
First Edition

APA Science Volumes

v

APA Decade of Behavior Volumes

Contents

Contributors

David A. Balota, PhD, Department of Psychology, Washington University, St. Louis, MO

Mahzarin R. Banaji, PhD, Department of Psychology, Yale University, New Haven, CT

Robert A. Bjork, PhD, Department of Psychology, University of California, Los Angeles

Kara Bopp, MA, Department of Psychology, Syracuse University, Syracuse, NY

Nelson Cowan, PhD, Department of Psychology, University of Missouri—Columbia

Fergus I. M. Craik, PhD, Department of Psychology and Rotman Research Institute, Baycrest Centre for Geriatric Care, University of Toronto, Toronto, Ontario, Canada

Randall W. Engle, PhD, School of Psychology, Georgia Institute of Technology, Atlanta

Monica L. Freedman, MA, Psychology Department, Rice University, Houston, TX

Arthur M. Glenberg, PhD, Department of Psychology, University of Wisconsin, Madison

Robert L. Greene, PhD, Department of Psychology, Case Western Reserve University, Cleveland, OH

Alice F. Healy, PhD, Department of Psychology, University of Colorado, Boulder

Sandra Hessels, BA, Department of Psychology, Washington University, St. Louis, MO

Larry L. Jacoby, PhD, Department of Psychology, Washington University, St. Louis, MO

Todd A. Kahan, PhD, Department of Psychology, University of Southern Mississippi, Hattiesburg

Roberta L. Klatzky, PhD, Department of Psychology, Carnegie Mellon University, Pittsburgh, PA

Susan J. Lederman, PhD, Department of Psychology, Queen's University, Kingston, Ontario, Canada

Randi C. Martin, PhD, Psychology Department, Rice University, Houston, TX

Bennet Murdock, PhD, Department of Psychology, University of Toronto, Toronto, Ontario, Canada

James S. Nairne, PhD, Department of Psychological Sciences, Purdue University, West Lafayette, IN

Ian Neath, PhD, Department of Psychological Sciences, Purdue University, West Lafayette, IN

James H. Neely, PhD, Department of Psychology, State University of New York at Albany

Lara Nugent, MA, Department of Psychology, University of Missouri—Columbia

James T. Parker, MA, Department of Psychology, University of Colorado, Boulder

Henry L. Roediger III, PhD, Department of Psychology, Washington University, St. Louis, MO

Scott Saults, PhD, Department of Psychology, University of Missouri—Columbia

Michael A. Stadler, PhD, Department of Psychology, University of Missouri—Columbia

Aimée M. Surprenant, PhD, Department of Psychological Sciences, Purdue University, West Lafayette, IN

Endel Tulving, PhD, Department of Psychology and Rotman Research Institute, Baycrest Centre of Geriatric Care, University of Toronto, Toronto, Ontario, Canada

Michael J. Watkins, PhD, Psychology Department, Rice University, Houston, TX

Jason M. Watson, MA, Department of Psychology, Washington University, St. Louis, MO

(*From left to right*) *Back row*: James S. Nairne, Henry L. Roediger III, Fergus I. M. Craik, Larry L. Jacoby, Endel Tulving, Bennet Murdock, Ian Neath, Randall W. Engle, Arthur M. Glenberg, Robert L. Greene, James H. Neely, Robert A. Bjork, and Michael J. Watkins. *Front row*: Alice F. Healy, Mahzarin R. Banaji, Randi C. Martin, Roberta L. Klatzky, Allison R. Marks, Aimée M. Surprenant, Nelson Cowan, David A. Balota, and Jason M. Watson.

Foreword

In early 1988, the American Psychological Association (APA) Science Directorate began its sponsorship of what has become an exceptionally successful activity in support of psychological science—the APA Scientific Conference program. This program has showcased some of the most important topics in psychological science, and the conference participants have included many leading figures in the field.

As we enter a new century, it seems fitting that we begin with a new face on this book series—that of the Decade of Behavior (DoB). The DoB is a major interdisciplinary initiative designed to promote the contributions of the behavioral and social sciences to address some of our most important societal challenges and will occur from 2000 to 2010. Although a major effort of the initiative will be related to informing the public about the contributions of these fields, other activities will be put into place to reach fellow scientists. Hence, the series that was the "APA Science Series" will be continued as the "Decade of Behavior Series." This represents one element in APA's efforts to promote the DoB initiative as one of its partner organizations.

Please note the DoB logo on the inside jacket flap and the full title page. We expect this logo will become a familiar sight over the next few years. For additional information about DoB, please visit http://www.decadeofbehavior.org.

As part of the sponsorship agreement with APA, conference organizers commit themselves not only to the conference itself but also to editing a scholarly volume that results from the meeting. This book is such a volume. Over the course of the past 12 years, we have partnered with 44 universities to sponsor 60 conferences on a variety of topics of interest to psychological scientists. The APA Science Directorate looks forward to continuing this program and to sponsoring other conferences in the years ahead.

We are pleased that this important contribution to the literature was supported in part by the Scientific Conferences program. Congratulations to the editors and contributors on their sterling effort.

Richard McCarty, PhD Virginia E. Holt
Executive Director for Science *Assistant Executive Director
for Science*

Preface

The Nature of Remembering: Essays in Honor of Robert G. Crowder, presents an overview on the state of knowledge in the experimental study of human memory. As the subtitle attests, it was written to honor Robert G. Crowder of Yale University, who had a long and distinguished career as a scholar, researcher, editor, textbook author, and leader in the field of cognitive psychology. All of the authors had a personal connection with Bob Crowder as a colleague, a student, a mentor, or a friend. The chapters both honor him and provide an overview of the state of their knowledge on critical topics in the psychology of memory.

In chapter 1, Henry Roediger III and Michael Stadler provide an overview of Bob Crowder's contributions to the field. They also describe and discuss the intellectual lineage, dating back to William James and John Dewey, in which Crowder worked. The following 18 chapters provide treatments of important topics in the field.

Chapters 2, 3, and 4 are, in one way or another, about episodic memory. Endel Tulving speculates on the origins of "autonoesis," or self-knowledge, which provides a defining characteristic of episodic memories. Larry Jacoby, Sandra Hessels, and Kara Bopp provide a new perspective on one of the oldest topics in the study of memory, namely, retroactive interference. The authors dissociate two forms of memory, recollection and accessibility bias, and show how their ideas can account for both classic and new findings in this critical area. Fergus Craik discusses how dividing attention during encoding and retrieval of material affects memory, with the surprise being that dividing attention during encoding has a much more powerful effect than does the same manipulation during a test. These three chapters provide interesting new insights into the operation of episodic memory.

In chapter 5, James Neely and Todd Kahan strike in a different direction. These authors explore the issue of whether semantic activation from reading a word is automatic (occurring without intention or effort). The research literature is conflicting on this point, and Neely and Kahan's review provides a careful analysis of this research and points the way to more methodologically secure experiments in the future. In chapter 6, Henry Roediger III, David Balota, and Jason Watson also explore the issue of activation in memory but in terms of how activation can create false episodic memories. They argue that certain types of false-memory phenomena can arise from spreading activation in semantic and lexical networks of associations. Chapter 7, by Mahzarin Banaji, is also about implicit phenomena of cognition, but she reports on her interesting work developing implicit measures of attitudes and the reaction of traditional social psychologists to this new approach. She contrasts the development of concepts of implicit memory and the reception of that body of work within cognitive psychology to the reaction by some social psychologists to work on implicit attitudes.

In chapter 8, Bennet Murdock marks the shift to a new direction. Murdock considers one of the venerable topics in the psychology of memory, namely, the serial position curve. That people remember the first few and last few elements of a series better than those in the middle has been often noted but never satisfactorily explained. Murdock provides a new analysis of the serial position curve that should guide future research. Whereas most research showing serial position effects has been conducted with materials such as lists of digits or words, in chapter 9 Alice Healy and James Parker consider serial position curves for information that is serially ordered but naturally occurring. In particular, they examine the serial position curves for recall of the names of U.S. presidents and vice presidents and argue for a new interpretation of such findings.

One factor that strongly affects the recency part of the serial position curve in immediate recall is modality of presentation—auditory presentation leads to greater recall or recognition than does visual presentation for the last few items in a list. This fact, which occupied so much of Bob Crowder's research and theorizing, is the subject of Michael Watkins's chapter (10). Watkins proposes his "gentle law" of speech ascendancy as a contender to understand the effect but uses the chapter as another chance to thunder against the "tyranny of reified memory." As always, his writing is interesting and provocative. Robert Bjork is also concerned with issues of time and position in chapter 11, starting with his research with William Whitten, who obtained remarkably regular serial position effects in the "through-list distractor paradigm" in the mid-1970s. The pursuit of understanding the distractor paradigm leads to fundamental and surprising insights about memory, which Bjork explains with his "new theory of disuse."

Chapter 12, by Roberta Klatzky and Susan Lederman, is also about modality of information, but this time the sense is touch. They describe ways in which information gathered by skin senses is unique and held in a specific fashion. Tactile information cannot be easily represented by other formats, such as those used to represent information gathered by other sensory–perceptual systems.

In chapter 13, returning to the issue of sound and speech, Ian Neath and Aimée Surprenant compare the effects of irrelevant speech and irrelevant sounds on memory tasks and, contrary to prior research, show that differences can be obtained between these two classes of events. Robert Greene's chapter 14 concerns a problem that was the subject of Bob Crowder's first scientific article, with Arthur Melton, in 1965, namely, the Ranschburg effect. This effect is observed in serial recall when an element of a list is repeated and, curiously, the repeated item is more poorly remembered than if a new item had been placed in that spot. Greene's new research implicates response inhibition as a probable cause of the effect and relates the Ranschburg effect to the response prefix effect, another topic that Crowder studied.

The next four chapters are in one way or another all concerned with short-term memory processes. In chapter 15, James Nairne provides a functional analysis of primary memory, emphasizing both compatibility of cues with stored traces and the distinctiveness of the representations themselves. His observations also have important implications for the understanding of long-term memory processes. In chapter 16, Randall Engle asks the fundamental question, "What is the capacity of working memory?" He considers ways in which this question has been addressed and concludes that the tasks used to measure working memory do measure the same core concept. Furthermore, working memory capacity seems related to fluid intelligence and is different from just holding information in a short-term store. In chapter 17, Nelson Cowan, Scott Saults, and Lara Nugent examine the hoary issue of forgetting over short time periods. They show that it is important to distinguish effects due to absolute amounts of time from those due to relative amounts of time. In chapter 18, Randi Martin and Monica Freedman provide a neuropsychological analysis of working memory capacity, addressing differences between input and output processes and showing how these might represent separate capacities. These four chapters on short-term memory processes provide state-of-the-art expositions on this critical concept in the study of human memory.

Like Bob Crowder, Arthur M. Glenberg, the author of chapter 19, received his PhD with Arthur Melton at Yale University. Glenberg considers the implications of the study of memory for using (and studying) language as well as the converse relation. He addresses many issues not typically considered in mainstream memory research and, therefore, provides a fitting capstone for the volume.

The Nature of Remembering grew out of a conference held at Yale University on June 11 and 12, 1999. Julie Crowder opened the event with touching personal remarks about how much she and Bob, as well as their children Bruce, Edward, and Lory, appreciated the event. Unfortunately, Bob Crowder was too ill to attend the conference. He died 13 months later, on July 27, 2000. He will be sorely missed by his students, collaborators, friends, and colleagues. Bob Crowder greatly furthered our understanding of the nature of remembering. We, the editors and authors of this volume, are pleased to honor his important contributions to the field by the work herein.

Acknowledgments

The festschrift conference in honor of Robert Crowder was generously sponsored by a grant from the Science Directorate of the American Psychological Association (APA), without which the conference would not have been possible. We greatly appreciate the support of APA. In addition, the Department of Psychology at Yale University generously supported the conference; special thanks also go to Alan Kazdin, chair of the Psychology Department at Yale, for his help and for the aid of his staff, particularly Ann Guarino. The Department of Psychology at Washington University in St. Louis also provided financial support for the conference. Marvin Chun and Mahzarin Banaji served as local organizers at Yale, and we appreciate their hard work. In addition, many Yale graduate students helped with audiovisual needs, videotaping the event, refreshments, and the myriad other chores that must be completed to have a conference run successfully. We are grateful to Adam Anderson, Amy Ciaschini, Martin Dennis, Emily Hsu, Yuhong Jiang, Kevin O'Connor, Ingrid Olson, Jennifer Pardo, Leon Rozenblit, Katie Shobe, and Heidi Wenk for generously spending their time to help make the conference a success. Production of this volume was made possible by the skilled professionals in APA's Books Department. We thank Mary Lynn Skutley (manager of acquisitions and development), Vanessa Downing (project editor), Judy Nemes (development editor), and Amy Clarke (production editor). The outstanding individuals at APA Books greatly helped to make this volume a reality.

THE
NATURE OF
REMEMBERING

John M. Yanson '99

Robert Crowder

CHAPTER 1

Robert G. Crowder and His Intellectual Heritage

Henry L. Roediger III
Michael A. Stadler

This chapter reviews the career of Robert G. Crowder, in whose honor this book was conceived. We describe some of the basic facts of his career, tell of his accomplishments and honors, describe his approach to scientific psychology, and discuss the intellectual tradition in which he worked. It is abundantly clear to us in undertaking this task how inadequate our means are to accomplish these goals. To capture in a few pages the power and sustained contributions of a career that spans nearly 40 years is impossible. We can only hope to provide a glimmer of Bob Crowder's many accomplishments and to sketch the ways that he inspired the authors of this volume (colleagues, friends, and students) and the entire field of cognitive psychology, in which he played so large a role. Any inadequacies in our treatment lie with us. The first author, one of Crowder's students, provided the remarks about his career. The second author, a grandstudent of Crowder through the first author, was more responsible for the intellectual genealogy provided.

Education

Robert Crowder received his undergraduate and graduate degrees from the University of Michigan. He seemed destined for a distinguished career even as an undergraduate, graduating Phi Beta Kappa and with high honors in psychology in 1960. In 1960–1961, he received a Fulbright Fellowship to study in France, with his instruction in French. He returned to Michigan in 1961 and received his PhD in 1965, working with Arthur W. Melton. After graduation, Crowder immediately accepted an assistant professor position at Yale University and spent his entire academic career at that institution, although he spent time at various other places, such as the Center for Advanced Study in the Behavioral Sciences in Palo Alto, California, while on leave from Yale.

Crowder's time at Michigan was an exciting one. The Human Performance Center was booming, a hotbed of exciting activity in the field of human experimental psychology, which would soon be christened "cognitive psychology" on the 1967 publication of Ulric Neisser's great book by that name. Bob attended Michigan with many other students who would also go on to outstanding careers. Irving Biederman, Don Dewsbury, Howard Egeth, Michael Posner, Edward Smith, Bob Sorkin, and Amos Tversky, among others, were students at Michigan in the same era as Crowder.

Topics of Investigation at Yale

After arrival at Yale, Crowder worked on problems of learning and memory in both rats and humans. His first published article, with Melton in 1965, was on the Ranschburg effect (Crowder & Melton, 1965; see chapter 14 in this volume for the latest on this topic). His dissertation (Crowder, 1967b) was published in the *Journal of Verbal Learning and Verbal Behavior* and shows how measurement of interpolated task performance in the Brown–Peterson (Brown, 1958; Peterson & Peterson, 1959) short-term memory paradigm could be used to infer covert rehearsal of list items in that task. In the same year, he published a study on proactive and retroactive interference in rats (Crowder, 1967a).

In retrospect, Crowder's first landmark publication was the one with John Morton on precategorical acoustic storage (PAS) in 1969 (Crowder & Morton, 1969). In that article, they described evidence supporting the concept of a brief auditory memory system that held information before it was categorized. They used the concept to explain both the modality effect in serial recall (superior recall of auditory to visual items) and its location (only for the last few items presented). The stimulus suffix effect, essentially conceived as a backward masking of the auditory information, also fit nicely into the story. A stimulus suffix is a redundant element presented at the end of a list of items that, in the case of auditory information, wipes out the recency effect and makes the serial position curve resemble that obtained with visual presentation. In the early 1970s, Crowder and his colleagues published a series of outstanding papers that provided many tests of the ideas proposed in 1969, with PAS theory riding high as an explanation of the modality effect, suffix effect, and related phenomena (e.g., see Morton, Crowder, & Prussin, 1971). The study of auditory perception of words led naturally to an interest in speech perception, and in many studies throughout his career, Crowder collaborated with members of the Haskins Laboratories, which is a neighbor of Yale in New Haven, CT.

Crowder's preoccupation with auditory cognition and his own personal interest in music led him to the study of psychomusicology, a topic on which he continued to publish throughout his career. To some psychologists, this field seems like an esoteric one. However, Crowder always made a strong case for its central importance to psychology. The production and appreciation of music permeate all cultures.

People respond to music on many levels. Just as the study of language provides one kind of light on the workings of the mind, so does the study of music. Bob Crowder published on many different topics within the psychology of music over the years— the perception of the major–minor distinction, mental imagery for music, and other topics. (A complete curriculum vita appears at the end of this book, including a chronological list of all of his published work.)

The study of audition led naturally to the study of time and how it is interwoven into memories. Whereas visual objects are usually spread out in space, auditory events are typically spread out in time (or at least time of occurrence is the principal feature in many cases). Collaborating primarily with Robert Greene and Ian Neath, Crowder published many articles in the 1980s and 1990s on distinctiveness of time as a critical dimension to memory. He also pioneered methods of studying these issues, such as the irregular list technique (Crowder & Greene, 1987). The study of serial position effects and time effects occupied much of his professional career (see the vita at the end of this book.)

Bob Crowder published on many other topics as well. The items mentioned above provide some highlights of his research career. A few other high points are worth mentioning. Crowder (1982a) published an influential article titled "The Demise of Short-Term Memory" that attracted much attention, focused the energies of the proponents of the concept, and led to the re-evaluation of the very idea of short-term memory. Somewhat later, with Mahzarin Banaji (Banaji & Crowder, 1989), he took on the growing "everyday memory movement" that, in the hands of some of its proponents, argues that psychologists interested in memory should close up their labs and go into the real world and use a more ethological approach to the study of memory. Researchers in this area have claimed that nothing much of importance had been, or could be, learned from laboratory studies of remembering (Neisser, 1978). Some mainstream memory researchers were won over by these claims, whereas most others were willing to ignore the everyday memory movement as a fad that would soon pass. Banaji and Crowder engaged its proponents directly, arguing that unless one can gain control of a situation to study cause and effect relations, no meaningful scientific inquiry could proceed. The debate grew contentious at times, although Banaji and Crowder's reply from the experimental camp simply echoed the strident nature of Neisser's (1978) original salvo. In retrospect, the interchanges seem to have had mutually beneficial effects for the field. The everyday memory researchers have tightened their procedures to permit stronger conclusions, and the experimentalists have broadened their purview to include more issues and phenomena than previously considered.

Books and Chapters

The preceding material sketched some of Bob Crowder's primary research efforts published in the format of journal articles. However, he is also well known for his other forms of publication. Chief among these is his 1976 book *Principles of Learning and Memory*. This text provided a wonderful, thorough overview of the greater part of the field of human learning and memory as it stood in that day. Following the books by McGeoch (1942) and its revision (McGeoch & Irion, 1952), Crowder's text was one of the few treating the topic with a complexity suitable for graduate student instruction. Nothing like it has been published since.

Crowder also published a well-received book on reading, *The Psychology of Reading: An Introduction* (Crowder, 1982b), which was translated into Italian and Spanish and revised by Richard Wagner, who became a coauthor (Crowder & Wagner, 1992). An edited volume on memory for odors was also published in 1995 in collaboration with Frank Schab (Schab & Crowder).

Bob Crowder was a frequent invitee to conferences, which resulted in edited volumes. He has many masterful chapters to his credit in these conference volumes. The first appeared in 1972 on "Visual and Auditory Memory" (which documented the accumulating evidence for PAS). Another important one, with Ian Neath (Crowder & Neath, 1991), introduced "the microscope metaphor" for scrutinizing issues of memory. His 1993 chapter, "Systems and Principles in Memory Theory: Another Critique of Pure Memory," also made a powerful contribution. Bob's chapters, like all his writings, are clear and engaging, with many interesting points and clever turns of phrase.

Honors, Awards, and Service

Although Bob Crowder was unusually modest for so eminent a scholar, honors sought him out, even if he did not seek them. Just out of high school he won the Oreon E. Scott Freshman Scholarship Award at Michigan and, as already noted, he won a Fulbright Fellowship to study in France for a year. Later in life he was elected to the Governing Board of the Psychonomic Society and served on its Publications Committee. He also edited *Memory & Cognition* for the society, and his action letters were models of thoughtfulness. His letters frequently made original contributions rather than merely summarizing reviewers' opinions. He enjoyed a year as a Fellow at the Center for Advanced Study in the Behavioral Sciences in Palo Alto and was elected to Fellow status of both the American Psychological Association and the American Psychological Society. Finally, he was elected to the Society of Experimental Psychologists, which is one of the highest honors of the field.

Besides his scholarly contributions, Bob Crowder helped carry on much of the department's business at Yale. He served as director of graduate studies for 3 years and director of undergraduate studies for a remarkable 13 years, providing advice to generations of Yale students. He even served as acting chair for 1 year at Yale but was relieved to be through with the job when the time passed.

The Functionalist Tradition

Bob Crowder was trained in the functionalist tradition of American psychology, founded in Chicago by James Rowland Angell (1869–1949). The functionalist tradition was, of course, rather amorphous, not a tight and tidy school with strongly held beliefs among its adherents. In Crowder's hands, the functionalist tradition manifested itself in clear theoretical statements that made testable predictions. His research was marked by straightforward (and often clever) experimental designs that were not overly complex or precious. His designs and experiments, the reporting of results, and his writing were marked by clarity rarely found in our field. The theories were verbally stated rather than cast in a mathematical form, but permitted predictions that could be falsified. Indeed, Crowder seemed to delight in designing experiments that would falsify predictions of his own theories.

The theory of precategorical acoustic storage provides a case in point. In the early 1970s, the theory seemed almost unassailable. The modality effect and the suffix effect, with their locations at the end of the list, seemed to provide powerful converging operations supporting the main tenets of the theory. Experiment after experiment conducted by Crowder and his collaborators at Yale and the Haskins Laboratories rolled in to support the theory: the "three-eared man" analog to the Sperling partial-report technique (Darwin, Turvey, & Crowder, 1972), the work showing differences between vowels and consonants in echoic memory (Crowder, 1971, 1973), and other aspects of the suffix effect (e.g., Morton et al., 1971) all fit the theory well.

Later, in the 1970s and early 1980s, evidence contrary to the PAS theory came in, a trickle at first but then a flood. The research on recall of lip-read and mouthed stimuli called the acoustic aspects of PAS into question because these types of silent presentation could mimic effects usually attributed to auditory presentation (Spoehr & Corin, 1978). Aspects of the suffix effect also came into question, such as finding long-delayed suffix effects (Watkins & Todres, 1980). The finding that the same physical suffix could have greater or lesser effects on recall of recent items called into question the designation of the effect as occurring precategorically (Ayres, Jonides, Reitman, Egan, & Howard, 1979). Characteristically, Crowder himself added tellingly to the evidence against his own theory, replicating some findings to be sure they were true, as well as adding additional critical observations of his own. Crowder also came to doubt the box-and-arrow models of memory that had dominated his thinking at one point—the idea of memory stores—and became inclined to a more procedural view of memory during the 1980s and 1990s (e.g., Crowder, 1993).

In recent years, Crowder prided himself on having produced (with Morton) a theory that was well defined enough to have (a) gained strong evidence in its favor but then (b) ultimately been rejected on the basis of remarkable new discoveries (those mentioned in the previous paragraph) that were not anticipated by (and could not be encompassed by) their theory. At the same time, Bob delighted in saying that he was wrong on all three counts: The memory phenomena he studied turned out to be not precategorical, not strictly acoustic, and not even storage.

The Intellectual Heritage

Crowder's scientific style was acquired from his mentor, Arthur Melton (1906–1978), whose own intellectual lineage could be traced back to John Dewey (1859–1952) and William James (1842–1910). (Figure 1.1 portrays Crowder's intellectual family tree.) It is worth spending a few pages on his predecessors because the Yale connections are much in evidence among his mentors.

FIGURE 1.1

Robert G. Crowder's intellectual predecessors.

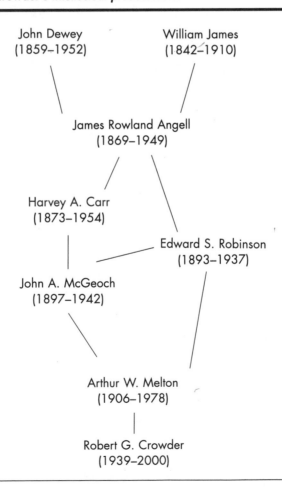

John Dewey
(1859–1952)

William James
(1842–1910)

James Rowland Angell
(1869–1949)

Harvey A. Carr
(1873–1954)

Edward S. Robinson
(1893–1937)

John A. McGeoch
(1897–1942)

Arthur W. Melton
(1906–1978)

Robert G. Crowder
(1939–2000)

Arthur Melton received a BA degree from Washington University in 1926, where he worked with John A. McGeoch (1897–1942); he then went to Yale to work with E. S. Robinson (1893–1937), receiving his PhD in 1932. Both mentors influenced Melton, but the topics and style of his later publications seem more similar to those of McGeoch, who was one of the founders of interference theory, than to those of Robinson (who died tragically just after Melton received his PhD). Melton published influential work on interference theory in the 1940s (e.g., Melton & Irwin, 1940, identified "factor X"—later identified as unlearning—as a source of retroactive interference). Crowder was devoted to Melton and kept his picture on his desk.

Melton rose to prominence because of his imposing style as much as for his research. He was a beacon of clear thinking and good judgment and held many important positions. He served as editor of the *Journal of Experimental Psychology* for 13 years, from 1950 through 1962, when it was one of only two or three significant publication outlets available to experimental psychologists. Melton was elected president of two divisions of the American Psychological Association (Experimental and Military), chair of the Governing Board of the Psychonomic Society, and president of the Midwestern Psychological Association. He was elected to the National Academy of Sciences, an honor few psychologists attain.

In Melton's obituary, Benton Underwood (1979), another of Melton's former students, wrote

> all these honors (and others) came to a man who in fact had published a relatively small number of papers, only a few of which were primarily reports of his own research. The fact is that Art Melton had trouble taking that final step in the research enterprise, that step of preparing a final report of the experiments completed. As late as 1960 he was studying results of experiments he had conducted in the late 1930s and early 1940s. . . . I do not mean to give the impression that Melton conducted many studies that were not published. In fact, after World War II, he did not carry out a large number of investigations. This may have been for the good of the discipline, because it allowed him time to concentrate on the use of his superb synthesizing skills. (p. 1172)

How did Melton then become so towering a figure in the field? He was noted for his wise summary statements on several matters (e.g., Melton, 1963, 1970), but he also attracted and trained great students. After leaving Yale, he became chair of the Psychology Department at the University of Missouri at the tender age of 29. He created an excellent master's program there, and many students left, after a few years of Melton's tutelage, to continue their studies elsewhere. Several of these former students (Arthur Irion, Alvin Liberman, David McClelland, Benton Underwood) went on to illustrious careers, propelled in part by Melton's master's program at Missouri.

In commenting on the University of Missouri program, Underwood (1979) provided insight into what working with Melton was like, although perhaps Melton had mellowed by the time Crowder was his student many years later:

> It became apparent that Art Melton made the program, and he attracted students who developed a fierce loyalty to him. Melton was a powerful teacher inside and outside the classroom. By some means, which remain something of a mystery, he made a student feel that experimental psychology was the most important profession in the world. But at the same time, it was patent that to become a member of this profession the student must be prepared to sacrifice. In particular, the student had to be prepared to stretch his or her mind to a point that had previously seemed unattainable. There was no compromise on this. For example, I enrolled as a graduate student with a very weak record as an undergraduate. At the first meeting of Melton's class in the fall term I was assigned the task of preparing a report on Boring's *Physical Dimensions of Consciousness* [1933]. I barely survived this introduction to Melton's program. (p. 1171)

Both of Melton's mentors were important figures in their own right. McGeoch received his PhD from Harvey Carr in the heyday of functionalism at the University of Chicago. His brief career was peripatetic because he left Washington University after only a few years to become chair at the University of Arkansas (1928–1930) but departed for Missouri, serving as chair for 5 years (1930–1935). (Melton succeeded him.) McGeoch went to Wesleyan in 1939 and then finally to the University of Iowa in 1939, where he died of a stroke in 1942 at age 45. McGeoch served as editor of *Psychological Bulletin* from 1935 until his death, was elected to the Society of Experimental Psychologists, and served as president of the Eastern Psychological Association. Perhaps his most famous article was "Forgetting and the Law of Disuse" in 1932, in which he undermined the decay theory of forgetting and championed retroactive interference as the primary cause of forgetting. Another notable accomplishment was his 1942 volume *The Psychology of Human Learning*, completed just before his death. This book was a standard text of the subject, and Crowder's *Principles of Learning and Memory* (1976) is similar in many ways in that it is a high level, synthetic graduate text. So McGeoch's influence lived on in Crowder's text.

E. S. Robinson, Melton's other mentor at Yale, also had a meteoric career cut short by tragedy. Like McGeoch, he got his PhD at Chicago (working with James Rowland Angell) in 1920. He taught briefly at Yale before returning to Chicago, then leaving for Harvard, and finally settling back in at Yale at age 34. Robinson had wide-ranging interests beyond basic experimental psychology, including social psychology and psychology and law. He served as editor of the *American Journal of Psychology*, *Journal of Social Psychology*, and *Psychological Bulletin*. Within the study of learning and memory, Robinson's memory lives in at least two ways. One is the Skaggs–Robinson hypothesis, which argues that retention of experience occurs according to a particular relation of similarity between the primary recall task and interpolated tasks. Efficiency of recall is hypothesized to be great when two tasks are highly similar or highly dissimilar but an interpolated task intermediate in similarity causes interference (see Robinson, 1927). Robinson's other main contribution to the field is his 1932 book *Association Theory Today*, in which he was more concerned with issues of animal conditioning than of human learning and memory, in keeping with the times.

Robinson died as a result of injuries from an accident at Yale. He was walking across campus one winter day when a bicyclist struck him hard. He fell, hit his head, and died of brain injuries two days later, never regaining consciousness. James Rowland Angell had been his mentor at Chicago and colleague at Yale, where Angell was president during Robinson's time there. He began his obituary of Robinson as follows:

> It is difficult to speak with restraint of Edward Stevens Robinson, whose sudden and untimely death on February twenty-seventh last brought a shock of deep grief to scores of his friends. It is peculiarly difficult for me to do this, for he had been a favorite student of mine at Chicago twenty years ago. I had followed his career with almost parental affection and interest, and I had been grateful for his companionship as a colleague at Yale for ten happy and fruitful years. To see him needlessly cut down in the full flower of his strength and while he was still steadily developing was a devastating experience. Following, as it did, so shortly after the equally premature death of his gifted wife, Florence Richardson Robinson, another of my pupils, it left me stunned and utterly dismayed. (Angell, 1937, p. 801)

Returning to the genealogy, Harvey Carr, who was McGeoch's mentor, received his PhD from Chicago under Angell. The academic job market was apparently tight (some things do not change over the years), so he taught high school in Texas for 1 year. He later wrote

> upon graduating in 1905, only two positions were open and I failed to land them. It was a discouraging summer, and through a friend I finally secured a high school position in Texas [where] this Yankee from the North was assigned two classes in the history of the Civil War. (Carr, 1936, p. 78)

He quickly left for a position at the Pratt Institute. After being there only 2 years, he was lured back to Chicago in 1908 to replace John B. Watson, who had just left for Johns Hopkins University. Carr had a long, distinguished career at Chicago and served as chair for 16 years (1922–1938), during which time the program produced 130 PhD graduates. Carr led the functionalists during those years. Boring (1950) commented in *A History of Experimental Psychology* that "Carr took, essentially, the point of view of this book—that functional psychology *is* American psychology" (p. 559).

James Rowland Angell was mentor to both Carr and Robinson. He firmly established the University of Chicago as the capital of the functional approach, and Chicago produced 50 doctorate graduates in psychology during Angell's time there (1884–1918), including John B. Watson and Walter S. Hunter. Angell provided an early and clear statement of the functional approach in his 1906 Presidential Address to the American Psychological Association, "The Province of Functional Psychology," which appeared in *Psychological Review* (1907). Angell was a leading light in American psychology, and his administrative talents were great. He became dean at the University of Chicago and was its acting president for 1 year. After World War I, he became chairman of the National Research Council and, in 1920, president of the Carnegie Corporation. In 1921, he was selected to be president of Yale University, a post he held for 16 years. It was during this time, and under Angell's strong leadership, that Yale enhanced its position as one of the world's premier universities. He greatly aided psychology at Yale. The Institute of Psychology was founded in 1921, the ambitious Institute of Human Relations was established in 1929, and Angell was instrumental in having the International Congress of Psychology convene at Yale in 1929. After leaving Yale, Angell worked at the National Broadcasting Corporation.

Angell worked with both John Dewey (at Michigan before he went to Chicago) and William James at Harvard. He received master's degrees under both mentors, which is about as impressive a pedigree as one might hope for. A curious fact, however, is that Angell never received a PhD in psychology. He came close, working with the philosopher Hans Vaihinger and the psychologist Benno Erdmann in Germany. Boring (1950) addressed the issue:

> The fact that James R. Angell never earned a Ph.D. did not seem to matter very much. He was a leader of thought, a university professor, a university president, and eventually was found in possession of 21 L.L.D.s, one Litt. D and one honorary Ph.D. It is extremely unlikely that a Ph.D. received in course would have affected his capacities any more than did these later distinctions. The fact is that Angell almost got his Ph.D. from Benno Erdmann in Halle, in 1893. Angell's thesis was accepted, subject to revision of its German style; but he would have had to remain at Halle without a stipend. He chose instead to return to America at Minnesota, where a position and a salary awaited him, a small salary but one large enough to enable him to marry. (p. 579)

In this time when many are asking what a person with only a master's degree in psychology can do, pointing to James Rowland Angell's career may be instructive. Of course, these are different times, and it is no longer possible to get master's degrees with William James and John Dewey.

We stop our genealogy of Robert Crowder's intellectual ancestors with William James and John Dewey and say little about them. Surely readers know of their distinction and contributions. The Crowder lineage has an auspicious beginning. Those of us who were his students and grand-students are proud to share it.

Of course, James and Dewey themselves had teachers and mentors. The first author of this chapter was surprised to learn, compliments of Endel Tulving, that one of William James's teachers in Switzerland, during his childhood, was Heinrich (German for Henry) Roediger. Allen (1967) wrote that James's father (Henry James, Sr.—the famous author was William's brother) enrolled three of his sons in "a boarding school, run by a German political exile named Achilles Heinrich Roediger" (p. 34). His father selected the school because few Americans were in the school and Henry, Sr., said "what he wanted most was for his boys to 'learn the languages'" (p. 34) that the other boys spoke. So although the first author was tempted to put "Henry Roediger" at the top of Figure 1.1, above James, the move might have seemed a bit extreme to most readers.

The functional tradition of James, Dewey, Angell, and others was brilliantly carried forward in the person of Robert Crowder. His research embodied the catholicity of spirit and interest in both basic and applied issues, which his intellectual ancestors promulgated. Crowder's students, both in the narrow sense of those who received PhDs under his direction and in the wider sense of those affected by him, his writing, and his editing, can be proud to carry forward in this functionalist tradition.

A Personal Note

We would like to end on a personal note, changing to the first-person voice of the first author: I entered graduate school at Yale in 1969 in the social psychology program. My undergraduate research had been concerned with human learning and memory, so I took Bob Crowder's course on Human Memory my first semester (reading Neisser's, 1967, *Cognitive Psychology* text as part of it) and the experience, literally, changed my life. I switched into the cognitive program shortly after that first semester, working on several projects with Bob Crowder, and continued with him (and Endel Tulving) throughout my graduate career.

For me, Robert Crowder was a perfect mentor. He had wide-ranging interests, even though his own research at that time was focused on short-term processes in auditory memory, the famous work related to the PAS theory. However, he delighted in thinking and reading about all topics in learning and memory (and beyond), and he was eager to advise students on whatever problems they chose to investigate. Bob was unfailingly helpful, never lost his temper (even when situations would have provoked most people to do so), and spent countless hours with his students. I would sometimes tell him about issues arising in other courses I was taking, and he would be fascinated. In particular, we had a long-running discussion (thanks to a great course I was taking with Dick Nisbett) on whether the concept of personality was valid. Did people really have personalities, or was the concept an attribution people made but with little concrete evidence for such traits? (Walter Mischel's, 1968, book *Personality and Assessment* was partly the impetus for the discussion.) During my years at Yale, Bob always attended not only the "Memory Lunch" and the cognitive colloquium series but also practically all the brown bags and colloquia in the department. Besides inherent interest in all these topics, Bob told me that he would often find that an issue in, say, social cognition and how scientists were thinking about that issue could influence his own work, even though it seemed, on the face of it, unrelated. The inquiring mind makes connections.

Now when his former students gather, we delight in telling each other stories of Bob's inquiring mind, his probing insights, and the generosity and helpfulness that he displayed to each of us during our times in graduate school and beyond.

Conclusion

Yale University has a long tradition of excellence in the study of learning and memory, both with humans and animals, to which Robert Crowder contributed over the past 35 years. Exhibit 1.1 is a list of Crowder's former PhD students— those who worked with him for most of their Yale years and others who he advised or served as chair of their dissertation committee. The records are not entirely clear in all cases, so some omissions from this list may have occurred.

The following chapters, many written by people listed in Exhibit 1.1, are intended to honor Robert Crowder for his fine achievements in experimental psychology, in general, and the study of human learning and memory, in particular. The authors contained herein comment on the specific influences Bob Crowder had on their careers.

EXHIBIT 1.1

Robert G. Crowder's PhD students

Marilyn J. Adler—1969	James S. Nairne—1981
Matthew H. Erdelyi—1969	Robert L. Greene—1984
Page Westcott—1969	Frank R. Schab—1989
Vicki P. Raeburn—1972	Lucinda De Witt—1989
Chao-Ming Cheng—1973	Mark A. Pitt—1989
Henry L. Roediger, III—1973	Ian Neath—1991
James H. Neely—1975	Aimée M. Surprenant—1992
Donald R. Rightmer—1975	Allison R. Marks—1994
William C. Wilkinson—1975	Heidi E. Wenk—1998

References

Allen, G. W. (1967). *William James: A biography.* New York: Viking.

Angell, J. R. (1907). The province of functional psychology. *Psychological Review, 14,* 61–91.

Angell, J. R. (1937). Edward Stevens Robinson (1893–1937). *Psychological Bulletin, 34,* 801–805.

Ayres, T. J., Jonides, J., Reitman, J. S., Egan, J. C., & Howard, D. A. (1979). Differing suffix effects for the same physical suffix. *Journal of Experimental Psychology: Human Learning and Memory, 5,* 315–321.

Banaji, M., & Crowder, R. G. (1989). The bankruptcy of everyday memory. *American Psychologist, 44*, 1185–1193.

Boring, E. G. (1933). *The physical dimensions of consciousness.* New York: Appleton-Century-Crofts.

Boring, E. G. (1950). *A history of experimental psychology.* New York: Appleton-Century-Crofts.

Brown, J. (1958). Some tests of the decay theory of immediate memory. *Quarterly Journal of Experimental Psychology, 10*, 12–21.

Carr, C. A. (1936). Harvey A. Carr. In C. Murchison (Ed.), *A history of psychology in autobiography* (Vol. 3, pp. 69–82). Worcester, MA: Clark University Press.

Crowder, R. G. (1967a). Proactive and retroactive inhibition in the retention of a T-maze habit in rats. *Journal of Experimental Psychology, 74*, 167–171.

Crowder, R. G. (1967b). Short-term retention for words with a perceptual-motor interpolated task. *Journal of Verbal Learning and Verbal Behavior, 6*, 753–761.

Crowder, R. G. (1971). The sound of vowels and consonants in immediate memory. *Journal of Verbal Learning and Verbal Behavior, 10*, 587–597.

Crowder, R. G. (1972). Visual and auditory memory. In J. F. Kavanagh & I. G. Mattingly (Eds.), *Language by ear and by eye: The relation between speech and learning to read* (pp. 251–276). Cambridge, MA: MIT Press.

Crowder, R. G. (1973). The sounds of speech in precategorical acoustic storage. *Journal of Experimental Psychology, 93*, 14–24.

Crowder, R. G. (1976). *Principles of learning and memory.* Hillsdale, NJ: Erlbaum.

Crowder, R. G. (1982a). The demise of short-term memory. *Acta Psychologica, 50*, 291–323.

Crowder, R. G. (1982b). *The psychology of reading: An introduction.* New York: Oxford University Press.

Crowder, R. G. (1993). Systems and principles in memory theory: Another critique of pure memory. In A. F. Collins, S. E. Gathercole, M. A. Conway, & P. E. Morris (Eds.), *Theories of memory* (pp. 130–161). East Sussex, NJ: Erlbaum.

Crowder, R. G., & Greene, R. L. (1987). On the remembrance of times past: The irregular list technique. *Journal of Experimental Psychology: General, 116*, 265–278.

Crowder, R. G., & Melton, A. W. (1965). The Ranschburg phenomenon: Failures of immediate recall correlated with repetition of elements within a series. *Psychonomic Science, 2*, 295–296.

Crowder, R. G., & Morton, J. (1969). Precategorical acoustic storage (PAS). *Perception & Psychophysics, 5*, 365–373.

Crowder, R. G., & Neath, I. (1991). The microscope metaphor in human memory. In W. E. Hockley & S. Lewandowsky (Eds.), *Relating theory and data: Essays on human memory in honor of Bennet B. Murdock* (pp. 111–126). Hillsdale, NJ: Erlbaum.

Crowder, R. G., & Wagner, R. K. (1992). *The psychology of reading: An introduction* (2nd ed.). New York: Oxford University Press.

Darwin, D. J., Turvey, M. T., & Crowder, R. G. (1972). An auditory analogue of the Sperling partial-report procedure. *Cognitive Psychology, 3*, 255–267.

McGeoch, J. A. (1932). Forgetting and the law of disuse. *Psychological Review, 39*, 352–370.

McGeoch, J. A. (1942). *The psychology of human learning.* New York: Longmans, Green.

McGeoch, J. A., & Irion, A. L. (1952). *The psychology of human learning* (2nd ed.). New York: Longmans, Green.

Melton, A. W. (1963). Implications of short-term memory for a general theory of memory. *Journal of Verbal Learning and Verbal Behavior, 2*, 1–21.

Melton, A. W. (1970). The situation with respect to the spacing of repetitions and memory. *Journal of Verbal Learning and Verbal Behavior, 9*, 596–606.

Melton, A. W., & Irwin, J. M. (1940). The influence of degree of interpolated learning on retroactive inhibition and the overt transfer of specific responses. *American Journal of Psychology, 53*, 173–203.

Mischel, W. (1968). *Personality and assessment.* New York: Wiley.

Morton, J., Crowder, R. G., & Prussin, H. A. (1971). Experiments with the stimulus suffix effect. *Journal of Experimental Psychology, 91*, 169–190.

Neisser, U. (1967). *Cognitive psychology.* New York: Appleton-Century-Crofts.

Neisser, U. (1978). Memory: What are the important questions? In M. M. Gruneberg, P. E. Morris, & R. N. Sykes (Eds.), *Practical aspects of memory* (pp. 3–24). London: Academic Press.

Peterson, L. R., & Peterson, M. J. (1959). Short-term retention of individual verbal items. *Journal of Experimental Psychology, 58*, 193–198.

Robinson, E. S. (1927). The "similarity" factor in retroaction. *American Journal of Psychology, 39*, 297–312.

Robinson, E. S. (1932). *Association theory today.* New York: Century.

Schab, F. R., & Crowder, R. G. (1995). *Memory for odors.* Mahwah, NJ: Erlbaum.

Spoehr, K. T., & Corin, W. J. (1978). The stimulus suffix effect as a memory coding phenomenon. *Memory & Cognition, 6*, 583–589.

Watkins, M. J., & Todres, A. K. (1980). Suffix effects manifest and concealed: Further evidence for a 20-second echo. *Journal of Verbal Learning and Behavior, 19*, 46–53.

Underwood, B. J. (1979). Arthur W. Melton (1906–1978). *American Psychologist, 34*, 1171–1173.

CHAPTER 2

Origin of Autonoesis in Episodic Memory

Endel Tulving

B ob Crowder and I shared a passionate interest in the experimental psychology of human memory throughout our professional careers, although we followed somewhat separate paths in pursuing the object of our love. These differences extended to both substance and style. Bob always took his science soberly and straight and treated it as a serious business in which rules and traditions that served us well in the past were observed and honored and not messed with. His way of doing memory science seemed to have been patterned after that of his great mentor, the late Arthur Melton. As for Melton, so for Crowder; psychology of learning and memory was "normal science" in Thomas Kuhn's terms, a matter of testing hypotheses within the accepted theoretical and methodological framework. Deviations from these "right" ways of thinking about problems and solving them are not welcome in normal science and are therefore to be resisted. I, however, have tended to think of the psychology of learning and memory as a preparadigmatic science in search of a paradigm. If so, the existing standards are to be viewed skeptically, as strictly temporary holding devices, sometimes even potential obstacles on the road to the goal of getting nature to reveal her secrets. Therefore, the standards are to be considered perennial candidates for modification and revision.

I professed the new science of "cognitive psychology" at Yale University in the early 1970s; so Bob was familiar with aspects of my less traditional work. One of these aspects had to do with recognition failure of recallable words, a phenomenon that Bob resolutely refused to believe until I demonstrated it to him personally, with him as the participant. Another aspect and central to the story here was the idea of episodic memory. This idea had arisen as an afterthought to a meeting at the University of Pittsburgh in March 1971. I wrote an essay about it in the volume of the conference papers (Tulving, 1972). The idea was that the "kind of memory" that had been studied in the psychological laboratories since Ebbinghaus was in

This research was supported by an endowment by Anne and Max Tanenbaum of research in cognitive neuroscience and by a grant from the Natural Sciences and Engineering Research Council of Canada.

some ways different from the "semantic memory" that several participants—Allan Collins and M. Ross Quilian, Walter Kintsch, and Peter Lindsay, Donald Norman, and David Rumelhart—had introduced at the Pittsburgh meeting. I called the "not-semantic" memory "episodic" and speculated about how the two differed.

Episodic Memory

The idea of episodic memory was frequently under discussion at the weekly "memory lunches" that Bob Crowder and I had organized at Yale. Bob quickly became an outspoken and persistent critic of the notion that episodic and semantic memories are different in any important way. Consequently, the discussions about episodic memory at our meetings were always spirited and sometimes even heated. The idea that the kind of memory involved in remembering things, such as what happened on one's recent trip to New York or what items had appeared in a recently seen list, is somehow different from the kind of memory involved in knowing that canaries have wings and lungs or that people imbibe lager in taverns was pure anathema to Bob. He thought it was not only "irresponsible" but also "sinful" (my terms, not his) to fractionate a perfect, beautifully coherent whole—long-term memory—into separate domains. The fact that in the 1972 article I referred to the two domains as memory "systems" only aggravated the error.

Bob played his role of the defender of the faith in his own inimitable fashion, of course: always polite, always sincere, always friendly, but always utterly unyielding. Because my position, taken objectively, was admittedly rather frail—there was nothing known at the time that could be considered to provide clear empirical support for the distinction between episodic and semantic memory—and Bob was very articulate; he usually came out on top in these debates. His authority in this matter was clearly revealed by the fact that none of the younger members of the group, mostly graduate students of psychology at Yale, either then or later, became an advocate of episodic memory. Indeed, one of them, Roddy Roediger, has remained one of the best-known critics and nonbelievers in the deeper significance of the distinction (Roediger, Buckner, & McDermott, 1999; Roediger, Weldon, & Challis, 1989).

I left Yale in 1974, returned to Toronto, and took my sinful ideas with me—thereby solving the problem of episodic memory at Yale. Elsewhere, the rebellion was treated in a way that today would be recognized as "politically correct": Many people adopted episodic and semantic memories as purely descriptive terms of two different categories of memory studies, namely, those with and those without specifically identified learning episodes, although refraining from much discussion about the reality of the distinction at any higher level.

This "heuristic" distinction between episodic and semantic memory served as a happy compromise until the publication of *Elements of Episodic Memory* (Tulving,

1983). In my book, I renewed the claims for separateness of episodic and semantic memory and made a more determined attempt to spell out the differences between the two systems. One aspect of the proposal was the idea that an important distinguishing characteristic of episodic memory is a unique "flavor" of the phenomenal "recollective experience" that accompanies retrieval from episodic memory. It represents a feeling of "warmth and intimacy," which William James wrote about in his *Principles of Psychology* (James, 1890), a feeling that is missing when one thinks about the knowledge in semantic memory. I suggested that because all researchers of laboratory studies of verbal learning and memory up to that time had only looked at the participants' behavior and had not been concerned with the flavor of the retrieval experience, the study of episodic memory had not yet begun.

These extended ideas about episodic memory did not sit well with the critics. A summary of the book, "Précis of Elements of Episodic Memory" (Tulving, 1984), was subjected to peer review in the journal *Behavioral and Brain Sciences*. In the course of the review, many shortcomings of the ideas in the book were discovered. Bob Crowder (1986) graciously agreed to write one of the reviews. In the first part, he provided a masterly overview of that section of *Elements of Episodic Memory* that deals with the distinction between episodic and semantic memory. Indeed, when I read it at the time, I felt that he might have been one of the very few readers of the book who had really understood what the new proposal was. Bob (Crowder, 1986), with his characteristic astuteness, went straight to the heart of the matter: "The heuristic distinction between episodic and semantic memory is now so widely accepted, it is easy to get well into the book before realizing that Tulving proposes here a radical new focus of episodic memory" (p. 566). This radical new focus was the idea, precisely put by Bob, that the "subjective experience of having a past event from one's life projected into the present is not just an additional criterion for defining episodic memory, it is the controlling definition of episodic memory" (p. 566).

Then after having precisely located the foreign intruder in the body psychologic, Bob, with the exquisite skill of a surgeon, proceeded to dissect the evidence that I had used in arguing the case for the distinction and the role of experience. When he had finished, there was little left of the episodic–semantic duality—just isolated bits and pieces of trivia in a shapeless and formless clutter.

After having thus disposed of the threat to the prevailing order, Bob had only wonderfully pleasant things to say about the rest of the book, the sections that dealt with phenomena of memory in the good old functionalist tradition of "let's do experiments and report and discuss the results."

In retrospect, it is easy to see that Bob Crowder was justified in resuming his 1972 stand in 1983. The picture of empirical support for the episodic–semantic distinction was brighter in 1983 than it had been in 1972 but not a lot brighter. In chapter 3 of *Elements of Episodic Memory*, I listed and discussed the differences between the two systems that were more numerous by then, but these were explicitly designated as hypotheses or as starting points of discussion. Although in another chapter of the book (chapter 5), I dealt with empirical evidence for the episodic–semantic distinction, the evidence was strained. Objectively, it was clear that the idea of the distinction was a bit ahead of solid data. At the time of the writing of *Elements of Episodic Memory,* the theoretical status of yet another then recently discovered "new" kind of memory, repetition or perceptual priming—episodic? semantic? procedural?—was unclear. This fact further contributed to the fuzziness of the whole scenario. Thus, by the middle of the 1980s, as Bob Crowder and other solid observers knew, the idea that episodic memory might be basically different from other kinds of memory was little more than an armchair thought in search of scientific respectability.

Changing Concepts

All this happened long ago. Today, *episodic memory* has become if not a household word then at least a less disruptive thought. Many students of memory, especially those with a neuropsychological orientation, have woven the concept into their own experiments and theories. In the meantime, the idea of episodic memory has also changed greatly. Compare two definitions. Consider first the following 1972 definition:

> Episodic memory is an information processing system that a) receives and stores information about temporally dated episodes or events, and about temporal–spatial relations among these events, b) retains various aspects of this information, and c) upon instructions transmits specific retained information to other systems, including those responsible for translating it into behavior and conscious awareness. (Tulving, 1972, p. 385)

This definition shows clear signs of having been shaped by the then-prevailing information-processing approach to studying verbal learning and memory in word-list experiments. The emphasis was on the processing of information about *events*, such as occurrences of words in a list: "receiving" (encoding), storing, and "transmitting" this information to output systems, in other words, retrieving it. The term *conscious awareness* was in the definition, but there was nothing unique about it, being shared by both episodic and semantic memory.

Now, consider the 1999 definition: Episodic memory is a recently evolved, late developing and early deteriorating, past-oriented memory system, and probably unique to humans. It makes possible mental "time travel" through subjective time, from the present to the past and to the future, and it allows re-experiencing, through autonoetic awareness, experiences as such. Its operations depend on semantic memory, and it is subserved by multiple brain regions including medial temporal lobes and prefrontal cortex.

Even a casual inspection shows that this definition is only superficially similar to the earlier one. The two formulations bear a family resemblance to each other, much like the resemblance of an adult to himself or herself in early childhood. In the current definition, no mention is made of processing information through the stages of encoding, storage, and retrieval because these stages characterize most memory systems. Past "events" become past "experiences" because it is necessary to distinguish between semantic memory events (e.g., "Lavoisier was guillotined during the French Revolution in Paris") and personal events ("I remember well my first visit to the Louvre"). Added are specific emphases on the past and "mental time travel" to underscore the fact that episodic memory is the only memory system whose explicit function is to allow the individual to re-experience (remember) the subjectively experienced past. Added also are ideas about the (phylogenetic) evolution and (ontogenetic) development of episodic memory, although factual information about the former is lacking and about the latter is still sparse. Furthermore, the 1999 definition mentions some neural substrates of episodic memory, a component of the definition that was not only impossible in 1972 but essentially unimaginable in the then current zeitgeist. Finally, the tentative proviso regarding the probable restriction of episodic memory to humans was inserted to distinguish episodic memory as defined here from episodic memory as used in the literature on memory of nonhuman animals. Although many nonhuman species possess sophisticated semantic memory (knowledge-of-the-world) systems, there is no evidence that any possess humanlike episodic memory (for a discussion, see Clayton & Dickinson, 1998; and Tulving & Markowitsch, 1998).

In the context of this chapter, the most important change in the definition of episodic memory is the shift from the general idea of "consciousness" that applied to both episodic and semantic memory in 1972 to "autonoetic consciousness" in 1999. What is this autonoetic consciousness? The remainder of this chapter revolves around this question. It is discussed here because it fits into the episodic memory story the beginnings of which Bob Crowder witnessed and partially shaped. The idea of autonoetic consciousness, or "autonoesis" as it is referred to henceforth, is a part of the continuation of the story.

The Remarkable Case of K. C.

The concept of autonoesis (autonoetic consciousness) literally has its roots in an accident. The accident was one that befell a now densely amnesic man known as K. C. whom we have been studying at the Rotman Research Institute in Toronto, Ontario, Canada, for many years. In 1981, at the age of 30, K. C. rode his motorcycle off the road and suffered brain damage of a highly unusual kind. Today, K. C. lives in Mississauga, near Toronto, in his parents' house. Because his mental state has not changed greatly over the intervening years, I describe K. C. in the present tense, although much of the evidence for the case comes from the studies conducted in the past (Hayman, Macdonald, & Tulving, 1993; Tulving, 1989b; Tulving, Schacter, McLachlan, & Moscovitch, 1988).

K. C.'s intellectual capabilities are in many ways indistinguishable from those of a healthy adult. His intelligence and language are normal, and he can read and write. He has no problem recognizing objects and naming them; he can close his eyes and give an accurate description of the CN Tower, Toronto's famous landmark, from imagining it. His knowledge of mathematics, history, geography, and other school subjects is not greatly different from other individuals at his educational level (a graduate of a community college); he can define and tell the difference between stalagmites and stalactites (a distinction either not yet mastered or already lost by some people who test him). His thought processes are clear; he can play the organ, chess, and various card games; he has no problem with immediate memory (his digit span has been measured to eight); his social manners are exemplary; and he possesses a quiet sense of humor.

Even K. C.'s memory, broadly speaking, seems normal in many ways. It would be inaccurate to say that his memory is impaired, because his brain damage did not noticeably affect most known forms of memory. He has no particular problems with many perceptual motor and cognitive skills, with the retrieval of premorbidly acquired general knowledge, or with short-term memory for recent (1 to 2 min. ago) happenings, as the examples in the previous paragraph show. When it comes to perceptual priming, his performance is embarrassingly higher than that of an average University of Toronto student (Tulving, Hayman, & Macdonald, 1991). He can readily answer questions, even about semantic (public, objective, shared) aspects of his autobiographical knowledge, such as his date of birth, the address of his home for the first 9 years of his life, the names of the some of the schools he attended, the make and color of the car he possessed, and the fact that his parents owned and still own a summer cottage. He knows the location of the cottage, can easily find it on the map, knows its distance (90 mi.) from his home, and how long it takes to drive there from Toronto in weekend traffic. He also knows that he has spent a lot of time there. All this accessible factual ("declarative," "cognitive," "propositional") knowledge, regardless of what it is about, is classified as semantic because it is impersonal, objective, public, and shared. K. C. knows things about himself and his past in the same way that he knows similar things about other individuals, friends, and family. It is knowledge of one's life from the point of view of an observer rather than that of a participant, the same kind of knowledge that people have about many other aspects of their world.

K. C.'s sole but substantial problem is that he cannot remember anything that has ever happened to him. However hard he tries and however powerfully he is prompted, he cannot bring into his conscious awareness a single event, happening, or situation that he witnessed or in which he participated. This global episodic amnesia covers the period from his birth to the present day: He cannot recollect anything from his life before or after the accident. He knows the address and, when standing in front of it, recognizes the house where he lived for the first 9 years of his life, but does not remember a single event that took place in the house. He does not remember a single visit to the family cottage and not a single event there in which he participated. Nor is he capable of remembering anything ever having happened in the house where he has now lived for over 30 years.

In the course of studying his amnesia, I collected descriptions of a number of poignant events from his life that would be regarded as highly memorable by everyone—a fight he had in a pub resulting in a broken arm that took him to the hospital; a traffic accident that caused his jaw to be "wired shut" for a week; the accidental death of his older brother to whom he was close; a huge chemical spill near his home that caused a 10-day evacuation of over 100,000 people in his neighborhood, including himself. The idea was to test his autobiographical memory with increasingly complete cues about the events. (I also made up a collection of descriptions of otherwise comparable events that had not happened to him and used these as controls.) The results are clear. Even when he was given full descriptions of the real events, his responses were the same as those he gave to the fabricated events: He said he did not remember the events and did not feel any familiarity toward them.

This contrast between what K. C. does not remember of his past and what he does know is very much in keeping with the hypothesis that episodic memory, memory of one's personal past, and semantic memory, general knowledge of the world, are subserved by different neural mechanisms. Although it must represent a one-in-a-million chance, it looks as if the brain damage that K. C. suffered from his accident resulted in a serious impairment in the functioning of the episodic memory system in the absence of a comparable impairment in the semantic system (Tulving et al., 1991).

From Episodic Memory to Autonoesis

The general pattern of K. C.'s lost and preserved mental capabilities can be economically described in terms of two kinds of consciousness. One is involved in tasks on which K. C. does very poorly. These are tasks that require him to mentally travel back in time to a particular episode, to relive it, to observe it again, to re-experience it. I named this kind of consciousness autonoetic (Tulving, 1985). *Autonoetic consciousness* (*autonoesis*) is defined as the neurocognitive capability of normal adults to become aware of their existence in subjectively experienced time. It includes but transcends self-awareness.

K. C. has normal self-awareness and has even learned his new "self" as revealed by trait judgments (Tulving, 1993; see also Klein, Loftus, & Kihlstrom, 1996). His autonoesis, however, is largely dysfunctional or perhaps even nonexistent. He lives in a timeless world, that is, in a permanent present. When he is asked to try to "travel back in time" in his own mind, back either a few minutes or many years, he says he cannot do it. When he is asked to describe the state of his mind when he tries to turn his mind's eye toward the past, the best he can do is to say that it is "blank." Nor can he think about the future. Thus, when asked, he cannot tell the questioner what he is going to do later that day, or the day after, or at any time in the rest of his life, any more than he can say what he did the day before or what events have happened in his life. When he is asked to describe the state of his mind when he thinks about his future, whether the next 15 minutes or the next year, he again says that it is blank. Indeed, when asked to compare the two kinds of blankness, one of the past and the other of the future, he says that they are "the same kind of blankness" (Tulving, 1985). Thus K. C. seems to be as incapable of imagining his future as he is incapable of remembering his past.

When K. C. is engaged in activities that do not require mental time travel into his own past or future, his awareness is normal. When he is asked the name of the capital of France, or the difference between stalagmites and stalactites, or thousands of other such facts, there is no sign of any deficiency. In these situations he is naturally consciously aware of what he is doing, but the kind of consciousness involved is different from autonoesis: It contains no awareness of personal time. I named the kind of consciousness that accompanies retrieval of impersonal factual information (semantic memory information) "noetic" (Tulving, 1985). (For the sake of completeness, a third kind of consciousness in memory, one corresponding to the lack of awareness of the mental contents of a task, was named "anoetic.") Thus, although K. C.'s autonoesis is severely impaired, his capability of conscious awareness of the world beyond subjective time, that is, his noetic consciousness or noesis, is well preserved.

It is important to note that K. C. has no greater difficulty in thinking about physical time than he has thinking about physical space. He knows and can talk about what most other people know about physical time units, structure, and measurement by clocks and calendars. But such knowledge of time in and of itself does not allow him to remember events as having happened at a particular time. It is necessary but not sufficient. Something else is needed, and this something else— the awareness of time in which one's experiences are recorded—seems to be missing from K. C.'s neurocognitive profile. He thus exhibits a dissociation between "knowing" time and "experiencing" time, a dissociation that parallels knowing the facts of the world and remembering experiences.

Remembering and Autonoesis

The story about K. C.'s two kinds of consciousness, one (autonoesis) dysfunctional, the other (noesis) largely preserved, is based on two critical assumptions. First, the claim that K. C.'s brain damage resulted in the loss of autonoesis but not noesis implies that before his accident, he, like any normal healthy non-brain-damaged person, possessed both of these kinds of consciousness: One cannot lose, or retain, something that one does not possess. If so, all normal human beings ought to be in possession of the same two kinds of consciousness. Second, the claim implies that there must exist specific, at least to some extent dissociable, neuronal correlates of the two kinds of consciousness in normal brains: One cannot lose, or retain, one of two functions of the brain if they are not neurally separable.

To test these two implications experimentally, one needs to solve two problems, among other things. The first consists in the creation in the laboratory of situations in which participants are known to be in one or the other conscious state: noetic or autonoetic. The second problem consists in the identification and measurement of brain activity that is correlated with the two mental states.

Note that the first problem is related to but goes beyond a problem that has already been tackled by students of memory who are interested in the relation between consciousness and memory. This standard problem concerns the separation of conscious from nonconscious processes of memory. The historically latest approach to the standard problem is associated with the concepts of priming and other forms of implicit memory (Roediger, 1990; Schacter, 1987; Toth, 2000; Tulving, Schacter, & Stark, 1982) and with the well-known process-dissociation procedure introduced by Jacoby (1991). Identification of autonoesis and noesis requires that we go beyond the standard problem inasmuch as the task calls not only for separating conscious from nonconscious processes but also for distinguishing one kind of consciousness from another. (For a further discussion, see Richardson-Klavehn, Gardiner, & Java, 1996.)

A beginning has been made in solving these problems. As a result, some initial evidence is available about neural correlates of autonoetic consciousness and its differences from noetic consciousness and nonconscious states.

The creation of autonoetic, noetic, and nonconscious (anoetic) mental states has become possible through what is known as the "remember/know paradigm" (Gardiner, 1988; Gardiner & Java, 1993; Gardiner & Richardson-Klavehn, 2000; Tulving, 1985). The basic idea is simple: When participants in an episodic memory test report that a particular event occurred at a particular time in a particular place they are further asked to describe the nature of the mental experience that accompanied the act of retrieval. Specifically, they are asked to offer either a "remember" or a "know" judgment. Remember designates recollection of the event of an item's occurrence in the study list, whereas know means that the participant's belief in the item's presence in the study has some other basis.

The initial remember/know experiments with word lists (a) show that people are capable of distinguishing between remembered and known successfully retrieved items and (b) provide a hint that the probability of occurrence of the two kinds of conscious awareness varies reliably and systematically with experimental conditions. Subsequent numerous studies confirmed the initial findings and generated a great deal of systematic data both with normal healthy participants (e.g., Gregg & Gardiner, 1991; Hockley & Consoli, 1999; Jones & Roediger, 1995; Mäntyla, 1997; Mungan

& Peynircioglu, 1999; Rajaram, 1993; Roediger & McDermott, 1995) and with special populations, such as amnesia patients (Knowlton & Squire, 1995; Yonelinas, Kroll, Dobbins, Lazzarra, & Knight, 1998), epilepsy patients with unilateral temporal lobectomies (Blaxton & Theodore, 1997), schizophrenia patients (Huron et al., 1995), Alzheimer's patients (Dalla Barba, 1997), and high-functioning people with autism (Bowler, Gardiner, & Grice, 2000). Space does not allow covering this research here; the burgeoning literature on remembering and knowing has been reviewed elsewhere (Gardiner & Richardson-Klavehn, 2000; Rajaram & Roediger, 1997; Wheeler, 2000). One of the unexpected methodological insights gained from all this research is that most of the research on recognition memory has inadvertently conflated the behavioral measures of two separable sets of processes. A corollary is that the conclusions about recognition drawn in research may hold for both, one, or neither of the two component processes taken individually.

For my present purposes, the important point made by the results of remember/know studies is that people can reliably distinguish between two states of conscious awareness and have no difficulty expressing the difference. These facts can be related to the dual-process theories of recognition that were proposed several decades ago (Atkinson & Juola, 1974; Jacoby, 1991; Mandler, 1980). The central idea in these theories is that episodic recognition can be based on one or both of two processes, recollection and familiarity. The nature of the relation between the two processes of dual-process theories and the two states of conscious awareness revealed by the remember/know paradigm is currently under intense scrutiny. The debate is enlivened by yet another theoretical stance according to which the processes and conscious states represent quantitative differences on a single continuum of recognizability (Donaldson, 1996; Gardiner & Gregg, 1997; Hirshman, 1998; Yonelinas, Dobbins, Szymanski, Dhaliwal, & King, 1996).

Autonoesis in the Brain

The remember/know paradigm can be used to create autonoetic and noetic states, thus solving the first of the two problems discussed earlier, and opening the doors to the search for their neural correlates. A handful of such studies have been conducted to date. The initial results can be described as variable but promising.

In an early study, Smith (1993), using the event-related potentials (ERP) technique (Rugg, 1995), reported a difference between the electrophysiological "signatures" of remembered and known word-recognition judgments. In a similar study, Düzel, Yonelinas, Mangun, Heinze, and Tulving (1997) added a novel feature to the basic design: By adopting the Deese–Roediger–McDermott (DRM) procedure (Deese, 1959; Roediger & McDermott, 1995), they created numerous discrete test events in which participants made false-positive judgments about test words that had not been physically presented for study ("critical lures"). Studies of the DRM procedure show that participants make both remembered and known judgments, even about such falsely recognized test words (Payne, Elie, Blackwell, & Neuschatz, 1996; Roediger & McDermott, 1995). The question concerned the similarities and differences between brain activity associated with true and false recognition.

The results of the Düzel et al. (1997) experiment show that autonoetic awareness is correlated with an increase in the amplitude of the ERP signal in the 500–800-ms time window, in relation to the no-recognition baseline, whereas noetic awareness is correlated with an amplitude decrease of the N400 component of the waveform and a decrease of the "negative going" waveform in the 500–800-ms window. Both these components have been observed in the studies of episodic memory retrieval (Rugg, 1995). The Düzel et al. (1997) experiment provides a basis for the interpretation of the earlier findings in terms of physiologically based states of conscious awareness. Remarkably, the same pattern of data was obtained for true and false recognition, that is, for hits and false alarms. This latter outcome reinforces the interpretation of the data in terms of qualitatively different states of conscious awareness, independent of the presence or absence of the specific physical stimuli in the study list.

Electrophysiological measures yielded by the ERP technique can provide evidence that differential brain activity, associated with a task or process, does occur, as does evidence about the temporal parameters of the differences. But they are relatively uninformative about "localization of function," about what brain regions are differentially involved in the tasks, processes, or mental states under scrutiny. Such information can be gained from the recently developed technique of event-related functional magnetic resonance imaging test (fMRI; Buckner, 2000; Nyberg & Cabeza, 2000). With this technique as with ERPs, behavioral and physiological data can be collected "on line" about any sequence of events, such as the presentation of items to study or test, and then sorted into different "bins" defined by the specified characteristics of the events. Thus, study events can be sorted into those that resulted in successful subsequent recognition and those that did not. When such an analysis is conducted, different brain regions are differentially active at encoding of subsequently recognized and nonrecognized items (Wagner et al., 1998).

Using the event-related fMRI technique, Henson, Rugg, Shallice, Josephs, and Dolan (1999) obtained evidence for differences in neuroanatomical regions where activity is correlated with the mental states that underlie "remember," "know," and "new" responses. In their study, they revealed a complex picture of brain activity associated with different states of conscious awareness of test events. Among other things, it looked as if remember judgments were more associated with left-hemispheric regions, especially in prefrontal and parietal cortices, whereas know judgments tended to be right localized. Future research no doubt will clarify the picture. For our immediate purposes, the important finding is that differences in neuroanatomical activation were associated with autonoetic and noetic states of awareness. Thus, at long last subjective phenomena of consciousness are becoming objective. The implications of this fact for the science of psychology are revolutionary.

Several researchers have suggested that frontal lobes play a critical role in autonoesis (Moscovitch & Melo, 1997; Tulving, 1993; Wheeler, Stuss, & Tulving, 1997). The results of Henson et al. (1999) provide initial direct support for these ideas. However, they also remind one that frontal lobes, like all other parts of the brain, do not do anything by themselves and that other brain regions are also involved.

Related Evidence

Other bits and pieces of empirical evidence that seem to fit into the developing pattern of data that forms the foundation for the story of autonoesis are worth mentioning. Clinical studies of patients with frontal lesions show that these patients have selective impairment in autobiographical remembering (DellaSala, Laiacona, Spinnler, & Trivelli, 1993; Kopelman, Stanhope, & Kingsley, 1999; Markowitsch et al., 1993; Markowitsch & Ewald, 1997; Rousseaux, Godfrey, Cabaret, Bernati, & Pruvo, 1997). Especially intriguing is the case of a young man, M. L., who suffered traumatic brain injury. He recovered most of his mental functions but was left with what appeared as a permanent impairment involving autonoesis (Levine et al., 1998; Levine, Freedman, Dawson, Black, & Stuss, 1999). The only observable brain damage was a lesion in the right-hemisphere uncinate fascicle, a fiber tract connecting prefrontal and temporal cortical regions. The patient's loss of autonoesis was accompanied by a seriously diminished affect and difficulties of self-regulation.

A related finding was reported by Markowitsch et al. (1999); they conducted a functional imaging study in which neural networks involved in the retrieval of "affect-laden" autobiographical material were compared with comparable fictitious material. The results show selective activations of the right amygdala and the right ventral prefrontal cortex near the uncinate fascicle associated with autobiographic material. In earlier research, Fink et al. (1996) described a positron emission tomography (PET) study where results revealed that a right-hemispheric network of cortical regions was involved in the ecphory (recovery) of affect-laden autobiographical information. To further complement the developing picture, Calabrese et al. (1996) reported a case of a postencephalitic patient, with brain damage mainly in the right temporofrontal region, which shows a severe and enduring loss of the ability to recollect premorbid personal experiences, and less severe loss of general knowledge. Finally, in a recent PET study, Craik et al. (1999) reported blood flow changes in a right-frontal region when participants made decisions about their own personality characteristics, thus hinting at the possibility that autonoesis associated with right-frontal regions may be analyzable into components related to "self" and "pastness."

In the realm of psychopharmacology, evidence has been reported that episodic memory retrieval but not semantic memory retrieval is impaired by various psychoactive drugs, such as benzodiazepines and ethanol, and that this impairment is limited to remembering and does not involve knowing (Bishop & Curran, 1995; Curran, Gardiner, Java, & Allen, 1993; Curran & Hildebrandt, 1999). Thus, the psychopharmacological approach, which allows the experimental creation of "reversible lesions" (Curran, 2000), shows promise as yet another window into the conscious mind.

Conclusion

There are two sciences of psychology, one of behavior and the other of the mind. The two share objectives, methods, and achievements, but in many ways they also differ. It is quite possible to study the lawfulness of behavior without even mentioning anything that has to do with the mind, and it is perfectly possible to study the mind at the same time using behavior merely as a measuring tool (Tulving, 1989a).

Here, I have told the story of how the idea of episodic memory spawned the idea of autonoesis (autonoetic consciousness), a human brain/mind capability that allows people to become consciously aware of their personal past and their personal future. Such awareness represents one of the truly unique human brain/mind capabilities. The story here is that empirical evidence is rapidly accumulating from a variety of sources and converging on the psychological and physiological reality of autonoesis. (A more thorough examination of these issues is available in Wheeler et al., 1997.)

The development of the story of autonoesis is interesting for several reasons. First, it symbolizes the emancipation of psychology as a science of the mind, or consciousness, as it was meant to be early in its history. Second, it illustrates how one can go beyond the traditional method to the study of consciousness that is based on the separation of conscious versus nonconscious phenomena and processes. Third, it points to what seems to be a radical shift in "doing" psychological science. The old "solo science" approach is being rapidly replaced by a new one based on multidisciplinary collaboration among experts of different backgrounds and with different skills but common objectives. Neuropsychological analyses of brain/mind relations provide outstanding examples of such a multidisciplinary approach. Functional brain imaging provides another. Finally, autonoesis may turn out to be a much more important player in the human drama than may be apparent now. One possibility, which I am exploring now, is that the evolutionary emergence of autonoesis, with backward and forward looking awareness of personal time ("palinscopic and proscopic chronesthesia") was a pivotal "driver" of the evolution of human culture and civilization. If so, autonoesis has played and is playing a highly crucial role in what humankind has been, is now, and will be in the future.

References

Atkinson, R. C., & Juola, J. F. (1974). Search and decision processes in recognition memory. In D. H. Krantz, R. C. Atkinson, R. D. Luce, & P. Suppes (Eds.), *Contemporary developments in mathematical psychology* (Vol. 1, pp. 243–293). San Francisco: Freeman.

Bishop, K., & Curran, H. V. (1995). Psychopharmacological analysis of implicit and explicit memory: A study with lorazepam and the benzodiazepine antagonist, flumazenil. *Psychopharmacology, 121,* 267–278.

Blaxton, T. A., & Theodore, W. H. (1997). The role of the temporal lobes in recognizing visuospatial materials: Remembering versus knowing. *Brain and Cognition, 35,* 5–25.

Bowler, D. M., Gardiner, J. M., & Grice, S. J. (2000). Episodic memory and remembering in adults with Asperger's syndrome. *Journal of Autism and Developmental Disorders, 30,* 295–304.

Buckner, R. L. (2000). Neuroimaging of memory. In M. S. Gazzaniga (Ed.), *The new cognitive neurosciences* (pp. 817–828). Cambridge, MA: MIT Press.

Calabrese, P., Markowitsch, H. J., Durwen, H. F., Widlitzek, H., Haupts, M., Holinka, B., & Gehlen, W. (1996). Right temporofrontal cortex as critical locus for the ecphory of old episodic memories. *Journal of Neurology, Neurosurgery, and Psychiatry, 61,* 304–310.

Clayton, N. S., & Dickinson, A. (1998). Episodic-like memory during cache recovery by scrub jays. *Nature, 395,* 272–274.

Craik, F. I. M., Moroz, T. M., Moscovitch, M., Stuss, D. T., Winocur, G., Tulving, E., & Kapur, S. (1999). In search of the self: A positron emission tomography study. *Psychological Science, 10,* 26–34.

Crowder, R. G. (1986). Remembering experiences and the experience of remembering. *Behavioral and Brain Sciences, 9,* 566–567.

Curran, H. V. (2000). Psychopharmacological perspectives on memory. In E. Tulving & F. I. M. Craik (Eds.), *The Oxford handbook of memory* (pp. 539–554). New York: Oxford University Press.

Curran, H. V., Gardiner, J., Java, R., & Allen, D. J. (1993). Effects of lorazepam on recollective experience in recognition memory. *Psychopharmacology, 110,* 374–378.

Curran, H. V., & Hildebrandt, M. (1999). Dissociative effects of alcohol on recollective experience. *Consciousness and Cognition, 8,* 497–509.

Dalla Barba, G. (1997). Recognition memory and recollective experience in Alzheimer's disease. *Memory, 5,* 657–672.

Deese, J. (1959). On the prediction of occurrence of particular verbal intrusions in immediate recall. *Journal of Experimental Psychology, 58,* 17–22.

DellaSala, S., Laiacona, M., Spinnler, H., & Trivelli, C. (1993). Autobiographical recollection and frontal damage. *Neuropsychologia, 31,* 823–839.

Donaldson, W. (1996). The role of decision making in remembering and knowing. *Memory & Cognition, 24,* 523–533.

Düzel, E., Yonelinas, A. P., Mangun, G. R., Heinze, H. J., & Tulving, E. (1997). Event-related brain potential correlates of two states of conscious awareness in memory. *Proceedings of the National Academy of Sciences, USA, 94,* 5973–5978.

Fink, G. R., Markowitsch, H. J., Reinkemeier, M., Bruckbauer, T., Kessler, J., & Heiss, W. D. (1996). Cerebral representation of one's own past: Neural networks involved in autobiographical memory. *Journal of Neuroscience, 16,* 4275–4282.

Gardiner, J. M (1988). Functional aspects of recollective experience. *Memory & Cognition, 16,* 309–313.

Gardiner, J. M., & Gregg, V. H. (1997). Recognition memory with little or no remembering: Implications for a detection model. *Psychonomic Bulletin and Review, 4,* 474–479.

Gardiner, J. M., & Java, R. I. (1993). Recognizing and remembering. In M. Conway & P. Morris (Eds.), *Theories of memory* (pp. 163–188). Hillsdale, NJ: Erlbaum.

Gardiner, J. M., & Richardson-Klavehn, A. (2000). Remembering and knowing. In E. Tulving & F. I. M. Craik (Eds.), *The Oxford handbook of memory* (pp. 229–244). New York: Oxford University Press.

Gregg, V. H., & Gardiner, J. M. (1991). Components of conscious awareness in a long-term modality effect. *British Journal of Psychology, 82,* 153–162.

Hayman, C. A. G., Macdonald, C. A., & Tulving, E. (1993). The role of repetition and associative interference in new semantic learning in amnesia. *Journal of Cognitive Neuroscience, 5,* 375–389.

Henson, R. N. A., Rugg, M. D., Shallice, T., Josephs, O., & Dolan, R. J. (1999). Recollection and familiarity in recognition memory: An event-related functional magnetic resonance imaging study. *Journal of Neuroscience, 19,* 3962–3972.

Hirshman, E. (1998). On the utility of the signal detection model of the remember/know paradigm. *Consciousness and Cognition, 7,* 103–107.

Hockley, W. E., & Consoli, A. (1999). Familiarity and recollection in item and associative recognition. *Memory & Cognition, 27,* 657–664.

Huron, C., Danion, J. M., Giacomoni, F., Grange, D., Robert, P., & Rizzo, L. (1995). Impairment of recognition memory with, but not without, conscious recollection in schizophrenia. *American Journal of Psychiatry, 152,* 1737–1742.

Jacoby, L. L. (1991). A process dissociation framework: Separating automatic from intentional uses of memory. *Journal of Memory and Language, 30,* 513–541.

James, W. (1890). *Principles of psychology.* New York: Holt.

Jones, T. C., & Roediger, H. L. (1995). The experiential basis of serial position effects. *European Journal of Cognitive Psychology, 7,* 65–80.

Klein, S. B., Loftus, J., & Kihlstrom, J. F. (1996). Self-knowledge of an amnesic patient: Toward a neuropsychology of personality and social psychology. *Journal of Experimental Psychology: General, 125,* 250–260.

Knowlton, B. J., & Squire, L. R. (1995). Remembering and knowing: Two different expressions of declarative memory. *Journal of Experimental Psychology: Learning, Memory, and Cognition, 21,* 699–710.

Kopelman, M. D., Stanhope, N., & Kingsley, D. (1999). Retrograde amnesia in patients with diencephalic, temporal lobe or frontal lesions. *Neuropsychologia, 37,* 939–958.

Levine, B., Black, S. E., Cabeza, R., Sinden, M., McIntosh, A. R., Toth, J. P., Tulving, E., & Stuss, D. T. (1998). Episodic memory and the self in a case of isolated retrograde amnesia. *Brain, 121,* 1951–1973.

Levine, B., Freedman, M., Dawson, D., Black, S., & Stuss, D. T. (1999). Ventral frontal contribution to self-regulation: Convergence of episodic memory and inhibition. *Neurocase, 5,* 263–275.

Mandler, G. (1980). Recognizing: The judgement of previous occurrence. *Psychological Review, 87,* 252–271.

Mäntyla, T. (1997). Recollections of faces: Remembering differences and knowing similarities. *Journal of Experimental Psychology: Learning, Memory, and Cognition, 23,* 1203–1216.

Markowitsch, H. J., Calabrese, P., Liess, J., Haupts, M., Durwen, H. F., & Gehlen, W. (1993). Retrograde amnesia after traumatic injury of the frontotemporal cortex. *Journal of Neurology, Neurosurgery, and Psychiatry, 56,* 988–992.

Markowitsch, H. J., & Ewald, K. (1997). Right-hemispheric fronto-temporal injury leading to severe autobiographical retrograde and moderate anterograde episodic amnesia— Implications for the anatomy of memory. *Neurology Psychiatry and Brain Research, 5,* 71–78.

Markowitsch, H. J., Reinkemeier, M., Thiel, A., Kessler, J., Koyuncu, A., & Heiss, W.-D. (1999). Autobiographical memory activates the right amygdala and temporo-frontal link: A PET study [Abstract]. *Acta Neurobiologiae Experimentalis, 59,* 219.

Moscovitch, M., & Melo, B. (1997). Strategic retrieval and the frontal lobes: Evidence from confabulation and amnesia. *Neuropsychologia, 35,* 1017–1034.

Mungan, E., & Peynircioglu, Z. F. (1999). Qualitative effects on directed forgetting on memory. *Turk Psikoloji Dergisi, 14,* 1–15.

Nyberg, L., & Cabeza, R. (2000). Brain imaging of memory. In E. Tulving & F. I. M. Craik (Eds.), *The Oxford handbook of memory* (pp. 501–519). New York: Oxford University Press.

Payne, D. G., Elie, C. J., Blackwell, J. M., & Neuschatz, J. S. (1996). Memory illusions: Recalling, recognizing, and recollecting events that never occurred. *Journal of Memory and Language, 35,* 261–285.

Rajaram, S. (1993). Remembering and knowing: Two means of access to the personal past. *Memory & Cognition, 21,* 89–102.

Rajaram, S., & Roediger, H. L., III. (1997). Remembering and knowing as states of consciousness during recollection. In J. D. Cohen & J. W. Schooler (Eds.), *Scientific approaches to the question of consciousness* (pp. 213–240). Hillsdale, NJ: Erlbaum.

Richardson-Klavehn, A., Gardiner, J. M., & Java, R. I. (1996). Memory: Task dissociations, process dissociations, and dissociations of consciousness. In G. Underwood (Ed.), *Implicit cognition* (pp. 85–158). Oxford, England: Oxford University Press.

Roediger, H. L. (1990). Implicit memory: Retention without remembering. *American Psychologist, 45,* 1043–1056.

Roediger, H. L., Buckner, R. L., & McDermott, K. B. (1999). Components of processing. In J. K. Foster & M. Jelicic (Eds.), *Memory: Systems, process or function?* (pp. 31–65). Oxford, England: Oxford University Press.

Roediger, H. L, & McDermott, K. B. (1995). Creating false memories: Remembering words not presented in lists. *Journal of Experimental Psychology: Learning, Memory, and Cognition, 21*, 803–814.

Roediger, H. L., Weldon, M. S., & Challis, B. H. (1989). Explaining dissociations between implicit and explicit measures of retention: A processing account. In H. L. Roediger, III, & F. I. M. Craik (Eds.), *Varieties of memory and consciousness: Essays in honour of Endel Tulving* (pp. 3–42). Hillsdale, NJ: Erlbaum.

Rousseaux, M., Godfrey, O., Cabaret, M., Bernati, T., & Pruvo, J. P. (1997). Retrograde memory after rupture of aneurysms of the anterior communicating artery. *Revue Neurologique, 153*, 659–668.

Rugg, M. D. (1995). Event related potential studies of human memory. In M. S. Gazzaniga (Ed.), *The cognitive neurosciences* (pp. 789–801). Cambridge, MA: MIT Press.

Schacter, D. L. (1987). Implicit expressions of memory in organic amnesia: Learning of new facts and associations. *Human Neurobiology, 6*, 107–118.

Smith, M. E. (1993). Neurophysiological manifestations of recollective experience during recognition memory judgements. *Journal of Cognitive Neuroscience, 5*, 1–13.

Toth, J. P. (2000). Nonconscious forms of memory. In E. Tulving & F. I. M. Craik (Eds.), *The Oxford handbook of memory* (pp. 245–261). New York: Oxford University Press.

Tulving, E. (1972). Episodic and semantic memory. In E. Tulving & W. Donaldson (Eds.), *Organization of memory* (pp. 381–403). New York: Academic Press.

Tulving, E. (1983). *Elements of episodic memory.* London, England: Oxford University Press.

Tulving, E. (1984). Précis of Elements of episodic memory. *Behavioral and Brain Sciences, 7*, 223–238.

Tulving, E. (1985). Memory and consciousness. *Canadian Psychology, 26*, 1–10.

Tulving, E. (1989a). Memory: Performance, knowledge, and experience. *European Journal of Cognitive Psychology, 1*, 3–26.

Tulving, E. (1989b). Remembering and knowing the past. *American Scientist, 77*, 361–367.

Tulving, E. (1993). Self-knowledge of an amnesic individual is represented abstractly. In T. K. Srull & R. S. Wyer, Jr. (Eds.), *The mental representation of trait and autobiographical knowledge about the self* (pp. 147–156). Hillsdale, NJ: Erlbaum.

Tulving, E., Hayman, C. A. G., & Macdonald, C. A. (1991). Long-lasting perceptual priming and semantic learning in amnesia: A case experiment. *Journal of Experimental Psychology: Learning, Memory, and Cognition, 17*, 595–617.

Tulving, E., & Markowitsch, H. J. (1998). Episodic and declarative memory: Role of the hippocampus. *Hippocampus, 8*, 198–204.

Tulving, E., Schacter, D. L., McLachlan, D. R., & Moscovitch, M. (1988). Priming of semantic autobiographical knowledge: A case study of retrograde amnesia. *Brain and Cognition, 8*, 3–20.

Tulving, E., Schacter, D. L., & Stark, H. A. (1982). Priming effects in word-fragment completion are independent of recognition memory. *Journal of Experimental Psychology: Learning, Memory, and Cognition, 8*, 336–342.

Wagner, A. D., Schacter, D. L., Rotte, M., Koutstaal, W., Maril, A., Dale, A. M., Rosen, B. R., & Buckner, R. L. (1998). Building memories: Remembering and forgetting of verbal experiences as predicted by brain activity. *Science, 282*, 1188–1191.

Wheeler, M. A. (2000). Episodic memory and autonoetic awareness. In E. Tulving & F. I. M. Craik (Eds.), *The Oxford handbook of memory* (pp. 597–608). New York: Oxford University Press.

Wheeler, M., Stuss, D. T., & Tulving, E. (1997). Toward a theory of episodic memory: The frontal lobes and autonoetic consciousness. *Psychological Bulletin, 121*, 331–354.

Yonelinas, A. P., Dobbins, I., Szymanski, M. D., Dhaliwal, H. S., & King, L. (1996). Signal detection, threshold, and dual process models of recognition memory: ROCs and conscious recollection. *Consciousness and Cognition, 5*, 418–441.

Yonelinas, A. P., Kroll, N. E. A., Dobbins, I., Lazzarra, M., & Knight, R. T. (1998). Recollection and familiarity deficits in amnesia: Convergence of remember/know, process dissociation, and ROC data. *Neuropsychology, 12*, 323–339.

CHAPTER 3

Proactive and Retroactive Effects in Memory Performance

Dissociating Recollection and Accessibility Bias

Larry L. Jacoby

Sandra Hessels

Kara Bopp

everal years ago at a conference, in discussing a problem for some people of easily becoming lost in new surroundings, Robert Crowder shared his strategy of stopping frequently to look back at the route he had just traversed, saying that doing so serves the important function of allowing one to see the route as it will appear when one returns. Stopping to look back is a generally useful strategy even when one cannot truly return. Looking back at his accomplishments, Bob has good reason to feel a great deal of pride. Among his greatest accomplishments are the students that he mentored, many who have gone on to become leading researchers and journal editors. Here, using Bob's strategy of looking back, we argue that much of the current research on memory has unknowingly returned to problems that have been investigated, specifically proactive and retroactive interference.

As described in Crowder's (1976) influential book, the interference theory of forgetting was seen as "the most comprehensive theoretical system in the field of human learning and memory" (p. 217). McGeoch (1932) argued that forgetting is the result of interference rather than decay with the passage of time or disuse. The prototype design used to investigate retroactive interference is owed to Müller and Pilzecker (1900, cited in Crowder, 1976). For that design, there are two conditions, both of which learn a first list of verbal items and later are tested for memory of that list (Table 3.1A). The control group is allowed to rest during the interval between the study and the test, whereas the experimental group learns another list of items,

This research was supported by grants from the National Institute on Aging (AG13845-02) and the Natural Sciences and Engineering Research Council of Canada (GP0000281).

TABLE 3.1

Example sequence of events in retroactive interference and misinformation effect

CONDITION	TIME 1	TIME 2	TIME 3
A. Retroactive interference			
Experimental	Learn A–B	Learn A–D	Test A–B
Control	Learn A–B	Rest	Test A–B
B. Misinformation effect			
Experimental	Mother–weekend	Mother–2 weeks	Test
Control	Mother–weekend	Rest	Test

an interpolated list, during that interval. The advantage in retention performance of the control condition over the experimental condition defines retroactive interference. The standard procedure for such experiments became paired-associate learning with the experimental condition conforming to an A–B, A–D paradigm: Two different responses, B and D, are learned in association to the same stimulus. By McGeoch's (1942) response competition theory, retrieval failures occur because some unwanted information is retrieved rather than the sought-after information. In the case of retroactive interference, the response learned in the second list (D) "blocks" retrieval of the first-list response (B). The basic idea is that forgetting results from blockage of retrieval (accessibility) caused by competing information rather than from actual loss of information from memory.

Crowder (1976) referred to McGeoch's (1942) theory as an independence hypothesis and contrasted that hypothesis with the unlearning hypothesis that later dominated theorizing about retroactive interference. The independence in question is between the learning of first- and second-list responses in the A–B, A–D paradigm. By McGeoch's theory, learning of a second association (A–D) does not influence the association of an earlier response (A–B) but, rather, has its effect on retention performance by providing a competitor for the earlier response. In contrast, the theory of unlearning holds that learning of a second association weakens the earlier association, a dependence hypothesis. The unlearning hypothesis originated from experiments by Melton and Irwin (1940) whose results show that the forgetting of paired associations from a first list could not be fully accounted for by interlist intrusions. Such intrusions, responses from the interpolated list that were mistakenly given in place of the first-list response, would be expected to account for all effects of retroactive interference if forgetting is caused by second-list learning competing with earlier learning. To explain the discrepancy, it was argued that learning of a response to a stimulus in an interpolated list requires unlearning or weakening of the earlier learned response. Retroactive interference was said to reflect both response competition and unlearning.

Postman and Underwood (1973) combined the notions of response competition and unlearning by proposing a two-factor theory of forgetting to account for proactive and retroactive interference. For proactive interference, it is the influence of prior learning that is of interest (Table 3.2A). The experimental group for proactive interference is the same as for retroactive interference except it is memory for the interpolated list that is tested. The control group "rests" rather than engaging in the prior learning. Proactive interference is measured as the retention advantage of the control over the experimental group and is said to result from response competition. Effects of unlearning are restricted to retroactive interference.

There was a great deal of controversy surrounding the question of whether unlearning or independence best describes the relation between responses paired with the same stimulus. Against the unlearning hypothesis, Martin (1971) showed that recall of a first-list response was stochastically independent of recall of a second-list response rather than the two being inversely related. An inverse relationship would be predicted if learning of the second-list response entailed unlearning of the first-list response. However, Hintzman (1972) argued that such conditionalized results cannot be used to establish independence. Some of the arguments against the independence hypothesis were later used against other claims of independence— the independence assumption in the process dissociation procedure (see the exchange between Jacoby, Begg, & Toth, 1997; Jacoby & Shrout, 1997; and Curran & Hintzman, 1997; Hintzman & Curran, 1997) and the proposed independence between recognition and recall put forth by Flexser and Tulving (1978; also see 1993; Hintzman, 1992, 1993; and Tulving & Flexser, 1992). The controversy surrounding the independence versus unlearning hypotheses was never really resolved. Rather, interests of memory researchers shifted to topics highlighted by the "cognitive revolution." Investigations of retroactive and proactive interference became unpopular, largely because of their having been couched in theorizing about associations and identified with "verbal learning," a tradition viewed as no longer fashionable.

At approximately the same time as interest in interference theory was declining in North America, it was used by British psychologists to describe exciting, new findings about the memory performance of people with amnesia. Warrington and

TABLE 3.2

Example sequence of events in proactive interference and action slip

CONDITION	TIME 1	TIME 2	TIME 3
A. Proactive interference			
Experimental	Learn A–B	Learn A–D	Test A–D
Control	Rest	Learn A–D	Test A–D
B. Action slip			
Experimental	Fly	Drive	Test
Control	Rest	Drive	Test

Weiskrantz (1970) tested memory by presenting a fragmented version of earlier studied words as cues for their retrieval and found that memory performance of people with amnesia was nearly equal to that of people with normally functioning memory. They described their results by saying

> it may not be too far-fetched to suggest that effective normal day-to-day memory demands that previous events be forgotten or suppressed and the inability to do so in the amnesic subject produces responses analogous to prior-list intrusions recorded in formal verbal learning experiments. (p. 630)

The notion is that people with amnesia are more vulnerable to interference than are normal people. Providing fragments as cues for retrieval was seen as having its effect by limiting interference in a way that allowed people with amnesia to eliminate incorrect, alternative responses just as do people with normal memories. The type of test used by Warrington and Weiskrantz later became known as an indirect or implicit test of memory, and there is now a great deal of evidence to show dissociations between performance on indirect and direct tests for people with normal memory (e.g., Roediger & McDermott, 1993) and for special populations such as people with amnesia (Shimamura, 1989) and older adults (Light & La Voie, 1993). Similar to the account of amnesia forwarded by Warrington and Weiskrantz, age-related differences in memory have been explained as resulting from the older adults being more susceptible to interference effects than are younger people (Hasher & Zacks, 1988; Winocur, 1982).

The "misinformation effect" (for a review, see Ayers & Reder, 1998) can be seen as an example of retroactive interference gained by using materials that are more interesting than are paired associates. In her classic experiments, Loftus (1975) showed that later presented, misleading information can influence memory reports about an earlier event in ways that are important for eyewitness testimony. Participants in her experiment viewed a scene that included a stop sign and were later asked a misleading question that implied that a yield sign, rather than a stop sign, appeared in the earlier scene. Participants in this experimental condition were much more likely to mistakenly report the presence of a yield sign in the earlier scene than were those in a control condition who were not asked the misleading question. The paradigm conforms to an investigation of retroactive interference with the stop sign corresponding to A–B and the misleading question about the yield sign corresponding to A–D learning. The misinformation effect refers to the worsened memory performance of the experimental as compared with the control condition just as does "retroactive interference."

Theoretical accounts of the misinformation effect have also been similar to those given for retroactive interference. Loftus (1975) claimed that the misleading question had its effect by altering the memory trace of the earlier event, a notion that is similar to unlearning. In contrast, McCloskey and Zaragoza (1985) suggested that misinformation effects are not reflective of memory change but, rather, are due to task demands and strategies that are similar to those accompanying response competition. The misleading information is seen to provide a competitor for response in the same way that a second-list response competes with a first-list response. Just as is found for retroactive interference, the misinformation effect is larger for older in comparison with younger adults (Cohen & Faulkner, 1989).

As described above, increased susceptibility of older adults to interference or misinformation effects means only that they are more likely to use incorrect or misleading information in tests of memory. Our goal is to better understand the basis for that difference. We forward a dual-process account of retroactive and proactive interference that differs in important ways from the traditional account that appeals to unlearning and response competition. Our approach distinguishes between recollection and automatic influences of memory (e.g., Jacoby, 1991) and seeks to measure the contributions of the two types of processes. Recollection refers to a consciously controlled use of memory whose impairment is largely responsible for amnesia and age-related differences in memory. Recollection is assumed to be independent of more automatic forms of memory that are largely preserved in people with amnesia and older adults and are, to some extent, revealed by performance on indirect tests. We argue that in contrast to alternative approaches, the greater susceptibility to interference shown by the older adults is a consequence rather than a cause of age-related differences in memory. We show that retroactive and proactive interference sometimes results from an effect on an automatic influence of memory that we term "accessibility bias" without changing ability to recollect.

"I Told You . . .": Analysis of a Misinformation Effect

Suppose that a wife tells her husband that her mother is going to visit for a weekend. After a delay of several days, she attempts to create a false memory by saying, "As I told you, my mother will arrive this weekend for a 2-week visit." The husband might accept the misinformation conveyed by the false "I told you . . ." claim, mistakenly concluding that he was earlier informed of the impending lengthy visit, whereas he would have correctly remembered the earlier conversation had it not been for the false claim (Table 3.1B). If the husband had challenged the "I told you . . ." claim, the wife might respond by accusing him of not paying full attention to their earlier conversation, suggesting that lack of attention has effects that are the same as those of misinformation. Although lack of attention can undoubtedly result in misinformation, we show that effects of the two are sometimes very different. We suspect that scenarios of the above sort are common and that the potential power of a false "I told you . . ." claim is widely known. As described later, false "I told you . . ." claims are a common ploy used to defraud older adults.

Our experiments investigating the "I told you . . ." effect used materials that are much less interesting than a visiting mother-in-law and, at most, no more interesting than the paired associates used in investigations of retroactive interference. Pairs of related words (e.g., knee bone) were presented for study. In one condition, participants devoted full attention to study. In a second condition, divided attention, participants studied the word pairs while simultaneously engaged in a listening task that involved monitoring for sequences of three consecutive odd numbers. Memory was tested by providing the lefthand member of each pair along with a fragment of the righthand member (knee b_n_) as cues for its recall. Immediately prior to the presentation of the recall test, a prime word was presented. The prime was the same as the target word (a valid prime), an alternative to the target word (an invalid prime), or a neutral nonword stimulus (a baseline prime). The design of the experiment is outlined in Table 3.3.

For now, consider only the invalid prime and baseline conditions, which correspond to the experimental and control conditions in a standard investigation of retroactive interference. The invalid prime condition was meant to correspond to a false "I told you . . ." claim. For that condition, a plausible alternative to the target word was used as the prime. The alternative was plausible in that, like the target, it was related to the context word and would complete the fragment. As expected, presentation of this invalid prime produced a misinformation effect, or retroactive interference, compared with the baseline condition in which a prime word was not presented (Table 3.4). That is, presentation of an invalid prime decreased the probability of correct recall and increased the probability of the prime being mistakenly reported as earlier studied. Dividing attention reduced the probability of correct recall and increased false recall for both the invalid prime and baseline conditions. The probabilities of correct and false recall add up to approximately 1.0 because materials were selected to allow only two possible responses to each test item, with those responses being ones that would come to mind for most people. Also participants were instructed to respond to each test item, guessing if necessary.

How did the invalid prime have its effect? One possibility is that the invalid prime replaced or altered memory for the earlier studied response (cf. Loftus, 1975). On this hypothesis, the reduction in correct recall produced by the invalid prime

TABLE 3.3

Basic procedure used for valid and invalid prime experiments

| STUDY PHASE CUE WORD AND TARGET | TEST PHASE | | TEST CONDITION |
	PRIME	WORD FRAGMENT	
bed sheet	sleep	bed s_ee_	Invalid prime
eagle bird	&&&&	eagle b__d	Baseline (no prime)
knee bone	bone	knee b_n_	Valid prime

TABLE 3.4

Probability of correct recall for prime conditions

| | PROBABILITY OF CORRECT RECALL | | |
| | TEST CONDITIONS | | |
STUDY CONDITION	VALID	BASELINE	INVALID
Full attention	.81 (.19)	.71 (.28)	.59 (.41)
Divided attention	.65 (.34)	.53 (.44)	.38 (.62)

| | ESTIMATES OF RECOLLECTION (R) AND ACCESSIBILITY BIAS (A) | |
STUDY CONDITION	R	A
Full attention	.41	.67
Divided attention	.04	.65

Note. Numbers in parentheses are the probabilities of false recall.

is not different in kind from the poorer recall produced by divided compared with full attention during the study. For both, the difference is because of poorer memory for the earlier studied list. However, there is another possibility: Perhaps the participant giving the invalid prime as a response was a consequence rather than a cause of poor memory. That is, perhaps participants gave the prime as a response only when they could not remember the earlier studied, target word. This account holds that the effect of an invalid prime is very different from that of dividing attention during the study. Rather than reducing memory for the earlier studied list, the invalid prime has its effect by means of accessibility bias: Presenting a word as a prime makes it more accessible as a response to be used when one is unable to recollect the studied word. By this view, dividing attention caused poor memory for the original list, whereas an invalid prime had its effect only after memory for the original list had failed.

If the prime exerts a simple bias effect that is based on accessibility, then the debilitating effect of an invalid prime should be mirrored by a facilitative effect of a valid prime. If the prime causes memory replacement, symmetry of this sort would not be predicted. Choosing between the two accounts, therefore, requires a third test condition, one for which a valid, rather than an invalid, prime is presented (Table 3.3). Results from the three test conditions can be combined to separate effects of the prime on accessibility bias from differences in recollection.

If presentation of a prime only influences accessibility bias, then, compared with the baseline condition, the increase in false recall produced by presentation of an invalid prime should be offset by an increase in correct recall produced by presentation of a valid prime. That is, the probabilities of correct recall for the valid and invalid prime conditions should be symmetrical around the baseline condition

(Table 3.4). To separate the contributions of recollection and accessibility bias, assume that for each of the test conditions, participants can sometimes recollect the studied word, with probability R. After a valid prime, when recollection fails $(1 - R)$, participants correctly give the prime as a response with a probability (A) that reflects accessibility bias influenced by the prime. For the valid prime condition then, the probability of a correct response is the sum of the probability of recollection of the correct word and the probability that accessibility bias results in the correct word when recollection fails: $P(\text{Correct Recall} \mid \text{Valid Prime}) = R + A(1 - R)$. The influence of the prime on accessibility bias is assumed to be the same for the valid and invalid prime conditions. Consequently, in the invalid prime condition, the prime is falsely reported only when recollection fails and the prime word is favored by accessibility bias: $P(\text{False Recall} \mid \text{Invalid Prime}) = A(1 - R)$.

With the use of these equations, the probability of recollection can be estimated by subtracting the probability of false recall (FR) in the invalid prime condition from the probability of correct recall (CR) in the valid prime condition, $R = P(\text{CR} \mid \text{Valid Prime}) - P(\text{FR} \mid \text{Invalid Prime})$. This measure rests on a rationale that is similar to that for subtracting false alarms from hits to measure "true" memory (see Snodgrass & Corwin, 1988, for a discussion of measures of recognition memory performance). Given an estimate of true memory (recollection), accessibility bias can be estimated using the probability of false recall in the invalid prime condition: $A = P(\text{FR} \mid \text{Invalid Prime})/(1 - R)$. Accessibility bias reflects use of the prime, a form of memory that is assumed to be independent of recollection of the target word.

Gaining estimates of R and A by means of the above equations shows that divided, compared with full, attention during study influenced recollection but left estimated accessibility bias unchanged (Table 3.4). Did presentation of a prime influence the probability of recollection? If it did not, one should be able to use the estimate of recollection gained from the valid and invalid prime conditions to predict performance in the baseline (no prime) condition. Because materials were balanced across replications, accessibility bias in the baseline condition should be equal for the two alternative responses $(A = .5)$. Combining estimates of R with this estimate of accessibility bias results in a predicted baseline performance equal to $R + (1 - R)$ $(.50)$. This equation almost perfectly predicts observed baseline performance for both the full-attention (.70 predicted vs. .71 observed) and divided-attention (.52 predicted vs. .53 observed) conditions, showing that presentation of a prime did not influence recollection.

The misinformation effect, or retroactive interference, observed in our experiment reflected only an influence on accessibility bias; ability to recollect was unchanged by presentation of a prime. In contrast, the manipulation of full versus divided attention produced an opposite dissociation by influencing recollection and leaving accessibility bias unchanged. Fitting a multinomial model to the results provides another means of gaining support for the same conclusions. The results are fit well by a multinomial model in which recollection and accessibility bias served as independent bases for responding. In the model, estimates of recollection were constrained to be the same across test conditions and estimates of accessibility bias were constrained to be the same across full- versus divided-attention conditions. Accessibility bias was set at .50 for baseline conditions.

Manipulating Accessibility Bias

Returning to the earlier example, the memory influence of an "I told you . . ." claim would be expected to depend on the validity of past claims from the same source. If the source were an unreliable one, having been often caught making erroneous claims, the "I told you . . ." claim might be ignored or, at least, might do much less to influence accessibility bias than it would if it had come from a credible source. At the extreme, an "I told you . . ." claim from an unreliable source might be treated as reason to reject the content of the claim and might show reactance by producing a response different from that dictated by the claim. In our situation, participants might strategically avoid giving a prime word as a response if the prime word is seldom valid.

In an experiment, Kara Bopp varied the probability of the prime being valid. In our earlier experiment, the prime was as likely to be valid as invalid, whereas in a "mostly valid" condition in Bopp's experiment the prime was valid on two thirds of the trials and invalid on only one third of the trials. Those probabilities were reversed in a "mostly invalid" condition. We expected accessibility bias to be larger when the prime was mostly valid.

The results are consistent with our expectations (Table 3.5). Probabilities of correct recall after valid and invalid primes were almost perfectly symmetrical around performance in the baseline condition in which a prime was not presented. This symmetry shows that presentation of a prime did not influence recollection but, rather, had its effect by means of an influence on accessibility bias. Estimates of recollection and accessibility bias were gained by the same means as in the earlier experiment. Comparisons of those estimates show that recollection did not differ for the mostly valid and mostly invalid conditions. However, accessibility bias did differ such that participants in the mostly valid condition were more likely to produce the prime as a response. The results are well fit by a multinomial model that constrained recollection to be equal across all conditions but allowed accessibility bias to differ between the mostly valid and mostly invalid conditions. Again, accessibility bias was set at .50 for baseline conditions.

Although not significant, there was a tendency for recollection to be higher in the mostly invalid than in the mostly valid condition. People might be more likely to attempt recollection when dealing with a low-credibility source of influence. Further analyses compared performance in the mostly valid and mostly invalid conditions during the last half of the experiment. Results from that analysis are the

TABLE 3.5

Memory effect of primes

BETWEEN-PARTICIPANT TEST CONDITIONS	PROBABILITY OF CORRECT RECALL		
	WITHIN-PARTICIPANT TEST CONDITIONS		
	VALID	BASELINE	INVALID
Mostly valid	.81	.67	.51
Mostly invalid	.77	.69	.60

BETWEEN-PARTICIPANT TEST CONDITIONS	ESTIMATES OF RECOLLECTION (R) AND ACCESSIBILITY BIAS (A)	
	R	A
Mostly valid	.32	.74
Mostly invalid	.38	.61

same as from the experiment as a whole except differences in accessibility bias were larger. This is to be expected because it takes time for participants to catch on that the prime is mostly valid or mostly invalid. However, a surprising result is that participants continued to favor the prime as a response even late in the experiment in the condition in which the prime was usually invalid. That is, participants never avoided the prime to the extent required for accessibility bias to drop to .50, let alone consistently avoiding the prime which would produce a value below .50. Perhaps effects of a prime on accessibility bias are automatic in the sense of being extremely difficult to avoid. Preliminary data collected by one of the present authors, Sandra Hessels, suggest that this is the case. In her experiment, participants heard the prime shortly before being presented with a recall test item. Telling participants to ignore the prime did not eliminate its effect. We suspect that in future experiments, we will be able to find conditions that allow participants to fully ignore the prime and conditions that result in reactance, that is, consistent avoidance of the prime as a response. Finding such conditions is important for applied purposes and for theory.

Misleading the Elderly Population

Our interest in misinformation effects that result from a false "I told you . . ." statement comes from our concern about fraudulent practices aimed at older adults. Older adults are a favorite target for scams and some of those scams involve a false "I told you . . ." statement (Jacoby, 1999). One example comes from home repairs. An older person may be approached by a dishonest salesperson with an offer of, for example, fixing pavement on a driveway for a very reasonable price. Later, when the job is completed, the amount demanded as payment is much higher than the price that was originally quoted. If the person complains, the dishonest salesperson responds, "I told you before that this was what it would cost." Out of uncertainty for what was originally agreed on, it is likely that the person will accept the false information and pay the increased price. Such scams take advantage of the impaired recollection of older adults by providing a response alternative that is in the scammer's best interest.

Jacoby (1999) compared the performance of younger and older participants using the procedures described above. A deficit in ability to recollect for older adults would give reason to expect them to show a larger effect of an invalid prime. Perhaps older adults are less often able to remember what was said earlier and, so, are more often open to the effects of accessibility bias. Jacoby attempted to equate recollection for one group of younger participants with that of older participants to see whether there were effects of aging beyond those on recollection. Younger participants in that group divided their attention during the study, the same manipulation that was found to reduce recollection in the first experiment described here. There were three groups of participants: older, young full attention, and young divided attention. The procedure was the same as outlined in Table 3.3. The probability of a prime being valid was .50.

Results reveal that for all groups, presentation of an invalid prime had its effect by means of an influence on accessibility bias. Compared with performance in the baseline condition, the decrease in correct responding produced by an invalid prime was approximately equal to the increase in correct responding produced by a valid prime (see Figure 3.1). Older participants were more susceptible to interference from an invalid prime than were young full-attention participants. However, they also show a larger positive priming effect. This pattern of results can be explained as produced by older participants' lessened ability to recollect. That is, older adults are more susceptible to a false "I told you . . ." claim than are the young full-attention participants because of a deficit in recollection. Greater susceptibility of young people can be produced by dividing attention during the study to reduce recollection. Dividing young participants' attention during the study produced results that were very similar to those found for older participants. Performance on baseline trials was nearly identical for older and younger divided-attention participants, suggesting that their ability to recollect was equated. The small difference in performance for the two groups after an invalid prime reflects a difference in accessibility bias. Young divided-attention participants were more likely to avoid using the prime as a response when they were unable to recollect than were older participants. This strategic avoidance of the prime increased accuracy after an invalid prime but produced an offsetting decrease in accuracy after a valid prime.

Summary and Implications for the Theory

Our "I told you . . ." experiments show the advantages of arranging conditions to examine retroactive effects on facilitation in combination with effects on interference.

FIGURE 3.1

The probability of correct recall for young divided-attention, young full-attention, and elderly population groups. From "Deceiving the Elderly: Effects of Accessibility Bias in Cued-Recall Performance," by L. L. Jacoby, 1999, Journal of Cognitive Neuroscience, 16, p. 428. Copyright 1999 by Psychological Press Ltd. Adapted with permission.

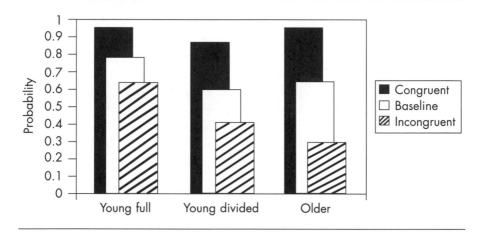

Traditional investigations of retroactive interference have included only a baseline and an interference condition (Table 3.1), and effects have been explained as due to response competition or unlearning. In contrast, we added a third condition to examine retroactive facilitation (valid prime) and retroactive interference (invalid prime). Doing so provides advantages that are the same as gained by examining hits and false alarms, rather than false alarms alone, in a standard investigation of recognition memory. Just as examining hits and false alarms allows one to separate effects on bias from those on memory, the addition of valid primes allows effects of accessibility bias to be separated from differences in recollection. Using that strategy shows that presentation of a prime did not influence memory in ways implied by the notion of unlearning. Instead, retroactive effects of the prime reflected only an influence on accessibility bias. Retroactive interference produced by an invalid prime was fully offset by retroactive facilitation produced by a valid prime. This symmetry of retroactive effects is expected if they reflect an influence of the prime on accessibility bias but would not be expected if presentation of a prime altered memory for the target. Had we examined performance only in the baseline and interference conditions, as is standard, we would have been unable to separate effects on bias from those on recollection of the earlier studied list. Similarly, Dosher, McElree, Hood, and Rosedale (1989) showed that priming in a recognition task reflects an influence on bias rather than increased discriminability. Presentation of semantically related primes improved performance on recognition judgments for target (old) items but worsened performance on recognition judgments for nontarget (new) items. As with our valid and invalid primes, semantic primes did not affect memory, but instead produced the symmetry characteristic of bias effects.

The effects of priming show that accessibility bias is dissociable from differences in recollection. Presentation of a prime and manipulating prime validity had an effect on accessibility bias but left recollection unchanged. Dividing attention during the study produced an opposite dissociation by reducing recollection and leaving accessibility bias unchanged. Age-related differences in susceptibility to interference were largely because of a deficit in recollection. Older participants were less likely to be able to recollect and, so, were more often open to effects of accessibility bias. That is, greater susceptibility to interference was a consequence rather than a cause of the older adult's poorer ability to remember the target word. Accessibility bias reflects a form or use of memory that is independent of recollection and is largely uninfluenced by aging. As described in the next section, using our approach to analyze proactive effects produced results that further support these conclusions.

Proactive Effects: Separating Habit and Recollection

Hay and Jacoby (1999) related the story of an aging math professor at the University of Manitoba who went to a conference in Chicago. When ready to return home, he was unable to find his airline ticket. After much searching, he bought another ticket and, arriving home, called his wife to pick him up at the airport. She replied that she would be unable to do so because he had driven their only car to Chicago. Such action slips demonstrate the influence of previously established habit on memory performance. If the professor did not usually travel to conferences by airplane, he would be unlikely to make such a mistake. Action slips are nothing more than instantiations of proactive interference (Table 3.2B).

Classic interference theory has explained proactive interference as due to response competition. An item comes to mind and, because of a loss of list differentiation, is mistakenly given as a response although it was appropriate for a prior list. According to this view, interference can be avoided only by retrieving list membership for each item that comes to mind and inhibiting response if the item is a member of the inappropriate list. Greater susceptibility to interference of people with amnesia (Warrington & Weiskrantz, 1970) and the elderly population (Hasher & Zacks, 1988) is said to be because of a lessened ability to suppress or inhibit inappropriate responses. In contrast to an inhibition account, greater susceptibility to interference might result from a deficit in recollection. When recollection of the target item fails, a guess is generated that is based on the first item that comes to mind. In the absence of recollection, habit determines item production. The argument is the same used to explain retroactive effects.

Hay and Jacoby (1996) separated the contributions of habit and recollection using materials that were the same used in our "I told you . . ." experiments. The procedures and underlying rationale were also similar except a manipulation of habit replaced the manipulation of priming. The first phase of their experiments was a training phase meant to develop a habit of a particular probability. Context words were presented along with a fragment of the target word and participants were asked to guess how the fragment would be completed. In Experiment 1, some fragments were completed with one word 75% of the time (e.g., knee b_n_; bone) and with the alternative word 25% of the time (knee b_n_; bend), whereas for other fragments the two alternatives were presented equally often (50/50). In a second phase of the experiment, participants saw short lists of the word pairs and were told to remember the pairs for a test that would immediately follow. During the test, the context words were presented with the fragments and were to be used as cues for recall of the target word in the short list. Incongruent test items were those in which the target was the nondominant response (the item presented 25% of the time during the training phase). Test items for which the target was presented 75% of the time were considered congruent. Items from the 50/50 condition served as a baseline against which effects of differential habit were evaluated.

The role served by congruent test items corresponds to that of valid primes in the "I told you . . ." experiments. Habit from prior training, a form of accessibility bias, would lead to the same response as recollection just as would a valid prime. For incongruent test items, in contrast, habit is opposed by recollection in the same way as are the effects of an invalid prime. By our view, then, effects of habit come about in the same way as those of priming with the obvious difference that habit produces proactive effects whereas priming effects are retroactive. The equations used by Hay and Jacoby (1996) to separate the contributions of habit and recollection are the same as described earlier for separating accessibility bias and recollection in our "I told you . . ." experiments.

Hay and Jacoby (1996) found that the probabilities of a correct response for congruent and incongruent test items were symmetrical around that for the baseline provided by items from the 50/50 training condition (.82, .63, and .72, respectively), a pattern of results that is the same as for valid and invalid primes in the "I told you . . ." experiments. The disadvantage for incongruent test items, compared with baseline, reflects proactive interference and was fully offset by proactive facilitation, the advantage for congruent items over baseline. Computing estimates revealed that estimated habit was higher for items from the 75/25 condition than for those from the 50/50 condition (.67 vs. .48), but estimated recollection was near identical for the two conditions (.45 vs. .43). Note that estimated habit shows probability matching—the estimate of habit was near the training probability (e.g., .67 vs. .75). Such probability matching is also found in other experiments reported by Hay and Jacoby and serves as converging evidence of the validity of assumptions underlying the estimation procedure (see Hay & Jacoby, 1996, for a discussion of this point along with a description of other converging evidence). A manipulation of response deadline produced a dissociation that was opposite to that produced by the manipulation of prior training (Experiment 3). Requiring participants to respond rapidly, rather than slowly, at the time of test reduced recollection but left habit unchanged. The effect on recollection was expected because recollection is generally assumed to be a slower process than is responding on the basis of habit. In a recent experiment, Jacoby, Debner, and Hay (in press) found that dividing attention during the study of the short lists reduced recollection but left estimated habit unchanged. That dissociation is the same as produced by dividing attention in the "I told you . . ." experiments.

Hay and Jacoby (1999) examined the effects of aging on recollection and habit. The results from their Experiment 1 (see the first two rows of Table 3.6) show that for incongruent test items, older adults were more likely than were the young to mistakenly give the response made dominant by prior training. That is, older adults were more susceptible to proactive interference or, stated differently, more likely to be influenced by a "bad" habit, or more likely to produce a "memory slip" akin to the action slip described at the beginning of this section. The result might be interpreted as evidence that older adults were less able to inhibit a habitual response (cf. Hasher & Zacks, 1988). A weakness in the inhibition account, however, is that it focuses only on the incongruent test items, a condition in which habit and recollection are in opposition. To gain a more complete account, one also needs to examine the situation where habit and recollection act in concert: congruent test items. The older adults were less likely to correctly respond to congruent test items. This disadvantage for older participants in a situation where habit is a source of correct responding would not be expected if they are impaired in their ability to inhibit habit-based responses. The effects can be better explained by a dual-process account in which recollection serves as an alternative to habit as a basis for responding. Estimates gained from our dual-process model show that the older adults were less able to recollect but did not differ from younger adults in their reliance on habit when recollection fails.

Can older participants be inoculated against effects of interference? An inhibition account would recommend teaching older adults to carefully examine the origin of

TABLE 3.6

Probability of dominant response and estimates

| | TRIAL TYPE | | ESTIMATES | |
GROUP	CONGRUENT	INCONGRUENT	RECOLLECTION	HABIT
Young participants	.88	.29	.60	.70
Elderly participants	.80	.50	.30	.74
Elderly participants[a]	.89	.31	.58	.73

Note. Data from Experiment 1 of Hay and Jacoby (1999). [a] This group was given elaborated instructions and had longer response deadlines. Data are from Experiment 3, distinctive condition only, of Hay and Jacoby (1999).

a response before making it overt to avoid being misled. The goal of this strategy is to enhance the editing function of consciousness (Jacoby, Kelley, & McElree, 1999). In contrast, we would seek to rehabilitate performance by finding conditions that encourage recollection. Hay and Jacoby (1999, Experiment 3) showed that when older people were provided with extra time at encoding and a longer retrieval deadline and explicit instructions to elaborate and integrate the pairs presented for study, their memory performance improved dramatically (bottom row, Table 3.6). These more supportive conditions made the older adults less susceptible to interference as shown by their better performance on incongruent test items and also improved their performance on congruent test items. Computing estimates show that the more supportive conditions served to enhance recollection for the older participants to a level that was as high as that of younger participants. Habit was unchanged. Thus, an effective way of reducing susceptibility to interference is to enhance an alternative basis for responding—recollection—rather than focus on interference alone.

Conclusion

Retroactive and proactive interference sometimes reflect only an influence on accessibility bias. This conclusion could not have been reached if we had relied on the experimental designs that have traditionally been used to investigate retroactive and proactive interference. Rather, it was necessary to examine performance in facilitation and interference conditions. Doing so allowed us to use a dual-process model to separate the contributions of recollection and accessibility bias. Support for the assumptions underlying that model is provided by findings of dissociations. As an example, contrary to an unlearning account of retroactive interference (Loftus, 1975; Postman & Underwood, 1973), presentation of an invalid prime did not alter memory for an earlier studied list but, rather, only influenced accessibility bias. In contrast, aging and dividing attention had their effects by reducing recollection and generally leaving accessibility bias unchanged. The greater susceptibility to interference shown by older adults was because of a deficit in recollection rather than a lessened ability to inhibit or suppress inappropriate responses (cf. Hasher & Zacks, 1988). Interference effects did not arise from a competitor that "blocked" retrieval of a correct response (cf. McGeoch, 1942). An account of that sort does not explain the symmetrical effects of valid and invalid primes or congruent and incongruent training. Such symmetry is expected if the effects arose from accessibility bias.

Our means of gaining estimates rests on the assumption that recollection and accessibility bias are independent contributors to overall performance. This approach to analyzing retroactive and proactive effects is the same as the process dissociation procedure (Jacoby, 1991) but creates conditions required to gain estimates in ways different than were originally used (for discussions of advantages of this change in means of creating conditions, see Hay & Jacoby, 1999; and Jacoby, 1998). The independence assumption underlying the process dissociation procedure has been its most controversial aspect (e.g., see Curran & Hintzman, 1997, and the reply by Jacoby et al., 1997). Findings of dissociations, of the sort described here, provide support for the independence assumption. However, dissociations should not always be expected. Differences in retroactive interference, as an example, might often reflect both differences in accessibility bias and a change in recollection. When primes were mostly invalid, rather than mostly valid, accessibility bias was reduced, and there was also a tendency toward an increase in recollection. The greater susceptibility of the older adults to interference produced by an invalid prime was largely because of their lessened ability to recollect. However, there was also a difference between young and old in accessibility bias. When unable to recollect, the older participants were more likely to rely on the prime than were younger participants. For these cases, it seems reasonable that differences in both recollection and accessibility bias were involved. It remains to be seen what effects are produced by manipulations that have been standard in investigations of retroactive and proactive interference, such as a manipulation of the retention interval between the study and the test.

The advance that we hope to gain from our approach is improved means of analyzing deficits in memory performance. Identifying older participants who are most vulnerable to a false "I told you . . ." claim is important to protect those individuals from attempted scams that plague older adults. Once identified as being vulnerable, it is necessary to diagnose the cause of that greater vulnerability. A deficit in recollection would be treated much differently than would an inappropriate accessibility bias. The latter might take the form of unwarranted trust or "gullibility" and be treated by warning older adults to be cautious and to strategically avoid being influenced by the memory reports of others. However, such caution is optimal only if one is in a generally hostile environment. Reducing accessibility bias has the benefit of reducing the probability of being misled by invalid claims but has the potentially large cost of also reducing the facilitation gained from valid claims. Similarly, reduced habit avoids action slips at the cost of facilitation that comes from an appropriate habit. The best defense against a false "I told you . . ." claim is to recollect what was truly said just as our forgetful university professor's best defense against the action slip of flying home would have been to have recollected that he drove to the conference. Measurement of recollection is the first step toward devising procedures that allow for its rehabilitation. The results from our preliminary attempts to rehabilitate recollection are encouraging (Hay & Jacoby, 1999; Jacoby, Jennings, & Hay, 1998).

The basis for forgetting can best be understood by looking at it not in isolation but in conjunction with instances of improved memory performance. This affords the use of a dual-process model that separates estimates of recollection from estimates of bias or habit. Separation of the two processes demonstrates that bias reflects a form or use of memory (implicit memory) that is largely uninfluenced by aging and even preserved by people with amnesia and that is independent of recollection. A dual-process model can easily be applied to more historical memory research concerned with the effects of interference. Crowder (1976) stated that "learning is not so much a matter of acquiring new behavior as it is a matter of organizing previously acquired behavior into new sequences" (p. 411). Looking back, it seems that our investigations aimed at explaining "I told you . . ." effects, habit effects and, in turn, the effects of aging are not unlike rearranging methods and principles that were investigated in great detail many years ago.

References

Ayers, M. S., & Reder, L. M. (1998). A theoretical review of the misinformation effect: Predictions from an activation-based memory model. *Psychonomic Bulletin and Review, 5,* 1–21.

Cohen, G., & Faulkner, D. (1989). Age differences in source forgetting: Effects of reality monitoring on eyewitness testimony. *Psychology and Aging, 4,* 10–17.

Crowder, R. G. (1976). *Principles of learning and memory.* Hillsdale, NJ: Halsted Press.

Curran T., & Hintzman, D. L. (1997). Consequences and causes of correlations in process dissociation. *Journal of Experimental Psychology: Learning, Memory, and Cognition, 23,* 496–504.

Dosher, B. A., McElree, B., Hood, R. M., & Rosedale, G. (1989). Retrieval dynamics of priming in recognition memory: Bias and discrimination analysis. *Journal of Experimental Psychology: Learning, Memory, and Cognition, 15,* 868–886.

Flexser, A. J., & Tulving, E. (1978). Retrieval independence in recognition and recall. *Psychological Review, 85,* 153–171.

Flexser, A. J., & Tulving, E. (1993). Recognition-failure constraints and the average maximum. *Psychological Review, 100,* 149–153.

Hasher, L., & Zacks, R. T. (1988). Working memory, comprehension, and aging: A review of a new view. In G. H. Bower (Ed.), *The psychology of learning and motivation* (Vol. 22, pp. 193–225). New York: Academic Press.

Hay, J. F., & Jacoby, L. L. (1996). Separating habit and recollection: Memory slips, process dissociations, and probability matching. *Journal of Experimental Psychology: Learning, Memory, and Cognition, 22,* 1323–1335.

Hay, J. F., & Jacoby, L. L. (1999). Separating habit and recollection in young and older adults: Effects of elaborative processing and distinctiveness. *Psychology and Aging, 14,* 122–134.

Hintzman, D. L. (1972). On testing the independence of associations. *Psychological Review, 79,* 261–264.

Hintzman, D. L. (1992). Mathematical constraints and the Tulving–Wiseman law. *Psychological Review, 99,* 536–542.

Hintzman, D. L. (1993). On variability, Simpson's paradox, and the relation between recognition and recall: Reply to Tulving and Flexser. *Psychological Review, 100*, 143–148.

Hintzman, D. L., & Curran, T. (1997). More than one way to violate independence: Reply to Jacoby and Shrout. *Journal of Experimental Psychology: Learning, Memory, and Cognition, 23*, 511–513.

Jacoby, L. L. (1991). A process dissociation framework: Separating automatic from intentional uses of memory. *Journal of Memory and Language, 30*, 513–541.

Jacoby, L. L. (1998). Invariance in automatic influences of memory: Toward a user's guide for the process-dissociation procedure. *Journal of Experimental Psychology: Learning, Memory, and Cognition, 24*, 3–26.

Jacoby, L. L. (1999). Deceiving the elderly: Effects of accessibility bias in cued-recall performance. *Journal of Cognitive Neuroscience, 16*, 417–436

Jacoby, L. L., Begg, I. M., & Toth, J. P. (1997). In defense of functional independence: Violations of assumptions underlying the process-dissociation procedure? *Journal of Experimental Psychology: Learning, Memory, and Cognition, 23*, 484–495.

Jacoby, L. L., Debner, J. A., & Hay, J. F. (in press). Proactive interference, accessibility bias, and process dissociation: Valid subjective reports of memory. *Journal of Experimental Psychology: Learning, Memory, and Cognition.*

Jacoby, L. L., Jennings, J. M., & Hay, J. F. (1998). Dissociating automatic and consciously controlled processes: Implications for diagnosis and rehabilitation of memory deficits. In D. J. Herrman, C. L. McEvoy, C. Hertzog, P. Hertel, & M. K. Johnson (Eds.), *Basic and applied memory research: Theory in context* (Vol. 1, pp. 161–193). Mahwah, NJ: Erlbaum.

Jacoby, L. L., Kelley, C. M., & McElree, B. D. (1999). The role of cognitive control: Early selection vs. late correction. In S. Chaiken & Y. Trope (Eds.), *Dual process theories in social psychology* (pp. 383–400). New York: Guilford Press.

Jacoby, L. L., & Shrout, P. E. (1997). Toward a psychometric analysis of violations of the independence assumption in process dissociation. *Journal of Experimental Psychology: Learning, Memory, and Cognition, 23*, 505–510.

Light, L. L., & La Voie, D. (1993). Direct and indirect measures of memory in old age. In P. Graf & M. E. J. Masson (Eds.), *Implicit memory* (pp. 207–230). Hillsdale, NJ: Erlbaum.

Loftus, E. F. (1975). Leading questions and the eyewitness report. *Cognitive Psychology, 7*, 560–572.

Martin, E. (1971). Verbal learning theory and independent retrieval phenomena. *Psychological Review, 78*, 314–332.

McCloskey, M., & Zaragoza, M. (1985). Misleading postevent information and memory for events: Arguments and evidence against memory impairment hypotheses. *Journal of Experimental Psychology: General, 114*, 1–16.

McGeoch, J. A. (1932). Forgetting and the law of disuse. *Psychological Review, 39*, 352–370.

McGeoch, J. A. (1942). *The psychology of human learning.* New York: Longmans, Green.

Melton, A. W., & Irwin, J. M. (1940). The influence of degree of interpolated learning on retroactive inhibition and the overt transfer of specific responses. *American Journal of Psychology, 53*, 173–203.

Postman, L., & Underwood, B. J. (1973). Critical issues in interference theory. *Memory & Cognition, 1*, 19–40.

Roediger, H. L., & McDermott, K. B. (1993). Implicit memory in normal human subjects. In H. Spinnler & F. Boller (Eds.), *Handbook of neuropsychology* (Vol. 8, pp. 63–131). Amsterdam, The Netherlands: Elsevier.

Shimamura, A. P. (1989). Disorders of memory: The cognitive science perspective. In F. Boller & J. Grafman (Eds.), *Handbook of neuropsychology* (Vol. 3, pp. 35–73). Amsterdam, The Netherlands: Elsevier.

Snodgrass, J. G., & Corwin, J. (1988). Pragmatics of measuring recognition memory: Applications to dementia and amnesia. *Journal of Experimental Psychology: General, 117*, 34–50.

Tulving, E., & Flexser, A. J. (1992). On the nature of the Tulving–Wiseman function. *Psychological Review, 99*, 543–546.

Warrington, E. K., & Weiskrantz, L. (1970). Amnesia: Consolidation or retrieval? *Nature, 228*, 628–630.

Winocur, G. (1982). Learning and memory deficits in institutionalized and noninstitutionalized old people: An analysis of interference effects. In F. I. M. Craik & S. Trehub (Eds.), *Aging and cognitive processes* (pp. 155–181). New York: Plenum Press.

CHAPTER 4

Effects of Dividing Attention on Encoding and Retrieval Processes

Fergus I. M. Craik

In this chapter, I review some recent work in my laboratory on encoding and retrieval processes in human memory. Like everyone else doing research in the field of human memory and learning at the present time, I have been greatly influenced by the ideas and findings produced by Bob Crowder over the past 35 years, and it is pleasant indeed to record that intellectual debt. As well as finding his *Principles of Learning and Memory* (1976) an invaluable source over the years, I had the pleasure of spending several months with Bob at the Stanford Center, where we organized a memory seminar and where I benefited greatly from his counsel and wisdom.

The work described in this chapter was carried out in collaboration with various colleagues—principally with Moshe Naveh-Benjamin from Ben Gurion University of the Negev in Israel and with Nicole Anderson from the University of Toronto (Toronto, Ontario, Canada). The starting point was the presumed similarity between encoding and retrieval processes based on the notions of encoding specificity (Tulving & Thomson, 1973), repetition of operations (Kolers, 1973), and transfer-appropriate processing (Morris, Bransford, & Franks, 1977; Roediger, Weldon, & Challis, 1989). All of these theoretical positions postulate that memory performance improves as the overlap between encoding and retrieval operations increases; ideally, retrieval processes should recapitulate the processes that occur when the event is originally encoded. If encoding and retrieval processes are essentially the same set of mental and neural activities carried out for somewhat different purposes, then it seems that other variables should have the same effect on the two of them. That is, variables that make encoding more or less effective should have parallel effects on retrieval. This appears to be true for some variables associated with decrements in memory performance—aging is one case in point—but less true of others. For example, both alcohol (Birnbaum, Parker, Hartley, & Noble, 1978) and benzodiazepines (Curran, 1991) seem to affect encoding processes but have little effect on retrieval.

Murdock (1965) showed that divided attention (DA) at the time of encoding was associated with marked reductions in later memory; it seems reasonable to assume that DA at retrieval would have similar effects. Surprisingly, however, Baddeley, Lewis, Eldridge, and Thomson (1984) reported that whereas DA at encoding reduced memory (thereby replicating the results of Murdock), DA at retrieval had little or no effect. This seemed such an unlikely result that Craik, Govoni, Naveh-Benjamin, and Anderson (1996) ran a similar series of studies in their laboratory. In these experiments, words or word pairs were encoded either under full-attention conditions or while the participant was simultaneously carrying out a demanding continuous reaction time (CRT) task. The subsequent retrieval tests (free recall, cued recall, or recognition) were also carried out under either full or divided attention.

The results largely replicate those of Baddeley et al. (1984). DA at encoding was associated with large reductions in memory performance in all cases, whereas DA at retrieval had much slighter effects. Table 4.1 shows the DA costs for both memory (percentage drop from performance under full attention) and the CRT task (increase in average reaction time [RT] per key press from performance under full attention) as a function of the memory paradigm used. The table shows that memory performance dropped substantially when the secondary task was performed at encoding (retrieval was under full attention) and that the losses were somewhat reduced for cued recall and recognition. For DA at retrieval (when encoding was under full attention), memory costs were much less than for DA at encoding, and the losses decreased from free recall to recognition. Performance of the CRT task slowed under dual-task conditions, more so for DA at retrieval in the case of free recall.

At first, this pattern appears to reflect a simple trade-off between memory and the CRT task—more attention was paid to memory retrieval than to memory encoding, perhaps because of the more immediate consequences of mental effort at retrieval. This cannot be the whole story, however, because RT costs are essentially the same for encoding and retrieval in the cases of cued recall and recognition, yet DA at encoding again has a larger effect on memory performance than does DA at retrieval. RT costs at encoding are greater for cued recall than for the other two paradigms,

TABLE 4.1

Memory and RT costs under divided-attention conditions

	MEMORY COSTS		REACTION TIME COSTS	
PARADIGM	**ENCODING**	**RETRIEVAL**	**ENCODING**	**RETRIEVAL**
Free recall[a]	40	12	48	134
Cued recall	33	9	77	68
Recognition	22	1	27	32

Note. Memory costs are shown as the percentage drop from full attention. Reaction time costs are given in milliseconds above baseline. This table is based on Experiments 1–4 of Craik, Govoni, Naveh-Benjamin, and Anderson (1996). [a]Free-recall results are averaged over two experiments.

presumably owing to the fact that participants must encode a pair of words on each trial in that case. Finally, RT costs at retrieval drop substantially from free recall to recognition memory.

Thus, the results of this first series of experiments generally confirm the conclusions of Baddeley et al. (1984) that whereas DA at encoding led to substantial memory deficits, DA at retrieval had remarkably slight effects. However, it does not seem possible to conclude that retrieval processes are "automatic," given the large secondary-task costs. The conclusions are therefore that retrieval is in some sense autonomous or obligatory, although resource demanding. Craik and his colleagues also have suggested that the pattern of declining costs from free recall through cued recall to recognition reflected the increasing amounts of "environmental support" associated with these respective paradigms (e.g., Craik, 1983). The observed asymmetry between the effects of DA on encoding and retrieval is thus in line with the effects of alcohol (Birnbaum et al., 1978) and depressive drugs (Curran, 1991), but it calls into question the theoretical notion that encoding and retrieval processes are essentially the same mental and neural operations. Some further experiments are described before reviewing the theory.

Effects of Divided Attention at Encoding

Previous studies of DA at encoding appear to show that any secondary task performed during the acquisition phase of a memory task results in a substantial reduction in later recollection. When words are learned and retrieved it does not seem to matter if the secondary task is an RT task involving simple visual stimuli and corresponding keys (Craik et al., 1996), card sorting (Baddeley et al., 1984; Murdock, 1965), or other verbal material (Fernandes & Moscovitch, 2000); large reductions in performance were observed in all cases. If qualitative similarity is not a factor, are there other aspects of secondary tasks that are important? An experiment conducted by Naveh-Benjamin, Craik, Gavrilescu, and Anderson (2000) shows that the task must use central resources to be effective.

Naveh-Benjamin et al. (2000) asked participants to learn and retrieve lists of 12 unrelated word-pairs presented auditorily. The lists were either encoded and retrieved under full attention, or a visual CRT task was also performed during either encoding or retrieval. The difficulty of the CRT task was varied in two ways: by having three or six choices (thereby varying decision difficulty) and by requiring the participant to make one press or two presses on the relevant key for each response (thereby varying motor difficulty). The main findings were that relative to full attention, DA at retrieval was associated with a small (8%) and statistically nonsignificant drop in memory performance. Also there was no further effect of increases in either decision difficulty or motor difficulty. In contrast, DA at encoding had a large detrimental effect (26% on average), and in this case variations in decision difficulty affected performance, whereas variations in motor difficulty did not. This result was obtained despite the further finding that the increase in RT costs was greater for motor difficulty than for decision difficulty. The conclusion was, therefore, that encoding processes are impaired by secondary tasks that consume central processing resources but not by tasks varying only in perceptual-motor difficulty.

A second question that may be asked is what is the nature of the "resource" that is withdrawn by secondary tasks? Is it simply time, for example? That is, the secondary task necessarily takes some time to perform; does the removal of this amount of processing time account for the observed reduction in memory? This question was addressed by using a procedure devised by Richard Govoni to study the trade-off between processing time (during encoding, e.g.) and subsequent memory performance. Full details of the procedure are given in Craik et al. (1996). The idea in brief is that word lists are first presented under full attention during encoding but at various rates. This procedure yields a curve relating encoding time to memory; slower rates are associated with higher levels of subsequent recall (see also Roberts, 1972). The CRT secondary task was also performed under single-task conditions to obtain a measure of baseline performance. The memory-encoding task (with words presented at a fixed rate of 4 s per word) was then combined with the CRT task in the DA procedure, and finally the word list was recalled under conditions of full attention. The results show first that memory performance after DA at encoding was lower than the level associated with a 4-s rate in the full-attention condition and second that the average key-press time in the CRT task was slower than the average RT in the single-task baseline condition.

The question was whether memory performance following DA at encoding could be predicted on the basis of the functional time available for encoding each word. On the simple assumption that memory encoding and the RT task share the same limited supply of attentional resources (represented here by the time available), Craik et al. (1996) asked whether the additional time taken to perform the CRT task under DA conditions is the functional time "allocated" to the memory task to carry out encoding operations. For example, if the CRT task took an average time of 500 ms per key press under single-task (baseline) conditions and 1,000 ms per key press under DA conditions, the assumption was that 500 ms in every second were used for memory encoding, and therefore the nominal encoding rate of 4 s per word was reduced to the functional rate of 2 s per word. This simple model predicts that memory performance following DA at encoding at a 4-s rate should be equivalent to performance at a 2-s rate under conditions of full attention.

The results of Craik et al. (1996) show that it was equivalent, provided that it was further assumed that memory encoding could also occur during the mechanical "motor time" component of each RT key press. The results also showed an unexpected finding, however. Encoding was carried out under three different conditions, in which the relative degrees of importance of the memory and RT tasks were varied by instructions to the participants. In one condition memory was emphasized, in a second the RT task was emphasized, and in a third the participants were told to allocate equal attention to the two tasks. Whereas memory performance in the "memory" emphasis condition fit the time–accuracy function well, the unexpected result was that levels associated with 50/50 and RT task emphasis fell progressively below the function. The researchers speculated that this might be due to a change in the qualitative type of encoding achieved when emphasis was shifted away from memory encoding. For example, the 50/50 and RT emphasis conditions might be associated with progressively shallower levels of encoding, so that their actual performance levels were lower than they "should be" based on a consideration of encoding times alone.

This hypothesis was explored by Dana Gavrilescu in an experiment reported in the article by Naveh-Benjamin et al. (2000). In her experiment, she first constructed three different time–accuracy functions relating encoding time to memory performance. Paired associate word lists were presented at rates of 2, 3, 4, and 6 s per pair in each of three conditions; the conditions themselves involved deep, medium, and shallow encoding instructions. This procedure resulted in three functions relating encoding time to memory, tracing out "cognitive contours" in which depth of encoding was also represented. The dual-task portion of the experiment was then conducted at a 6-s rate of presentation and under three different conditions of relative emphasis. Figure 4.1 shows the time–accuracy curves or "calibration functions" linking encoding times to memory performance under the deep, medium, and shallow encoding conditions. The data points all appear to asymptote around 4 s, so straight-line functions were fitted to the points for 2, 3, and 4 s, given that the observed values for memory performance in the DA conditions all fell between 3 and 4 s of (functional) encoding times. These data points for the DA conditions were collected under three conditions of relative emphasis of the memory encoding and CRT tasks: memory, 50/50, and RT, as previously indicated. The three points shown in Figure 4.1 (marked x, o, and +) plot the observed number of words recalled against the functional time allocated to encoding. This latter value, in turn, was calculated from the amount of slowing observed in the CRT task, in the manner described above. As an example, the memory emphasis condition yielded a recall score of 5.6 words and a functional encoding time of 3.8 s. Given that the actual presentation rate was 6 s per word, this means that 2.2 s of each 6 s were taken up by the decision times of the CRT task, leaving 3.8 s in each 6 s for memory encoding.

Figure 4.1 shows that the observed values for the memory, 50/50, and RT conditions of emphasis in the DA part of the experiment fell systematically between the deep and medium time–accuracy functions. Functional encoding times also fell slightly from memory to RT conditions, but the reduction in numbers of words recalled was greater than predicted on the basis of any one time–accuracy function. The conclusion drawn by Naveh-Benjamin et al. (2000) was therefore that the greater emphasis on the CRT task is associated both with a reduction in functional encoding

FIGURE 4.1

Encoding time, depth of processing, and recall under full or divided attention.

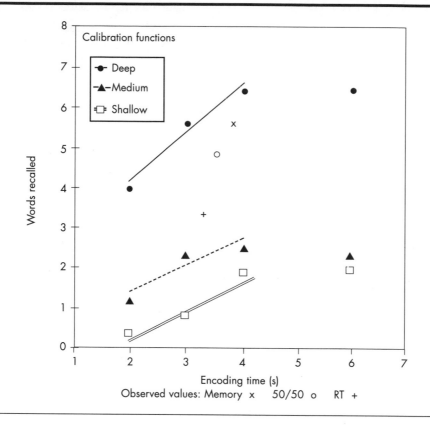

time and with a qualitative change (from deeper to shallower processing) in the type of processing achieved.

A third question relating to the effects of DA on encoding concerns the degree of semantic elaboration accomplished. It is known that greater degrees of encoded elaboration are associated with higher levels of subsequent recall (Craik & Tulving, 1975), so it seems likely that at least part of the drop in memory performance associated with DA is due to a reduction in elaboration. Having said that, the relations among DA, elaboration, and memory could take one of two forms, as illustrated in Figure 4.2. The more likely possibility (Figure 4.2A) is that, relative to full attention, encoded representations under DA are less elaborate but fall on the same function relating amount of elaboration to later memory. An alternative possibility (Figure 4.2B) is that the DA function relating elaboration to memory falls at a lower level than the full-attention function; this would suggest that memory performance is lower for DA than for full attention, given the same degree of elaboration.

FIGURE 4.2

Functions relating recall to degree of elaboration at encoding under full or divided attention.

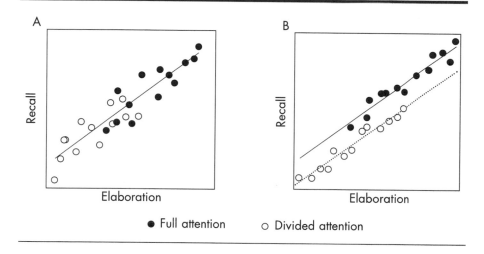

Jill Kester, Aaron Benjamin, and I have carried out several unpublished experiments to explore this issue. In one study, we presented word-pairs to participants and asked them to rate the elaborateness of the connection they could form between each pair of words. The rating scale ranged from 0 (*unable to form any meaningful connection*) to 5 (*a strong, meaningful connection*). Our assumption was that degree of rated elaboration would correlate positively with later recall of the second word of each pair given the first word as a cue. Half of the participants performed the word-pair rating task (which we regarded as the encoding phase) under full-attention conditions, and the other half performed the task under DA. The word-pairs were presented visually, and the DA participants simultaneously performed an auditory digit-monitoring task.

The results are shown in Table 4.2A. Levels 0 and 1 were collapsed into one category, as were levels 4 and 5, due to the small number of ratings given to these levels. The table shows that, as expected, cued-recall performance increases as the rated degree of elaboration increases and that this happens for both full-attention and DA conditions. Unexpectedly, however, performance for the DA group was substantially lower than for the full-attention group at every level of elaboration. This surprising result means that for the same subjective rating, participants encoding under DA conditions recalled fewer words in the cued-recall phase than did those working under full-attention conditions. One possible reason for the result is that DA participants perhaps did not really *process* the word-pair as such but merely judged the semantic relatedness of the pair without much real mental involvement. This seems somewhat unlikely given the strong relation between rated degree of

TABLE 4.2

Proportions of words recalled

ATTENTION	A. DEGREE OF ELABORATION			
	0 + 1	2	3	4 + 5
Full	.36	.47	.50	.61
Divided	.10	.17	.23	.31

	B. RATED ELABORATION				
	0	1	2	3	4
Full	.64	.82	.81	.79	.86
Divided	.46	.68	.67	.64	.78

Note. The data are from the unpublished experiments of Kester, Craik, and Benjamin.

elaboration and subsequent recall, but it seemed preferable to run a further version of the experiment in which the degree of elaboration could be measured more objectively.

In this second version, pairs of words were again presented; but in this case, the participants were instructed to generate a sentence using both words. They were also asked to make the sentence as richly meaningful as possible. As in the previous experiment, half of the participants performed this sentence generation task under full-attention conditions, and half performed it while simultaneously carrying out a card-sorting task. The generated sentences were later transcribed, mixed randomly, and given to judges who rated the semantic richness, complexity, and coherence of each sentence on a scale from 0 to 4. A rating of 0 meant that the participant was unable to come up with a sentence within the 6-s time limit and so simply repeated back the two words. A rating of 4 was given to richly elaborate sentences. Following the generation phase, all participants performed a cued-recall task under full-attention conditions; the first words from each pair were re-presented, and participants attempted to recall the original paired second word in each case. The results are shown in Table 4.2B, and it may be seen that they essentially replicate the pattern shown in Table 4.2A. Again there were significant effects of attention and of degree of elaboration but no interaction between the factors. Recall levels were higher in the second version of the experiment, probably because it involved only 48 pairs (vs. 80 pairs in the first version) and possibly because of the greater effectiveness of sentence generation as an encoding manipulation. The main point remains, however; for the same degree of semantic elaboration, fewer words were recalled after encoding them under DA conditions.

The results shown in Table 4.2 suggest that DA at encoding reduces memory performance in some way other than by reducing the richness of the semantic elaboration achieved. The results of Gavrilescu's experiment (Naveh-Benjamin et al., 2000) suggest that DA impairs the qualitative depth of encoding, but the present experiments show that DA is associated with lower performance even when such qualitative factors are equated between DA and full attention. Kester, Craik, and Benjamin speculated that DA may affect some processes of binding and consolidation that do not have any correlates in subjective experience. This point is discussed again briefly after a consideration of the effects of division of attention at the time of retrieval.

Effects of Divided Attention at Retrieval

The experiments conducted by Craik et al. (1996) confirm the surprising findings by Kellogg, Cocklin, and Bourne (1982) and by Baddeley et al. (1984) that DA at retrieval had relatively slight effects on memory performance. These researchers also have shown that instructions to emphasize either the memory task or the RT task had large effects at encoding but no systematic effects at retrieval. This latter result is thus in line with the suggestion of Baddeley et al. (1984) that retrieval processes are automatic, but Baddeley et al.'s suggestion is disconfirmed by the finding that retrieval consumes more processing resources than does encoding, as measured by the reduction in secondary task performance (Johnston, Griffith, & Wagstaff, 1972; see also the free-recall results shown in Table 4.1). Retrieval processes may thus be "automatic" in the sense that they are not very amenable to conscious control, but they are clearly not automatic in the sense that they can be run off without the expenditure of attentional resources. On the contrary, they appear to require considerable resources.

Although the conclusion that DA at retrieval has little or no effect on memory performance is well supported by the previously cited results, findings from other studies appear to set limits on the generality of the conclusion. Jacoby (1991) reported two experiments in which DA at retrieval reduced performance markedly, especially for words that had been encoded deeply and semantically (anagram solution) compared with words encoded by reading. Jacoby suggested that DA at retrieval reduced or eliminated the participants' ability to use recollection processes as a component of overall recognition, leaving them to rely on familiarity, which is virtually unaffected by the DA procedure. Normally, anagram solution generates information that is used in recollection, but DA at retrieval reduces the advantage typically associated with anagrams over read words. One possible way to resolve the apparent difference between the results of Jacoby (1991), on the one hand, and those of Baddeley et al. (1984) and Craik et al. (1996), on the other, is that performance in the latter cases depended heavily on familiarity rather than on recollection. The finding that DA at retrieval has a small but significant effect on free recall, a smaller effect on cued recall, and no effect on recognition (see Table 4.1) is in line with this suggestion. Jacoby's second experiment used his exclusion paradigm, in which participants must make a decision about the source of each item (e.g., visual or auditory presentation during the previous encoding phase) while also making the recognition judgment. Perhaps the necessity to recollect source makes retrieval processes vulnerable to division of attention.

I have run some experiments to test this possibility. In one version, single words were presented visually or auditorily, and this variable was crossed with the orienting task performed on each word—participants either reported the number of syllables or rated the word for pleasantness. These 2 × 2 encoding conditions were performed under full attention, but the subsequent recognition test was carried out under either full or DA conditions. The recognition test was unpaced (participants checked off their responses on a typed sheet), and participants were asked first whether they recognized each word and, if so, whether it had been presented visually or auditorily, and with the syllable or pleasantness orienting task. Table 4.3A shows the item recognition data (hits minus false alarms) for the four encoding conditions; it is clear that DA had only a small effect on performance. What about recognition of source information? Table 4.3B shows the probabilities of making the correct modality judgment (auditory–visual) and task judgment (syllable–pleasantness) given that the word itself was correctly recognized. That is, Table 4.3B gives conditional probabilities. Again it is clear that any decrements associated with DA at retrieval were small and unsystematic. These results are thus in line with those of Baddeley et al. (1984) and Craik et al. (1996).

TABLE 4.3

Effects of divided attention at retrieval

	ENCODING CONDITION					
ATTENTION	VIS–SYLL	AUD–SYLL	VIS–PLEASANT	AUD–PLEASANT	SYLL	PLEASANT
A. Item recognition						
Full	.51	.55	.81	.81		
Divided	.47	.51	.79	.79		
B. Attribute recognition (conditional on item recognition)						
Modality						
Full	.68	.77	.70	.74		
Divided	.73	.72	.74	.73		
Orienting task						
Full	.87	.89	.89	.82		
Divided	.84	.87	.85	.85		
C. R estimates						
Full					.45	.71
Divided					.21	.27

Note. vis = visual presentation; aud = auditory presentation; syll = syllable task; pleasant = pleasantness rating.

However, a second version of the experiment yielded very different results. Words were again encoded under full attention and with the same 2 × 2 combination of modality and orienting task. Retrieval was carried out under either full or DA conditions, and the process dissociation procedure was used (Jacoby, 1991). In this, words were all presented visually at retrieval and at a 2-s rate. In the "inclusion" condition, participants responded positively to any previously presented word, and in the "exclusion" condition, they responded positively only to words that had originally been presented auditorily. Visual words and new (distractor) words were given a negative response. This technique thus necessitates that both an item judgment and a source judgment be made within 2 s. Table 4.3C shows the estimates of conscious recollection (R; see Jacoby, 1991, for details) as a function of attention and type of orienting task. In this case, DA is associated with a substantial reduction in performance, and this reduction is greater for words encoded deeply with the pleasantness ratings. An analysis of variance showed significant effects of attention, type of processing, and the interaction between these factors. It thus appears that DA at retrieval does reduce memory performance markedly when a source judgment is required, and the retrieval processes must be carried out under time pressure.

A second qualification on the general conclusion that retrieval processes are immune to the effects of DA concerns the similarity of the secondary task to the memory task. In all of the experiments described thus far, these tasks have been rather dissimilar; typically the memory task involved verbal materials and the DA task involved either a perceptual-motor task or monitoring a long series of digits for specified targets. Fernandes and Moscovitch (2000) conducted experiments in which both memory and secondary tasks involved verbal materials and found substantial effects of DA at retrieval under these conditions. The memory task was free recall of a list of words, and the secondary task consisted of monitoring a long sequence of visually presented words for the occurrence of targets defined as three successive words denoting man-made objects or (in another condition) three successive 2-syllable words. Recall performance dropped by 37% for the man-made task and by 33% for the syllable task. These decrements in retrieval are obviously much greater than the 12% drop observed in DA at retrieval for free recall reported by Craik et al. (1996) and shown in Table 4.1.

Nonetheless, Fernandes and Moscovitch (2000) confirmed some aspects of the original results reported by Craik et al. (1996) by showing that the man-made and syllable-monitoring tasks caused an even larger drop in performance when they were performed during encoding; the decrements in performance were now 53% and 52%, respectively. In further experiments, Fernandes and Moscovitch compared the man-made monitoring task with a task involving a long series of 2-digit numbers that participants monitored for the occurrence of three successive odd numbers. These tasks were carried out during either encoding or retrieval of a free-recall list. For DA at retrieval, the reductions in performance were 30% for the man-made task but only 13% for the digit task; clearly this latter result is quite comparable to the

12% drop reported by Craik et al. (1996). Finally, when Fernandes and Moscovitch had participants perform their monitoring tasks at encoding, the drops were 56% and 50% for man-made and digit monitoring, respectively.

Fernandes and Moscovitch (2000) concluded that DA at retrieval reduces memory performance when both tasks compete for the same verbal representational system. It should also be noted that their man-made task involved a considerable working memory load, as the string of words held in mind must be continually updated. They also concluded that DA at encoding reduces memory performance regardless of the similarity between the memory task and the secondary task; in this case, it appears that any competition for general processing resources affects performance. Finally, in line with the previous studies described in the present chapter, they also reported an asymmetry between DA at encoding and DA at retrieval, with the same secondary task having a larger detrimental effect in the former case.

Conclusion

The series of experiments discussed in this chapter had their origin in the assumption that encoding and retrieval processes are similar. Following the notions of encoding specificity (Tulving & Thomson, 1973), repetition of operations (Kolers, 1973), and transfer-appropriate processing (Morris et al., 1977; Roediger et al., 1989), my interpretation of the evidence is that successful retrieval processes essentially recapitulate the same mental and neural processes that occurred during encoding (Craik, 1983). However, the evidence from the studies reviewed here suggests that encoding and retrieval processes show more differences than similarities. First, DA has a much greater detrimental effect at encoding than at retrieval, and this asymmetry does not appear to be due simply to a differential trade-off with secondary task performance. Second, encoding appears to be more controlled, more sensitive to emphasis instructions (Craik et al., 1996), and differentially affected by secondary tasks that involve central decision making (Naveh Benjamin et al., 2000). Third, DA at encoding appears to result in a shallower type of processing (Naveh-Benjamin et al.) and may also impair the efficiency of binding and consolidation processes (unpublished experiments of Kester et al.).

Nonetheless, retrieval processes are very resource demanding, especially with retrieval tasks that are low in environmental support (Craik, 1983; Craik et al., 1996). DA at retrieval impairs the recollection of context more than the recollection of item information (Table 4.3; Jacoby, 1991). Finally, Fernandes and Moscovitch (2000) showed that similarity between the memory and secondary tasks plays a greater role at retrieval than it does at encoding.

Must one therefore conclude that encoding and retrieval processes are different in nature? If so, how does one reconcile these differences with such well-established principles as encoding specificity and transfer-appropriate processing? One possible line of resolution is that these principles refer to the necessary similarity between the qualitative representations of events that are formed at encoding and reactivated at retrieval. Logically, it seems necessary for encoding and retrieval processes to have something in common, given that the two sets of processes refer to the same external event. At the same time, the differences between the processes may reflect major differences in the control processes that guide encoding and retrieval, respectively.

Evidence on these points is beginning to emerge from studies of cognitive neuroimaging, although the evidence itself is still somewhat contradictory and its implications for behavioral studies somewhat conjectural. In the HERA (hemispheric encoding–retrieval asymmetry) principle, Tulving, Kapur, Craik, Moscovitch, and Houle (1994) suggested that encoding processes are associated with activation of the left-prefrontal cortex, whereas episodic retrieval processes are associated with right-prefrontal activation. This suggestion is in line with the notion that the control processes underlying encoding and retrieval are different. However, some recent studies (e.g., McDermott, Buckner, Petersen, Kelley, & Sanders, 1999; Wagner et al., 1998) report similar prefrontal activations for encoding and retrieval, with verbal encoding and retrieval activating left-frontal regions, and nonverbal encoding and retrieval activating right-frontal regions. In addition, McDermott et al. distinguished such "code-specific" activations from "set-specific" activations, with the further observation that a region of the right-frontal polar cortex shows set-specific activation in that it tends to be more active during retrieval than encoding. These suggestions lead to the reasonable position that some mental processes (and their neural correlates) necessarily overlap between encoding and retrieval, whereas others (representing different "sets" or different control processes) are substantially different. It seems likely that further collaborative interchanges between the classical experimental psychology described by Crowder (1976) and others and the burgeoning new field of cognitive neuroscience will further clarify the similarities and differences between the processes involved in encoding and retrieval.

References

Baddeley, A. D., Lewis, V., Eldridge, M., & Thomson, N. (1984). Attention and retrieval from long-term memory. *Journal of Experimental Psychology: General, 113*, 518–540.

Birnbaum, I. M., Parker, E. S., Hartley, J. T., & Noble, E. P. (1978). Alcohol and memory: Retrieval processes. *Journal of Verbal Learning and Verbal Behavior, 17*, 325–335.

Craik, F. I. M. (1983). On the transfer of information from temporary to permanent memory. *Philosophical Transactions of the Royal Society of London, Series B302*, 341–359.

Craik, F. I. M., Govoni, R., Naveh-Benjamin, M., & Anderson, N. D. (1996). The effects of divided attention on encoding and retrieval processes in human memory. *Journal of Experimental Psychology: General, 125*, 159–180.

Craik, F. I. M., & Tulving, E. (1975). Depth of processing and the retention of words in episodic memory. *Journal of Experimental Psychology: General, 104*, 268–294.

Crowder, R. G. (1976). *Principles of learning and memory.* Hillsdale, NJ: Erlbaum.

Curran, H.V. (1991). Benzodiazepines, memory and mood: A review. *Psychopharmacology, 105*, 1–8.

Fernandes, M. A., & Moscovitch, M. (2000). Divided attention and memory: Evidence of substantial interference effects at retrieval and encoding. *Journal of Experimental Psychology: General, 129*, 155–176.

Jacoby, L. L. (1991). A process dissociation framework: Separating automatic from intentional uses of memory. *Journal of Memory and Language, 30*, 513–541.

Johnston, W. A., Griffith, D., & Wagstaff, R. R. (1972). Speed, accuracy, and ease of recall. *Journal of Verbal Learning and Verbal Behavior, 11*, 512–520.

Kellogg, R. T., Cocklin, T., & Bourne, L. E., Jr. (1982). Conscious attentional demands of encoding and retrieval from long-term memory. *American Journal of Psychology, 95*, 183–198.

Kolers, P. A. (1973). Remembering operations. *Memory & Cognition, 1*, 347–355.

McDermott, K. G., Buckner, R. L., Petersen, S. E., Kelley, W. M., & Sanders, A. L. (1999). Set- and code-specific activation in the frontal cortex: An fMRI study of encoding and retrieval of faces and words. *Journal of Cognitive Neuroscience, 11*, 631–640.

Morris, C. D., Bransford, J. D., & Franks, J. J. (1977). Levels of processing versus transfer appropriate processing. *Journal of Verbal Learning and Verbal Behavior, 16*, 519–533.

Murdock, B. B., Jr. (1965). Effects of a subsidiary task on short-term memory. *British Journal of Psychology, 56*, 413–419.

Naveh-Benjamin, M., Craik, F. I. M., Gavrilescu, D., & Anderson, N. D. (2000). Asymmetry between encoding and retrieval processes: Evidence from divided attention and a calibration analysis. *Memory & Cognition, 28*, 965–976.

Roberts, W. A. (1972). Free recall of word lists varying in length and rate of presentation: A test of total time hypotheses. *Journal of Experimental Psychology, 92*, 365–372.

Roediger, H. L., III, Weldon, M. S., & Challis, B. H. (1989). Explaining dissociations between implicit and explicit measures of retention: A processing account. In H. L. Roediger III & F. I. M. Craik (Eds.), *Varieties of memory and consciousness: Essay in honour of Endel Tulving* (pp. 3–41). Hillsdale, NJ: Erlbaum.

Tulving, E., Kapur, S., Craik, F. I. M., Moscovitch, M., & Houle, S. (1994). Hemispheric encoding/retrieval asymmetry in episodic memory: Positron emission tomography findings. *Proceedings of the National Academy of Sciences, 91*, 2016–2020.

Tulving, E., & Thomson, D. M. (1973). Encoding specificity and retrieval processes in episodic memory. *Psychological Review, 80*, 352–373.

Wagner, A. D., Poldrack, R. A., Eldridge, L. L., Desmond, J. E., Glover, G. H., & Gabrieli, J. D. E. (1998). Material-specific lateralization of prefrontal activation during episodic encoding and retrieval. *Neuroreport, 9*, 3711–3717.

CHAPTER 5

Is Semantic Activation Automatic?

A Critical Re-Evaluation

James H. Neely
Todd A. Kahan

I n this chapter, we evaluate evidence from the past 25 years relevant to Posner and Snyder's (1975) and Neely's (1977) claim that words automatically activate their meanings, a claim recently called a myth (Besner, Stolz, & Boutilier, 1997; Stolz & Besner, 1999). According to Posner and Snyder's (1975) seminal treatment and some of the subsequent refinements made by Neumann (1984) and Bargh (1989, 1994), an automatic process (a) is fast acting, (b) is capacity free, (c) can occur without intention, (d) is involuntary or uncontrollable, and (e) can occur without conscious awareness. Although these five criteria were originally given equal weighting, they have not been examined to the same extent. Because of page limitations, we focus on whether semantic activation (SA) is capacity free and can occur without intention. We chose the former because it has not been extensively investigated and in our opinion may prove to be an informative area for future research. We chose the latter because it has been extensively used as a virtual litmus test for SA automaticity. (For more extensive treatments of the other criteria, see Bargh & Chartrand, 1999; Carr, 1992; Dosher, 1998; Draine & Greenwald, 1998; Greenwald & Draine, 1998; Johnston & Dark, 1986; Kahneman & Treisman, 1984; and Merikle & Reingold, 1998.)

We thank Jeanette Altarriba, Dave Balota, Tram Neill, and Roddy Roediger for their helpful comments on drafts of this chapter. We especially thank Derek Besner and Jennifer Stolz for discussing with us many of the issues covered in this chapter. Although we have taken many aspects of their discussion into account, our acknowledgment of their input should not be misconstrued as indicating that they endorse our arguments. We also thank Alice Healy for alerting us to the issues we raise concerning Besner, Stolz, and Boutilier's (1997) work in the section on effects of intraword spatially focused attention.

Semantic Activation

Almost all theories of reading assume that a word has at least three distinct kinds of mental representations: orthographic (corresponding to its visual letter patterns), phonological (corresponding to how it sounds when pronounced), and semantic (corresponding to its meaning). Because data from the Stroop (1935) and semantic priming (Meyer & Schvaneveldt, 1971) paradigms serve as cornerstones for the claim that SA is automatic, we focus on them here. In the standard single-word semantic priming paradigm (see Neely, 1991, for a review), a person either pronounces or makes a lexical (word–nonword) decision to a word target (e.g., *nurse*) after silently reading a prime that is either semantically–associatively related to it (e.g., *doctor*) or unrelated to it (e.g., *curtain*). Evidence for SA is provided by the semantic priming effect, the finding that reaction times (RTs) or response accuracy to the target is typically facilitated by the related prime relative to the unrelated prime. In the standard Stroop paradigm (see MacLeod, 1991, for a review), people name the ink color in which a word (representing a color name) is printed. The standard Stroop effect is that RTs to name the ink color are longer when the word names a color different from that ink color than when it names that ink color. According to Posner and Snyder (1975), this effect is not caused by SA for the word inhibiting the ink color's activation of its phonological–semantic representations. Instead, it is the rapid prior entry of the word's articulatory representation into a one-item verbal output buffer that interferes with (delays) the output of the more slowly activated ink color's articulation.

Although Stroop (1935) and semantic priming effects are typically taken as evidence for a word's SA, one can question whether either effect is due to the word's semantic representation having actually been activated. Consider semantic priming studies. In over 95% of them, the prime and target are associatively related, that is, the target is likely to be given as a free association to the prime. Although most of these prime–target pairs (e.g., *lion* and *tiger*, *reply* and *answer*) are also semantically related, some are not (e.g., *book* and *worm*). Although associatively related items clearly produce priming, it is more controversial whether semantic similarity in the absence of association yields priming (see McRae & Boisvert, 1998, for a review of these findings). This issue becomes difficult to resolve if semantic similarity between two words is based on their noncontiguous co-occurrence in text and discourse (e.g., Landauer & Dumais, 1997; Lund & Burgess, 1996) or if priming occurs through mediated associations (e.g., *lion* primes *stripes* because both are associated to *tiger* as shown by Balota & Lorch, 1986; see also McNamara, 1992; cf. McKoon & Ratcliff, 1992). Because of these interpretive problems, in this chapter we accept as evidence for SA any priming (or Stroop interference) effect that is based on either associative or semantic relations established outside the laboratory.

Most researchers have assumed that the standard Stroop interference effect is based on the activation of the word's semantic representations, but this need not be so. To see why, consider the highly similar flanker effect (e.g., Eriksen & Eriksen, 1974) in which people respond with a key press to a fixated target item. When the items flanking the target are associated with a key press different from the target's, RTs are slower than when they are associated with the target's key press or no key press. If the stimuli were different meaningless squiggles, one could attribute flanker interference to task-relevant response competition, without any involvement of extra-experimental semantics. By analogy, Stroop interference from color words could be produced entirely by nonsemantic, task-relevant response competition, in which case Stroop interference per se is ill suited for investigating SA.[1] However, if Stroop interference is produced by both nonsemantic, task-relevant response competition and semantically based response competition, one must isolate these two sources of competition to assess the automaticity of each.

Because we allow extra-experimental associative relations to serve as a basis for inferring SA, the strongest evidence that SA is directly involved in Stroop interference comes from Klein's (1964) and Dalrymple-Alford's (1972) findings that interference from a noncolor word that has a strong association to a color (e.g., *sky, lemon*) is greater than interference from a noncolor word with no association to a particular color name (e.g., *put, table*). If the interference were due only to nonsemantic task-relevant response competition, *sky* should not have slowed responding relative to *put* because both should have activated their equally task-irrelevant articulatory codes to the same degree. However, as Posner and Snyder (1975) argued, if extra-experimental semantic–associative information is activated during the Stroop task, representations associated with ink colors are globally primed because the task is to name ink colors. Thus, *sky* would produce more interference in saying "red" because its globally primed associate "blue" would be activated more than *put*'s globally unprimed associate "place." This articulatory-based interference account, supplemented by semantic priming, can also explain why words naming the ink colors used in the experiment produce more Stroop interference than words naming other (less globally primed) colors, which in turn produce more interference than (globally unprimed) noncolor words (Klein, 1964). Thus, to assess the automaticity of SA in the Stroop paradigm, one can compare ink-color-naming RTs for a color-related noncolor distractor (e.g., *sky*) and for a color-unrelated noncolor distractor (e.g., *put*). (For brevity, we refer to this as the *sky–put* Stroop design.) This comparison is analogous to one made by Warren (1974). He found that RTs to name the ink color in which *dog* is printed are longer if *dog* has been primed by *cat* than if it has been primed by *wall*, which basically demonstrates that semantic priming occurs

---

[1] An even stronger challenge to the use of Stroop paradigm to test for SA automaticity is that many Stroop effects can be accommodated by a parallel distributed-processing model (Cohen, Dunbar, & McClelland, 1990) that does not explicitly appeal to the concept of automaticity or have semantic representations. However, for purposes of this chapter if SA is shown to be involved, we accept Stroop interference as a useful tool for examining SA automaticity.

when the response to the target is ink-color naming rather than lexical decision or pronunciation.

Automaticity

Before turning to the evidence, we make some general comments about the kinds of inferences one can make about the automaticity of SA. First, Kahneman and Chajczyk (1983) suggested that a strongly automatic process should not be enhanced or diminished by the allocation of resources to or from that process. Although this is true for the process, it is not necessarily true for its associated behavioral effects. For example, priming may originate from an expectancy mechanism and automatic SA. That is, when the proportion of trials containing a semantically related prime and target (the relatedness proportion) is high, people use a prime word to generate an expectancy for potential targets related to that prime, if they are given enough time to do so. This leads to an increase in priming as relatedness proportion increases, the relatedness proportion effect, but only when the stimulus onset asynchrony (SOA) between the prime and target is greater than 500 ms (e.g., den Heyer, Briand, & Dannenbring, 1983; Stolz & Neely, 1995). Because this attention-demanding expectancy mechanism can increase the facilitation observed from a related prime without affecting SA itself, if an attentional manipulation reduces semantic priming it could be due to its effect on expectancy and not SA, in which case the reduced priming would not be evidence against SA. Hence, to conclude that manipulations are affecting SA, one must be sure that they are not affecting performance through a concurrently operating mechanism (such as expectancy) that can also affect performance in that task. In the semantic priming paradigm, this means showing that the manipulation is affecting priming at a short SOA that fails to yield a relatedness proportion effect (cf. Stolz & Neely, 1995). When data purportedly providing evidence against SA automaticity come from experiments that do not show that a reduction in priming is due to SA rather than expectancy, we say they suffer from the "expectancy" problem.

Of course, one can differentiate between a manipulation's reducing an effect versus eliminating it, which would seem to be ironclad evidence against the layperson's notion of SA automaticity (i.e., that SA always occurs). But even if one ignores the statistical problems associated with establishing a null effect, the absence of priming or Stroop interference must be interpreted with caution: Once again, one must distinguish between a variable's affecting performance versus its affecting SA. For example, in the priming task, if a manipulation on the prime greatly delayed the initiation of target processing, automatic SA from the prime might have been unaffected, but no priming would occur because that SA would have decayed before target processing began (this is referred to as the "decay problem"). Alternatively, if a manipulation were to totally degrade visual feature integration from the word's letters, the absence of priming or Stroop interference under that circumstance would tell us more about "seeing" than about SA. (This is referred to as the "visual feature integration problem."[2]) To rule out the visual feature integration problem, one needs to show that a manipulation is having a direct effect on SA rather than an indirect effect on SA through impaired visual feature integration. In the semantic priming paradigm, the strongest possible demonstration of a direct effect would be to show that the manipulated variable eliminates semantic priming while leaving repetition priming completely unaffected. If the manipulated variable produced equal reductions for repetition and semantic priming and if SA makes a contribution to repetition priming beyond lexical activation's contribution, then the results would be ambiguous. They would be ambiguous because the equal reduction could be interpreted as having been due either to reduced SA or to impaired visual feature integration. Finally, related to problems associated with interpreting null effects other than the issue of statistical power, the behavioral measure used to assess SA may not be sensitive enough to detect its presence, such that an alternative measure might reveal it. With these caveats in mind, we now turn to an evaluation of the evidence.

Is Semantic Activation Capacity Free?

An automatic process does not consume attentional resources to begin or to run to completion. This implies that the amount of SA that a written word produces is not affected by concurrently operating attention-demanding mental operations or by the number of elements in the display in which it occurs. Stated another way, if SA is strongly automatic, SA from a foveally presented task-irrelevant word should occur full blown even when attention should be fully allocated to other task-relevant events in the display; this should be so regardless of the type of processing (linguistic or otherwise) that must be performed on those task-relevant events. Because these issues are closely tied to the intentionality criteria to be discussed, in this section the focus is on whether SA is affected by dual-task demands or is affected by the number of other items in the display in which the word producing that SA is embedded. Later, we address whether SA is affected by spatial attention and the type of processing required to meet task demands.

Dual-Task Interference

If SA is automatic, its ability to produce priming in the semantic priming paradigm and interference in the *sky–put* Stroop design should not be affected by the require-

---

[2]Becker and Killion's (1977) finding that reducing the visual intensity–contrast of the prime did not reduce priming is not necessarily evidence against the visual feature integration problem because intensity may only affect the rate of feature integration and not its asymptotic level. If a clearly presented prime and a prime presented in visual noise produced equal priming, our visual feature integration argument would be undermined.

ment to perform some other concurrent task. Because of its long history in the study of attention, it is somewhat surprising that the dual-task interference methodology has not often been used to examine the automaticity of SA from words in either the Stroop or semantic priming paradigms. (One possible explanation for this is the thorny methodological issues associated with this approach; see Neumann, 1984.) However, it has been reported that verbal shadowing (Posner, Sandson, Dhawan, & Shulman, 1989) and nonverbal tone monitoring (Henik, Tzelgov, & Friedrich, 1993) sometimes reduce or eliminate semantic priming in a lexical decision task but never affect repetition priming under similar conditions. The dissociation between repetition and semantic priming is important because it shows that shadowing and tone monitoring were not affecting visual feature integration but rather seemed to be selectively affecting SA itself. Hence, taken at face value, these findings seem problematic for the automaticity of SA. However, there are reasons to question them. First, the conditions under which dual tasks did reduce semantic priming (Henik et al., 1993; Posner et al., 1989, Experiments 1 & 3) were highly similar to conditions under which dual tasks did not reduce semantic priming (Henik, Nissimov, Priel, & Umansky, 1995; Posner et al., 1989, Experiments 4 & 5). This makes it difficult to know which of the two outcomes is the "true" effect. Second, because the relatedness proportion was .5 or greater (counting repetition trials as semantically related) and the SOA was 400 ms or more,[3] these experiments suffer from the expectancy problem. However, there were three cases across both the Posner et al. (1989) and Henik et al. (1993) studies in which a dual task eliminated priming. This is much more convincing, but there are three reasons for restraint in embracing this as evidence against SA automaticity. First, it is not clear why priming was eliminated in only these cases, as they were procedurally similar to several other cases in which priming was not eliminated or even reduced. Second, if the dual task delayed the response to the lexical decision target by enough time, there is a decay problem. Third, these results conflict with data obtained by Fuentes, Carmona, Agis, and Catena (1994) in experiments better designed to examine the role of expectancy mechanisms, experiments to which we now turn.

Fuentes et al. (1994) had two prime words appear simultaneously, one at fixation (the attended prime) and the other to the right of fixation (the unattended prime). At an SOA of 850 ms, a lexical decision target appeared at fixation. In different single- versus dual-task blocks, the same people made a lexical decision to the target either as the only task or while shadowing text. Shadowing reduced priming from the attended word but not from the unattended prime. Moreover, when the two primes were presented for only 30 ms and immediately masked (the SOA was still 850 ms), the attended and unattended primes produced similar priming

---

[3]In Henik et al.'s (1993) experiments, the reported data were averaged across SOAs that ranged between 240 and 1,840 ms.

effects that were quite comparable to the priming produced by the unmasked, unattended primes in the single- and dual-task conditions. Taken together, these data suggest that dual-task interference occurs for attended primes (by affecting expectancy) but not for unattended or masked primes, which produce priming only through SA and not through expectancy. Hence, there is no dual-task interference for SA, suggesting that SA is automatic.

Display Load: The Stroop Dilution Effect

Kahneman and Chajczyk (1983) introduced a modified Stroop task in which a fixated color patch rather than a word carried the to-be-named color. Simultaneous with its presentation, on some trials a single word could appear randomly above or below the color patch. This word could name the color of the ink patch (the congruent color); could name some other color (the conflicting color, which named one of the other ink colors used in the experiment); or could be a neutral, noncolor word. Relative to the neutral word, the congruent word produced facilitation, and the conflicting word produced interference. These facilitation and interference effects were reduced when another neutral noncolor word also appeared in the opposite (above vs. below) location. Because the presence of another word in the display reduced the Stroop effect observed when only one word appeared, Kahneman and Chajczyk called this the "Stroop dilution effect." This effect seems problematic for SA being automatic. (Here, we assume that SA was involved in these Stroop effects, although to be sure one would need to replicate this dilution using the *sky–put* design.) That is, it seems that the SA producing the Stroop effect was inhibited by the addition of another to-be-ignored word that required no response.

However, results from Brown, Roos-Gilbert, and Carr (1995) weaken the implications these results have for SA automaticity. Although Brown et al. found that including up to three more neutral words in the display led to proportionally more Stroop dilution, the dilution was even greater from distractors made up of nonrepetitive letterlike elements. (See Fuentes & Tudela, 1992, Experiment 2, for a conceptually similar finding for semantic priming.) Brown et al. also ruled out an attentional capture account that says that Stroop dilution occurs because (a) people can only attend to one word at a time; (b) a color word produces a Stroop effect only if it is attended (which is against SA automaticity); and (c) the more neutral words appear in the display, the less likely it is that the color word will capture attention first, so that it can produce a Stroop effect. This attentional capture account was ruled out (see also Yee & Hunt, 1991) because the Stroop dilution effect still occurred (albeit in attenuated form) when the color word rather than the neutral word was fixated, such that the color word should have captured attention first. Because the amount of dilution depended on the visual properties of the added distractors, Brown et al. argued that dilution is due to a visual feature degradation effect for the color word that is reduced when the color word is fixated. Hence, Stroop dilution experiments suffer from the visual feature integration problem.

Display Load: Semantic Priming

Dark, Johnston, Myles-Worsley, and Farah (1985, Experiments 2 and 5) examined how display load during prime presentation affects priming. For the prime frames, people were to press a key whenever an animal name appeared in one of eight locations. Each prime frame consisted of one to four unrelated words. A visually degraded target word that gradually became less degraded followed about 10% of the prime frames. Priming was the identification time for the degraded target when it was unrelated to all of the words in the prime frame minus the identification time for the target when it was related to one of them. Facilitatory priming occurred when only a single word appeared in the prime frame, but not when one or three additional words appeared, a result perfectly analogous to Kahneman and Chajczyk's (1983) Stroop dilution effect. However, unlike Kahneman and Chajczyk's study in which the interfering word and the dilution words all appeared in unattended spatial locations (because the color patch always appeared at fixation), in Dark et al.'s study the priming word and the dilution words all appeared in attended spatial locations. But, as was so for Stroop dilution effects, Dark et al.'s (1985) load–dilution effects on semantic priming cannot be taken as strong evidence against SA. Indeed, the finding that similar load–dilution effects occurred for identity priming (Experiment 8) provides additional support for Brown et al.'s (1995) claim that the presence of multiple words in a display affects visual feature integration rather than SA per se.

Summary

Although Posner et al. (1989) and Henik et al. (1993) have shown that dual tasks sometimes reduce or eliminate semantic priming, this is not compelling evidence against SAs being capacity free because the reductions in priming could have been mediated by expectancy and the elimination of priming was not consistently observed under highly similar conditions. Moreover, the Fuentes et al. (1994) dual-task data provide strong support for SA automaticity by showing that dual-task interference occurs for attended primes (presumably by affecting expectancy) but not for unattended or masked primes, which produce priming only through SA and not expectancy. Finally, the effect that the load–dilution variable has on Stroop interference and on semantic priming cannot be taken as strong evidence against SA automaticity because this variable seems to be affecting SA indirectly through visual feature integration rather than affecting SA directly. Thus, based on the totality of the evidence, we believe that SA satisfies the capacity-free criterion of automaticity.

Can Semantic Activation Occur Without Intention?

If SA for a word is automatic, it should occur even when the word is task irrelevant and the person performing the task is, therefore, not intending that SA for that word occur, that is, is not allocating any attentional resources toward producing SA for that word. This situation is different from the dual-task situation, in which study participants are attending to the word to perform one of the tasks on that word. If SA occurs for a word even when the person does not intend that SA occur for that word, this would provide very strong evidence for the automaticity of SA. In this section, we distinguish between two different reasons for a person not to allocate attentional resources to a word, that is, to "ignore" that word. One basis is spatial relevance, namely, the word is presented in a part of the visual display that does not contain the task-relevant targets to which responses must be made. The second basis is information relevance, namely, semantic information about the word cannot be used to aid task performance.

Despite its common acceptance as the prototype task for assessing SA automaticity, the standard Stroop task does not satisfy either the spatial or informational irrelevance criterion. That is, the person must attend to the spatial location in which the word occurs to see its ink color. Also, as noted by MacLeod (1991), if processing the meaning of the word *red* facilitates saying "red" to red ink, when the experiment contains congruent Stroop trials, there may be some motivation to allocate attentional resources to producing SA for the words, even though there may be a behavioral cost in doing so when the color word conflicts with the ink color. The best way to conduct a Stroop study to maximize the likelihood that the words will be ignored is to use the *sky–put* design and (a) have people name the color of a patch presented in a location different from the simultaneously presented word, as in the Kahneman and Chajczyk (1983) and Brown et al. (1995) studies, and (b) have the color of the patch never match the color associated with the color-related noncolor word (e.g., never present a blue patch with *sky*). It is interesting to note that most Stroop researchers have not followed both of these two prescriptions in testing for the automaticity of SA (so we cannot be sure if the word was truly "ignored"). Instead, they either have manipulated the probability that the color word is congruent with or conflicts with the to-be-named ink color (see MacLeod, 1991, pp. 176–177, for a summary) or whether the congruent or conflicting word appears in the same location as the "object" bearing the to-be-named color. As for the semantic priming paradigm, because one must include related primes to assess SA, the role of information relevance is examined by manipulating whether semantic information is relevant to tasks that people perform on the prime or target.

Effects of Word-Level Spatially Focused Attention

Kahneman and Henik (1981, Experiment 2) presented displays containing a circle and a square, randomly appearing on opposite sides of fixation, each of which circumscribed a word written in colored ink. People were to name the ink color of the word in the circle. Because the attended word (in the circle) and the unattended word (in the square) were equidistant from fixation, they should have fallen on areas of the retina having equal acuity. The words could either both be neutral (the baseline condition for assessing the effects of the color word), or one could be neutral and the other a congruent or conflicting color word. The conflicting color word produced a 202-ms interference effect when attended and only a 50-ms (although still significant) interference effect when unattended. This suggests that SA depends on spatial attention. However, because the baseline–conflict comparison compares interference from task-irrelevant versus task-relevant responses, one cannot be sure the effect is being produced by differences in SA per se. Also because the unattended word sometimes was congruent with the attended ink color, there may have been some motivation to process the unattended word. Thus, these procedures need to be used in a *sky–put* design with no congruent colors, especially because Fuentes et al. (1994) found strong evidence in favor of the automaticity of SA in semantic priming experiments using similar spatial attention manipulations, evidence to which we now turn. (See Fuentes & Tudela, 1992, for a review of spatial attention effects on semantic priming.)

Fuentes et al. (1994) showed that a word in an unattended location 4.3° to the right of an attended location produced a significant 18-ms priming effect, albeit reduced from the 63-ms effect that occurred when the prime was in the attended location. But because the SOA was 850 ms and the priming emanating from the attended location was affected by a dual-task requirement and by visual masking, whereas priming from the unattended location was not, these data suggest that priming from the word in the attended location was expectancy based, whereas priming from the word in the unattended location was based solely on capacity-free SA. However, Dark et al. (1985) failed to find priming from an unattended location in a focused-attention variant of their load–dilution paradigm described earlier. In this variant, for the priming frames people were to press a key only if the animal name appeared in one of four relevant locations and to ignore words (animal names and otherwise) appearing in four irrelevant locations. When there was only one item in the priming display, semantic priming and repetition priming were each statistically equivalent for words in the attended and unattended locations. However, when there were two words in the display, semantic priming for a word in an attended location was reduced from 150 ms to a nonsignificant 15 ms in an unattended location. This elimination of priming from an unattended location with two-item displays seems to conflict directly with Fuentes et al.'s (1994) finding of significant priming. However, there were four attended and four unattended locations in which stimuli could appear in Dark et al. and only one attended and one unattended location in which stimuli always appeared in Fuentes et al. More important, because Dark et al. did not test identity priming under the same conditions, spatial attention could have been affecting visual feature integration and not SA per se. (See earlier discussion of Dark et al.'s load effects.) Thus, we believe the best evidence favors the claim that when there is no requirement for attention to be focused on a word's individual letters, words in spatially unattended locations automatically activate their meanings.

Effects of Intraword Spatially Focused Attention

Thus far, we have discussed the effects of spatial attention when it is directed to whole words occupying attended locations. A different kind of spatial attention manipulation was introduced by Kahneman and Henik (1981, Experiment 3) in the Stroop paradigm. In each two-word display, one word, randomly to the left or right of fixation, either had all of its letters or only a single letter in colored ink. All other letters were in black ink, and people were to name the ink color of the word or single letter. The words could either both be neutral (the baseline condition for assessing the effects of the color-bearing word) or one could be neutral and the other a conflicting color word. (Because there were no congruent color words, there should have been no motivation at all to attend to the "meaning" of any word.) When the color word was attended (color bearing), Stroop interference was significantly greater when all of its letters were colored (a 159-ms effect) relative to when only one of its letters was colored (a 94-ms effect). When the color word was unattended, it produced 0 ms of interference when all of the letters of the neutral word were colored and a (nonsignificant?) 21 ms of interference when only a single letter in the neutral word was colored. These findings suggest that (a) Stroop interference is not produced by a word in an unattended location when that location can be selected against on the basis of its not containing task-relevant information (but see Brown et al., 1995, Experiment 4, for a different result) and (b) Stroop interference produced by a color word in an attended location is greater when that word is processed holistically.

Besner, Stolz, and associates have extended Kahneman and Henik's (1981, Experiment 3) findings in several very interesting ways. In Experiment 1 of Besner et al. (1997), people saw only a single letter string in which either all or a randomly determined one of its letters was colored (with the remaining letters in white). The letter string could be either a congruent or conflicting color word. Stroop interference was reduced by only a single letter being colored relative to all letters being colored. However, even for the single colored letter, Stroop interference remained substantial, perhaps because the inclusion of congruent color words caused people to attend to the word. To test this, in Experiment 2, only incongruent color words were used and the "neutral" baseline was a nonword that had the same first two letters as one of the color words (e.g., *yenile, blat*). Under these conditions, the 34-ms Stroop interference obtained for the color words relative to the nonwords when all of their letters were colored was completely eliminated when only one of their letters was colored. However, this finding should be treated with caution. Although there was a difference between the interference produced by *yellow* and *yenile* when all of the letters were colored, this may have been due to an orthographic–phonological difference rather than an SA difference. This is possible because noncolor words that have the same first letter or rhyme with color words (e.g., *clean* for *green*) produce interference relative to an orthographically–phonologically unrelated word (see MacLeod, 1991, p. 171, for relevant studies). Thus, the "low" in *yellow* may be causing more interference than the "ile" in *yenile*, but only if spatial attention is distributed across these distinguishing letters. Another problem is that had a more neutral word (i.e., one not containing multiple letters from the name of one of the task-relevant ink colors) been used as a baseline, one might discover that the interference was not entirely eliminated when only one of the letters was colored.

Besner and Stolz (1999a) also showed that the amount of Stroop interference a color word produces is also affected by a general processing set that is induced by the kinds of displays that appear on other trials in the experiment. Specifically, they showed that Stroop interference from a word with all of its letters colored occurred when other trials in the experiment contained a single colored letter presented in isolation but not when they contained a single colored letter that appeared in a randomly selected position among "noncolored" (white) ASCII characters (e.g., $#h&%). These data suggest that Stroop interference occurs when people have a general set for spreading their attention across a single visual object to extract its ink color but not when they focus their attention so as to extract the ink color of only a part of an object.

As interesting as the findings of Kahneman and Henik (1981, Experiment 3), Besner et al. (1997), and Besner and Stolz (1999b) are, they could all be due to the fact that when spatial attention is focused on only a single letter within a word, visual feature integration for other letters in that word is impaired. If so, the elimination–reduction of Stroop interference would be based on an indirect effect on SA, through impaired visual feature integration rather than on a direct effect on SA per se. However, this visual feature integration explanation is challenged by Besner and Stolz's (1999b) particularly interesting finding that a set to focus spatial attention on a constituent within a visual object is not a sufficient condition for eliminating Stroop effects. In their study, a congruent or conflicting color word appeared above or below the ink-color-bearing item. For one group of people, the ink-color-bearing item was a neutral noncolor word (e.g., *square*, *circle*) with either all or only one of its letters colored. Conceptually replicating prior findings, Stroop interference from the adjacent color word was eliminated when the ink-color-bearing neutral word had only a single letter within it colored but not when all of its letters were colored. For another group, the ink-color-bearing item was a geometric figure (e.g., *square* or *circle*) with either all of its outline colored or only a segment of its outline colored. Now Stroop interference occurred whether only a part or all of the geometric figure's outline was colored. On the basis of these results, Besner and Stolz (1999b) argued that to eliminate Stroop effects, spatially focused attention must be focused on linguistic elements. Such domain specificity in the effects of spatial attention would seem to rule out a visual feature integration explanation for why a set to focus attention on only a single letter of a word eliminates the Stroop interference that it or an adjacent color word produces. That is, for both the partially colored geometric figures and words, spatial attention should have been equally focused and hence should have had the same effect on visual feature integration for the adjacent color word producing the Stroop interference. However, instead of reflecting domain specificity, this within-word versus within-shape difference could have been due to spatial attention being more narrowly focused when it was focused on an object embedded in other objects (i.e., a letter in other letters) rather than on a part of a single object (the shape). If so, even this word versus shape effect could have been due to differential effects of spatial attention on visual feature integration rather than to differential effects of attention being focused on linguistic versus nonlinguistic elements.

Effects of Levels of Processing on the Prime

The results most often cited as evidence against SA automaticity come from the letter-search paradigm originated by Smith (1979) and reviewed by Maxfield (1997). Unless otherwise noted, in each letter-search study we cover, a single letter is duplicated above each letter of the prime word and the task is to indicate whether that letter appears in the prime, with the letter-search response being made immediately and with the lexical decision target appearing from between 200 ms to 2 s later. Although prime letter search almost always eliminates semantic priming, this finding is not necessarily compelling evidence against SA automaticity because it may reflect a decay problem or a spatial attention effect on visual feature integration, as we now discuss.

The results concerning whether letter search affects SA or visual feature integration are mixed. Smith (1979) found that when letter search was performed on both the prime and target there was an elimination of the semantic priming that occurred when letter search was performed on only the target. However, because repetition priming was eliminated as well, the effect seems to have been due to visual feature integration, not to SA per se. Friedrich, Henik, and Tzelgov (1991) found that repetition and semantic priming effects were 56 ms and 19 ms, respectively, when the prime was named and 40 ms and 6 ms (nonsignificant), respectively, when there was a letter search on the prime. However, because repetition and semantic priming were equally reduced (by 16 ms and 13 ms, respectively), the letter-search effect could have been due to visual feature integration impairment rather than diminished SA per se. Finally, Stolz and Besner (1998, Experiment 3) found a nonsignificant 11-ms semantic priming effect when there was a prime letter search but also found a significant 51-ms morphological priming effect (prime: *marked*; target: *mark*) relative to an orthographic control baseline (prime: *market*; target: *mark*). However, because the magnitudes of morphological and semantic priming were not assessed in the absence of letter search, one does not know the degree to which letter search reduced both kinds of priming. If they were reduced by the same amount, these results would be ambiguous, as were the Friedrich et al. (1991) results. (In fairness, Stolz & Besner, 1998, were focusing more on whether morphological and semantic representations are distinct than on SA automaticity.)

Other experiments have been conducted to examine the timing of the letter search on the prime. Chiappe, Smith, and Besner (1996) found that semantic priming was eliminated by a prime letter search that began as soon as the prime was presented, whether that letter search was interrupted or ran to completion. Friedrich et al. (1991, Experiment 4) and Stolz and Besner (1996) have shown that if prime processing was given a head start before letter search began, the letter search did not shut down the SA that had already been initiated. The finding that letter search in a word precludes that word's initiation of SA would be good evidence against SA automaticity, but only if there were no visual feature integration or decay problem.

To determine if SA occurs but then decays before the target appears, Henik, Friedrich, Tzelgov, and Tramer (1994) used a delayed letter-search procedure in which people waited until after the lexical decision response to the target before giving their letter-search or naming response to the prime. Thus, Henik et al. were able to use a 240-ms prime–target SOA, during which SA from the prime, had it occurred, should not have decayed. A prime–target SOA of 840 ms was randomly intermixed with the 240-ms SOA. Different groups received relatedness proportions of .2 or .8. Within each relatedness proportion, half of the people performed letter search on the prime in the first half of the experimental session and then named the prime in the second half, whereas the other half performed these two tasks in the reverse order. Averaged across the two relatedness proportions, when the prime-naming and prime letter-search tasks were performed first, at the 240-ms SOA they both yielded priming effects of about 50 ms, whereas at the 840-ms SOA only the prime-naming task yielded a significant (62-ms) priming effect. (For letter search, the priming effect was 1 ms.) This suggests that letter search does not eliminate SA but rather causes it to decay much more rapidly.

When prime letter search eliminates semantic priming, is this due to intraword spatially focused attention or to shallow processing of the prime? Several findings suggest that it may be a spatial attention effect. For example, when all of a prime's letters are in the same color and people are to respond on the basis of ink color (a perceptually shallow task in which spatial attention can be distributed across all of the word's letters), Chiappe et al. (1996) obtained standard semantic priming effects whether the prime colors were easy or difficult to discriminate. Moreover, the elimination of semantic priming by prime letter search seems to be specific to having the search letter duplicated above each letter of the prime word, a situation likely to induce a spatially focused letter-by-letter matching strategy. Indeed, when the search letter appeared only once above the middle of the prime, Kaye and Brown (1985) found that semantic priming was not significantly reduced. Also, Besner, Smith, and MacLeod (1990) had people decide if two simultaneously presented words (one above the other) shared a letter. RTs to respond "yes" were 195 ms slower for related pairs such as *table chair* relative to unrelated pairs such as *fable chair*. Congruent with Kaye and Brown's (1985) findings, this inhibitory semantic priming effect shows that SA does occur when letter search is less likely to occur on the basis of attention being serially focused on only one of the prime's letters at a time.

This is not to say that all levels-of-processing effects on the prime are due to intraword spatially focused attention. In a lexical decision task, Smith, Theodor, and Franklin (1983) found that priming was eliminated when people responded as to whether or not an asterisk appeared beside the prime. (Although not an example of intraword spatially focused attention, this is likely a spatial attention effect rather than a "levels" effect.) Smith et al. also showed that when people had to report the number of syllables in a visually presented prime, there was less priming than when people had to respond on the basis of the prime's meaning. Although this particular levels effect was not due to spatial attention, it could have been due to linguistic decomposition of the prime being required, rather than to differences in levels of holistic prime processing. (However, Smith et al. also found more priming when the prime was semantically processed than when it was read silently. Presumably, prime processing was holistic in both of these cases.) Using the same prime syllable-counting task, Friedrich, Kellogg, and Henik (1982) found that priming was very similar to that observed when the prime was named (25 ms vs. 29 ms). These data seem to support a (phonological) levels rather than a prime decomposition interpretation. However, in the prime syllable-counting task, when the prime contained more than one syllable, there was a nonsignificant inhibitory 12-ms priming effect; for monosyllabic primes, there was a 62-ms facilitatory semantic priming effect. (For prime naming, priming effects were virtually identical for mono- vs. polysyllabic words.) These data suggest that when a word is decomposed into its constituents, it does not produce SA. However, SA may have occurred but decayed during prime decomposition.

Another study potentially relevant to levels of processing on the prime was reported by Stolz and Besner (1997). They presented either an 80-ms or 288-ms immediately masked prime, and at a prime target SOA of 716 ms presented a lexical decision target. With a relatedness proportion of .5, when people saw only the 80-ms or 288-ms primes, both yielded significant and highly similar semantic priming effects; however, when they saw them randomly intermixed, the 80-ms primes did not produce semantic priming whereas the 288-ms primes did (see also Smith, Besner, & Miyoshi, 1994). Although this absence of priming from the intermixed 80-ms primes seems to argue against SA automaticity, Stolz and Besner also found that with a relatedness proportion of .25, the 80-ms primes now yielded a significant priming effect highly similar to that found for the 288-ms primes, even when these different duration primes were intermixed. According to Stolz and Besner's analysis, although SA is not automatic (i.e., does not occur when attention is spatially misdirected or is focused on one of a word's letters or on a nonsemantic processing domain), SA does occur when the default processing mode for words is engaged.

To account for why the 80-ms masked primes did not yield priming when intermixed with the 288-ms primes and the relatedness proportion was .5, Stolz and Besner (1997) appealed to Carr and Dagenbach's (1990) and Dagenbach and Carr's (1994) center-surround theory. According to this theory, a brief masked prime does automatically produce SA. However, when people are actively trying to retrieve this difficult-to-see word's meaning, to facilitate their conscious identification of that word, they "center" attention on that word's "lexical" representation. If conscious identification fails and this center mechanism remains engaged, this inhibits the "semantic surround" of that word through a lateral-inhibition-like mechanism. Depending on the proportion of successful versus failed identification trials, the net priming effect can be facilitatory, inhibitory, or null. According to Stolz and Besner, when the relatedness proportion is .50 and half of the primes are presented long enough that people become consciously aware that the primes and targets are often related, they try to retrieve the 80-ms prime's meaning, thereby engaging the center-surround mechanism. When retrieval fails, the resulting inhibition offsets the facilitation from SA, thereby producing a null effect. When the relatedness proportion is only .25 or there are no longer duration primes in the experiment, people passively process the prime (i.e., do not engage the center-surround mechanism), such that the SA it produces results in a full-blown priming effect. Although logically consistent with the data, their analysis would be more strongly supported if it were shown that under conditions in which semantic priming was eliminated, there was enhanced repetition priming (because the center mechanism would have increased the activation level of the prime's lexical representation; cf. Bushell, 1996; Carr & Dagenbach, 1990). If repetition priming were not enhanced, this would suggest that the center-surround mechanism was not operating, and the absence of semantic priming could then be taken as evidence against SA.

Can semantic priming be eliminated by inducing a shallow level of processing on the prime without requiring prime decomposition or using conditions that might engage the center-surround mechanism? In a relevant lexical decision study conducted in our laboratory by VerWys, Stolz, and Neely (nonpublished study; see Snow & Neely, 1987), shallow processing on the prime (and perhaps the target as well) was induced by having a large proportion of the prime–target pairs be physically identical (PI). Specifically, in a PI group, on 70% of the trials, word primes and their word targets were PI, and on equal percentages (10% each) of the remaining trials, they were either nominally identical (i.e., *CAT cat*), semantically related, or unrelated. In a semantic group, the percentages of PI and semantically related trials were exchanged. To ensure that the PI group would need to process the prime (and target) holistically (e.g., could not respond "word" on the basis of noting a few shared letters between the prime and target), for nonword targets there were, with comparable percentages, corresponding PI (e.g., *NURSE NARSE*), nominally identical (e.g., *NURSE narse*), semantically related (e.g., *DOCTOR NARSE* or *DOCTOR narse*), and unrelated (e.g., *TANGLE NARSE* or *TANGLE narse*) prime–target pairs. The most important result is that in the PI group at a 150-ms SOA (and a 750-ms SOA as well), there was no hint of a semantic priming effect (a 2-ms effect), even though

PI priming (52 ms) and nominal identity priming (32 ms) were quite substantial, suggesting that the primes were processed holistically. However, in the semantic group, semantic priming (+27 ms) was equivalent to nominal identity priming (+32 ms) and (anomalously) greater than PI priming (a nonsignificant 8-ms effect). These data suggest that shallow, holistic prime processing eliminates semantic priming. Because PI and nominal identity priming were as large or larger in the PI group than in the semantic group, the visual feature integration problem is ruled out. Thus, the elimination of semantic priming in the PI group would seem to be strong evidence against SA automaticity. However, RTs for semantically related nonword targets (e.g., *DOCTOR narse*) show a significant 16-ms inhibition effect relative to unrelated nonword targets (e.g., *TANGLE narse*) in the PI group. This suggests that SA occurred and that nonword RTs may be more sensitive to picking up SA effects than are word RTs!

One final study that shows a reduction of semantic priming that may be due to the level of holistic prime processing was reported by Neely, VerWys, and Kahan (1998). They used a two-prime procedure in which the first, 33-ms lowercase prime was masked and the second, 150-ms uppercase prime preceded the lexical decision target with a 300-ms SOA. The second prime was related to its target with a relatedness proportion of .25. When the two primes were unrelated (and the first prime was also unrelated to the target), averaged across two experiments, the second prime produced a significant 31-ms semantic priming effect when it was related to the target. However, when the two primes were nominally identical (i.e., the second prime was primed by itself), semantic priming was reduced to a nonsignificant 9 ms. However, Neely and VerWys (1996) showed that repetition priming is enhanced, not eliminated, with the same procedures. This rules out impaired visual feature integration as the source of the semantic priming reduction and suggests that the center-surround mechanism may have been operating (cf. Carr & Dagenbach, 1990). Thus, Neely et al. (1998) suggested that the elimination of semantic priming might be due to the masked first prime having engaged the center-surround mechanism such that the surround inhibition from the first prime might have offset the facilitatory priming from the second prime. However, this account is refuted by our unpublished finding that semantic priming is also eliminated by immediate prime repetition even when the first prime is clearly visible (see also Dagenbach, in press), such that the center-surround mechanism should not have been operating.

The elimination of semantic priming from immediate repetition of the prime would be strong evidence against SA automaticity if one could be sure that other priming mechanisms such as expectancy were not involved. Because Neely et al.'s (1998) SOA between the second prime and the target was only 300 ms and the relatedness proportion they used was only .25, Neely et al. assumed that expectancy was not operating in their experiments. However, to be sure of this, Hutchison, Neely, and Johnson (in press) sought to show that semantic priming without prime repetition would not be affected by variations in relatedness proportion using Neely et al.'s (1998) procedures. Instead, they showed that with Neely et al.'s procedures, priming from a nonrepeated prime increased from 34 to 71 ms as relatedness proportion increased from .25 to .75, but prime repetition reduced priming by 19 ms at the .25 relatedness proportion and by 31 ms at the .75 relatedness proportion. However, when the SOA between the second prime and target was reduced from 300 to 167 ms, priming from a nonrepeated prime was equivalent for the .75 and .25 relatedness proportions, demonstrating that expectancy was not operating at the 167-ms SOA. Most important, now when there was direct evidence that expectancy was not operating, priming from a repeated prime was overall 2 ms greater than priming from a nonrepeated prime. This suggests that immediate repetition priming of a prime is reducing semantic priming by affecting expectancy, not SA. Thus, the Neely et al. (1998) results do not provide evidence against SA automaticity.

Effects of Levels of Processing on the Target

Although numerous studies have been conducted to examine the effects of levels of processing on the prime on SA, only a few studies have been conducted to examine whether SA occurs for shallow levels of target processing. One relevant finding is Smith's (1979) observation that semantic priming occurred when there was a letter search on the target (but not the prime). However, Blum and Johnson (1993) were unable to replicate this effect conceptually or "directly" in that they found that priming was eliminated when there was a letter search on the target. In another relevant paradigm, Warren (1974) had people perform the perceptually shallow task of naming the ink color in which a target word was presented and found that semantic priming led to *slower* RTs (i.e., more Stroop interference). This is strong evidence for SA automaticity in that SA occurs even when it only hurts performance, such that there should be a strong motivation to suppress or not allocate attentional resources to the prime's or target's meanings. Friedrich, Kellogg, and Henik (1983) replicated Warren's effect and, analogously to what they found for lexical decisions to targets, showed that there was no inhibitory (or facilitatory) semantic priming effect in target color naming when there was a prime letter search.

In a recent variation of Warren's (1974) paradigm, Rouibah, Tiberghien, and Lupker (1999) asked people to decide if a word's ink color matched or mismatched the color of a preceding square that was followed by a 49-ms backward-masked word prime. At a 98-ms prime–target SOA, the ink-bearing word target was presented. The observed 24-ms facilitatory semantic priming effect is very strong evidence for SA automaticity because (a) the level of processing on the target was nonsemantic and shallow, (b) the relatedness of the prime and target provided no information about the correct response in Rouibah et al.'s Experiment 5, (c) the relatedness proportion was low and the SOA was short, and (d) the briefly presented prime was masked.

The strongest evidence for SA automaticity would be to show that SA occurs even when semantic information does not facilitate performance such that there would be no motivation to produce it. But how then could one demonstrate that SA had occurred? Although the only way out of this bind would seem to be to use tasks in which SA only hurts performance (as in the Warren, 1974, paradigm), an alternative approach can be found in a clever paradigm developed by Besson, Fischler, Boaz, and Raney (1992). In a study phase, they manipulated levels of processing on simultaneously presented word pairs. In a shallow graphemic-processing task, people decided if the first and last letters of the two words matched in terms of their being vowels or consonants; in the deep-processing task, people decided if the two words matched or mismatched in terms of their referents' animacy. Semantic priming occurred in the deep- but not the shallow-processing task. Taken at face value, these data are evidence against SA automaticity. However, Besson et al. were able to show that even though semantic priming did not facilitate (nor hurt) performance in the graphemic-processing task, SA had indeed occurred. First, in subsequent episodic-recognition and word-fragment completion tests involving pairs of words, the difference in performance on related versus unrelated pairs was much greater if the words in these pairs had been presented together during the study phase than if they had not. This shows that SA had occurred during study. Because this effect occurred to the same degree for both levels of prior processing, SA was apparently just as great in the shallow graphemic task as in the deep animacy task, even though SA had not facilitated online performance in the graphemic-processing task. The second result of Besson et al. that shows that SA occurred to the same degree for the shallow- and deep-processing tasks was the finding that the significant difference in event-related potentials for related versus unrelated pairs was statistically equivalent for the graphemic- and animacy-processing tasks. These two results occurred even when people did not know about the subsequent episodic-recognition and word-fragment completion tests. Hence, in the shallow graphemic task, in which semantic relatedness did not facilitate performance, there would have been no reason whatsoever to produce SA. Thus, the Besson et al. findings provide strong evidence of SA automaticity.

Summary

As expected when numerous studies are conducted to address a relatively complex issue, the data relevant to whether SA can occur without intention are mixed. However, we believe that the weight of the evidence favors the following conclusions:

- Misdirected spatial attention can impair visual feature integration and hence indirectly affect SA (e.g., Dark et al., 1985; almost all of the research by Besner & Stolz).

- When semantic information is task relevant and spatial attention is not specifically being focused on only one of a word's letters, SA for that word occurs even when attention is misdirected to a location not occupied by that word and converging evidence (no dual-task decrement, masking) shows that the effect of SA is not expectancy based (Fuentes et al., 1994). Evidence that SA has not occurred in such tasks is compromised as follows:

(a) SA may not be mediating the effect that is being reduced or eliminated by the spatially misdirected attention (as in Stroop interference from color words).

(b) The effect may not be reliable (Kahneman & Henik, 1981, Experiment 2; vs. Brown et al., 1995, Experiment 4).

(c) The SA reduction or elimination may be due to visual feature integration impairment (Dark et al., 1985).

- In tasks in which semantic information may be task relevant, when spatial attention is being focused on only one of a word's letters, SA for that word may not occur (e.g., Besner & Stolz's Stroop research; Smith's, 1979, letter-search paradigm). However, this kind of attentional manipulation is likely impairing visual feature integration (e.g., Smith, 1979) or the decay of SA, not its initiation (Henik et al., 1994).

- In shallow-processing tasks in which a word is processed holistically, SA occurs even when semantic information is not directly task relevant (Rouibah et al., 1999) or does not even facilitate on-line performance (Besson et al., 1992).

- Neely et al.'s (1998) finding that prime repetition greatly reduces semantic priming is not evidence against SA automaticity because the reduction in semantic priming occurs only under conditions in which expectancy is shown to be operating.

Conclusion

So is SA automatic? If one accepts a layperson's definition of an automatic process (i.e., that it always occurs) the answer is clearly *no*, but it could hardly be otherwise. If the question is the somewhat more interesting one of whether SA is automatic in that it is unaffected by spatial attention, the answer is also clearly "no" (as Stolz & Besner, 1999, correctly argued). Thus, SA is not automatic by Posner and Snyder's (1975) and Neely's (1977) definitions, which strongly implied, but did not explicitly say, that spatial attention plays no role in SA. However, if the focusing of spatial attention on individual letters within a word impairs visual feature integration for other letters in that word such that the word is not "seen" (perceptually encoded even at a nonconscious level), even the staunchest supporter of SA automaticity would not argue that SA should occur under those conditions.

The more interesting question concerning SA automaticity is the following: When visual feature integration is not impaired, is SA unaffected by the allocation of attentional resources and does it occur without intention? Because any single experimental design can be criticized for not controlling all possible variables or optimally ruling out all possible alternative interpretations, to answer this question one must examine evidence across experiments, weighting that evidence according to its empirical strength and the optimality of the experimental design in which it was observed. On the basis of the preponderance of evidence using this approach, we conclude that unless visual feature integration is impaired through misdirected spatial attention, SA is indeed automatic in that it is unaffected by the intention for it to occur and by the amount and quality of the attentional resources allocated to it.

References

Balota, D. A., & Lorch, R. (1986). Depth of automatic spreading activation: Mediated priming effects in pronunciation but not in lexical decision. *Journal of Experimental Psychology: Learning, Memory, and Cognition, 12*, 336–345.

Bargh, J. A. (1989). Conditional automaticity: Varieties of automatic influence in social perception and cognition. In J. S. Uleman & J. A. Bargh (Eds.), *Unintended thought* (pp. 3–51). New York: Guilford Press.

Bargh, J. A. (1994). The four horsemen of automaticity: Awareness, intention, efficiency, and control in social cognition. In R. S. Wyer, Jr., & T. K. Srull (Eds.), *Handbook of social cognition* (2nd ed., pp. 1–40). Hillsdale, NJ: Erlbaum.

Bargh, J. A., & Chartrand, T. L. (1999). The unbearable automaticity of being. *American Psychologist, 54*, 462–479.

Becker, C. A., & Killion, T. H. (1977). Interaction of visual and cognitive effects in word recognition. *Journal of Experimental Psychology: Human Perception and Performance, 3*, 389–401.

Besner, D., Smith, M. C., & MacLeod, C. M. (1990). Visual word recognition: A dissociation of lexical and semantic processing. *Journal of Experimental Psychology: Learning, Memory, and Cognition, 16*, 862–869.

Besner, D., & Stolz, J. A. (1999a). Context dependency in Stroop's paradigm: When are words treated as nonlinguistic objects? *Canadian Journal of Experimental Psychology, 53*, 374–380.

Besner, D., & Stolz, J. A. (1999b). Unconsciously controlled processing: The Stroop effect reconsidered. *Psychonomic Bulletin and Review, 6*, 449–455.

Besner, D., Stolz, J. A., & Boutilier, C. (1997). The Stroop effect and the myth of automaticity. *Psychonomic Bulletin and Review, 4*, 221–225.

Besson, M., Fischler, I., Boaz, T., & Raney, G. (1992). Effects of automatic associative activation on explicit and implicit memory tests. *Journal of Experimental Psychology: Learning, Memory, and Cognition, 18*, 89–105.

Blum, T. L., & Johnson, N. F. (1993). The effect of semantic priming on the detection of letters within words. *Memory & Cognition, 21*, 389–396.

Brown, T. L., Roos-Gilbert, L., & Carr, T. H. (1995). Automaticity and word perception: Evidence from Stroop and Stroop dilution effects. *Journal of Experimental Psychology: Learning, Memory, and Cognition, 21,* 1395–1411.

Bushell, C. M. (1996). Dissociated identity and semantic priming in Broca's aphasia: How controlled processing produces inhibitory semantic priming. *Brain and Language, 55,* 264–288.

Carr, T. H. (1992). Automaticity and cognitive anatomy: Is word recognition "automatic"? *American Journal of Psychology, 105,* 201–237.

Carr, T. H., & Dagenbach, D. (1990). Semantic priming and repetition priming from masked words: Evidence for a center-surround attentional mechanism in perceptual recognition. *Journal of Experimental Psychology: Learning, Memory, and Cognition, 16,* 341–350.

Chiappe, P. R., Smith, M. C., & Besner, D. (1996). Semantic priming in visual word recognition: Activation blocking and domains of processing. *Psychonomic Bulletin and Review, 3,* 249–253.

Cohen, J. D., Dunbar, K., & McClelland, J. L. (1990). On the control of automatic processes: A parallel distributed processing account of the Stroop effect. *Psychological Review, 97,* 332–361.

Dagenbach, D. (in press). A constraint on elimination of semantic priming by repeating a prime. *American Journal of Psychology.*

Dagenbach, D., & Carr, T. H. (1994). Inhibitory processes in perceptual recognition: Evidence for a center-surround attentional mechanism. In D. Dagenbach & T. H. Carr (Eds.), *Inhibitory processes in attention, memory, and language* (pp. 327–357). San Diego, CA: Academic Press.

Dalrymple-Alford, E. C. (1972). Associative facilitation and interference in the Stroop color-word task. *Perception and Psychophysics, 11,* 274–276.

Dark, V. J., Johnston, W. A., Myles-Worsley, M., & Farah, M. J. (1985). Levels of selection and capacity limits. *Journal of Experimental Psychology: General, 114,* 472–497.

den Heyer, K., Briand, K., & Dannenbring, G. (1983). Strategic factors in a lexical decision task: Evidence for automatic and attention driven processes. *Memory & Cognition, 11,* 374–381.

Dosher, B. A. (1998). The response-window regression method—Some problematic assumptions: Comment on Draine and Greenwald (1998). *Journal of Experimental Psychology: General, 127,* 311–317.

Draine, S. C., & Greenwald, A. G. (1998). Replicable unconscious semantic priming. *Journal of Experimental Psychology: General, 127,* 286–303.

Eriksen, B. A., & Eriksen, C. W. (1974). Effects of noise letters upon the identification of a target letter in a nonsearch task. *Perception and Psychophysics, 16,* 143–149.

Friedrich, F. J., Henik, A., & Tzelgov, J. (1991). Automatic processes in lexical access and spreading activation. *Journal of Experimental Psychology: Human Perception and Performance, 17,* 792–806.

Friedrich, F. J., Kellogg, W., & Henik, A. (1982, November). *Effects of mode of processing on semantic activation.* Paper presented at the annual meeting of the Psychonomic Society, Minneapolis, MN.

Friedrich, F. J., Kellogg, W., & Henik, A. (1983). The dependence of semantic relatedness effects upon prime processing. *Memory & Cognition, 11*, 366–373.

Fuentes, L. J., Carmona, E., Agis, I. F., & Catena, A. (1994). The role of the anterior attention system in semantic processing of both foveal and parafoveal words. *Journal of Cognitive Neuroscience, 6*, 17–25.

Fuentes, L. J., & Tudela, P. (1992). Semantic processing of foveally and parafoveally presented words in a lexical decision task. *Quarterly Journal of Experimental Psychology: Human Experimental Psychology, 45A*, 299–322.

Greenwald, A. G., & Draine, S. C. (1998). Distinguishing unconscious from conscious cognition—Reasonable assumptions and replicable findings: Reply to Merikle and Reingold and Dosher. *Journal of Experimental Psychology: General, 127*, 320–324.

Henik, A., Friedrich, F., Tzelgov, J., & Tramer, S. (1994). Capacity demands of automatic processes in semantic priming. *Memory & Cognition, 22*, 157–168.

Henik, A., Nissimov, E., Priel, B., & Umansky, R. (1995). Effects of cognitive load on semantic priming in patients with schizophrenia. *Journal of Abnormal Psychology, 104*, 576–584.

Henik, A., Tzelgov, J., & Friedrich, F. (1993). Dissociation of lexical and semantic aspects in word processing. *Israel Journal of Medical Sciences, 29*, 597–603.

Hutchison, K. A., Neely, J. H., & Johnson, J. D. (in press). With great expectations, can two "wrongs" prime a "right"? *Journal of Experimental Psychology: Learning, Memory, and Cognition.*

Johnston, W. A., & Dark, V. J. (1986). Selective attention. *Annual Review of Psychology, 37*, 43–75.

Kahneman, D., & Chajczyk, D. (1983). Tests of the automaticity of reading: Dilution of Stroop effects by color-irrelevant stimuli. *Journal of Experimental Psychology: Human Perception and Performance, 9*, 497–509.

Kahneman, D., & Henik, A. (1981). Perceptual organization and attention. In M. Kubovy & J. R. Pomerantz (Eds.), *Perceptual organization* (pp. 181–211). Hillsdale, NJ: Erlbaum.

Kahneman, D., & Treisman, A. M. (1984). Changing views of attention and automaticity. In R. Parasurman & D. R. Davies (Eds.), *Varieties of attention* (pp. 29–61). New York: Academic Press.

Kaye, D. B., & Brown, S. W. (1985). Levels and speed of processing effects on word analysis. *Memory & Cognition, 13*, 425–434.

Klein, G. S. (1964). Semantic power measured through the interference of words with color-naming. *American Journal of Psychology, 77*, 576–588.

Landauer, T. K., & Dumais, S. T. (1997). A solution to Plato's problem: The latent semantic analysis theory of acquisition, induction, and representation of knowledge. *Psychological Review, 104*, 211–240.

Lund, K., & Burgess, C. (1996). Producing high-dimensional semantic spaces from lexical co-occurrence. *Behavior Research Methods, Instruments and Computers, 28*, 203–208.

MacLeod, C. M. (1991). Half a century of research on the Stroop effect: An integrative review. *Psychological Bulletin, 109*, 163–203.

Maxfield, L. (1997). Attention and semantic priming: A review of prime task effects. *Consciousness and Cognition: An International Journal, 6,* 204–218.

McKoon, G., & Ratcliff, R. (1992). Spreading activation versus compound cue accounts of priming: Mediated priming revisited. *Journal of Experimental Psychology: Learning, Memory, and Cognition, 18,* 1155–1172.

McNamara, T. P. (1992). Theories of priming: I. Associative distance and lag. *Journal of Experimental Psychology: Learning, Memory, and Cognition, 18,* 1173–1190.

McRae, K., & Boisvert, S. (1998). Automatic semantic similarity priming. *Journal of Experimental Psychology: Learning, Memory, and Cognition, 24,* 558–572.

Merikle, P. M., & Reingold, E. M. (1998). On demonstrating unconscious perception: Comment on Draine and Greenwald. *Journal of Experimental Psychology: General, 127,* 304–310.

Meyer, D. E., & Schvaneveldt, R. W. (1971). Facilitation in recognizing pairs of words: Evidence of a dependence between retrieval operations. *Journal of Experimental Psychology, 90,* 227–234.

Neely, J. H. (1977). Semantic priming and retrieval from lexical memory: Roles of inhibitionless spreading activation and limited-capacity attention. *Journal of Experimental Psychology: General, 106,* 226–254.

Neely, J. H. (1991). Semantic priming effects in visual word recognition: A selective review of current findings and theories. In D. Besner & G. Humphreys (Eds.), *Basic processes in reading: Visual word recognition* (pp. 264–336). Hillsdale, NJ: Erlbaum.

Neely, J. H., & VerWys, C. A. (1996, November). *Repetition priming of the prime eliminates semantic priming.* Paper presented at the annual meeting of the Psychonomic Society, Chicago.

Neely, J. H., VerWys, C. A., & Kahan, T. A. (1998). Reading "glasses" will prime "vision," but reading a pair of "glasses" will not. *Memory & Cognition, 26,* 34–39.

Neumann, O. (1984). Automatic processing: A review of recent findings and a plea for an old theory. In W. Prinz & A. F. Sanders (Eds.), *Cognition and motor processes* (pp. 255–293). Berlin: Springer-Verlag.

Posner, M. I., Sandson, J., Dhawan, M., & Shulman, G. L. (1989). Is word recognition automatic? A cognitive–anatomical approach. *Journal of Cognitive Neuroscience, 1,* 50–60.

Posner, M. I., & Snyder, C. R. R. (1975). Attention and cognitive control. In R. L. Solso (Ed.), *Information processing and cognition: The Loyola Symposium* (pp. 55–83). Hillsdale, NJ: Erlbaum.

Rouibah, A., Tiberghien, G., & Lupker, S. J. (1999). Phonological and semantic priming: Evidence for task-independent effects. *Memory & Cognition, 27,* 422–437.

Smith, M. C. (1979). Contextual facilitation in a letter search task depends on how the prime is processed. *Journal of Experimental Psychology: Human Perception and Performance, 5,* 239–251.

Smith, M. C., Besner, D., & Miyoshi, H. (1994). New limits to automaticity: Context modulates semantic priming. *Journal of Experimental Psychology: Learning, Memory, and Cognition, 20,* 104–115.

Smith, M. C., Theodor, L., & Franklin, P. E. (1983). The relationship between contextual facilitation and depth of processing. *Journal of Experimental Psychology: Learning, Memory, and Cognition, 9,* 697–712.

Snow, N., & Neely, J. H. (1987, November). *Reduction of semantic priming from inclusion of physically or nominally related prime-target pairs.* Paper presented at the annual meeting of the Psychonomic Society, Seattle, WA.

Stolz, J. A., & Besner, D. (1996). Role of set in visual word recognition: Activation and activation blocking as nonautomatic processes. *Journal of Experimental Psychology: Human Perception and Performance, 22,* 1166–1177.

Stolz, J. A., & Besner, D. (1997). Visual word recognition: Effort after meaning but not (necessarily) meaning after effort. *Journal of Experimental Psychology: Human Perception and Performance, 23,* 1314–1322.

Stolz, J. A., & Besner, D. (1998). Levels of representation in visual word recognition: A dissociation between morphological and semantic processing. *Journal of Experimental Psychology: Human Perception and Performance, 24,* 1642–1655.

Stolz, J. A., & Besner, D. (1999). On the myth of automatic semantic activation in reading. *Current Directions in Psychological Science, 8,* 61–65.

Stolz, J. A., & Neely, J. H. (1995). When target degradation does and does not enhance semantic context effects in word recognition. *Journal of Experimental Psychology: Learning Memory, and Cognition, 21,* 596–611.

Stroop, J. R. (1935). Studies of interference in serial verbal reactions. *Journal of Experimental Psychology, 18,* 643–662.

Warren, R. E. (1974) Association, directionality, and stimulus encoding. *Journal of Experimental Psychology, 102,* 151–158.

Yee, P. L., & Hunt, E. (1991). Individual differences in Stroop dilution: Tests of the attention-capture hypothesis. *Journal of Experimental Psychology: Human Perception and Performance, 17,* 715–725.

CHAPTER 6

Spreading Activation and Arousal of False Memories

Henry L. Roediger III
David A. Balota
Jason M. Watson

To understand how the mind works, one must understand associative processing. This idea is as old as Aristotle's first theories of mind, in which he speculated about the factors that create mental associations (contiguity, similarity, contrast). Succeeding generations of scholars and researchers have repeatedly affirmed, both in their theories and in experimental research, that the mind is an exquisitely tuned device for holding associative information. This theme permeates modern cognitive psychology. Activation of a concept in episodic or semantic memory is believed to spread among neighboring concepts, partially arousing them, and thereby influencing mental life.

The associative effect of one concept on another has been studied in many paradigms in cognitive psychology. For example, in a standard semantic priming paradigm (e.g., Neely, 1977, 1991; see also Neely & Kahan, chapter 5, this volume), the speed of deciding that a letter string (*doctor*) is a word is increased if it has been preceded by an associatively related word (*nurse*) relative to an unrelated word (*house*). The basic explanation is that activation of *nurse* spreads through an associative–semantic network, thereby partially activating the related word *doctor* so that it can be identified faster. Similarly, in the false-recognition paradigm used by Underwood (1965), the presence of a word such as *table* in a list increased false recognition of a related word such as *chair*, relative to unrelated concepts such as *screen*. A straightforward interpretation of this finding is that presentation of the word *table* may have aroused an implicit associative response, as Underwood called it, to *chair* when *table* was encoded. When *chair* later was presented for a recognition

This research was supported by a contract from the Office of Technical Services of the U.S. Government and Grant NIA-PO1-AGO3991 from the National Institute on Aging. The authors benefited from comments from David A. Gallo and Kathleen B. McDermott.

decision, its partial activation earlier caused it to be falsely recognized. Spreading activation through associative–semantic networks may be responsible for both phenomena.

Although associative processes are routinely invoked to explain both semantic priming phenomena and false-recognition phenomena, systematic examination of possible commonalities between these two areas of inquiry has not been carried out. One purpose of this chapter is to begin such exploration of the connections between activation processes within an interrelated network and the development of false memories. In pursuit of this goal, we first provide a brief review of the use of the spreading activation metaphor in explaining phenomena beyond simple semantic priming effects.

Beyond Semantic Priming and Spreading Activation

As Anderson (1983) pointed out, the priming paradigm is ideally suited to investigating the spreading activation mechanism. Hence, we briefly review evidence concerning some of the core aspects of spreading activation from a series of semantic and episodic priming tasks. The findings indicate that (a) there are clear similarities across semantic and episodic tasks, (b) activation spreads across multiple links within both episodic and semantic networks, and (c) activation summates on concepts in memory. After this review, we then turn to the relevance of this mechanism for the study of false memories.

The metaphor of spreading activation within an interrelated network of associated concepts (see Figure 6.1) has been central in models of letter processing (McClelland & Rumelhart, 1981), semantic priming (Collins & Loftus, 1975), speech production (Dell, 1986), and memory and problem solving (e.g., Anderson, 1976). In fact, this mechanism is the major retrieval process in both the human associative memory and the adaptive control of thought models developed by Anderson (e.g., 1976; Anderson & Bower, 1973) and is the primary retrieval mechanism invoked in connectionist models (see McClelland & Rumelhart, 1986). The widespread appeal of this framework is that it (a) has potential quantitative tractability, (b) relies on straightforward associative learning principles, and (c) has at least some similarity to the notion of neural connections within interrelated ensembles of neurons.

Although the metaphor of spreading activation has been widely used, one might question the utility of such a spreading activation process beyond simple semantic priming paradigms. All learning systems that have been studied are sensitive to associative co-occurrence. If this is the case, then one might ask if this framework provides explanatory power above and beyond conditioning principles that have been well established in other arenas. The verbal learning and memory tradition (elegantly reviewed in chapter 8 of Crowder, 1976) has clearly established the importance of associative information in paired-associate paradigms. Again, what

FIGURE 6.1

Hypothetical semantic network of concepts related to sleep.

are the novel predictions of the spreading activation framework? We now briefly review some evidence suggesting that the same spreading activation processes empirically documented in semantic priming paradigms extend to some standard effects observed in the episodic memory literature. This converging evidence provides the foundation for extending the spreading activation metaphor to the study of false memories.

Spacing by Retention Interval Interaction

Crowder (1976) argued that one of the more powerful ways to dissociate two memory systems or processes is to find a variable that affects the two different memory processes in opposite directions, that is, a variant of the functional dissociation approach. Many such variables exist, but one that is particularly intriguing arose from an experiment by Peterson, Wampler, Kirkpatrick, and Saltzman (1963). They showed that the spaced study of paired associates provides a benefit over massed study in a delayed testing situation (the usual spacing effect). However, they also showed that on an immediate test, the opposite effect emerges—massed repetition provides better retention than spaced repetition. At Yale University, this effect became known as the "Peterson paradox," owing to Endel Tulving, because of the paradoxical outcome that spacing can have opposing effects on memory performance depending on the delay between the second presentation and the test. Balota, Duchek, and Paulin (1989) replicated these surprising effects in both younger and older adults. Crowder (1976, p. 294) viewed this finding particularly difficult to accommodate within the standard models of memory and appealed to Estes's (1955) stimulus sampling model as one way to account for this interaction.

Can one find a similar Spacing × Retention Interval interaction in a priming situation, or is this interaction limited to episodic memory performance? If one could find a similar pattern in a priming paradigm, then this would increase the general applicability of the spreading activation metaphor in accommodating how information becomes accessible in memory. This was the goal of a study by Spieler and Balota (1996). This experiment was modeled after the Peterson et al. (1963) study with the subjects' simple task being to name two semantically unrelated words on each of 500 trials, with some pairs repeated. Spieler and Balota manipulated both the spacing between the repeated word pairs and the distance (intervening items or time) between the last presentation and the test trial. The speed to name the second word when it was paired with the same earlier presented word, compared with when it was paired with a new word, across repetitions was the measure of activation from the prime to the target. The results of this study are clear and are shown in Figure 6.2: The Spacing × Retention Interval interaction did occur in a priming paradigm in which episodic memory retrieval is unlikely to be involved. Thus, the priming paradigm does show a parallel effect to a powerful episodic memory phenomenon under conditions that minimize strategic attentional operations. As Crowder (1976, chapter 9) emphasized, the Spacing × Retention Interval interaction is a fundamental aspect of memory performance and permeates both human and animal learning studies.

Does Activation Really "Spread" Within the Memory Network?

Of course, all that we have demonstrated so far is that an intriguing finding originally obtained in standard paired-associate studies (the Spacing × Retention Interval interaction) can be extended to an automatic type of episodic priming paradigm. However, if the spreading activation metaphor has real value, then one should be able to find that activation does not simply influence a directly related concept but

FIGURE 6.2

Mean episodic priming effects (unrelated prime – repeated prime) in speeded naming performance as a function of retention interval and spacing. Data from Spieler and Balota (1996).

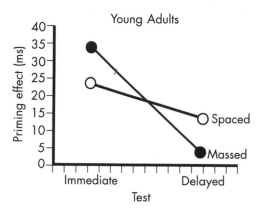

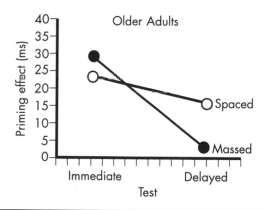

also extends beyond directly related concepts to more distant concepts in memory. This is a relatively difficult issue to explore because there is often a weak relation between more distance concepts in memory. The strategy researchers have used to answer this question is to construct triads of words in which two words that are themselves unrelated are related to a third word. Consider the words *lion–tiger–stripes*. The words *lion* and *stripes* are only related through the mediator *tiger*. If one finds priming from *lion* to *stripes*, then one would have evidence for activation spreading multiple steps within the memory network.

The first person to conduct such research was de Groot (1983), and her initial attempt to find such mediated or two-step priming failed to provide any evidence for priming from concepts such as *lion* to *stripes* using the lexical decision task. de Groot viewed this null outcome as a problem for the spreading activation metaphor. However, Balota and Lorch (1986) argued that de Groot's failure to find such multiple step activation may have been due to her use of the lexical decision task, which encourages backward checking processes. That is, evidence exists that subjects check back for a relation to the prime word when they respond to the target word (see Neely, 1991), and this fact may have minimized the sensitivity to mediated priming effects. Specifically, if subjects checked for a relation between *stripes* and *lion,* they usually would fail to find one (especially at a 250-ms stimulus onset asynchrony), and hence the words may be treated as an unrelated pair. Balota and Lorch switched the dependent measure to speeded naming in which any postlexical checking process is minimized. It is interesting to note that in this study, there was clear evidence for mediated priming. In a later study, McNamara and Altarriba (1988) also found evidence for multiple step activation processes in a version of the lexical decision task that minimizes the backward postlexical check process. They found that activation not only spreads two steps but actually can spread three steps, for example, from *mane* to *lion* to *tiger* to *stripes.*

Of course, one might again question whether the phenomena produced in a semantic memory task would also extend to an episodic memory task. Specifically, can one find multiple step activation processes within an episodically instantiated memory network? To pursue this issue, Balota and Duchek (1989) asked participants to study a set of paragraphs that were linked such that the predicate of sentence *N* was the subject of sentence *N* + 1. Examples of such sentences and the corresponding network (see Ratcliff & McKoon, 1981) are displayed in Figure 6.3. After the sentences are stored in memory, one can then test episodic memory recognition for a given target word when it is briefly primed by a word that varies in distance from that target. For example, the target word *guest* could be primed by a word close within the network (e.g., *rug*) or a word more distant within the network (e.g., *workman*). In the Balota and Duchek experiment, the primes were presented for varying durations (200, 600, or 1,000 ms), and the subjects were asked to simply make speeded yes–no episodic recognition decisions only on the target. Interestingly, there was priming compared with a neutral baseline (the word *blank*) for both the near and the distant conditions, but the distant condition produced less priming (50 ms) than did the near condition (72 ms). Thus, the metaphor of spreading activation across multiple nodes within a memory network occurs not only in semantic memory networks but also in networks established by recent episodic encodings and with an episodic recognition task.

Does Activation Summate?

If the activation metaphor is useful in accounting for encoding and retrieval processes, one should find evidence that multiple sources of activation produce greater priming

FIGURE 6.3

Propositional network and example paragraph for simple linear networks.

1. The umbrella protects the carpet.
2. The carpet is under the workman.
3 The workman moves the rug.
4. The rug impresses the guest.
5. The guest hears the doorbell.

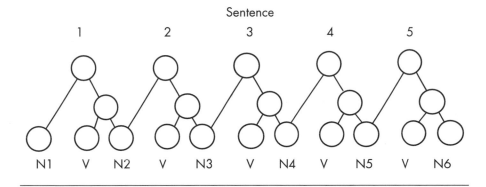

than a single source of activation. Balota and Paul (1996) identified three theoretically intriguing ways that activation might combine at a particular concept in memory. The first is an underadditive pattern in which two sources of activation may provide less effect than the sum of the individual sources. For example, if a single prime produces a near asymptotic level of activation, an additional prime can no longer boost activation beyond this asymptote. The second pattern is simple additivity in which the influence of two sources of priming may add together, so that the combined effect would be their sum. This seems to be the implicit assumption of most activation-based models, although this issue is typically not addressed in the models. The third interesting pattern is superadditivity in which the sum of the individual primes is greater than their simple additive effects. Superadditivity of priming might be expected if multiple sources of activation converge and direct conscious processing to the highly activated node. If neither prime alone would do so, but their combination does, an overadditive priming effect would occur.

Although the extent to which multiple sources of activation combine is a seemingly straightforward issue, this topic has received relatively little attention in the semantic priming literature (see Balota & Paul, 1996; Brodeur & Lupker, 1994; and Schmidt, 1976). The real trick in this research is to minimize the influence of the first prime on the second prime, which often occurs because three words are likely to be interrelated (e.g., *doctor–nurse–patient*). Balota and Paul attempted to avoid this problem by developing a multiple prime paradigm in which primes were unrelated to each other but converged on a target word. Examples of the four critical conditions are shown in Table 6.1: related–related, related–unrelated, unrelated–related, and unrelated–unrelated. Also note that in the related–related (*lion–stripes*) condition, the first and second primes are not directly related to each other. In this way, Balota and Paul could investigate the influence of multiple primes on target activation while avoiding the influence of direct relations between the primes.

The results of five experiments, which include both lexical decision and naming tasks (and other manipulations), yielded remarkably consistent evidence for simple additivity of priming, as shown in the data in Table 6.1. Specifically, one can predict the influence of two primes in the related–related condition by simply adding the priming effect from the related–unrelated and the unrelated–related conditions, compared with the unrelated–unrelated condition. This pattern of additivity occurred both when the target words were ambiguous (had two meanings, each of which was primed, e.g., *kidney–piano–organ*) and when the targets were unambiguous (or had one meaning, *lion–stripes–tiger*). Therefore, additivity of priming seems fairly general.

Extensions of Spreading Activation to False-Memory Paradigms

In the previous sections we have argued that activation within both episodic and semantic memory networks causes priming, spreads across multiple links, and summates. In this next section we apply the spreading activation metaphor to the

TABLE 6.1

Additivity of priming

Target	Prime type	Prime 1	Prime 2	Target	Mean	Priming effect
Unambiguous						
	RR	*Lion*	*Stripes*	*Tiger*	539	29
	UR	*Fuel*	*Stripes*	*Tiger*	551	17
	RU	*Lion*	*Shutter*	*Tiger*	555	13
	UU	*Fuel*	*Shutter*	*Tiger*	568	
Ambiguous						
	RR	*Kidney*	*Piano*	*Organ*	550	24
	UR	*Wagon*	*Piano*	*Organ*	560	14
	RU	*Kidney*	*Soda*	*Organ*	566	8
	UU	*Wagon*	*Soda*	*Organ*	574	

Note. R = related; U = unrelated. Priming effects are computed in ms with respect to the UU baseline for each target type. The predicted (UR + RU) priming effect of 26 ms equaled the observed priming effect of 27 ms in the RR condition, collapsing across the two types of items.

understanding of false recall and false recognition. We began the chapter with the example from Underwood's (1965) research on false recognition, in which the study of one word (*table*) increased false recognition of an associated word given later (*chair*). However, false recognition effects in Underwood's paradigm are very small. Therefore, we rely on a different paradigm that produces robust false-memory effects as assessed in both recall and recognition.

The procedure is one developed by Roediger and McDermott (1995), based on earlier research by Deese (1959), and is known as the Deese–Roediger–McDermott (DRM) paradigm. In this situation, subjects hear a list of 15 words that are related to a critical nonpresented word (e.g., *bed, rest, awake, tired, dream, wake, snooze, blanket, doze, slumber, snore, nap, peace, yawn,* and *drowsy*). The words are the first 15 associates to *sleep* in the Russell and Jenkins (1954) norms. Although *sleep* is not presented, the intriguing finding from many experiments is that critical nonpresented words such as *sleep* are both falsely recalled and falsely recognized at very high levels. For example, in single trial free recall in Roediger and McDermott's (1995) experiments, the probability of recalling the critical missing word approximated (Experiment 1) or even exceeded (Experiment 2) the probability of recalling words that had occurred in the middle of the list. Similarly, the false alarm rate for these items in a recognition test after many lists have been presented equaled the hit rate of the studied items, with .81 and .79 probability of an "old" response for these two types of items, respectively. In addition, when subjects were asked to make remember–know judgments using Tulving's (1985) procedure, they reported "remembering" the nonpresented words at about the same level (.58) as words that actually were presented (.57). This pattern is in clear contrast to false alarms made for unrelated words, which occurred with low frequency (.11, showing that sheer guessing was not a problem) and were mostly judged to be known (.09) rather than remembered (.02). The DRM paradigm, therefore, produces high levels of false remembering in both recall and recognition performance.

Consider these findings within the spreading activation framework shown in Figure 6.1. The simplest interpretation is that the activation from the multiple words presented in the list converges on and primes the critical nonpresented item. If this high degree of convergence produces as much activation for the critical items that are not presented as for list items that are actually studied and if activation during study partly determines recall and recognition, then the spreading activation metaphor can be useful in understanding these phenomena. It is worth noting that McDermott (1997) showed that if the critical item is presented in the list, it is better recalled than if it is not presented (the standard DRM procedure). One interpretation of this outcome (which was replicated by Miller & Wolford, 1999) is that additional activation accrues from the study of the word relative to the standard condition (see Wixted & Stretch, 2000, for more formal specification of these ideas within a signal detection framework).

Although the basic DRM results are consistent with the activation metaphor, asking more detailed questions permits the analogy to be extended and should provide better evidence about the relevance of the framework. We now turn to these questions.

Do False Memories Summate?

The strongest prediction of an automatic spreading activation account of the DRM phenomenon is that false recall and false recognition should increase as the total amount of activation for that critical item increases. This prediction follows naturally from Balota and Paul's (1996) summation of priming studies reviewed above. In a direct test, Robinson and Roediger (1997) presented 3, 6, 9, 12, or 15 items from the DRM lists and tested memory for the lists, for both accurate and false recall and recognition. The results are shown in Figure 6.4, where it can be seen that probability of recall of list items drops with length of the list (the usual list length effect; Murdock, 1961), but recall of the critical items increases as a function of list length.

FIGURE 6.4

Mean percentage of veridical and false recall as a function of number of list items presented from the DRM lists. Data are from Robinson and Roediger (1997).

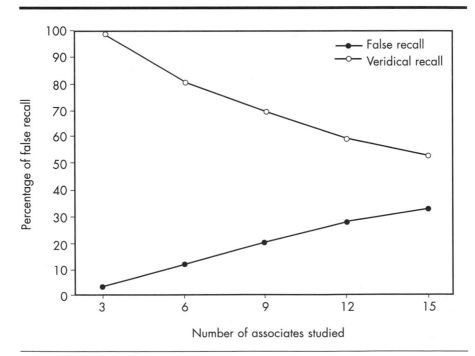

This latter finding is consistent with a spreading activation account, which predicts that activation should summate for critical items in a way that is similar to the summation of activation in semantic priming experiments. The data in Figure 6.4 came from an experiment in which only varying numbers of related words were presented, so that list length was confounded with number of related items. Robinson and Roediger (1997) conducted a second experiment in which unrelated filler words were added to the varying numbers of related words to bring all lists to 15 items, so that (for example) the list of 6 related items now included 9 unrelated fillers. It is interesting to note that adding unrelated fillers depressed the level of recall of list items but had no effect on recall of the critical items. Therefore, false recall appears to be driven by the sum of associative strength from list items to the critical item rather than the average strength because adding filler items leaves the total associative strength constant but reduces the mean strength.

Roediger, Watson, McDermott, and Gallo (in press) conducted a regression analysis that also strongly implicates the associations between list items and the critical item as determining false memories in this paradigm. They conducted a multiple regression analysis in which they entered eight factors having to do with both list characteristics and features of the critical items for 55 DRM lists. The 55 lists include 36 lists from a published study (Stadler, Roediger, & McDermott, 1999) and 19 lists developed separately (Gallo & Roediger, 2000). The range of false recall produced by these lists is .01 to .65, even though all of the lists were constructed in the same general manner by selecting the first 15 associates to a word from various word norms. The reliability of the lists in producing false recall is high, with a split-half correlation of .90.

The question of interest is what factor or factors determine the propensity of the lists to elicit false recall? Of eight factors considered, that of backward associative strength (of items in the list to the missing critical item) turned out to be the most strongly correlated with probability of false recall. That is, the degree to which the list items evoke associations to the critical item nicely predicts false recall. The correlation between backward association strength and false recall was .73, and the scatter plot is shown in Figure 6.5. Deese (1959) reported an even stronger correlation between these variables in his data, .87, but on a smaller number of lists. Backward associative strength accounted for 35% of the variance in the Roediger, Watson, et al. (in press) multiple regression analysis, far more than the only other two significant factors. This outcome strongly supports the spreading activation interpretation of the phenomenon: The more strongly associated list items are to the critical item, the more likely the critical item is to be activated, and the more likely it is to be recalled and recognized. Of course, the data in Figure 6.5 are correlational, but those in Figure 6.4 provide an experimental analysis leading to the same conclusion. The more list items tend to elicit the critical item, the greater is false recall and false recognition and, of course, associative strength also determines semantic priming effects (e.g., Balota & Duchek, 1988; Lorch, 1982). McEvoy, Nelson, and Komatsu

FIGURE 6.5

Scatter plot of backward associative strength and probability of false recall of the critical nonpresented item across 55 lists. Data are from Roediger, Watson, McDermott, and Gallo (in press).

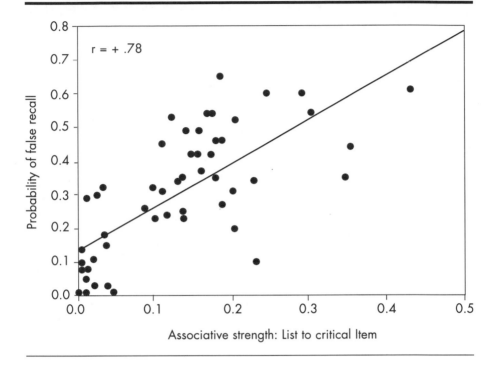

(1999) also implicated the role of backward associative strength in producing false recall.

Is Conscious Processing of the List Items Necessary to Produce False-Memory Effects?

Evidence exists that two types of mechanisms underlie semantic priming effects. One mechanism reflects the automatic spread of activation within a memory network, as we have been discussing, whereas a second mechanism reflects a more attention-demanding process in which subjects generate conscious expectancies about the upcoming target from the prime (Neely, 1977; Posner & Snyder, 1975). One strong piece of evidence that activation can truly be automatic is that significant priming can occur for primes presented very briefly (e.g., 20 ms) and followed by a visual mask (Balota, 1983; Fowler, Wolford, Slade, & Tassinary, 1981; Marcel, 1983). These primes are clearly at or below threshold levels of identification (for a review, see Holender, 1986), and so there is very little possibility of conscious attentional mechanisms producing these priming effects.

In this context, an interesting question emerges regarding the DRM paradigm: If spreading activation is a useful metaphor to understand false memories in this paradigm, do lists presented very fast (too fast for conscious processing of the items) still elicit false recall and false recognition? In the typical DRM paradigm with relatively slow presentation rates, the critical items may become consciously activated during study of the list (McDermott, 1997). If such conscious activation of the list items were necessary to produce the phenomenon, then fast rates of presentation should eliminate the effect. However, if false memories are also aroused by automatic spreading activation, one might expect the phenomenon to persist even under fast rates of presentation. Of course, both automatic and conscious mechanisms may be at work.

To address these issues, Roediger, Balota, and Robinson (2000) presented the DRM lists at very fast durations of 20, 80, 160, or 320 ms per word, with a constant 32-ms interstimulus interval. At the fastest rate, all 15 words flashed by in less than 1 s (780 ms), with the phenomenal result that maybe one or two words were actually perceived by the subjects. After each list, subjects were required to recall as many items as possible from the list. The results show remarkable regularity between veridical and false recall. The recall of list words and the recall of critical items increased in a one-to-one fashion with progressively slower presentation rates. The probability of veridical recall was .10, .22, .28, and .31 over the four rates of presentation (from 20 to 320 ms), whereas false recall was .10, .25, .31, and .33, respectively. Assuming activation of list items increased as the rate slowed, then false recall increased in direct proportion to activation.

How might more strategic processes affect false recall? At some point, when strategic operations kick in, one might expect the relations between veridical and false recall to break down, with there being a discontinuity in false recall. Toglia, Neuschatz, and Goodwin (1999) and Gallo and Roediger (2000) discovered that at much slower rates of presentation, there is actually a negative association between veridical and false recall. In Gallo and Roediger's Experiment 2 with lists that produce high levels of false recall, slowing presentation across rates of .5, 1, and 3 s/item increased the probability of veridical recall from .58 to .65 to .73. However, probability of false recall decreased from .48 to .41 to .28 across these same rates. At these slower rates, when strategic processes have come into play, greater study time decreases false recall. Obviously, this pattern is inconsistent with a simple activation account of false memories—greater study time would normally lead to greater activation—and therefore suggests that other processes must be involved.

The positive correlation between study time and false recall at fast rates and the negative correlation at slow rates argue, of course, that the function relating study time to arousal of false memories is at least nonmonotonic and probably an inverted ∪. However, the data just discussed come from different experiments. Can both patterns be obtained in the same experiment by sampling rates from a wider range? McDermott and Watson (in press) conducted the critical experiment demonstrating that this is so and bearing out the conclusion that the function is discontinuous. Their data are shown in Figure 6.6. Level of false recall rose over fast rates and then dropped at slower rates, confirming the points made above, but within the context of a single experiment with other variables controlled.

How might one account for this nonmonotonic relation between presentation rate and veridical and false recall? With increases in presentation duration after relatively short delays, one might expect increases in both false and veridical recall as a result of spreading activation mechanisms. However at longer delays, it is possible that recollection of specific information about list items is sufficiently strong such that participants no longer rely on global activation to drive a memory response. For example, would one expect false recall with only a three-item list? The answer is *no* because veridical recall would be sufficiently good that the participant would rely only on item-specific information (see Robinson & Roediger, 1997). Thus, one possible way to accommodate the nonmonotonic relation between presentation rate and veridical and false memories is to consider the distinctiveness of item recall.

FIGURE 6.6

Nonmonotonic relation between presentation rate and veridical and false recall. Data are from McDermott and Watson (in press).

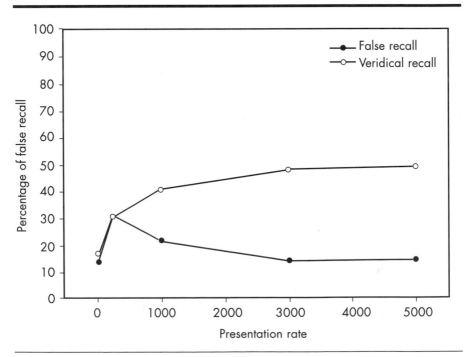

When item specific information is accessible, participants may be less likely to consider global activation from list items as enough to drive a recall or recognition response (for a discussion of this point, see Balota, Cortese, et al., 1999; and Kensinger & Schacter, 1999).

To return to the central issue of this section, evidence from Roediger, Balota, and Robinson (2000) leads to the conclusion that the critical item can be elicited by an automatic spread of activation among semantic associates. False recall occurred even at rates of 20 or 80 ms/item, conditions in which conscious activation of the lure during study is unlikely. (Indeed, conscious activation of most list items is questionable at these rates.) Seamon, Luo, and Gallo (1998) reached similar conclusions about the automaticity of false memories when they obtained robust recognition of critical items under conditions that minimized conscious awareness of the study words. These conditions included both rapid presentation rates and division of attention during study. This outcome establishes another similarity between research on semantic priming and false memory and extends the spreading activation metaphor, at least at relatively fast presentation rates, to the domain of false memories.

Individual Differences in the DRM Paradigm

If false memories within the DRM paradigm are created by an automatic spread of activation among semantic associates, then interesting predictions can come from research on populations besides healthy young subjects. In particular, research with older adults and individuals with dementia of the Alzheimer's type (DAT) shows a pattern of intact automatic activation of information but impaired attentional processes. For example, both groups demonstrate robust semantic priming effects (Balota & Duchek, 1991; Balota, Watson, Duchek, & Ferraro, 1999; Ober & Shenaut, 1995). The automatic spreading activation component of priming is also intact in these populations, but the more attentional mechanism appears to break down (Balota, Black, & Cheney, 1992; Ober & Shenaut, 1995). If the creation of false memories reflects the automatic spread of activation among semantic associates, then one might predict that healthy older adults and individuals with DAT would be likely to produce false memories. Indeed, if the breakdown in attentional control and monitoring processes fails to inhibit false memories, as may occur in younger adults, then the tendency to false recall and false recognition may even be exaggerated in these populations. In fact, several researchers have shown exactly this pattern: Relative to young adults, older adults and DAT patients show worse recall of list items in the DRM paradigm, but relatively greater false recall (Balota, Cortese, et al., 1999; Norman & Schacter, 1997; Tun, Wingfield, Rosen, & Blanchard, 1998). Therefore, comparisons among groups provide converging evidence regarding the role of spreading activation in producing false memories.

Hybrid-Cue False-Memory Paradigms: Limits to the Spreading Activation Analogy

In the remaining portion of this chapter, we consider one situation in which the parallel between spreading activation in a short-term priming paradigm and in the DRM false-memory paradigm does not hold. Watson, Balota, and Paul (2000) used naming and lexical decision tasks to address whether priming would summate with primes that tapped semantic and orthographic–phonological dimensions using the multiprime paradigm shown in Figure 6.1. In the related condition, subjects received semantic (*rest*), orthographic–phonological (*weep*) primes, or both that converged on a target (*sleep*). Priming occurred from both types of prime independently (10 ms from semantic primes, 15 ms from orthographic–phonological primes), and the combination of primes across the semantic and orthographic–phonological codes nearly added together (a 22-ms priming effect). This additive pattern is consistent with the original Balota and Paul (1996) studies with semantic primes.

Watson, Balota, and Roediger (2000; see also Watson, Balota, & Sergent-Marshall, in press) extended this mixed code procedure to the DRM paradigm by developing lists that had either semantic associates, orthographic–phonological associates, or both types of items (hybrid lists) that converged on a critical nonpresented item. For example, in the hybrid list condition, with the critical item *sleep*, the list items were *bed, steep, rest, weep, tired, sleet, awake, bleep, dream, slope, snore,* and *seep,* among others. It is interesting to note that Watson, Balota, and Roediger obtained a different pattern of results in the DRM paradigm relative to the data from speeded naming experiments regarding mixed codes, reviewed above. The hybrid lists produced a much higher probability of false recall (.64) than predicted from an additive combination of independent estimates of semantic (.33) and orthographic–phonological (.17) proba-bilities of false recall. Although this outcome appears to limit the application of the spreading activation metaphor to account for the creation of false memories, we believe the activation account is still viable—both types of primes activate the critical item—but that an extra factor creates the superadditivity.

What might produce the superadditive recall of critical items in the hybrid-cue condition? Although future research will be needed to fully address this issue, we suspect that this outcome results from an interplay between semantic and orthograph-ic–phonological networks which, although absent in priming measures, is present in the episodic retrieval environment and influences recall. Rubin and Wallace (1989) provided direct evidence for such a mechanism in a word generation task. Subjects who were given meaningful cues such as "a mythical being" did not produce *ghost;* similarly, those who were given the cue "rhymes with *ost*" failed to produce *ghost.* However, if given the cue "a mythical being that rhymes with *ost*," they produced *ghost* every time. The independent cues were ineffective in evoking the response, but the compound cue always did. The reason is that the two cues converge on a single concept, whereas the independent cues could elicit many concepts. This pattern of specificity in recall is also consistent with Watkins's (1975) arguments about cue overload, that is, having a more distinctive cue environment greatly augments recall—but in this case false recall. (See chapter 15 by J. S. Nairne for the importance of distinctiveness in retrieval processes.) In our pure lists, the critical concept could be activated either by the semantic or the orthographic–phonological items, but many items were activated. However, in the hybrid lists, the critical item was uniquely specified by the activation of two intersecting dimensions; so conditions at retrieval were most effective in eliciting recall of the critical item, even though it was not presented.

Clearly, additional research will be necessary to determine the exact cause of the false recall–priming paradox that is observed with hybrid cues, but we think the intersecting activation from two sources that more distinctively specifies the target may hold the key. Whatever the cause of the superadditivity, the hybrid list condition produces the largest false-recall effects ever observed in the literature. Subjects falsely recalled the critical concept on 64% of the trials.

Another study is directly relevant here. Sommers and Lewis (1999) also obtained high levels of false recall and false recognition by presenting subjects with lists of items that all come from the same "neighborhood" of words, in terms of Luce and Pisoni's (1998) neighborhood activation model of speech perception. If a subject studies words such as *hat, bat, cot,* and *cab*, all from the same word neighborhood as *cat,* false recall of *cat* is high. The model assumes that spoken words activate neighbors during perception. Therefore, when many neighbors converge on the same word, it is activated many times, which leads to false recall and false recognition. Sommers and Lewis's (1999) work further supports the idea that activation processes are critically important in the creation of false memories.

Conclusion and Caveats

The focus of this chapter has been on the relevance of spreading activation, as typically measured by priming paradigms, for the creation of false memories. We believe the evidence is persuasive in validating our analogy between activation in short-term priming phenomena and in the DRM false-memory paradigm. We reviewed several lines of evidence that support this framework. However, we do not want to leave the impression that activation during encoding is the *only* factor at work in the DRM paradigm. Clearly, the same spreading activation that has been reviewed in this chapter is likely to occur both at encoding and during retrieval. Indeed, Roediger and McDermott (1995, 2000; also see Roediger, McDermott, & Robinson, 1998) have discussed a multiplicity of processes during both encoding and retrieval that may operate in this situation, and many other perspectives (e.g., the fuzzy trace theory by Reyna & Brainerd, 1995) have been useful in aiding the understanding of these phenomena. In this chapter, we emphasize encoding processes and, relatively speaking, neglected retrieval processes. However, we firmly believe that a more complete account of these interesting and puzzling phenomena must include factors operating at encoding, at retrieval, and in their interaction (Roediger, 1999). We tell only part of the story in this chapter, but our intent is to show that activation plays a critical role in priming and in the creation of false memories.

References

Anderson, J. R. (1976). *Language, memory, and thought*. Hillsdale, NJ: Erlbaum.

Anderson, J. R. (1983). A spreading activation theory of memory. *Journal of Verbal Learning and Verbal Behavior, 22,* 261–295.

Anderson, J. R., & Bower, G. H. (1973). *Human associative memory*. Washington, DC: Winston.

Balota, D. A. (1983). Automatic semantic activation and episodic memory encoding. *Journal of Verbal Learning and Verbal Behavior, 22,* 88–104.

Balota, D. A., Black, S., & Cheney, M. (1992). Automatic and attentional processing in young and old adults: A reevaluation of the two-process model of semantic priming. *Journal of Experimental Psychology: Human Perception and Performance, 18,* 485–502.

Balota, D. A., Cortese, M. J., Duchek, J. M., Adams, D., Roediger, H. L., McDermott, K. B., & Yerys, B. E. (1999). Veridical and false memories in healthy older adults and in dementia of the Alzheimer's type. *Cognitive Neuropsychology, 16,* 361–384.

Balota, D. A., & Duchek, J. M. (1988). Age-related differences in lexical access, spreading activation, and simple pronunciation. *Psychology and Aging, 3,* 84–93.

Balota, D. A., & Duchek, J. M. (1989). Spreading activation in episodic memory: Further evidence for age independence. *Quarterly Journal of Experimental Psychology, 41,* 849–876.

Balota, D. A., & Duchek, J. M. (1991). Semantic priming effects, lexical repetition effects, and contextual disambiguation effects in healthy aged individuals and individuals with senile dementia of the Alzheimer type. *Brain and Language, 40,* 181–201.

Balota, D. A., Duchek, J. M., & Paulin, R. (1989). Age-related differences in the impact of spacing, lag, and retention interval. *Psychology and Aging, 4,* 3–9.

Balota, D. A., & Lorch, R. F. (1986). Depth of automatic spreading activation: Mediated priming effects in pronunciation but not in lexical decision. *Journal of Experimental Psychology: Learning, Memory, and Cognition, 12,* 336–345.

Balota, D. A., & Paul, S. T. (1996). Summation of activation: Evidence from multiple primes that converge and diverge within semantic memory. *Journal of Experimental Psychology: Learning, Memory, and Cognition, 22,* 827–845.

Balota, D. A., Watson, J. M., Duchek, J. M., & Ferraro, R. F. (1999). Cross-modal semantic and homograph priming in healthy young, healthy old, and in Alzheimer's disease individuals. *Journal of the International Neuropsychological Society, 5,* 626–640.

Brodeur, D. A., & Lupker, S. J. (1994). Investigating the effects of multiple primes: An analysis of theoretical mechanisms. *Psychological Research, 57,* 1–14.

Collins, A. M., & Loftus, E. F. (1975). A spreading-activation theory of semantic processing. *Psychological Review, 82,* 407–428.

Crowder, R.G. (1976). *Principles of learning and memory.* Hillsdale, NJ: Erlbaum.

Deese, J. (1959). On the prediction of occurrence of particular verbal intrusions in immediate recall. *Journal of Experimental Psychology, 58,* 17–22.

de Groot, A. M. B. (1983). The range of automatic spreading activation in word priming. *Journal of Verbal Learning and Verbal Behavior, 22,* 417–436.

Dell, G. S. (1986). A spreading activation theory of retrieval in sentence production. *Psychological Review, 93,* 283–321.

Estes, W. K. (1955). Statistical theory of spontaneous recovery and regression. *Psychological Review, 62,* 145–154.

Fowler, C. A., Wolford, G., Slade, R., & Tassinary, L. (1981). Lexical access with and without awareness. *Journal of Experimental Psychology: General, 110,* 341–362.

Gallo, D. A., & Roediger, H. L. (2000). *Variability among word lists in evoking associative memory illusions.* Manuscript in preparation, Washington University, St. Louis, MO.

Holender, D. (1986). Semantic activation with and without conscious identification in dichotic listening, parafoveal vision, and visual masking: A survey and appraisal. *Behavioral and Brain Sciences, 9,* 1–23.

Kensinger, E. A., & Schacter, D. L. (1999). When true memories suppress false memories: Effects of aging. *Cognitive Neuropsychology, 16,* 399–415.

Lorch, R. F. (1982). Priming and search processes in semantic memory: A test of three models of spreading activation. *Journal of Verbal Learning and Verbal Behavior, 21,* 468–492.

Luce, P. A., & Pisoni, D. B. (1998). Recognizing spoken words: The neighborhood activation model. *Ear and Hearing, 19,* 1–36.

Marcel, A. J. (1983). Conscious and unconscious perception: Experiments on visual masking and word recognition. *Cognitive Psychology, 15,* 197–237.

McClelland, J. L., & Rumelhart, D. E. (1981). An interactive activation model of context effects in letter perception: Part 1. An account of basic findings. *Psychological Review, 88,* 375–407.

McClelland, J. L., & Rumelhart, D. E. (Eds.). (1986). *Parallel distributed processing: Explorations in the microstructure of cognition* (Vol. 2). Cambridge, MA: MIT Press.

McDermott, K. B. (1997). Priming on perceptual implicit memory tests can be achieved through presentation of associates. *Psychonomic Bulletin and Review, 4,* 582–586.

McDermott, K. B., & Watson, J. M. (in press). The rise and fall of false recall: The impact of presentation duration. *Journal of Memory and Language.*

McEvoy, C. L., Nelson, D. L., & Komatsu, T. (1999). What's the connection between true and false memories? The differential roles of interitem associations in recall and recognition. *Journal of Experimental Psychology: Learning, Memory, and Cognition, 25,* 1177–1194.

McNamara, T. P., & Altarriba, J. (1988). Depth of spreading activation revisited: Semantic mediated priming occurs in lexical decision. *Journal of Memory and Language, 27,* 545–559.

Miller, M. B., & Wolford, G. L. (1999). The role of criterion shift in false memory. *Psychological Review, 106,* 398–405.

Murdock, B. B., Jr. (1961). The retention of individual items. *Journal of Experimental Psychology, 62,* 618–625.

Neely, J. H. (1977). Semantic priming and retrieval from lexical memory: Roles of inhibition-less spreading activation and limited capacity attention. *Journal of Experimental Psychology: General, 106,* 226–254.

Neely, J. H. (1991). Semantic priming effects in visual word recognition: A selective review of current findings and theories. In D. Besner & G. Humphreys (Eds.), *Basic processes in reading: Visual word recognition* (pp. 264–336). Hillsdale, NJ: Erlbaum.

Norman, K., & Schacter, D. L. (1997). False recognition in younger and older adults: Exploring the characteristics of illusory memories. *Memory & Cognition, 25,* 838–848.

Ober, B. A., & Shenaut, G. K. (1995). Semantic priming in Alzheimer's disease: Meta-analysis and theoretical evaluation. In P. A. Allen & T. R. Bashore (Eds.), *Age differences in word and language processing* (pp. 247–271). Amsterdam: Elsevier.

Peterson, L. R., Wampler, R., Kirkpatrick, M., & Saltzman, D. (1963). Effects of spacing presentations on retention of paired associates over short intervals. *Journal of Experimental Psychology, 66,* 206–209.

Posner, M. I., & Snyder, C. R. R. (1975). Attention and cognitive control. In R. L. Solso (Ed.), *Information processing in cognition: The Loyola Symposium* (pp. 55–85). Hillsdale, NJ: Erlbaum.

Ratcliff, R., & McKoon, G. (1981). Does activation really spread? *Psychological Review, 88,* 454–462.

Reyna, V. F., & Brainerd, C. J. (1995). Fuzzy-trace theory: An interim synthesis. *Learning and Individual Differences, 7,* 1–75.

Robinson, K. J., & Roediger, H. L. (1997). Associative processes in false recall and false recognition. *Psychological Science, 8,* 231–237.

Roediger, H. L. (1999). Why retrieval is the key process in understanding human memory. In E. Tulving (Ed.), *Memory, consciousness, and the brain: The Tallinn Conference* (pp. 52–75). Philadelphia: Psychology Press.

Roediger, H. L., Balota, D. A., & Robinson, K. J. (2000). *Automatic mechanisms in the arousal of false memories.* Manuscript in preparation, Washington University, St. Louis, MO.

Roediger, H. L., & McDermott, K. B. (1995). Creating false memories: Remembering words not presented in lists. *Journal of Experimental Psychology: Learning, Memory, and Cognition, 21,* 803–814.

Roediger, H. L., & McDermott, K. B. (2000). Tricks of memory. *Current Directions in Psychological Science, 9,* 123–127.

Roediger, H. L., McDermott, K. B., & Robinson, K. J. (1998). The role of associative processes in creating false memories. In M. A. Conway, S. E. Gathercole, & C. Cornoldi (Eds.), *Theories of memory* (Vol. II, pp. 187–246). Hove, Sussex, England: Psychological Press.

Roediger, H. L., Watson, J. M., McDermott, K. B., & Gallo, D. A. (in press). Factors that create false recall: A multiple regression analysis. *Psychonomic Bulletin and Review.*

Rubin, D. C., & Wallace, W. T. (1989). Rhyme and reason: Analyses of dual retrieval cues. *Journal of Experimental Psychology: Learning, Memory, and Cognition, 15,* 698–709.

Russell, W. A., & Jenkins, J. J. (1954). *The complete Minnesota norms for responses to 100 words from the Kent–Rosanoff word association test* (Tech. Rep. No. 11, Contract N8 ONR 66216, Office of Naval Research). Minneapolis: University of Minnesota.

Schmidt, R. (1976). On the spread of semantic excitation. *Psychological Research, 38,* 333–353.

Seamon, J. G., Luo, C. R., & Gallo, D. A. (1998). Creating false memories of words with or without recognition of list items: Evidence for nonconscious processes. *Psychological Science, 9,* 20–26.

Sommers, M. S., & Lewis, B. P. (1999). Who really lives next door: Creating false memories with phonological neighbors. *Journal of Memory and Language, 40,* 83–108.

Spieler, D. H., & Balota, D. A. (1996). Characteristics of associative learning in younger and older adults: Evidence from an episodic priming paradigm. *Psychology and Aging, 11,* 607–620.

Stadler, M. A., Roediger, H. L., & McDermott, K. B. (1999). Norms for word lists that create false memories. *Memory & Cognition, 27,* 494–500.

Toglia, M. P., Neuschatz, J. S., & Goodwin, K. A. (1999). Recall accuracy and illusory memories: When more is less. *Memory, 7,* 233–256.

Tulving, E. (1985). Memory and consciousness. *Canadian Psychologist, 26,* 1–12.

Tun, P. A., Wingfield, A., Rosen, M. J., & Blanchard, L. (1998). Response latencies for false memories: Gist-based processes in normal aging. *Psychology and Aging, 13,* 230–241.

Underwood, B. J. (1965). False recognition produced by implicit verbal responses. *Journal of Experimental Psychology, 70,* 122–129.

Watkins, M. J. (1975). Inhibition in recall with extralist "cues." *Journal of Verbal Learning and Verbal Behavior, 14,* 294–303.

Watson, J. M., Balota, D. A., & Paul, S. T. (2000). *Summation of activation with multiple semantic, orthographic, and phonological primes: Assessing the influence of hybrid cues in naming and lexical decision.* Manuscript in preparation, Washington University, St. Louis, MO.

Watson, J. M., Balota, D. A., & Roediger, H. L. (2000). *The role of semantic and phonological activation in the creation of false memories.* Manuscript in preparation, Washington University, St. Louis, MO.

Watson, J. M., Balota, D. A., & Sergent-Marshall, S. D. (in press). Semantic, phonological, and hybrid veridical and false memories in healthy elder adults and in dementia of the Alzheimer's type. *Neuropsychology.*

Wixted, J. T., & Stretch, V. (2000). The case against a criterion-shift account of false memory. *Psychological Review, 107,* 377–383.

CHAPTER 7

Implicit Attitudes Can Be Measured

Mahzarin R. Banaji

The title of this essay is bold and unoriginal. It is, as those of advanced age or schooling will recognize, a variation of L. L. Thurstone's (1928) landmark article "Attitudes Can Be Measured," in which he described his general method of equal appearing intervals, introducing the topic thus:

> The natural first impression about these two concepts [attitude and opinion] is that they are not amenable to measurement in any real sense. It will be conceded at the outset that an attitude is a complex affair which cannot be wholly described by any single numerical index. For the problem of measurement this statement is analogous to the observation that an ordinary table is a complex affair which cannot be wholly described by any single numerical index. So is a man such a complexity

This chapter was difficult to write, in part, because of the nature of the subject matter to be tackled and, in part, because it was a painful reminder of Bob Crowder's death. He will never get to read it, but I know exactly the parts that would have made him smile.

Not only did R. Bhaskar and Richard Hackman encourage that these ideas be put into print (if only to stop my increasing groaning about them), but their presence is palpable in every paragraph, except this one. Tony Greenwald brilliantly produced the Implicit Association Test (IAT); need I say more. Claude Steele provided affirmation that the IAT effect was the phenomenon of interest, independent of immediate prediction. Many colleagues provided comments on short notice: Roddy Roediger made observations and corrections without which the scholarship would be poorer by several just noticeable differences. Paul Bloom, Siri Carpenter, Wil Cunningham, Buju Dasgupta, Thierry Devos, Stephanie Goodwin, Jack Glaser, Tony Greenwald, Larry Jacoby, Kristin Lane, Kristi Lemm, Brian Nosek, Jason Mitchell, Wayne Steward, Laurie Rudman, and Bethany Teachman provided invaluable comments.

For many years, Susan Bouregy and Suzanne Polmar of Yale University's Faculty of Arts and Sciences Committee on Research on Human Subjects have provided unflagging support, in spite of the disproportionate amount of "business" my group sends their way. National Science Foundation (NSF) Grants SBR 9422241 and 9709924 and National Institute of Mental Health (NIMH) Grant MH-57672 supported the research and writing. I am grateful beyond dollars. Especially, I thank Carolyn Morf of NIMH and Steven Breckler of NSF for their vigilant monitoring. These grants compensate for my working at a university with a small course-based respondent pool and provide support for the finest graduate students there are (who dared to come here anyway).

which cannot be wholly represented by a single index. Nevertheless we do not hesitate to say that we measure the table. The context usually implies what it is about the table that we propose to measure. We say without hesitation that we measure a man when we take some anthropometric measurements of him . . . his height or weight or what not. Just in the same sense we shall say here that we are measuring attitudes. . . . The point is that it is just as legitimate to say that we are measuring attitudes as it is to say that we are measuring tables or men. (pp. 530–531)

With these words, Thurstone launched into the specifics of his idea that evenly graduated opinions could be so arranged that equal steps or intervals on the attitude scale represented equally noticeable shifts in attitude. Of interest to me here is not the particular method Thurstone devised but rather the radical assessment offered by his generation of social psychologists—the idea that the fundamental act of evaluation, of mentally appraising an object along a good–bad dimension, could itself be measured. Until then, attitude and associated constructs such as feeling, evaluation, and preference were considered to be sufficiently intractable as to elude capture in the laboratory. This, of course, explains Thurstone's insistence that attitudes could indeed be measured, even though the need for such exhortation must surely seem quaint to early-21st-century psychologists.

It would appear that research on attitudes, established in 1935 as social psychology's "most central and indispensable construct" (Allport, 1954), should provide sufficient preparation for future developments of both theory and measurement. It would also appear that the secure early groundwork for attitude measurement should provide a sturdy enough foundation to explore even unorthodox possibilities for this cornerstone construct. Yet surprisingly, that does not seem to be the case as the field confronts new, previously undetected forms of attitudes. Persistent questions arise about the measurement of certain attitudes, especially when they appear not in their familiar, conscious form but as they materialize in ways that elude conscious awareness, seem oblivious to conscious intention, and defy conscious control.

I should assure readers that the troubles that such attitudes and their measurement elicit are not imaginary issues created largely for my own delectation. Although not yet available in print, they have been persistently posed and with a passion atypical of the sterility of normal academic exchange. Large numbers of individuals, both academic colleagues and lay audiences, have raised questions in the course of many presentations (over 100 conference and colloquia presentations in the last 5 years by members of the lab), in the course of submissions to the Yale University Psychology Department's Committee on Research on Human Subjects and in the form of written communications. Their interest in this work has been marked by an admirable curiosity and the deepest insight about a phenomenon that can, at times, be disconcerting. I am deeply obliged to the individuals whose comments improved the research and directly influenced this report. That said, this chapter contains responses to what I regard to be an orthodoxy that needs to be challenged if a new generation is to probe in more intrepid fashion the existence of implicit attitudes and their measurement.

Interestingly, in this particular line of work, issues and questions raised by experts and lay audiences appear to be equal in sophistication. Here, I raise primarily those issues that have a broad consensus across both communities, with obvious deference to issues of scientific rather than social or political import. The particular implicit measures of attitude with which I am concerned consist of identifying an attitude *object* (which could be anything: the NASDAQ index, single malt scotch, Timothy McVeigh, the African National Congress, or god) and pairing it in a variety of ways with *evaluative* attributes (i.e., the concepts of pleasant or unpleasant, good or bad). The speed of responding to say "god" when it is paired with "pleasant" than "unpleasant" is taken as a measure of the individual's strength of positivity or negativity toward the concept "god." A great deal of work has now been produced that uses variations of measures of automatically activated attitudes (see Banaji, Lemm, & Carpenter, in press; Fazio, in press; Greenwald & Banaji, 1995).

Because the theme of this book is memory, I would have liked to create a two-way street with equal traffic along attitude and memory lanes. However, in this chapter, I necessarily emphasize implicit attitudes and beliefs with comparisons to unconscious memory. Invisibly beneath the analysis lies an assessment offered by Gordon Allport (1954) in his famous tract, *The Nature of Prejudice*—namely, that the concepts of attitude (prejudice) and belief (stereotype) are deeply rooted in the ordinary ways in which humans perceive, categorize, and remember (see Banaji & Bhaskar, 1999, for implications of this view for the bounded rationality of social judgment). In addition, because the analyses presented here necessitate connecting constructs that arbitrarily happen to sit in distinct academic spheres (i.e., attitude belief in social psychology and memory in cognitive psychology), some of what I say may seem either too obvious or too unfamiliar to readers with differing intellectual alliances. I take this risk happily, in part because of a comment Bob Crowder once made about my uneasy perch at the intersection of areas—"but we are both interested in how people think," he said—a comment that was as comforting more than a dozen years ago as it is now, when the demand for an integrated analysis of mind and society appears to have raised new possibilities.

In this chapter, I point out difficulties with the concept of implicit attitude and possible reasons for them. The discussion focuses on the two main questions that arise most persistently in response to the use of the Implicit Association Test (IAT; Greenwald, McGhee, & Schwartz, 1998), and the goal is to provide interim answers to each. The first question may be boiled down to this: Are implicit attitudes really attitudes at all? More to the point, are presumed measures of implicit attitudes (i.e., measures of the strength of association between evaluation and attitude object) detecting attitudes at all? Second, how valid are implicit attitudes? In particular, what are they related to and distinct from, and what do they predict in the so-called real world? I address these issues here in part because my thinking about implicit processes (not to mention the real world) was shaped by a dozen years of interaction with Bob Crowder, most directly through his weekly "memory lunch" meetings.

Less nostalgically, I see the constructs of attitude and memory as deeply intertwined, and I am recklessly optimistic that any assessments of implicit attitudes that are misguided, including my own, will fade when considered in the context of parallel developments in the study of implicit memory. Conversely, questions concerning the reliability of implicit measures of memory and the relationship among such measures that are sometimes swept under the rug may be clarified in the light of discoveries about implicit evaluation and attitude.

Are Implicit Attitudes Attitudes?

Construals of Implicit Memory

There is incomplete agreement regarding the use of the term "implicit memory" ("unconscious memory" and "indirect measure of memory" are other contenders). I nevertheless use it here because in my own work, I have made use of that term when applied to social cognition (see, e.g., Banaji, Hardin, & Rothman, 1993; Greenwald & Banaji, 1995). I begin with the construct of implicit memory and the family of tasks that constitute its main measures. As students of memory know, the concept of unconscious or implicit memory came into prominence in the late 1970s and early 1980s because of an exciting convergence of evidence from patient and college samples using both clinical observations and experimental methods. This body of research revealed the existence of new forms of memory that lay well concealed from conscious recollection yet were starkly present on indirect measures, such as lexical decisions, perceptual identification, and other seemingly irrelevant judgments (Jacoby, 1994; Richardson-Klavhen & Bjork, 1988; Roediger, 1990; Roediger & McDermott, 1993; Schacter, 1987). Such research followed on the heels of a previous decade of work (Meyer & Schvaneveldt, 1971; Neely, 1977), active even today, that used a lexical decision judgment to gauge automatic processes in semantic memory. Taken together, such research made the psychological study of two central facets of consciousness immensely more tractable: the study of memory as it operated outside conscious awareness and memory as it operated without conscious control.

To investigate alternative forms of memory, one needed new measures, and a remarkably ingenious set came to be devised within a short span of time to allow discoveries of dissociated memory processes or memory systems. In addition to the heavily used lexical decision task, other tasks such as perceptual identification, word-stem completion, word- and picture-fragment naming, and a host of judgment tasks (e.g., fame of a name, liking for an object, brightness and loudness estimates) served as indirect measures of implicit memory, with the signature finding being a dissociation between conscious and unconscious forms.

In regard to the results from such experiments, it should not be overlooked that a paradigm shift had occurred. Measurement and theory worked hand-in-hand to produce breakthroughs that transformed the understanding of the nature of memory. Memory, which for 100 years had been generally equated with recollection (as in the act of reflecting consciously on things past), became stretched to accommodate a broader meaning. This expanded meaning of memory, at least superficially, bore faint resemblance to the older conception of what memory meant to laypeople and to scientists. Nowhere was the difference more striking than in the measurement tools themselves, which no longer required conscious recollection on the part of the participant. Compared with traditional, face-valid measures of free recall and recognition, measures of implicit memory could, at least to the naked eye, seem alien. The comfortable assumption, that everybody and their uncle Chet could accept, was that if memory for the past is required, well then, just ask. Implicit measures, however, require imagining the improbable: For example, one takes the speed (or ability) to respond to a quickly flashing word, or the proficient completing of a word fragment, as an indicator of memory. Or even more absurd to the unprepared mind, one takes subjective assessments of a stimulus, such as the perceived fame of a name or expressed liking for a polygon or a human face, as a measure of memory.

Difficult as such leaps may have been, these seemingly alien measures were seen to reveal something new about memory. The important point is that the novel nature of these measures did not lead investigators to scramble around for a new construct or to become baffled about which was the "real" memory (the one that responded with sensitivity to free recall, for instance, or the one that showed no budging on free recall but an almost aesthetic sensitivity to perceptual identification).[1] Seeing that the old and the new were possibly part and parcel of the same construct of memory seemed possible not so much on the basis of grand theory but rather as a bottom-up attempt to make sense of intriguing phenomena—about dissociated memory processes in people with ordinary memory and in the stark observations of amnesia patients that implied a deep separation of memory systems. In any event, the same construct of memory came to be expanded to now include varyingly named extensions, such as unconscious memory, implicit memory, automatic memory, indirect memory, and procedural memory.

---

[1]Pioneers of research on unconscious forms of memory have pointed out there was resistance to the concept of unconscious memory when it was first introduced that may still linger. Yet one has to assume that such reactions were marginalized because research on implicit memory is thriving and has been an important player in the new mind sciences. Both Roddy Roediger and Larry Jacoby (personal communications, January 26–27, 2000) noted that there were indeed those who did not accept that measures of implicit memory revealed memory at all. A reviewer of Jacoby and Dallas (1981), for instance, thought the article interesting but not about memory; the article is now widely regarded as an important contribution to the understanding of memory.

Construals of Implicit Attitudes

It is awkward to discuss metamethodological issues concerning implicit attitudes and their parallels to memory without a clear sense of just what is meant by implicit attitudes. I therefore move to a discussion of definitions and the properties of particular measures. To allay fears that implicit attitudes are not really attitudes, Jason Mitchell (personal communications, May 2000) used an amusing strategy of plotting an array of three definitions in his lectures. His goal was to show the correspondence between the two firmly established definitions of attitude and implicit memory and the resulting definition of implicit attitudes. If attitude is "a psychological tendency that is expressed by evaluating a particular entity with some degree of favor or disfavor" (Eagly & Chaiken, 1998, p. 269) and if implicit memory is "revealed when previous experiences facilitate performance on a task that does not require conscious or intentional recollection of these experiences" (Schacter, 1987, p. 501), then implicit attitudes are "introspectively unidentified (or inaccurately identified) traces of past experience that mediate favorable or unfavorable feeling, thought, or action toward social objects" (Greenwald & Banaji, 1995, p. 8).

At the level of abstract concepts, as reflected in the definitions, there is reassuring congruity. But this, as seen later, is not at issue. Difficulties begin when particular measures do not sit well with established notions of how the attitude construct is being conceptualized now, in contrast to the past, or to its lay meaning. These aspects of measurement, rather than any definitional imbalances, appear to be the source of concern.

The family of implicit attitude measures is becoming increasingly diverse (see Fazio, in press), a positive state of affairs insofar as it does not result in "camps" on the basis of task rather than theory. I describe two variations, evaluative priming and the IAT, although this family of tasks, including the affective Stroop task, the affective flanker task, and other response competition tasks, contains many similarities and surprising dissimilarities (De Houwer, 1999).

Evaluative Priming as a Measure of Attitude

Perhaps the greatest amount of published research on automatic attitudes to date uses an evaluative priming task, brought to prominence by Russ Fazio and his colleagues (see, e.g., Fazio, Sanbonmatsu, Powell, & Kardes, 1986). The evaluative priming task closely follows the procedure used to measure semantic priming (see Fazio et al., 1986; see also Bargh, Chaiken, Govender, & Pratto, 1992; and Glaser & Banaji, 1999). In evaluative priming, primes (attitude objects) are followed by targets (evaluative words), and the speed to judge the target is taken as an indicator of the strength of evaluative association between attitude object and evaluation. In essence, the assumption is that if an attitude object (e.g., flowers, ice cream) evokes a positive evaluation, it should facilitate response to other evaluatively congruent (i.e., positive) co-occurring information; likewise, if an attitude object (e.g., insects, anchovies) evokes a negative evaluation, it ought to be easier to respond to evaluatively negative co-occurring material.

In an evaluative priming task, a prime containing the attitude object (e.g., flower, insect, ice cream, anchovies) is presented for a short duration (say 200 ms) followed by an evaluatively congruent or incongruent but semantically unassociated target (e.g., friend, agony). Responses of "good or bad," "word or nonword," or mere pronunciation of the target are facilitated to the extent to which prime and target are evaluatively related. This evaluative priming effect has been taken to be a measure of automatic attitude. Such findings, and even their interpretation, appear to be well accepted—certainly my own research using such a procedure both in the domain of attitudes (Glaser & Banaji, 1999) and implicit beliefs or stereotypes (Banaji & Hardin, 1996; Blair & Banaji, 1996) has been interpreted as such—measures of implicit attitude or stereotype. It is important to note that a further interpretation of the strength of evaluative associations to social groups, Black and White, reveals the strength of anti-Black prejudice, has also been offered (Fazio, Jackson, Dunton, & Williams, 1995), and preliminary evidence of its validity affirmed through the prediction of a nonverbal measure of prejudicial behavior. That is, implicit pro-White attitude (prejudice), as measured by the strength of evaluative association between Black + bad, White + bad (and likewise of association with "good" as well), predicted the degree of anti-Black, nonverbal action.

The Implicit Association Test

Since 1995, another measure of automatic attitudes, the IAT, has been in use, although the first article on it appeared much later (Greenwald et al., 1998) to ensure satisfactory parameter testing. The IAT relies on a response latency indicator obtained in the process of pairing the attitude object (e.g., a social group such as old–young) with an evaluative dimension (e.g., good–bad) or specific attributes that may not be purely evaluative (e.g., self–other, home–career, science–arts). In the computerized version, the pairing is achieved by using a keyboard key (e.g., a left key) to be pressed in response to items from the two paired categories (e.g., old + bad) while another key (e.g., a right key) is used for the other pair (e.g., young + good). The speed to complete this pairing compared with the opposite one is interpreted as a measure of the strength of implicit evaluation (attitude). Likewise, the strength of association between concept + attribute (i.e., old–young with home–career) is interpreted to be a measure of the strength of implicit belief (stereotype). In the case of the IAT, association between attitude object and evaluation is achieved by pairing many instances of the attitude object (e.g., flower: daffodil, rose, tulip) with instances of a particular evaluative category (e.g., good: vacation, cake, truth) through arbitrary assignment to a response key (left or right). For example, if implicit attitudes toward flowers are to be measured, a contrasting category is generated (e.g., insects) and the task requires all instances of the category flower and the category good to be assigned to a single (e.g., left) response key, while all instances of the category insect and the opposing evaluative category bad are assigned to a different (e.g., right) response key. Responses in the condition (flower + good and insect + bad) are compared with responses made in the opposite pairing (flower + bad and insect + good). The difference in response latencies to items in these two conditions of alternating pairings is taken as the measure of implicit attitude toward flowers versus insects. The IAT effect is a difference score reflecting a relative attitude that shows both the direction (positive vs. negative) of implicit attitude and the magnitude of the attitude (larger numbers reflecting larger differences between pairings in milliseconds).

Evaluative priming and IAT tasks share several basic assumptions: (a) that strength of evaluative association can be measured; (b) that the extent to which concepts share evaluative meaning (independent of semantic meaning) is revealed in the ease with which they can be mentally paired; (c) that one way to measure the strength of evaluative association is to measure the speed of object + evaluation pairs; and (d) that the strength of evaluative association as measured under conditions of speeded responding is a measure of automatic attitude. Most important, both tasks measure the strength of evaluative association in some way, and both take the strength of that evaluative association to reflect the strength of automatic attitude— that is their fundamental commonality. To be sure, there are many obvious and subtle differences between these methods, and among the goals for future research lies the task of understanding the processes that each taps and its unique prediction of the downstream effects of social judgment.

So Are Implicit Attitudes Attitudes?

Having offered definitions of implicit attitudes and provided a summary of two measures, I redirect the discussion to the question of the meaning of implicit attitudes. One issue concerns just how tightly an experimental operation or specific task should be tied to the psychological construct assumed to be underlying it. Although semantic priming provided a measure of the strength of association between prime and target pairs, the findings were not interpreted as indicative merely of measures of associative strength alone (although surely that was the implied mechanism) but rather as measures of semantic memory. Likewise, data from word-stem completion tasks were not regarded as speaking to the question of accessibility alone (although surely that is a reasonable description of what prior exposure does) but rather as evidence of savings in memory. Whatever may have been the informal discussions among investigators at the time the paradigm was shifting, the outcome, as known today, is this: Although new measures and emerging new conceptualizations of memory bore no family resemblance to their ancestors, they were regarded as speaking to the question of memory, not some interim process such as accessibility or associative strength alone. The extension to implicit attitudes is simple: I would claim that it is attitude, as defined conventionally, that these new measures speak to, albeit in a form that differs from the conventional one. The lack of intuitive appeal of measures of implicit attitude should not detract from the expansion of the attitude construct to include such measures.

In selecting an example target to demonstrate the difficulty of imagining new measures of old constructs, I have taken the conventional South Indian position that those easiest to exploit to support one's parochial position are those who are closest, that is, one's own family. Here, I shamelessly use a group to which I am tightly bound by ties of affection including collaboration, car rides, and babysitting—a segment of Yale's Psychology Department that constitutes a committee on which I have myself served many a time. The following local example is therefore used to illustrate the mental hurdle I describe concretely.

Psychologists at Yale University may encounter two committees on ethics concerning human research: a Faculty of Arts and Sciences Committee and a second, departmental committee, whose role is to determine whether the proposed research additionally meets an educational goal if participants are to be drawn from Introductory Psychology courses. Although my research has always been routinely approved by both committees, it has elicited a peculiar scrutiny from the departmental committee—along a dimension that some may even regard to be outside the purview of the committee's task. That is, the departmental committee has chosen to specify the theoretical interpretation that participants may receive during debriefing and the theoretical interpretation that is likewise prohibited. I quote from two letters written recently by this committee: "The IAT should be described as a measure of implicit associations rather than a measure of implicit attitudes, beliefs, preferences, or stereotypes" (a letter to Brian Nosek, a student colleague of mine, dated January 23, 2000), and similarly, "the first concern [of this committee] has to do with your reference to the IAT, as a measure of attitudes (a claim some Committee members are uncomfortable with) instead of a measure of implicit associations (which none are uncomfortable with)" (a letter to Kristin Lane, a student colleague of mine, dated January 23, 2000).

I should be clear that the views of this committee are widely shared among its members and have been consistently expressed over time. As a result, I take these assessments with the utmost seriousness, in the sense that I adhere to the prescriptions of the committee. Nevertheless, I remain unpersuaded by its assessment, about as unpersuaded as somebody studying memory using a lexical decision task might be if told that "the first concern of this committee has to do with your reference to the lexical decision task as a measure of memory (a claim some committee members are uncomfortable with) instead of a measure of automatic association (which none are uncomfortable with)." The fact that such an issue arises suggests a genuine inability to accommodate a new manifestation of even a familiar and well-worn concept.

The nature of debriefing here offers an opportunity to examine the different standards that are set when a procedure is unfamiliar. It is, of course, important in any education of participants in a research enterprise to take seriously the interpretation of the specific procedures of the experiment offered. In the case of the experiments in question, participants should be (and are) made aware that what was measured is the speed to respond to concept terms (e.g., old–young) when paired with Attribute A (e.g., good) relative to the speed when paired with (a typically complementary) Attribute B (e.g., bad). Furthermore, participants should also be made aware that this speed to respond to particular pairings of stimuli has been viewed, over decades of research, to be indicative of the strength of association between concepts (e.g., between doctor–nurse vs. doctor–butter).

To leave it at that, however easy it appears, seems dissatisfying, not to mention the ethical dilemma it poses. In the spirit of full debriefing, there is an obligation to offer participants the understanding available at present that implicit evaluations have been regarded, by experts, to reveal attitude since at least 1986 (Fazio et al., 1986). Also such an interpretation remains within the bounds of widely endorsed definitions of attitudes, as a "psychological tendency that is expressed by evaluating a particular entity with some degree of favor or disfavor" (Eagly & Chaiken, 1998, p. 269). On the basis of 2 decades of research (see Bargh et al., 1992; Fazio, Chen, McDonel, & Sherman, 1982; Fazio et al., 1986; Glaser & Banaji, 1999) in which the automatic association between a concept and an evaluative attribute has routinely been discussed as an attitude, should one not be able to speak about the construct using that term? These questions are not the banal ones they may seem about the language of debriefing in a chapter on the measurement of implicit attitudes. Instead, they get to the heart of how one may responsibly go about determining the construct validity of these measures.

A Personal Perspective

When I first came to consider the idea of unconscious social cognition, it was not without difficulty that I cut loose from the dominant view of attitudes as conscious and therefore as open to change by sheer dint of will. My mind was changed through the insights and discoveries of others, primarily by the two sources I mention here. I report them not because I wish to drag readers through the Sisyphean development of my own thinking but because I regard one of these sources to be of historical importance in the development of the concept of automatic attitude (Fazio et al., 1982, 1986) and the other source to have provided a useful metaphor to think about the idea of proceduralism (Crowder, 1989). Together, they provided me with guides to move to an emerging construct of implicit social cognition.

A first foothold along slippery terrain was Russell Fazio's work on automatic attitudes. Almost 2 decades ago, Fazio et al. (1982) made a unique connection between attitude and memory through the construct of accessibility:

Consequently, the present paper focuses upon a somewhat different indication of the "strength of an attitude"—the speed and ease with which the attitude can be accessed from memory. Attitude accessibility is a particularly relevant and important variable, for, unlike other potential indicants of attitude strength, attitude accessibility is obviously involved in the attitude-to-behavior process. If an attitude is to "guide" behavior, the attitude must first be accessed from memory. (p. 340)

Later in the same article, they stated for the first time to my knowledge what is now the received view of automatic attitudes (at least among those who believe that evidence for them exceeds that for cold fusion): "Essentially, then, an attitude can be viewed as an association between a given object and a given evaluative category" (p. 341).

I regard this statement as marking a leap forward for the study of attitudes and for the study of all related mental constructs. Why is this? Because unlike previous definitions that had perhaps assumed but never directly stated it, Fazio et al. (1982) took a measure of the strength of evaluative associations to be a measure of attitude. Later, Fazio et al. (1986) accomplished a shift in the paradigm through a series of demonstrations of the automatic association between attitude object and evaluation. In so doing, they made further debate and development possible (Bargh et al., 1992; Glaser & Banaji, 1999). Fazio's work allowed me to shed my orthodox assumption that attitudes were measurable only in conscious form and, more important, it provided a way to conceive of evaluative associations as an individual difference measure of attitude valence and attitude strength.

A second source of influence that dragged me out of my orthodoxy was a simple analogy offered by Bob Crowder in his attempt to capture the idea of proceduralism. In an essay honoring the contributions of Endel Tulving (Crowder, 1989) he wrote that

once memory is regarded as a by-product of information processing, the implicit concept of an all-purpose memory store dissolves. To me, a comfortable language to describe this attitude is to say that memory is not a storage process as such; it is simply the property of information processing that extends in time afterwards. In much the same way, the neutrinos detected at several international observatories starting on February 24, 1987, were not a sort of time capsule, laid down by Supernova 1987A for our benefit. The neutrinos represent part of that original event itself, in a galaxy called the Large Magellanic Cloud—an event that occurred 163,000 years ago and a billion billion miles away from here. And so it is with at least some kinds of memories. The retention is just an aspect of the original episode itself, manifest at some temporal remove. (p. 272)

This way of thinking about memory, not as a storage device but rather as a property of information processing, detected at a time and in a place distant from the original episode (in response to an appropriate probe) provided me with the brace to view apparently different constructs in a similar way—attitudes, beliefs, and their by-products in social cognition. It seemed that just as it had become possible to think about memory not as a store in which memories lay waiting to be selectively (re)collected by the mind's conscious hand, so it should be with at least some kinds of attitudes and beliefs. A few years later, we wrote about implicit attitudes in the same spirit of proceduralism (Greenwald & Banaji, 1995), and it has been central to our work on implicit social cognition with special focus on prejudice and stereotypes. Not surprisingly, because the terms *prejudice* and *stereotype* have clear meaning in ordinary parlance, they resist molding (even more so than the parent concepts of *attitude* and *belief*) in all ways that violate the texture of their everyday, colloquial meaning. But surely this should be regarded as an impediment, and as such, it requires correction, if these constructs are to be treated not on the basis of how hard they tug at one's intuition but as the objects of scientific scrutiny.

Déjà Vu All Over Again

The leap forward that is required in understanding implicit attitudes is no different from the advances in measurement in the early decades of the 20th century. In 1928, the idea that attitudes could be measured was novel enough that Thurstone (1928) needed to make an argument for it by drawing a parallel to the measurement of the dimensions of a physical object, a table. The title and tone of his article show clearly that his ideas concerning measurement were not commonly accepted. In particular, a footnote shows that there may have been resistance to his proposal that what he was measuring was indeed an attitude. Here is a part of the footnote: "Professor Faris, who has been kind enough to give considerable constructive criticism to the manuscript for this paper, has suggested that we may be measuring opinion but that we are certainly not measuring attitude" (Thurstone, 1928, p. 532).

Thurstone (1928) then went on to argue in the footnote why it is the case that what he was measuring was not an opinion but an attitude. A century ago the very idea of measuring evaluation or attitude was sufficiently radical to provoke disagreement about whether this new mental contraption was indeed reflecting an "attitude." I should therefore suppress my surprise if the idea of unconscious attitude encounters similar doubt, this time because speeded judgments that tap the strength of evaluative associations simply do not intuitively capture attitude as we have come to (not) know and love that construct. The process, the contemporary Professor Faris said, may be measuring something, but it is certainly not measuring attitude: "More generally, there is little evidence to suggest that the IAT has anything at all to do with attitudes, either implicitly or explicitly" (see Karpinski & Hilton, 1999).

There may be two lessons from this history for students of implicit attitudes and implicit social cognition more generally: First, in addition to cogent theory, the study of implicit attitudes needs to be deeply grounded in an understanding of the psychometric properties of new measures and in setting rigorous standards for measurement in a manner similar to the first century of research on explicit attitudes.[2] Yet at the same time, understanding the nature of these new measures cannot come from an unthinking adoption of criteria developed for the different family of explicit measures. Second, it is necessary to resist any and all orthodoxy that challenges developments of the concept of implicit attitudes on the grounds that the measures do not bear a likeness to instinctual accounts of how attitudes should be measured or how they have been measured in the past. To put it baldly, that sentiment is as misplaced today as it was in 1928.

It is perhaps the case that early in the development of any construct, there are moments of understandable and even required confusion about the appropriate manner in which the construct should be treated. With psychological constructs (vs. many physical ones), the problem has an added peculiarity identified by William James in his discussion of the scientific study of self, that is, that the knower and known are one and the same. For many constructs like memory, attitude, or consciousness, the knower and known have a close relationship, a condition ripe for delusions that derive from intuitive notions of what memory, attitude, or consciousness ought to be. Among the most invidious of traps when investigating mental constructs with which one's own thinking apparatus has intimate familiarity is the demand that the constructs ought to feel "real," even to the scientist. Several years ago, Bob Crowder and I noted what appeared to us to be such a peculiarity in the study of memory: the demand that the workings of memory ought to be studied in their natural habitat because of an assumption that methods that were ecologically valid would naturally yield results that are more valid (Banaji & Crowder, 1989). To the contrary, our view was that the appearance of the ecological validity of the probe used to study memory ought not to primarily guide investigations, in spite of the comfort that accompanies such a strategy.

A similar argument, quoted here in full, was made by Crowder in a commentary titled "The Brain, the Kidney, and Consciousness" in the early 1990s of which I retain only a draft copy that was circulated for comment by him.[3] (Crowder's mention of *consciousness* here refers to intuitive theories of how mental systems work; he is not against the scientific study of consciousness.)

---

[2]That is why Greenwald et al. (1998) published the first article years after the task was first designed. Hundreds of people have now participated in dozens of parameter-testing studies at the University of Washington and Yale University, conducted not for publication but for understanding. I warn against the use of implicit measures without a deep understanding of them (Karpinski & Hilton, 1999, being the best example); the technique can appear to be easy to construct.

[3]As Bob Crowder's students recently discovered, he did not always enter citations to his published work in his curriculum vita (a fact I attribute to his intense modesty rather than disorganization). I have been unable to locate the full citation to this commentary, although I am certain that it was published. I am grateful to Julie Crowder for locating the most recent version on Bob's computer—the citation here is from that version.

Consciousness of the mind is precisely the same as consciousness of kidney function. Both the brain and the kidneys are organs that result in bodily processes. Leaving aside truly theological issues, they could not, possibly, be anything else, other than bodily functions. For both, we can observe the states that result from activity in the system, but we have no special access to how either works. We have only the evident products of each to consider and from which to fabricate models of process. Naive theoretical models result from observations of the products of the system and scientific models (right or wrong) result from scientific methods.

Our intuitions based on experience, or consciousness, are of equal value for the study of mental and renal function. They are not, by the way, of no value at all: We laymen carry with us a naive theory of kidney function based on observed input–output relationships. I call this the "asparagus and beer" process. It can lead to some valid conclusions, with careful enough observation and enough time. But it is entirely extracurricular with regard to the agenda of natural science. The development of kidney physiology depended surely on histology, anatomy, and physiological laboratory experiments, not on more and more thoughtful theories based on kidney consciousness.

Experimental psychology seems to be the appropriate natural science to investigate how the mind works. The study of consciousness of mental life will inform ideas on how the brain works no more than awareness of other bodily functions informed their corresponding branches of science. To deny this means to accept that the brain is translucent in process whereas other organs are opaque. Why should this be the case?

Are kidneys too banal a system to use as an example? Then take vision, another bodily function resulting from identified physiological substrates. Indeed, this is an excellent example because retinal tissue is authentically a part of mind. The careful analysis of visual consciousness—after images, contrasts, illusions—has occasionally informed visual science, but experiments are usually needed to bring these phenomena under control, for they are, after all, largely unconscious.

In auditory cognition, we simply cannot become aware, however hard we try, of the cues that guide perception of things like speech (formants). Nor can we count the vibrations that make up periodic sound. This said, can we be optimistic about the contribution auditory consciousness could make to our understanding of audition? Would we want to deny that auditory cognition is mental? These systems, kidney function, visual function, and auditory function, can serve as parables for how science can deal with mundane experience: Above all, by abandoning that experience and using the methods of natural science to find more adequate ways of describing how the system works. This recommendation is no different in the mental domain than in the renal. Consciousness of any of these systems comes "after the fact" and cannot clarify the process.

In one regard, Crowder and I were "kindred spirits," an honor he once heaped on me that marked the beginning of humorous written exchanges that resulted in several published works (see Banaji & Crowder, 1989, 1991, 1994). We were both prone to speaking our mind about a need for the ordinary, and hence respectful, treatment of psychological constructs, and we were prone to stating such opinion, to put it politely, in plain language. In this next section, I comment on work that, in one sense, has nothing to do with the work of my kindred spirit and, in another sense, has everything to do with him because the approach and interpretations have required speaking plainly, and the encouragement to do so was inspired by Crowder's own unvarnished words about matters such as kidney consciousness.

Are Implicit Attitudes Valid?

Prediction, Prediction. Did You Hear Me? Prediction!

Some constructs elicit curious early demands of a particular form of validity, especially criterion validity, both of the predictive and concurrent sort. This demand is, for example, more true of constructs like attitude (not to mention prejudice) rather than, say, force (not to mention tension, surface tension, or hypertension). The insistence with which the "validity" question regarding a concept and its measurement is raised may be inversely related to the "toughness" of the concept's scientific standing—the stronger the assumption that a concept has already earned admission to the mansion of science, the lower may be the demand to immediately prove just what the particular procedure and the construct it presumably captures really predict.

The problem of validity shows up in at least two ways. First, there is a demand to show whether the measure predicts some criterion. For example, if the measure were one that measured romantic feelings, the question that sometimes arises quickly is how well it can predict Joe Schmoe's problem of a broken heart. In fact, the criterion variable of fixing the broken heart assumes great importance, often without regard to the question of how well understood the criterion (heartstrings, heartthrob) itself is. This is an important issue because as McGuire (1989) pointed out, we as a field have a far better grasp over matters of mind (i.e., mental constructs like attitude or memory) and their measurement than we do over behavior and its measurement. In addition, the fact that the criterion (often a behavior that is of the "real world") is often far less understood can make measurement of the criterion itself, let alone the relationship, weak. Relationships in areas that have an underdeveloped understanding of the behavior have a low probability of being detected (even if they exist), and quickly, in consequence, a sense can develop that the construct is not valid because of poor prediction. When done right, mental states will predict behavior (see Bargh, Chen, & Burrows, 1996), but to understand the mental construct, the behavior, and their relationship is not a simple or quick task.

We as a field did not ask in the early 1970s what lexical decision tasks predicted about other forms of automatic memory, and similarly, we did not ask in the 1980s what word-stem completion would predict about anything at all. Certainly, there has been no scurrying around to test whether performance on a word-stem completion in the "lab" would predict how well Jane would do on her fifth-grade fill-in-the-blank test in the "school." That attempt would be preposterous because the purpose of a task such as stem completion was to understand something about how memory works. It is equally premature to clamor for immediate criterion validity of evaluative priming, the evaluative Stroop, or the IAT at this stage. In other parts of social cognition, I have no recollection of similar demands being made. For example, in the past two decades of important research programs provoked by Higgins, Rholes, and Jones (1977) on construct accessibility, there was no great criterion validity crisis of whether the "Donald" task (a dependent variable that assessed the degree to which a primed construct influenced judgment) predicted impression formation at cocktail parties. Pushing the criterion validity problem early and strongly can have at least two negative outcomes: It can stop research through early dismissal of a tool, and it can provoke misuse of the construct based on early and insufficient tests of predictive validity (a case in point being the now multimillion dollar international enterprise of emotional intelligence testing based on a shamefully nonexistent understanding of the construct), a point the psychologists who developed the original construct have repeatedly emphasized (Salovey, Mayer, & Caruso, in press).

The task of building the case for a phenomenon using a particular task and through comparisons with other procedures is a slow and hard process. Fazio (in press) offered a brief review of largely theoretical issues involved in investigations of evaluative priming in which an underlying theme becomes clear—there is a seamless connection between explorations of phenomena that have a decidedly theoretical focus (what are the competing theories, mechanisms, moderators, etc.)—and many demonstrations show the validity of evaluative priming in an incremental way—some show how basic cognitive processes such as attention, categorization, judgment, and behavior are affected by automatic evaluation. Some studies clarify the construct validity of automatic attitudes using the evaluative priming procedure. Later, studies show concurrent criterion validity by emphasizing that the strength of the automatic attitude activation effect using racial stimuli predicts the magnitude of nonverbal prejudicial behavior. But understanding automatic attitude or any such fundamental process takes time. For example, the idea of an automatic attitude–evaluation link was first described in 1982 (Fazio et al.), whereas the famous criterion validity study was conducted over a decade later (Fazio et al., 1995).

Over the course of that decade, a great deal more of the "nomological net" described by Cronbach and Meehl (1955) to track the development of the validity of a construct was carefully constructed for evaluative priming as a measure of automatic attitude. The tolerance sought in the assessment of a new measure of the same underlying construct, the IAT, is the same—the time to develop the meaning of what a task, with its unique properties, can teach about unconscious attitudes. Pushing fast and furiously to "show me what it predicts" may be counterproductive. One first needs to understand the construct before asking what it may or may not predict. The fields of intelligence testing and of testing in selection contexts such as organizations highlight some of the issues here, and profound discussions concerning validity may be found in Jenkins's (1946) "Validity for What?" in Weitz's (1961) "Criteria for Criteria," and in Wallace's (1965) "Criteria for What?" These may be worth paying attention to before issuing subpoenas.[4]

But why is this demand for prediction in some domains more so than in others? One obvious possibility is the presumed social value and social interest of the particular construct under scrutiny. If social interest in the topic is high (e.g., stereotypes, prejudice), questions concerning prediction arise faster than one can say "Jackie Robinson." As hard a realization as this may be for those who study memory, people do not give as much of a hoot about implicit memory as they do about implicit prejudice. This was perhaps the fortunate circumstance in which even the construct of automatic attitudes, when studied outside the race–prejudice context, was able to prosper. Attitudes about neckties grab about the same attention as does memory for neckties. So the difference here may be less in the construct (attitude vs. memory) than in the content of what is being measured—good reason for closely monitoring the sources of displeasure or impatience. Yet unless attitudes that reveal social group preferences are subjected to questions of criterion validity in a manner no more or less urgent than the same questions about the predictive validity of blood flow as a measure of brain activity, or response time as a measure of memory, one endures the risk of driving the best minds away from fields where exploration of socially relevant constructs needs to become accepted as an intrinsic, scientific good.

In that same 1928 article with which I began this chapter, Thurstone said the following about his interest in attitude measurement, even if no prediction of behavior were possible:

> In the present study we shall measure the subject's attitude as expressed by the acceptance or rejection of opinions. But we shall not thereby imply that he will necessarily act in accordance with the opinions that he has endorsed. Let this limitation be clear. The measurement of attitudes expressed by a man's opinions does not necessarily mean the prediction of what he will do. If his expressed opinions and his actions are inconsistent, that does not concern us now, because we are not setting out to predict overt conduct. We shall assume that it is of interest to know what people say that they believe even if their conduct turns out to be inconsistent with their professed opinions. Even if they are intentionally distorting their attitudes, we are measuring at least the attitude which they are trying to make people believe that they have. (p. 533)

---

[4]My collaborator, Tony Greenwald, while agreeing with my sentiment, thinks differently. He believes that reasonable (and unreasonable) demands for predictive validity can have positive consequences for the field in the form of initiating and completing research faster than in the absence of such demands. He is a better person than I.

Dreading the Nonintuitive

Another sense in which the validity problem arises is to assume that the measure should "feel" valid. A statement such as "I used to be an atheist, but I gave it up for Lent" (attributed to the character Max Klinger of the television series *M*A*S*H*) intuitively feels like a statement of a personal belief (and belief change) in the same way that asking for free recall intuitively feels like a measure of memory. To the contrary, a task that measures the strength of association in response latencies between me + atheist has less of that intuitive advantage as a measure of implicit belief, in the same way that measuring the strength of association between doctor + nurse seems intuitively less to be a measure of semantic memory. Justifying a method of exploration on grounds of such intuition was exactly what Crowder was complaining about in his piece on kidney consciousness.

Yet I hope it is clear that I am not saying that the constructs one should engage cannot be ones that already have lay meaning. What I am saying, especially when it comes to constructs like attitude and prejudice, is that one proceeds with validation without a simple judgment of the similarity between the surface features of the measure and its likeness to the intuitive representation of the construct. It is "work" to write papers, but that lay sense of what "work" means is neither expected to, nor does it, bear isomorphic mapping with the same construct as defined in the science that has studied it. As millions of students have memorized for physics exams, work is said to be done when the point of application of a force moves (Sears, 1980; but see Feynman, 1963, for a discussion of the difference between physical work, physiological work, and the phrase "workers of the world, unite!," pp. 14-1–14-2). I think people have inadequately come to terms with the idea that constructs of attitude and prejudice are objects of scientific scrutiny. If they had, they would make less of a demand that a measure of attitude must feel like a measure of attitude, by first passing some personally and communally comforting threshold of validity.

It may be best to turn to what is already known about the particular task in question (the IAT) and ask whether in the few years it has received attention, progress has been made to form a strong first stage of the "nomological net" set forth as the requirement for developing construct validity (Cronbach & Meehl, 1955). To address questions about the psychometric properties of data from implicit measures, I begin with a description of the findings themselves. In the course of doing so, responses to the question of validity are intermixed and evidence is provided that rules out some alternative explanations, leaving others as contenders for further experimentation. The question of validity is a slippery one, in part because there is no clear adjudication of a measure as valid or invalid, just those that have garnered greater or lesser evidence in support. Cronbach and Meehl (1955) suggested that often an investigator believes that no single criterion is available to meet his or her standards of perfect criterion validity and that, under these circumstances, an interest in construct validity must come to the fore. It is the trait or quality that underlies the measure that is of central importance rather than the test behavior or the score on the criterion variable.

In a previous section, it was noted that in studies of semantic priming, while speaking about strength of association as the immediate explanatory device, investigators have been clear in their assessment that their data spoke to the question of semantic memory. Cronbach and Meehl (1955) offered a direct general statement that addressed this issue: The question of construct validity would not arise if the goal was merely to say that the pattern of response latencies on a lexical decision task reveals faster responding to concepts that are semantically related, or that the evaluative priming task captures faster responding to tasks that are affectively related. No question of construct validity would arise because "no interpretation has been made" (p. 283). However, as soon as such data are interpreted to reflect memory or to reflect attitude, the question of construct validity becomes important.

Furthermore, if one were interested in speaking to a single practical question, a criterion variable may be easy to set up and appropriate tests of prediction may be conducted. But if one labors under the illusion of building general theories of social cognition (as do many psychologists, including my colleagues and I), one must remain engaged with the question of construct validity no matter what the demands are to do otherwise. Drawing from Thurstone, Cronbach and Meehl (1955) wrote,

> it used to be common to define validity as the correlation between a test score and some outside criterion. We have reached a stage of sophistication where the test criterion correlation is too coarse. It is obsolete. If we attempted to ascertain the validity of a test for the second space-factor, for example, we would have to get judges [to] make reliable judgments about people as to this factor. Ordinarily their [the available "judges"] ratings would be of no value as a criterion. Consequently, validity studies in the cognitive functions now depend on criteria of internal consistency. (p. 283)

Lessons learned 40 years ago seem to be lost in the demand for a single type of (predictive) validity.

Toward Validation of the Implicit Association Text: Implicit Race Attitudes

This last section presents a thin slice of a developing net of results, many of which are only recently available (for a more general review of the literature on unconscious social cognition, see Banaji, Lemm, & Carpenter, in press). The findings presented here address the challenges that have been posed to the IAT, at least with a single attitude object, race, with validity in a variety of ways already available. Early in its development, the IAT technique seemed both to be of scientific interest while also providing a uniquely captivating experience. It was capable, at times, of dramatically highlighting the ease of some associations over others, much in the same way that the Stroop task leaves the respondent cognizant of the response competition that hinders some associations compared with others. For these reasons, the developers of the IAT decided to make the task available in more than one way: first to other scientists for research use in 1995, even prior to publication of the first article (Greenwald et al., 1998). Second, after approximately 4 years of experience and dozens of parameter-testing experiments in two labs (Yale University and University of Washington), a website was created at which various tasks can be sampled primarily as an (un)consciousness-raising device[5] for the public at large (http:// www.yale.edu/implicit).[6] By April 2000, well over 700,000 IATs using a variety of attitude objects were completed (see Nosek, Banaji, & Greenwald, 2000, for a summary).

In my mind, the appeal of and perhaps resistance to the IAT derive in part from the relatively stark experience the task provides to the respondent of the mental interference that makes some associations (e.g., Black + good) harder to perform than others (White + good). The discomfort in the case of the race task may stem from exactly such awareness of (a) an evaluative disparity between conscious attitudes and unconscious evaluations and (b) a lack of control over one's responses on a task that has personal meaning and value. Certainly the developers of the technique were themselves taken aback by their own first performance because their data on this measure sat in direct contradiction to their presumed attitude. From the various responses to date, it appears that acknowledging that both the consciously available and the unconsciously elicited attitude can be true renditions, each of a different form of the same attitude object and within the same mind, appears to be an acquired taste.[7]

When data from amnesia patients or college students show stark dissociations between conscious and unconscious memory, one can see this as theoretically

---

[5]John Jost first proposed the use of the phrase "(un)consciousness raising" (Jost, Banaji, & Greenwald, 1994).

[6]The creation of this website would not have been possible without the expertise and determination of Brian Nosek, currently a graduate student at Yale, who serves not only as web master and primary data analyst but also as the architect of more general possibilities for web-based research.

[7]Roddy Roediger pointed out that implicit attitude research appears to have constructed a debate about whether such attitudes reflect "real" attitudes more so than do explicit ones. To him (a favorer of transfer appropriate processing), such an issue seems to be a nonstarter. Both measures can be valid indicators of different types of attitudes and behavior (personal communication, January 25, 2000). I could not agree more. In fact, when considering how individuals or societies must prepare themselves for decisions of great personal or societal consequence or in building aspirations for the future, the more I learn about the presence of implicit social cognition, the more I am struck by the importance of conscious thought and action in human affairs (an idea to be developed more seriously in a DeVane Lecture, the collaborative course being devoted to the future of American democracy, to mark Yale's tercentennial in 2001).

exciting and as marking a major step forward in understanding. When the vast majority of respondents who hold consciously egalitarian attitudes (the theoretical equivalent of amnesia patients for the purpose because they can reveal disparities between conscious and unconscious attitude) show marked dissociation between conscious and unconscious attitudes toward Black and White Americans (and in several other attitude conditions), the occasion should be cause for similar theoretical interest and debate. I need to say something banal here, in the sense that most all agree with it: Tasks and findings ought not to be judged by the level of comfort they provide about acceptable views of human nature or the personal comfort the findings afford. John Bargh (1999) made the wise observation that just because we as humans may like the idea of being able to exert control over stereotypes and prejudice is no reason to believe that we can or to reject findings that show that we cannot. It is not surprising when a lack of synchrony between our view of ourselves as unbiased ("I am a morally good person") and evidence of ourselves as biased ("I am not a morally good person") controls assessments of the finding of such discrepancies on the part of laypeople; it is a bit embarrassing when the same is possibly true of scientists themselves.

This chapter contains descriptions of laboratory data in the usual sense but also e-data obtained at a website that opened in September 1998 and at which various demonstrations that tap implicit attitudes and beliefs can be sampled (for details, see Nosek, 1999; and Nosek et al., 2000). These particular e-data are interpreted with caution because participants were self-selected visitors to the website, who self-selected the tasks to complete and the number of times they completed each task. However, these e-data have a unique strength because of the sample size of completed tests (well over 1,000,000 tests completed between September 1998 and December 2000). Additionally, the e-data provide a sample that is in some regard more diverse than the college samples typically tested (see Nosek et al., 2000). Reassuringly, the patterns of e-data collected at the demonstration site conform excellently to data collected under more controlled conditions, and they also conform to theory.

Automatic Preference for White

There are several findings of interest in the race data, shedding light on the role of group membership and the cultural value assigned to social groups in determining attitude. Several independent data collections show a strong pro-White preference[8] among White Americans, even when using conservative cutoffs for computing prefer-

---

[8]For ease of description I refer to findings as revealing attitudes that are pro and anti toward the attitude object. In all contexts, a proattitude object bias (e.g., proyoung) refers to a greater ease of pairing that category (young) with evaluatively positive concepts (good or pleasant words or pictures) than negative concepts (bad or unpleasant words or pictures). All reports here are based on a task that always includes a contrast category (e.g., the elderly population), as in the original specification of the IAT. An alternative task that avoids the inclusion of a single contrasting category is currently being developed.

ence. The original article by Greenwald et al. (1998) first shows this pattern, and it has now been obtained in every data set they have collected since then, with effect sizes (Cohen's d) that are usually in the large range (.8 and greater).

Beyond Familiarity

The most common early alternative posed in response to these data from White (and other non-Black) respondents concerns differential familiarity. The pro-White preference, it can be argued, really reveals an effect of relatively greater familiarity with White than Black stimuli, rather than reflecting anything like an implicit preference for one group or another. This issue has been addressed by Dasgupta, McGhee, Greenwald, and Banaji (2000) and Ottaway, Hayden, and Oakes (in press). Even when Black and White names are statistically equated for familiarity, a preference for White over Black remains, suggesting that familiarity cannot explain the obtained pro-White preference. Additionally, using multiple social groups, Rudman, Greenwald, Mellott, and McGhee (1999) showed that the IAT effect is not an artifact of familiarity.

Culture or Person?

The finding of a pro-White effect among White Americans has persistently raised the possibility that what the IAT detects is not a reflection of the individual's own implicit attitude but rather a preference that resides in some clearly separable culture out there. If culture is offered as the source of learning that determines the content of the automatic preference, there is only agreement. But if the measure is assumed to have detected something other than that individual's temporary representation of the attitude object (i.e., it is seen as a measure of something else called "culture"), I would disagree. There is no question that the IAT (like other attitude measures) reflects a learned preference as dictated by one's culture and group membership. For example, a semantic priming task roughly detects repeated cultural pairing (moderated through individual experience) of, for example, the concepts *doctor* and *nurse.*

In the same way, the IAT roughly detects repeated cultural pairing (moderated through individual experience) of Black + bad and White + good, most clearly among non-Black inhabitants of the United States. But just as the strength of association between doctor and nurse in a given person reflects how those constructs have come to be paired in the mind of a particular individual, so does the variation in pro-White bias reflect the strength of association between White + good in an individual's mind, however culturally "caused."

The following example should clarify the reason for the mistaken belief that the preference being measured has little to do with an individual's preference. It should surprise no one when I say that it is through cultural learning that children in South India learn to eat and love very hot pickles (even though all infants, including South Indian ones, spit them out with vigor). What is interesting is "whose" attitude toward pickles one then believes the eventual adult attitude to be. I would argue that one sees this attitude as belonging to the individual (i.e., as Suparna's attitude or Kavitha's attitude), however obvious may be the cultural influence. As a field, we believe that attitudes, although showing cultural variation (e.g., some Americans liken the taste of Indian pickles to that of gasoline, whereas millions of Indians cannot get through a meal without them), also reflect the attitudes of individuals embedded in that culture. In addition, to social psychologists, it is the individual differences in those attitudes that are important and interesting, in addition to group differences. Indeed, it is individual variability that is at the core of the construct of attitude.

This being the case, and an agreeable issue when one speaks about pickles, it is interesting that the IAT-detected attitude is said not to reflect an individual's implicit attitude but rather a cultural bias that is independent of the individual's own attitudes. For example, "in other words, perhaps the IAT tells us little about people's conscious or unconscious beliefs or attitudes, but tells volumes about their environments" (Karpinski & Hilton, 1999). To my mind, the idea that the IAT (or evaluative priming) attitudes are seen not as a reflection of an individual's mind is at best an oddity that will prove in time to be misguided.

But why is there such a compelling sense that the implicit attitude that is being picked up is not one's own? The fallacy may arise from assuming that there is a bright line separating one's self from one's culture, an assumption that is becoming less tenable as researchers discover the deep reach of culture into individual minds (Fiske, Kitayama, Markus, & Nisbett, 1998). Implicit attitudes, as I see it, reflect traces of experiences within a culture that have become so integral a part of the individual's own mental and social makeup that it is artificial, if not patently odd, to separate such attitudes into "culture" versus "self" parts.

But the more important observation here may be the following: The experience that implicit attitudes, as measured by the IAT, may not reflect an individual's own attitude but rather that of the culture may lie in the dominant popular understanding of attitudes—as things that are under conscious awareness, intention, and control. In addition, this is a meaningful experience and a distinction that consciously held attitudes certainly allow. That is, one can consciously have the compelling experience of holding a belief or attitude that is discrepant with those of individual others (e.g., "My senator likes the NRA, but I don't") or beliefs that are discrepant from a culture or subculture (e.g., "97% of all Americans and 95% of physicians believe in God, but I don't"). The human ability to consciously "know" one's own attitude or belief, and to "know" its separation from the attitudes and beliefs of others, is an important marker of conscious social cognition. The ability to be able to consciously reflect on one's own mind, a fundamentally unique human ability, is what appears to be causing the confusion regarding implicit attitudes. One desires to see a separation between culture and person in the same way with implicit attitudes as with explicit attitudes; this distinction is imposed on the data, so powerful is the assumption of individual–culture separation (for a clear example of this fallacy, see Karpinski & Hilton, 1999). The expectation is that just as conscious attitudes are malleable by volition, so must be the case with automatic attitudes. When implicit attitudes do not respond to the call of free will, the source of the attitude becomes suspect— whose attitude is it? "Not mine," is the answer. "I can't seem to control it, and surely if it were mine, I would be able to do so." Add to this the unpalatable nature of the observed dissociation between conscious and unconscious race attitudes, and one may see why a manufactured distinction between self and culture can seem so compelling, even if incorrect.

Perhaps the struggle to find a place to point the finger, to take the burden of possession off one's self, comes from the inherently political nature of such assessments. One certainly does not see the same agitation when one cannot seem to remember a list of words for which one shows intact priming. Individuals are the transducers of cultural experience—they provide the physical, social, and psychological shell through which culture speaks. Yet when revealed attitudes are not palatable, the reaction is to look for an answer elsewhere, and pointing to culture (not as the environment in which the attitude is learned but rather as the "thing" whose attitude is being measured) is perfectly understandable and perfectly wrong.

Is Group Membership All That Matters?

Among the most intriguing of questions concerning implicit race attitudes concerns the performance of Black Americans themselves. The discussion rests primarily on e-data because of the sheer size of the numbers of Black Americans available at the demonstration website. Black Americans show a notable deviation in automatic attitude from White Americans, with pro-Black preference being revealed to a greater extent than it is among White Americans. However, Black American data do not show strong pro-Black preference. Black Americans show an average difference score close to zero (no bias in either direction). These data support a theoretical expectation I had about Black Americans. To the extent that the IAT captures a preference that stems from group membership (rooted in a preference for self and hence attributes associated to the self, see Greenwald et al., 2000), Black Americans show a more positive automatic attitude toward the group to which they belong than do White Americans, who do not possess group membership. Yet to the extent that the IAT reveals a learned negativity toward Black Americans that is inherent in the culture, approximately half the members of the group of reported Black Americans in this sample do not (or one might say, cannot) show implicit positive attitude toward their own group as do members of many other more culturally privileged groups. This is in stark contrast to the strong progroup attitudes that Black Americans show on explicit measures that are even stronger than those shown by White Americans (see Banaji, Greenwald, & Rosier, 1997). So group membership does matter, but because all groups do not show equal implicit positive associations to their own groups, I entertain the possibility that culturally imposed notions of good and bad infiltrate and shape individual attitudes toward one's own social group.

Third Parties

The influence of culture on individual attitudes may be gleaned in another way—from third-party members. If attitudes are a function of both group membership (i.e., preference for one's own group) and cultural value assigned to the group, then respondents who belong to a third group (i.e., those who do not hold membership in either of two groups) can provide useful information about the reach of culture. Asian participants provide useful data in this regard. Of the 8,012 Asians who took the Black–White IAT, 73% showed a pro-White bias, that is, an effect commensurate with that shown by White Americans. Likewise, with the many implicit attitudes studied that cannot include group membership (e.g., insect–flower, math–arts), the attitude may be informative about individual differences toward the object, even though no membership is implied. At times, even here, known-groups validation is available, as in the finding that entomologists show greater liking for insects than do nonentomologists (Citrin & Greenwald, 1998), and omnivores show greater liking for meat than do vegetarians (Swanson, Rudman, & Greenwald, in press). More than anything, this finding does verify that the long reach of culture affects even third parties who do not hold membership in the target groups.

Social Neuroscience: Attitudes and Brain Activation

In a previous context, I mentioned Robert Crowder's belief that the brain, like other organs involved in bodily functions, should be studied through experimental treatment of behavior and not from deeper and deeper intuitions about the working of the organ. In the context of research on attitudes, Phelps and I postulated that dissociations between implicit and explicit attitudes observed on measures of automatic associations should find validation in brain activity (see Ochsner & Lieberman, 2000, for a review of extant research on social neuroscience). In particular, there ought to be a mapping between individual learning (as revealed by IAT and other measures) and activity in a subcortical structure known to be involved in emotional learning. Phelps et al. (2000) focused on the amygdala, obtaining a measure of activation in response to unfamiliar Black and White faces during scanning. The difference in Black–White activation was significantly correlated with measures of race bias obtained on the IAT ($r = .58$) and potentiated eye-blink startle ($r = .56$) that also used unfamiliar Black versus White faces. Two findings of a lack of correlation are also of theoretical interest. First, such correlations were not obtained when faces of familiar and liked Black and White individuals were used. Second, no correlation between amygdala activity and a measure of conscious race attitudes and beliefs, the Modern Racism Scale (MRS), was obtained. Their point is the opposite of the simplistic notion that "racism is in the brain." Instead, they suggested that cultural learning is the cause of the effects observed in both amygdalar activity as well as IAT and potentiated startle. For the purpose of this chapter, the finding of interest lies in the congruence between the responses of a brain center known to be involved in emotional learning and the automatic expressions of preference on "behavioral" tasks such as the IAT and startle. Culture is the ether in which learning occurs, and such learning reveals something specific about the internalized attitude of the individual; searching for a ghost named "culture" in the mind's machine will likely produce the same successes as other searches for ghosts.

Ethnocentrism

With its roots in the postwar exodus to the United States, scholars especially from the Frankfurt School favored a theory regarding a complex of mental and social processes that produced a personality type they referred to as "the authoritarian personality," a signature feature of such a personality being ethnocentrism, or a generalized dislike of all groups foreign to one's own. The notion of authoritarian ethnocentrism produced a great deal of research, but such work did not touch the mainstream of social psychology nor did it leave a lasting impact on the field. Cunningham, Nezlek, and Banaji (2000) analyzed ethnocentrism using both classic explicit and IAT measures, including five social groups for assuring generality of the findings—attitudes toward Black–White, gay–straight, poor–rich, foreign–American, and Jewish–Christian. This research shows that the strength of automatic evaluations of good–bad with each of these pairs reveals not only a stable implicit ethnocentrism factor but also one that is psychometrically distinct from the latent factor that taps explicit attitudes. This work marks the beginning of a program of research to provide construct validity for implicit measures with both convergent and divergent measures. By including measures of general rigidity in thinking and authoritarianism this research shows that unconscious attitudes and broader personality structures operated in concert.

Psychometrics of Implicit Attitude Measures

Many conversations at conferences in recent months have focused on the problem of the lack of relationship among various measures of implicit attitudes and between measures of implicit and explicit attitudes (e.g., National Science Foundation Construct Validity/Implicit Social Cognition Workshop, May 1999, Zion, IL). These questions lie at the heart of many of the challenges that are being posed to implicit measures of social cognition more generally. Some investigators have selected a single explicit measure of attitude as the criterion (this itself may indicate the dominance of explicit measures, that they are naturally assumed to be the criterion!) and attempted to see if the implicit measure "measures up" to it. For example, Karpinski and Hilton (1999) did just that, arguing that if the attitude topic is one not affected by social demands, implicit measures ought to relate to explicit ones. That such an assessment was offered only indicates my own ineffectiveness in pointing out the expected dissociation between such measures, even when social desirability is not at issue. One can see these two families of measures (implicit and explicit) as distinct not merely as an empirical convenience (i.e., experimenters need to keep the hypothesis hidden from participants' awareness, so they must use measures that bypass such awareness) but as theoretical necessities; that is, these two modes are fundamentally different, even when they are partially related (Cunningham et al., 2000; Greenwald & Banaji, 1995).

The facts as they currently stand suggest that implicit and explicit attitudes are indeed dissociated and sometimes doubly (e.g., positive attitudes on an explicit measure, negative attitudes on an implicit measure) or they may be partially dissociated (both attitudes may be positive or negative, yet each accounting for a unique portion of the variance). In the research world in which conscious and unconscious attitudes are seen to be conceptually distinct, the low correlation or lower correlation between measures within the same family is taken as evidence of validity, not a challenge to it. Thus, when Fazio et al. (1995) found a lack of correlation between evaluative priming and the MRS, a theoretical prediction was confirmed; when Phelps et al. (2000) found that IAT and brain activity were correlated but that MRS and brain activity were not, convergent and incremental validity were demonstrated; when Cunningham et al. (2000) showed that implicit attitudes toward five social groups formed a single factor that was separable from (but related to) explicit attitudes, convergent and divergent validity were demonstrated.

Just as across family (implicit–explicit) comparisons are of interest, so are within family (implicit–implicit) comparisons. A worry is that various versions of implicit measures, theoretically belonging to the same family, are not related to each other. Certainly, if that were the case, the outcome would be similar to research on memory: Multiple implicit measures of memory tapping differing processes are not expected to be related to each other even though they sit theoretically in roughly the same family. With attitudes, such data have begun to be reported (e.g., Cameron, Alvarez, & Bargh, 2000). Nevertheless, it is likely that low and unsystematic correlations are more likely to be a function of the lack of power of experimental designs and statistical analyses rather than reflecting a genuine lack of correlation. It is reckless to affirm low or no correlations without effectively ruling out Type II errors (see Cunningham, Preacher, & Banaji, in press). Reaction time data are notorious for insensitivity to internal consistency, but when internal consistency is controlled for, the stability of the data over time increases dramatically. Various researchers have conducted studies in which multiple measures (across time) of multiple tasks (all variations of implicit attitude measures) are used and good convergence between implicit measures is found (Cunningham et al., in press). Why is this? Unlike other tests, the substantial power both in sample size and data analytic techniques has been ensured, calling into doubt one's own and others' reports of a lack of convergence within implicit measures (see also Rudman & Kilianski, 2000). The moral of the story here is that it is too early to proclaim dissatisfaction with the reliability or stability of implicit measures. The overwhelming likelihood is that, when appropriately conducted, theoretically expected relationships between implicit measures indeed emerge.

Shifting Implicit Attitudes Follow Shifting Construals

Mitchell, Nosek, and Banaji (1998, 2000) used explicitly liked Black athletes (e.g., Michael Jordan) and explicitly disliked White politicians (e.g., Jesse Helms) as stimuli but with varying group labels in the IAT. Validating the correspondence between conscious and unconscious attitudes, the implicit attitude revealed stronger associations between Black + good and White + bad when athlete and politician were the labels. But when the classification dimension was changed to race (e.g., Jordan classified as Black, Helms as White), the positive implicit attitude toward the same Black athletes was eliminated. This dissociation is remarkable, given that the two attitude tasks were conducted in sequence and the explicit attitudes were strongly in favor of Black athletes and not White politicians. The cultural imposition of negativity toward the group Black interfered with the positive associations to particular favored members of the group. Mitchell et al. took these and other similar data to be evidence of the impact of the group frame in which individuals are viewed. Strong liking can turn to no liking when a shift in the construal of the attitude object is even slightly engineered.

Mitchell et al. (1998) did not take these findings to reflect opposing attitudes toward the same target; instead, they took the disjunction between the two implicit attitudes to reveal what Solomon Asch had pointed out many years ago—that the difference in attitude when performing the athlete–politician task renders a different construal of the attitude object than when performing the Black–White task. Such data lead them to view attitudes as malleable and sensitive to context and framing and suggest a departure from the assumption that attitudes come in stable, monolithic form (see Wilson, Lindsey, & Schooler, 2000, for a related but distinct view).

Malleability of Implicit Attitudes

Assumptions about the nature of implicit attitudes had led me to the conclusion that such attitudes would be hard to change, in part because the underlying associations are ones learned over a long period of time. To my great surprise, data from other labs (and now mine as well) are pointing to a contradictory assessment about the nature of implicit attitudes. Dasgupta and Greenwald (in press) showed that when respondents are primed with photos and descriptions of admired Black individuals (e.g., Martin Luther King, Jr.) and notorious White individuals (e.g., Timothy McVeigh) they show a reduction in implicit pro-White attitude (see also Rudman, 1999, for a classroom intervention that provides a similar reduction). Blair and Ma (2000) showed that the imagining strong women leads to a reduction in the association of women as weak (relative to male as strong). Carpenter and Banaji (2000) showed the same and, in addition, that such priming effects are specific (i.e., they are restricted to change on strong–weak beliefs but do not influence good–bad attitude judgments). This line of research shows that associations between attitude object and evaluation or between belief object and attribute are more transient than previously assumed. That they can be shifted with minimal intervention is exciting both in what it reveals about the structure of attitudes and about attitude change (as perhaps not requiring deep interventions with long-lasting effects but rather as shallow interventions with shorter lasting but no less real change).

Conclusion

I have addressed, in idiosyncratic fashion, two related questions that most commonly emerge in response to research on implicit attitudes using the IAT: Are they really attitudes, and what do they predict? I suggested, through parallels with research on memory, that these questions are legitimate in some respects and inappropriate in other respects. An idea that I did not tackle is the question of implicit attitude measurement for its own sake, simply as a measure of attitude (independent of whether it relates to conscious attitudes, etc., or not, whether it is "better" or "worse" than conscious measures or not). This idea was brought home to me forcefully in an observation offered by Roddy Roediger (personal communication, April 5, 2000) that I expand on here to make the point. There is certainly some interest in knowing whether people believe they have a good memory or not, and if that question is the one of interest, one would merely ask for estimates of memory ability. But would one use a person's estimate of their memory ability when it comes to learning about memory? Or the accuracy of a person's eyesight when it comes to a decision about whether they can fly an airplane or not? Just as personal estimates would be laughable in such contexts, so too it should be with attitudes. The point is that some of these new measures are of interest simply because they allow one to firmly get away from verbal self-report measures and as such they expand the horizon of what can be learned about attitudes. In so doing, they offer a window into a mental world to which the conscious mind is not privy. Explicit attitude measures may always remain of interest given the theoretical question at hand. But implicit measures may be of interest in their own right if a measure independent of conscious feeling is sought. It may be as quaint to rely on self-reported attitude for some purposes, as it currently would seem if one relied on people's estimates of their own intelligence as the basis of providing them admission to college.

Looking at these two areas of research on attitudes and memory has been beneficial to me, if for no reason other than to bring to the fore that differing assessments can emerge of the same underlying processes. Almost 30 years ago, researchers of implicit memory gained momentum in part through observations that amnesia patients showed intact priming but poor conscious recollection (Warrington & Weiskrantz, 1968). A decade later, Nisbett and Wilson (1977) wrote an article I regard to be among the more important contributions to psychology over the past 100 years, in which they presciently described how we, as a field, may have overestimated people's ability to introspect on the contents of their mind and the rationale for their behavior. They warned that social psychologists ought to bear in mind the dissociations between what people say and what they do, between the actual and presumed reasons for action. Although that article is well known, I do not believe its advice was taken seriously until recent years, when a focus on unconscious processes came to be of interest in its own right. Both fields of research on memory and attitude have gained enormously from breaking away from the fold of traditional measurement. The goal of this chapter was to highlight two main issues concerning what implicit attitudes are and their validity. As well, it provided an opportunity to stand on a soapbox to warn about a few matters: the strangely different standards for assessing the value of research on implicit memory versus implicit attitudes, a confusion regarding whether attitudes reveal about the individual or the culture, and the potential resistance to the idea of a lack of control over the attitudes and beliefs that are dear to the hearts of most Americans (viz., a strong sense of racial equality and egalitarianism in general).

I recall that when Bob Crowder was vastly impressed with an idea, the highest praise that he would offer in his understated way was the following: "You know, it changed my mind." So to my kindred spirit, I can simply say, "You changed my mind." But far more important than the changing of single minds lies the task, even the hope, that the work of a new generation vigorously understanding how attitudes and beliefs operate in unconscious and conscious modes will change so many minds that the arguments posed here will seem anachronistic, even defunct.

References

Allport, G. W. (1954). *The nature of prejudice.* Cambridge, MA: Addison-Wesley.

Banaji, M. R., & Bhaskar, R. (1999). Implicit stereotypes and memory: The bounded rationality of social beliefs. In D. L. Schacter & E. Scarry (Eds.), *Memory, belief and brain* (pp. 139–175). Cambridge, MA: Harvard University Press.

Banaji, M. R., & Crowder, R. G. (1989). The bankruptcy of everyday memory. *American Psychologist, 44,* 1185–1193.

Banaji, M. R., & Crowder, R. G. (1991). Some everyday thoughts on ecologically valid methods. *American Psychologist, 46,* 78–79.

Banaji, M. R., & Crowder, R. G. (1994). Experimentation and its discontents. In P. E. Morris & M. Gruneberg (Eds.), *Aspects of memory* (2nd ed., pp. 296–308). New York: Routledge.

Banaji, M. R., Greenwald, A.G., & Rosier, M. (1997, October). *Implicit esteem: When collectives shape individuals.* Paper presented at the Preconference on Self, Toronto, Ontario, Canada.

Banaji, M. R., & Hardin, C. D. (1996). Automatic stereotyping. *Psychological Science, 7,* 136–141.

Banaji, M. R., Hardin, C., & Rothman, A. J. (1993). Implicit stereotyping in person judgment. *Journal of Personality and Social Psychology, 65,* 272–281.

Banaji, M. R., Lemm, K., & Carpenter, S. J. (in press). Automatic and implicit processes in social cognition. In A. Tesser & N. Schwartz (Eds.), *Blackwell handbook of social psychology: Intraindividual processes.* London, England: Blackwell.

Bargh, J. A. (1999). The cognitive monster: The case against the controllability of automatic stereotype effects. In S. Chaiken & Y. Trope (Eds.), *Dual-process theories in social psychology* (pp. 361–382). New York: Guilford Press.

Bargh, J. A., Chaiken, S., Govender, R., & Pratto, F. (1992). The generality of the automatic attitude activation effect. *Journal of Personality and Social Psychology, 62,* 893–912.

Bargh, J. A, Chen, M., & Burrows, L. (1996). Automaticity of social behavior: Direct effects of trait construct and stereotype activation on action. *Journal of Personality and Social Psychology, 71,* 230–244

Blair, I. V., & Banaji, M. R. (1996). Automatic and controlled processes in stereotype priming. *Journal of Personality and Social Psychology, 70,* 1142–1163.

Blair, I., & Ma, J. (2000). *Imagining stereotypes away: The moderation of automatic stereotypes through mental imagery.* Manuscript submitted for publication, University of Colorado, Boulder.

Cameron, J. A., Alvarez, J. M., & Bargh, J. A. (2000, February). *Examining the validity of implicit and explicit measures of prejudice: Is there really a bona fide pipeline?* Paper presented at the first annual meeting of the Society for Personality and Social Psychology, Nashville, TN.

Carpenter, S., & Banaji, M. R. (2000). *Implicit gender attitudes: Group membership, cultural construal, and malleability.* Unpublished manuscript, Yale University, New Haven, CT.

Citrin, L. B., & Greenwald, A. G. (1998, April). *Measuring implicit cognition: Psychologists' and entomologists' attitudes toward insects.* Paper presented at the annual meeting of the Midwestern Psychological Association, Chicago.

Cronbach, L. J., & Meehl, P. E. (1955). Construct validity in psychological tests. *Psychological Bulletin, 52,* 281–302.

Crowder, R. G. (1989). Modularity and dissociation in memory systems. In H. L. Roediger & F. I. M. Craik (Eds.), *Varieties of memory and consciousness: Essays in honor of Endel Tulving* (pp. 271–294). Hillsdale, NJ: Erlbaum.

Cunningham, W. A., Nezlek, J. B., & Banaji, M. R. (2000). *Conscious and unconscious ethnocentrism: Revisiting the ideologies of prejudice.* Manuscript in preparation, Yale University, New Haven, CT.

Cunningham, W. A., Preacher, K. J., & Banaji, M. R. (in press). Psychometric properties of implicit attitude measures: Internal consistency, stability, and convergent. *Psychological Science.*

Dasgupta, N., & Greenwald, A. G. (in press). Exposure to admired group members reduces automatic intergroup bias. *Journal of Personality and Social Psychology.*

Dasgupta, N., McGhee, D. E., Greenwald, A. G., & Banaji, M. R. (2000). Automatic preference for White Americans: Eliminating the familiarity explanation. *Journal of Experimental Social Psychology, 36,* 316–328.

De Houwer, J. (1999). *Understanding irrelevant feature paradigms: Why is Stroop Stroop and Simon Simon?* Unpublished manuscript, University of Southampton, Southampton, England.

Eagly, A. H., & Chaiken, S. (1998). Attitude structure and function. In D. T. Gilbert, S. T. Fiske, & G. Lindsay (Eds.), *The handbook of social psychology* (4th ed., Vol. 1, pp. 269–322). New York: McGraw-Hill.

Fazio, R. H. (in press). On the automatic activation of associated evaluations: An overview. *Cognition and Emotion.*

Fazio, R. H., Chen, J. M., McDonel, E. C., & Sherman, S. J. (1982). Attitude accessibility, attitude–behavior consistency, and strength of the object–evaluation association. *Journal of Experimental Social Psychology, 18,* 339–357.

Fazio, R. H., Jackson, J. R., Dunton, B. C., & Williams, C. J. (1995). Variability in automatic activation as an unobtrusive measure of racial attitudes: A bona fide pipeline? *Journal of Personality and Social Psychology, 69,* 1013–1027.

Fazio, R. H., Sanbonmatsu, D. M., Powell, M. C., & Kardes, F. R. (1986). On the automatic activation of attitudes. *Journal of Personality and Social Psychology, 50,* 229–238.

Feynman, R. P. (1963). *Lectures in physics* (Vol. 1). Reading, MA: Addison-Wesley.

Fiske, A. P., Kitayama, S., Markus, H. R., & Nisbett, R. E. (1998). The cultural matrix of social psychology. In D. T. Gilbert & S. T. Fiske (Eds.), *The handbook of social psychology* (4th ed., Vol. 2, pp. 915–981). Boston: McGraw-Hill.

Glaser, J., & Banaji, M. R. (1999). When fair is foul and foul is fair: Reverse priming in automatic evaluation. *Journal of Personality and Social Psychology, 77,* 669–687.

Greenwald, A. G., & Banaji, M. R. (1995). Implicit social cognition: Attitudes, self-esteem, and stereotypes. *Psychological Review, 102,* 4–27.

Greenwald, A. G., Banaji, M. R., Rudman, L. A., Farnham, S. D., Nosek, B. A., & Rosier, M. (2000). Prologue to a unified theory of attitudes, stereotypes, and self-concept. In J. P. Forgas (Ed.), *Feeling and thinking: The role of affect in social cognition and behavior* (pp. 308–330). New York: Cambridge University Press.

Greenwald, A. G., McGhee, D. E., & Schwartz, J. L. K. (1998). Measuring individual differences in implicit cognition: The implicit association test. *Journal of Personality and Social Psychology, 74,* 1464–1480.

Higgins, E. T., Rholes, W. S., & Jones, C. R. (1977). Category accessibility and impression formation. *Journal of Experimental Social Psychology, 13,* 141–154.

Jacoby, L. L. (1994). Measuring recollection: Strategic vs automatic influences of associative context. In C. Umilta (Ed.), *Attention and performance, XV* (pp. 661–679). Cambridge, MA: Bradford.

Jacoby, L. L., & Dallas, M. (1981). On the relationship between autobiographical memory and perceptual learning. *Journal of Experimental Psychology: General, 3,* 306–340.

Jenkins, J. G. (1946). Validity for what? *Journal of Consulting Psychology, 10,* 93–98.

Jost, J. T., Banaji, M. R., & Greenwald, A. G. (1994, June). *Experiments on (un)consciousness raising: Exploring the false fame bias in feminist samples.* Paper presented at the annual meeting of the American Psychological Society, Washington, DC.

Karpinski, A., & Hilton, J. L. (1999). *Validating attitude measures: The implicit association test as a cautionary tale.* Manuscript submitted for publication, University of Michigan, Ann Arbor.

McGuire, W. J. (1989). The structure of individual attitudes and attitude systems. In A. R. Pratkanis, S. J. Breckler, & A. G. Greenwald (Eds.), *Attitude structure and function* (pp. 37–69). Hillsdale, NJ: Erlbaum.

Meyer, D. E., & Schvaneveldt, R. W. (1971). Facilitation in recognizing pairs of words: Evidence of a dependence between retrieval operations. *Journal of Experimental Psychology, 90,* 227–234.

Mitchell, J., Nosek, B., & Banaji, M. R. (1998, June). *A rose by any other name? Dissociated attitudes toward social group members.* Paper presented at the annual meeting of the American Psychological Society, Washington, DC.

Mitchell, J., Nosek, B., & Banaji, M. R. (2000, February). *Category salience determines implicit attitudes toward Black female and White male targets.* Paper presented at the first annual meeting of the Society for Personality and Social Psychology, Nashville, TN.

Neely, J. H. (1977). Semantic priming and retrieval from lexical memory: Roles of inhibitionless spreading activation and limited-capacity attention. *Journal of Experimental Psychology: General, 106,* 226–254.

Nisbett, R. E., & Wilson, T. D. (1977). Telling more than we can know: Verbal reports on mental processes. *Psychological Review, 84,* 231–259.

Nosek, B. A. (1999, August). *Reaction time research on the Internet.* Paper presented at the 107th Annual Convention of the American Psychological Association, Boston.

Nosek, B. A., Banaji, M. R., & Greenwald, A. G. (2000). *Harvesting implicit group attitudes and beliefs from a demonstration website.* Manuscript under review, Yale University, New Haven, CT.

Ochsner, K. N., & Lieberman, M. D. (2000). *The social cognitive neuroscience approach.* Unpublished manuscript, Harvard University, Cambridge, MA.

Ottaway, S. A., Hayden, D. C., & Oakes, M. A. (in press). Implicit attitudes and racism: The effect of work familiarity and frequency in the implicit association test. *Social Cognition.*

Phelps, E. A., O'Connor, K. J., Cunningham, W. A., Gatenby, J. C., Funayama, E. S., Gore, J. C., & Banaji, M. R. (2000). Amygdala activation predicts performance on indirect measures of racial bias. *Journal of Cognitive Neuroscience, 12,* 729–738.

Richardson-Klavehn, A., & Bjork, R. A. (1988). Measures of memory. *Annual Review of Psychology, 39,* 475–543.

Roediger, H. L. (1990). Implicit memory: Retention without remembering. *American Psychologist, 45,* 1043–1056.

Roediger, H. L., & McDermott, K. B. (1993). Implicit memory in normal human subjects. In F. Boller & J. Grafman (Eds.), *Handbook of neuropsychology* (Vol. 8, pp. 63–181). Amsterdam, The Netherlands: Elsevier.

Rudman, L. A. (1999, May). *Predictive utility for the implicit association test.* Paper presented at the Conference on Construct Validity in Implicit Social Cognition, National Science Foundation, Zion, IL.

Rudman, L. A., Greenwald, A. G., Mellott, D. S., & McGhee, D. E. (1999). Measuring the automatic components of prejudice: Flexibility and generality of the implicit association test. *Social Cognition, 17,* 1–29.

Rudman, L. A., & Kilianski. S. E. (2000). Implicit and explicit attitudes toward female authority. *Personality and Social Psychology Bulletin, 26,* 1315–1328.

Salovey, P., Mayer, J. D., & Caruso, D. (in press). The positive psychology of emotional intelligence. In C. R. Snyder & S. J. Lopez (Eds.), *The handbook of positive psychology.* New York: Oxford University Press.

Schacter, D. L. (1987). Implicit memory: History and current status. *Journal of Experimental Psychology: Learning, Memory, and Cognition, 13,* 501–518.

Sears, F. (1980). *University physics* (5th ed.). Reading, MA: Addison-Wesley. (Original work published 1902)

Swanson, J. E., Rudman, L. A., & Greenwald, A. G. (in press). Using the Implicit Association Test to investigate attitude–behavior consistency for stigmatized behavior. *Cognition and Emotion.*

Thurstone, L. L. (1928). Attitudes can be measured. *American Journal of Sociology, 33,* 529–554.

Wallace, S. R. (1965). Criteria for what? *American Psychologist, 20,* 411–417.

Warrington, E. K., & Weiskrantz, L. (1968). New method of testing long-term retention with special reference to amnesic patients. *Nature, 217,* 972–974.

Weitz, J. (1961). Criteria for criteria. *American Psychologist, 16,* 228–231.

Wilson, T. D., Lindsey, S., & Schooler, T. Y. (2000). A model of dual attitudes. *Psychological Review, 107,* 101–126.

CHAPTER 8

Analysis of the Serial Position Curve

Bennet Murdock

As a Yale University PhD who preceded Bob Crowder's arrival, I was asked to give a few reflections on Yale at that time. I entered Yale as a graduate student in 1947, and my very first class there was almost my last. It was the Proseminar, and the 12 of us new students were regaled by Clark Hull (who had retired the year before) accompanied by page turners Neal Miller and Carl Hovland. It seemed like the Holy Trinity: the father, son, and the Holy Ghost. Hull inaugurated the proceedings by asking our opinion about psychology as a science, and we went around the table so each could venture an opinion. As luck would have it, I was the very last one in line, and smart aleck that I was, I had to give an answer that was very different from everyone else's. The triumvirate was not pleased, and I almost got up and walked out.

At the time, Yale was not only the mecca for animal learning but also the top experimental psychology department in North America. Doug Lawrence was running rats 20 hours a day in the ground floor of the Institute of Human Relations; Julian Jaynes was sleeping in the subground floor (he could not afford an apartment); and all of us were co-opted into taking Neal Miller's learning course, which is not what I had come to graduate school for. The highlight of the course was the approach–avoidance conflict, and if one could understand the double approach–avoidance conflict, one would get an *A* in the course. I am not sure I would have survived had it not been for Fred Sheffield's encouragement and mentoring.

Not only was there no course in perception, but the word *attention* was verboten. Could anyone give a satisfactory operational definition (the hallmark of a science) for attention? Finally in our last year, a few of us were bold enough to request an informal course in perception, and with considerable reluctance, one of the esteemed verbal learners in the department was persuaded to lead us. He frankly admitted he knew nothing about perception but was willing to learn along with us.

This work was supported by Grant APA-146 from the Natural Sciences and Engineering Research Council of Canada. I thank Steve Lewandowsky, Dave Smith, and Ian Neath for helpful comments on earlier drafts of this chapter and Dave Smith for writing the scoring program for Figure 8.10.

When it came time for my thesis proposal, an article by Anchard Zeller ("An Experimental Analogue of Repression," 1950) had just appeared in the *Journal of Experimental Psychology*. I was intrigued by this article, and it was much closer to my interests than animal learning. However, my committee (which included Neal Miller) was not that excited about this topic, and after much give and very little take, I ended up with an acceptable topic: "The Effects of Failure and Retroactive Inhibition on Mediated Generalization" (Murdock, 1952). At least it got me my degree.

When it came time for us to graduate, our supervisors got on the telephone and got us jobs. Doug Lawrence went to Stanford University, Julian Jaynes (eventually) went to Princeton University, George Mandler (and later Herbie Kelman) went to Harvard University, Seymour Feshback went to the University of Pennsylvania, and I went north. I left before Gordon Bower was a graduate student and before Tex Garner and Bob Crowder arrived. But the winds of change were blowing, and things have not been the same since.

To turn to the subject at hand, in this chapter I discuss serial order effects and the serial position curve in particular. I think serial order effects were Bob Crowder's main interest in the memory area. He saved the best until last (see Crowder, 1976, chapter 12). On the empirical side, there were his many studies of prefix and suffix effects and on the theoretical side his work with John Morton on the precategorical acoustic store (Crowder & Morton, 1969).

The U-shaped serial position curve is one of the oldest, if not the oldest, finding in the experimental study of human memory. It antedated Ebbinghaus (1885/1964); to my knowledge, it was first reported by Nipher (1876) and reprinted by Stigler (1978). Nipher used a binomial distribution to describe the pattern of errors he found in his data. The typical serial position curve looks very much like the Big Dipper with a round bottom; it has an extensive primacy effect and a slight recency effect (upturn at the end), though the recency effect depends on experimental conditions and method of scoring. An example is shown in Figure 8.1. There have been many attempts to explain the serial position curve. Here I briefly discuss three different approaches: hierarchical models, two-factor models, and models based on the concept of distinctiveness.

Hierarchical Models

Hierarchical models generally assume a very limited memory span and postulate some hierarchical structure to explain why the serial position curve spans a greater range. Examples of such models would be the fractional anticipatory goal response model of Sheffield (1961), the chunking model of N. F. Johnson (1972), the organizational model of Anderson and Bower (1973), and the perturbation model of Estes (1972, 1997). These are all discussed in some detail in Crowder (1976)—and I return to the chunking notion later.

FIGURE 8.1

Serial position curves for an 8-item list after 1 and 20 s of shadowing. Data are from Parkinson (1972).

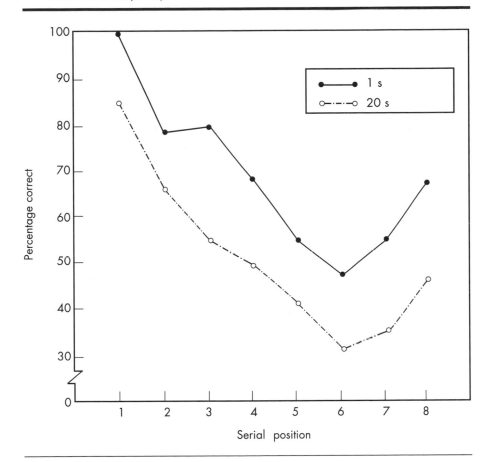

Two-Factor Models

Two-factor models assume two separate factors, one to explain primacy and the other to explain recency. The main two-factor models to be discussed are the retroactive–proactive model of Foucault (1928), a possible modification mentioned by Crowder (1976), and the start–end model of Henson (1998).

Retroactive–Proactive Model

Foucault (1928) suggested that proactive inhibition could account for the primacy effect and retroactive inhibition could account for the recency effect. There are no items that precede the first item and no items that follow the last item, so he used this to estimate the magnitude of proactive inhibition and retroactive inhibition. Then he used an additive combination rule to predict performance on the intervening items. Memory for each intervening item would be the sum of the proactive and retroactive inhibition from other items. However, the obtained forgetting was much greater than the predicted forgetting (see Murdock, 1974, for further details).

Crowder's Modification

Then in 1976, Bob Crowder suggested

> another way of accomplishing the same thing [i.e., a U-shaped curve] would be to have linear rather than negatively-accelerated functions relating inhibition to list position but to combine the two functions in a multiplicative function. (p. 447)

I was curious about this and worked out an example that is shown in Figure 8.2. The linear proactive inhibition and retroactive inhibition functions for a five-item list are shown in the left-hand panel, and the multiplicative combination is shown in the right-hand panel. The primacy and recency effects could not be better.

However, this simple model requires four parameters (a slope and intercept for each of the linear functions), and the multiplicative combination is much too finely tuned. One must have exactly the right parameter values to produce a minimum at serial position 4, but serial position curves are very robust, and the same curve shows up under a variety of conditions. Also one gets parallel serial position curves when one compares an immediate with a delayed condition (Figure 8.1), and proactive inhibition builds up over time.

I doubt that Bob Crowder would be too upset about these problems. The only reference to his patch on the Foucault model was the quotation given above, and he did not pursue the matter further.

FIGURE 8.2

Linear retroactive interference and proactive interference gradients (left side) that combine multiplicatively to produce the serial position curve (right side).

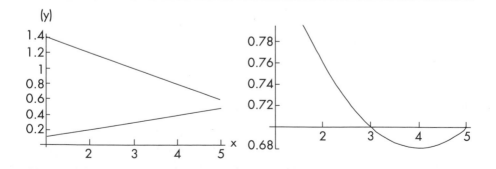

Start-End Model

The start–end model of Henson (1998) assumes that there are end anchors, and each item in a list is associated with both anchors. Because these associations are assumed to be graded in strength, he is able to explain not only the classic U-shaped serial position effect but many other serial order effects as well. This is a very impressive model, and it shows how much progress has been made over the years. However, it does have a problem.

The problem is this: If one is seeing a list for a single presentation, how does one have an end anchor to associate to each list item? An experiment by Crowder (1969) highlights this problem. This experiment used a between-subjects design with a single presentation of each list and two conditions—constant and variable context. In the constant-context condition, all lists were 9 items long; but in the variable-context condition, list length ranged unpredictably from 9 to 23 items. There were some 9-item lists in the variable-context condition, so the experimental contrast of interest was the comparison of the 9-item lists in the constant versus the variable context.

The results are shown in Figure 8.3. The context manipulation had a big effect on primacy but no effect at all on recency. It is hard to see how associations to an end anchor could be identical under the two conditions when there is so much uncertainty in the variable-context condition as to when the end of the list is coming.

Other Models

There are other models that assume some sort of underlying process that produces primacy if not recency. For instance, the chaining model (Lewandowsky & Murdock, 1989) and the primacy model (Page & Norris, 1998) assume an attenuation process that automatically results in primacy. In oscillator-based associative recall (OSCAR; Brown, Preece, & Hulme, 2000), an assumed oscillation results in progressively greater phase differences as one goes through the list. These and other current models are discussed in Lewandowsky (1999). Two factors may be involved in primacy and recency, but it would be better if they fell out of more basic assumptions. If they are simply assumed directly, then one may simply be assuming what needs to be explained.

Distinctiveness

Another approach to serial position effects is the notion of distinctiveness. Distinctiveness was popular in the 1950s, and in 1960 I proposed a possible quantification (Murdock, 1960). I suggested a D scale that was based on the summed similarity differences between each item in the list and all other list items. In a way it implemented the remote associations that were the standard explanation for serial position effects in the 1940s (McGeoch, 1946). Although the metric was based on a logarith-

FIGURE 8.3

Serial position curves for constant and variable context conditions. From "Behavioral Strategies in Immediate Memory," by R. G. Crowder, 1969, Journal of Verbal Learning and Verbal Behavior, 8, 1969, p. 525. Copyright 1969 by Academic Press. Reprinted with permission.

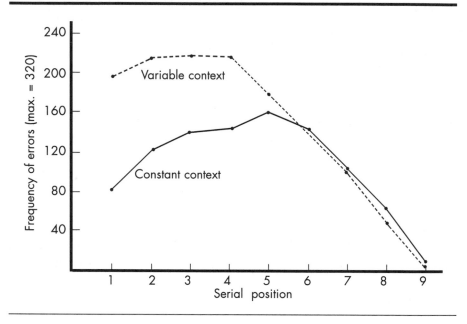

mic transform of the ordinal position values, still it was a zero-parameter model where primacy and recency effects fell out of the underlying assumptions. It predicted U-shaped serial position curves for absolute judgment and serial recall.

There have been many applications of the distinctiveness notion. It was used by Glenberg (1987) to explain the long-term recency phenomenon (Bjork & Whitten, 1974), by Einstein and McDaniel (1987) to explain the facilitating effects of bizarre images, and by Lockhart and Craik (1990) as a possible basis for the levels effect (Craik & Lockhart, 1972), although now *elaboration* seems a more useful concept (see chapter 4 by Craik). G. J. Johnson (1991) fitted an impressive amount of serial learning data to the distinctiveness model with only a single free parameter. Distinctiveness has been used to explain the efficacy of self-generated cues in recall (Mäntyla & Nilsson, 1988) and organization in free recall (Hunt & Reed, 1996). The distinctiveness notion was used for the recall of order information by Cunningham, Marmie, and Healy (1998), although this notion does not work so well for the recall of presidents and vice presidents from semantic memory (see chapter 9 by Healy and Parker). Bower (1971) made three main criticisms of the original distinctiveness model. First, from a Gedanken experiment, he argued that it could not explain results with very small differences in distinctiveness. He also claimed that it could not explain differences in degree of learning (although see G.J. Johnson, 1991). Finally, he pointed out that it was not a process model; one could describe the results, but how did they come about?

Neath (1993) and Neath and Crowder (1996) have tested and extended the distinctiveness model, and Neath, Brown, McCormack, and Chater (2000) proposed a modification of the model (local rather than global distinctiveness) to answer the first criticism of Bower (1971). However, it cannot explain extralist factors such as the buildup and release from proactive inhibition (Wickens, Born, & Allen, 1963) or the nature of serial-order intrusions (Conrad, 1959). The distinctiveness model may or may not be a good model for the serial-position curve, but I do not think it is the right model for the serial-order effects in general.

Binomial Model

As I prepared for the conference preceding this book, I thought it would be worthwhile to develop a simple hierarchical model based on chunking to see how far it would go. It is a binomial model in that it specifies binomial distributions as the underlying distributions. Underlying distributions should be built into any model at the start rather than added on at the end when needed. It is deliberately not a two-factor model; I wanted to see if one could develop a model that would generate primacy and recency (or at least primacy) without building them into the model. It would be nice if one could have a model where serial position curves would fall out of the model as a consequence of more basic assumptions.

Assume that subjects form chunks when asked to study and recall a serial list. The model specifies two distributions: chunk size and recall probability given chunk size. The model predicts run length (the distribution of the number of correct responses before the first error) and, from this, one type of serial position curve can be derived. It is the serial position curve that results when the data are scored up to the point of the first error.

There are many methods of scoring serial recall data and different experimental procedures as well. Because item scoring gives different results than position scoring (Drewnowski & Murdock, 1980), for the study-test procedure subjects could recall the items in order or recall the order of the items; also they could be instructed to indicate blanks or not be allowed to leave blanks. I decided to use run length as the dependent variable to circumvent these problems. The model would become much more complicated otherwise, but the price for this simplification is that the model makes no predictions about errors nor can it generate a recency effect.

Chunk-Size Distribution

There is much evidence that optimum chunk size is about 3–4 (N. F. Johnson, 1972; Ryan, 1969; Wickelgren, 1964). So for a 7-item list, chunks of 5, 6, or 7 should be progressively less common; at the lower end, chunks of 2, 1, or 0 should also be progressively less common. (A chunk of zero implies that nothing was stored.) Consequently, the chunk-size distribution should be binomial with a probability value close to .5. Call this probability value p_c; a binomial distribution with $p_c = .5$ and $N = 7$ is shown in the left-hand panel of Figure 8.4.

Recall Distribution

What about the recall distribution? The recall distribution is the probability that 0, 1, 2, . . ., n items will be recalled in the correct order from a chunk of size n. If the chunk size is 7 then the probability that all items would be correctly recalled is essentially zero. If the chunk size is about 3 or 4 the probability is close to 1.0, and for a "chunk" size of 1 it essentially equals 1.0. A reasonable approximation can be obtained by assuming another underlying binomial distribution and cumulating from the top down. An example of the cumulative version of a binomial is shown in the right-hand panel of Figure 8.4.[1]

Chunks are formed at the time of study, and recall proceeds as follows: Let L be list length, then the first chunk will be size 0, 1, 2, . . . up to a maximum of L. Assume some number of items are recalled from the first chunk. If all the items from the chunk are recalled, unless the first chunk is size L, one moves on to the second round where the upper limit on chunk size is determined by the number of items yet to recall; call it U_2. The number of unrecalled items on round 1 (U_1) is always equal to L. If all the items are not recalled then recall (or at least our

FIGURE 8.4

Binomial chunk-size distribution (offset by 1) with $p_c = .5$ *and* $N = 7$ *(left side) and cumulative binomial of the same distribution (right side).*

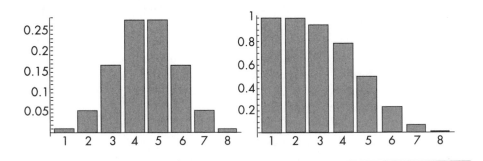

---

[1]The chunk-size distribution and the recall distributions are different binomials, but in Figure 8.4, the cumulative aspect of the recall distribution with the chunk-size distribution is illustrated.

scoring) stops. The possible chunk sizes on round 2 will be 0, 1, 2 . . ., U_2. Following the same logic, on round 3 the number of possible chunk sizes will be 0, 1, 2, . . ., U_3, and this continues until all items have been recalled or the process stops. So on each round there is a possible distribution of chunk sizes and, within that, a set of recall distributions for each possible chunk size.

This process is shown in Figure 8.5 by means of a tree diagram for $L = 3$. The numbers in the diamonds indicate the value of U at the start of each round; thus,

FIGURE 8.5

Tree diagram for a three-item list. The number in the diamonds indicates the number of items yet to recall on each trial, and the circles indicate the chunk sizes.

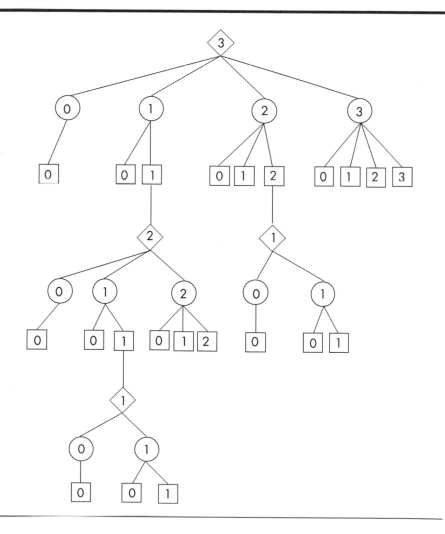

$U_1 = L = 3$, $U_2 = 2$ or 1, and $U_3 = 1$. The circles indicate the possible chunk sizes on each round; 0, 1, 2, or 3 for round 1, then 0, 1, or 2 for $U_2 = 2$ or 0 or 1 for $U_2 = 1$ on round 2, or 0 or 1 for $U_3 = 1$ on round 3.[2] For each round, under each chunk (circle) the possible run-length values are shown in the boxes. Recall continues to the next round by that path if and only if all the items from the chunk on the previous round are recalled, provided that the previous chunk size is greater than 0 and less than U_r.

Although the probabilities are not shown in Figure 8.5, the computation would be like any tree diagram—probabilities multiply as one goes down the tree, and the outcome is determined by the final destination. Thus, multiplication and addition (no convolution!) are all that is required to determine the predicted run-length values for any set of distributions. However, it is tedious even with $L = 3$, $L = 4$ is doable but not great fun, and $L = 5$ is pushing the limits (at least of my patience). Fortunately there is a simpler way, but before I get to that it is necessary to say a bit more about the distributions.

It might seem as if one needs a multiplicity of distributions; separate distributions for each chunk size on each round and, within that, separate recall distributions for each chunk size on each round. In fact, one does, but fortunately both sets of distributions (one for chunk size, one for recall probabilities given chunk size) can be obtained from the two original distributions by cumulating. The two original distributions are the chunk-size binomial with probability p_c and the recall or run-length distribution with probability p_r. Let me illustrate with a numerical example.

If the chunk-size probabilities are .1, .3, .4 and .2 for $L = U_1 = 3$, then the probabilities are .1, .3 and .6 for $U_2 = 2$ and .1 and .9 for $U_2 = U_3 = 1$. That is, there is a ceiling effect imposed by the value of U_r and the truncated distributions must be formed by the cumulative process illustrated in this numerical example. Exactly the same reasoning applies for the run-length distribution. If the run-length probabilities are .2, .5, .18 and .12 for a chunk of 3, they must be .2, .5, and .3 for a chunk of 2 and .2 and .8 for a chunk of 1. Thus, all one needs are two binomials, for chunk size with probability p_c and for run length given chunk size with probability p_r and one can compute the run-length distributions for any value of L.

To expedite the computation, set up the chunk-size distribution for each value of U on each round as a column vector and the associated conditional recall distributions as the row entries in a matrix. If each element in each row in the matrix is multiplied by the corresponding element in the column vector, then the result is the run-length probabilities for that value of U on that round. The predicted run-length values can be obtained by weighting each outcome with the carryover probability from the previous round and summing over rounds.

---

[2]The number of possible chunk sizes on round r for any list length L is $\binom{L-1}{r-1}$.

I used a three-step procedure to generate serial position curves from the model: fit memory-span functions, use the resulting parameters to get the run-length function, then get serial position curves from the run-length functions. The memory-span functions (Figure 8.6) come from Crannell and Parrish (1957), and they had five conditions: words unlimited, words limited, letters unlimited, letters limited, and digits. For both words and letters, the limited condition was a fixed-set procedure where the same items were presented on every trial, so only order information was required. In the unlimited condition the items were different on every trial, so both item and order information were required.

Each of the five curves in Figure 8.6 is a list-length function; it is percentage correct as a function of L. Given run-length curves for each value of L, the last value in the run-length function should correspond to the list-length percentage correct for that value of L. Consequently, I did a grid search (in steps of .01) to find the best fitting set of run-length curves for each condition. There were two free parameters for each condition, p_c and p_r. The binomial N (N_c) for the chunk-size binomials was set to 7, 8, 9, 10, and 11 for the five conditions because these were the list-length values at which the memory-span functions were essentially zero (see Figure 8.6). As mentioned above, the binomial N (N_r) for the run-length functions was always the same as N_c.

The results are shown in Table 8.1. The standard errors are the average sum of the squared deviations between predicted and observed. Although the fits are very good, a total of 10 free parameters (two probability values for each of five conditions) is not very satisfying. However, a plot of the parameter space for the digits conditions (Figure 8.7) shows that variations in p_c have relatively little effect on the goodness of fit, and this is true for all five conditions. Consequently, the data were refit with p_c fixed at .99 with one free parameter (p_r) for each condition.

The results of this second fit are shown in Table 8.2. Again the fit is very good, and there was only a small variation in p_r. Finally, I took the average value of p_r (.59), generated the list-length curves for all five conditions, and the resulting

TABLE 8.1

Parameter estimation results for the memory-span data

CONDITION	TYPE	N_c	SE	p_c	p_r
1	Words unlimited	7	.00167	.99	.59
2	Words limited	8	.0015	.84	.59
3	Letters unlimited	9	.00117	.99	.59
4	Letters limited	10	.00044	.66	.54
5	Digits	11	.000007	.86	.61

Note. In these fits p_c and p_r were free parameters for each condition, N_c was set in advance, and SE is the standard error. Data from Crannell and Parrish (1957).

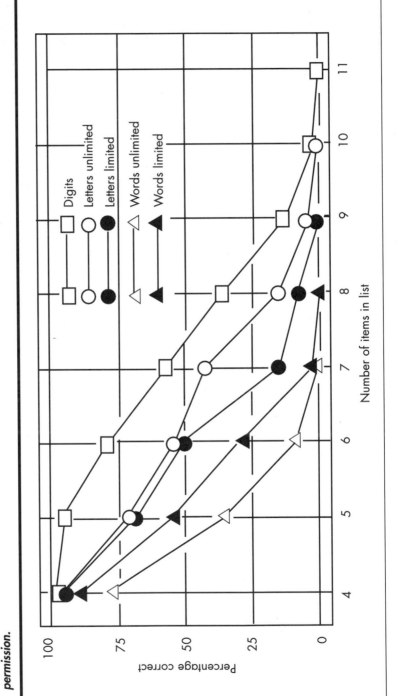

FIGURE 8.6

Percentage correct as a function of list length for five types of material. From "A Comparison of Immediate Memory Span for Digits, Letters, and Words," by C. W. Crannell and J. M. Parrish, 1957, Journal of Psychology, 44, p. 322. Copyright 1957. Reprinted with permission.

FIGURE 8.7

Three-dimensional plot of the parameter space in three steps of .01 on both sides of the optimum for Condition 5 of Crannell and Parrish (1957). The vertical axis is the standard error (SE), the right-hand axis is p_c, and the left-hand axis is p_r.

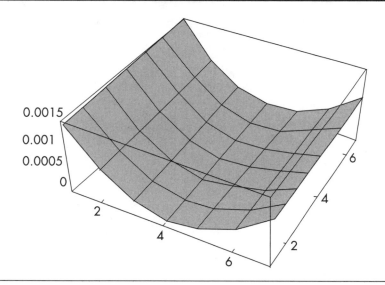

standard error was .0067. Thus, in effect, the complete Crannell and Parrish (1957) set of curves can be fit with one free parameter (p_r) with a standard error less than .01.

The predicted memory-span functions with these parameter values (i.e., $p_c = .99$ and $p_r = .59$) are shown in Figure 8.8. There are some slight irregularities in the functions not seen in the original data, but surely the model predictions capture the main features of the data. What about the predicted run-length functions? These

TABLE 8.2

Parameter estimation results for the data when p_c was fixed at .99 for all conditions

CONDITION	TYPE	N_c	SE	p_c	p_r
1	Words unlimited	7	.00167	.99	.59
2	Words limited	8	.0032	.99	.60
3	Letters unlimited	9	.00117	.99	.59
4	Letters limited	10	.0020	.99	.57
5	Digits	11	.00007	.99	.61

Note. In these fits, p_c and p_r were free parameters for each condition, N_c was set in advance, and *SE* was the standard error. Data are from Crannell and Parrish (1957).

FIGURE 8.8

Predicted curves for p_c = .99 and p_r = .59 for the data of Crannell and Parrish (1957).

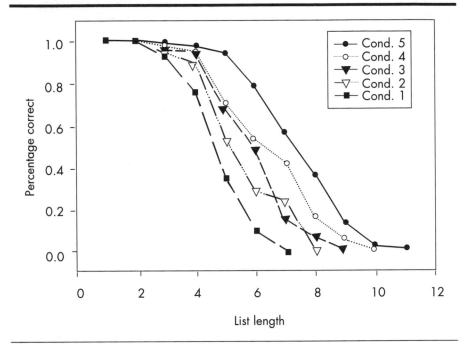

are shown in Figure 8.9 as cumulative (or distribution) and not probability density functions to facilitate comparison with Figure 8.1. They were plotted for $L = 3$, 5, and 7, and they were obtained from the predicted run-length functions as described above. As can be seen, there is really only one curve; given the way these curves were obtained (i.e., by cumulating) the shorter curves must always lie on top of the longest curve.

What do actual run-length functions look like? Some data from a recent experiment by Duncan and Murdock (2000) are shown in Figure 8.10. All subjects were given 5-, 6-, and 7-item lists from the Toronto word pool. There were two conditions, precued and postcued. In the precued condition, the subjects knew in advance what the list length and test type would be. In the postcued condition, they did not. The results for the precued condition are shown in the left-hand panel and the results for the postcued condition are shown in the right-hand panel. For all practical purposes, the curves in the postcued condition are superimposed.

Discussion

What do these results mean? They mean that under these conditions, subjects do not chunk. To chunk means to segment, and a p of .99 means that the list is not

FIGURE 8.9

Predicted run length curves for L = 3, 5, and 7 with p_c = .99 and p_r = .59.

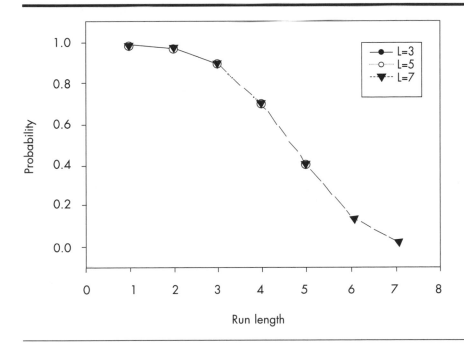

Run length

divided into parts.[3] To me, this was a very surprising result; it was certainly nothing I expected. However, it is indisputable that the fits would be poorer if the values of p_c were less than .99.

The phrase "under these conditions" may be important; the presentation rate in the Duncan and Murdock (2000) experiment was fast (4 items/s) and there was only a 250-ms blank interval before the recall cue (a row of asterisks) appeared. However, I once did an unpublished experiment to test the decay theory of memory using digits with a presentation rate (as near as I could manage) of 10 items/s or 1 item/s with $L = 10$, and there was little difference in the results. Also the model fits the Crannell and Parrish (1957) data well, and there the presentation rate was 1 item/s.

Perhaps in my enthusiasm for the chunking notion, I have overlooked another factor that certainly needs consideration. By segmenting a list, each chunk or part is easier to recall than the entire list, but then there is the problem of accessing the chunks in the right order. N. F. Johnson (1972) showed that most of the errors occur in accessing the chunks; these are the transition-error probabilities, and they

---

[3]The value of p_c is really 1.0 not .99 but the program would crash if $p_c = 1.0$.

increase with chunk size. So there is a cost associated with chunking; perhaps, under these conditions, the cost outweighs the benefit.

This is not to say that subjects never chunk or that the chunking notion is wrong. Personally, I still believe in the chunking notion as much as I ever did but, under these conditions, apparently there is no chunking. With repetition (Martin & Noreen, 1974) or experimenter-imposed grouping (N. F. Johnson, 1972; Ryan, 1969), subjects may chunk, and the value of p_c would be different. In this connection, Ryan (1969) suggested that chunking might occur with grouping because the pauses allow time for chunking, so this might well be an important factor.

In general, this simple model shows that one can get accurate run-length curves without proactive inhibition or retroactive inhibition assumptions or, indeed, without any of the standard two-factor assumptions that guarantee primacy and recency. Although I started out with 10 free parameters, I was able to reduce it to 1 free parameter and the binomial model could still fit the list-length functions of memory-span studies and generate run-length curves that matched the data when list length was varied. The only assumptions were that both chunk size and run length were binomially distributed. No derivations or simulations were needed; all one needed to do was work out the predictions from the appropriate tree diagram.

I should reiterate that this binominal model is limited in scope. It does not explain errors; it cannot predict recency or the distance functions of Estes (1972) or Nairne (1990); it cannot predict conditional probability functions (Murdock, 1968; Schweickert, Chen, & Poirier, 1999); it cannot explain the Ranschburg effect (see chapter 14 by R. L. Greene); and it cannot begin to explain how chunking might come about. The conclusion about p_c might be different if the underlying assumptions were changed. It is not even a process model although it could be implemented in the chunking model or the power-set model described elsewhere (Murdock, 1995). However, it is a simple quantitative model that can make some surprisingly accurate predictions for a few basic serial order effects, and I think it

FIGURE 8.10

Run-length curves for 5-, 6-, and 7-item lists for precued (left side) and postcued (right side). Data are from Duncan and Murdock (2000).

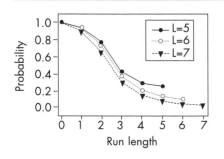
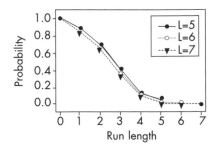

is very much in the functionalist tradition of Bob Crowder that has been pointed out in many other chapters in this volume.

The conclusion is very simple. One can describe the memory-span function and the serial position positional curve with a single binomial distribution with a probability of about .6 and an N of 7 or more, depending on the type of material. Nipher (1876) had the right distribution,[4] but he applied it to errors, not to run length, and apparently he did not see the advantage of cumulating.

---

[4]A binominal with $p = .6$.

References

Anderson, J. R., & Bower, G. H. (1973). *Human associative memory*. Washington, DC: Winston.

Bjork, R. A., & Whitten, W. B. (1974). Recency-sensitive retrieval processes in long-term free recall. *Cognitive Psychology, 6,* 173–189.

Bower, G. H. (1971). Adaptation-level coding of stimuli and serial position effects. In M. H. Appley (Ed.), *Adaptation-level theory* (pp. 175–201). New York: Academic Press.

Brown, G. D. A., Preece, T., & Hulme, C. (2000). Oscillator-based memory for serial order. *Psychological Review, 107,* 127–181.

Conrad, R. (1959). Errors of immediate memory. *British Journal of Psychology, 50,* 349–359.

Craik, F. I. M., & Lockhart, R. S. (1972). Levels of processing: A framework for memory research. *Journal of Verbal Learning and Verbal Behavior, 11,* 671–684.

Crannell, C. W., & Parrish, J. M. (1957). A comparison of immediate memory span for digits, letters, and words. *Journal of Psychology, 44,* 319–327.

Crowder, R. G. (1969). Behavioral strategies in immediate memory. *Journal of Verbal Learning and Verbal Behavior, 8,* 524–528.

Crowder, R. G. (1976). *Principles of learning and memory,* Hillsdale, NJ: Erlbaum.

Crowder, R. G., & Morton, J. (1969). Precategorical acoustic storage (PAS). *Perception and Psychophysics, 5,* 365–373.

Cunningham, T. F., Marmie, W. R., & Healy, A. F. (1998). The role of item distinctiveness in short-term recall of order information. *Memory & Cognition, 26,* 463–476.

Drewnowski, A., & Murdock, B. B. (1980). The role of auditory features in memory span for words. *Journal of Experimental Psychology: Human Learning and Memory, 6,* 319–332.

Duncan, M., & Murdock, B. (2000). Recall and recognition with precuing and postcuing. *Journal of Memory and Language, 42,* 301–313.

Ebbinghaus, H. (1964). *Über das gedächtnis: Untersuchungen zur experimentellen pscyhologie* [Memory: A contribution to experimental psychology] (H. A. Ruger & C. E. Bussenius,

Trans.; Dover Press ed.). New York: Teachers College, Columbia University. (Original work published 1885)

Einstein, G. O., & McDaniel, M. A. (1987). Distinctiveness and the mnemonic benefits of bizarre imagery. In M. A. McDaniel & M. Pressley (Eds.), *Imagery and related mnemonic processes: Theories, individual differences and applications* (pp. 78–102). New York: Springer-Verlag.

Estes, W. K. (1972). *Coding processes in human memory*. Washington, DC: Winston.

Estes, W. K. (1997). Processes of memory loss, recovery, and distortion. *Psychological Review, 104,* 148–169.

Foucault, M. (1928). Les inhibitions internes de fixation. *Annee Psychologique, 29,* 92–112.

Glenberg, A. M. (1987). Temporal context and recency. In D.S. Gorfein & R. R. Hoffman (Eds.), *Memory and learning: The Ebbinghaus Centennial Conference* (pp. 173–190). Hillsdale, NJ: Erlbaum.

Henson, R. N. A. (1998). Short-term memory for serial order: The start–end model. *Cognitive Psychology, 36,* 73–137.

Hunt, R. R., & Reed, R. E. (1996). Accessing the particular from the general: The power of distinctiveness in the context of organization. *Memory & Cognition, 24,* 217–225.

Johnson, G. J. (1991). A distinctiveness model of serial learning. *Psychological Review, 98,* 204–217.

Johnson, N. F. (1972). Organization and the concept of a memory code. In A. W. Melton & E. Martin (Eds.), *Coding processes in human memory* (pp. 125–159). Washington, DC: Winston.

Lewandowsky, S. (1999). Reintegration and response suppression in serial recall: A dynamic network model. *International Journal of Psychology, 34,* 434–446.

Lewandowsky, S., & Murdock, B. B. (1989). Memory for serial order. *Psychological Review, 96,* 25–57.

Lockhart, R. S., & Craik, F. I. M. (1990). Levels of processing: A retrospective commentary on a framework for memory research. *Canadian Journal of Psychology, 44,* 87–112.

Mäntyla, T., & Nilsson, L. G. (1988). Cue distinctiveness and forgetting: Effectiveness of self-generated cues in delayed recall. *Journal of Experimental Psychology: Learning, Memory, and Cognition, 14,* 502–509.

Martin, E., & Noreen, D. L. (1974). Serial learning: Identification of subjective subsequences. *Cognitive Psychology, 6,* 421–435.

McGeoch, J. A. (1946). *The psychology of human learning*. New York: Longmans, Green.

Murdock, B. B. (1952). The effects of failure and retroactive inhibition on mediated generalization. *Journal of Experimental Psychology, 44,* 156–164.

Murdock, B. B. (1960). The distinctiveness of stimuli. *Psychological Review, 67,* 16–31.

Murdock, B. B. (1968). Serial order effects in short-term memory. *Journal of Experimental Psychology Monograph Supplement, 76,* 1–15.

Murdock, B. B. (1974). *Human memory: Theory and data*. Potomac, MD: Erlbaum.

Murdock, B. B. (1995). Developing TODAM: Three models for serial-order information. *Memory & Cognition, 23,* 631–645.

Nairne, J. S. (1990). Similarity and long-term memory for order. *Journal of Memory and Language, 29,* 733–746.

Neath, I. (1993). Contextual and distinctive processes and the serial-position functions. *Journal of Memory and Language, 32,* 820–840.

Neath, I., Brown, G. D. A., McCormack, T., & Chater, N. (2000). *Distinctiveness models of absolute identification: Evidence for local, not global, effects.* Manuscript submitted for publication, Purdue University, West Lafayette, IN.

Neath, I., & Crowder, R. G. (1996). Distinctiveness and very short-term serial-position effects. *Memory, 4,* 225–242.

Nipher, F. E. (1876). On the distribution of errors in numbers written from memory. *Transactions of the Academy of Science of St. Louis, 3,* ccx–ccxi.

Page, M. P. A., & Norris, D. (1998). The primacy model: A new model of immediate serial recall. *Psychological Review, 105,* 761–781.

Parkinson, S. R. (1972). Short-term memory while shadowing: Multiple-item recall of visually and of aurally presented letters. *Journal of Experimental Psychology, 92,* 256–265.

Ryan, J. (1969). Grouping and short-term memory: Different means and patterns of grouping. *Quarterly Journal of Experimental Psychology, 21,* 137–147.

Schweickert, R., Chen, S., & Poirier, M. (1999). Reintegration and the useful life time of the verbal memory representation. *International Journal of Psychology, 34,* 447–453.

Sheffield, F. D. (1961). Theoretical considerations in the learning of complex sequential tasks from demonstration and practice. In A. A. Lumsdaine (Ed.), *Student response in programmed instruction* (Pub. No. 943, pp. 13–32). Washington: National Academy of Sciences–National Research Council.

Stigler, S. M. (1978). Some forgotten work on memory. *Journal of Experimental Psychology: Human Learning and Memory, 4,* 1–4.

Wickelgren, W. A. (1964). Size of rehearsal group and short-term memory. *Journal of Experimental Psychology, 68,* 413–419.

Wickens, D. D., Born, D. G., & Allen, C. K. (1963). Proactive inhibition and item similarity in short-term memory. *Journal of Verbal Learning and Verbal Behavior, 2,* 440–445.

Zeller, A. (1950). An experimental analogue of repression. *Journal of Experimental Psychology, 40,* 411–422.

CHAPTER 9

Serial Position Effects in Semantic Memory

Reconstructing the Order of the U.S. Presidents and Vice Presidents

Alice F. Healy

James T. Parker

There is no doubt that parsimony is a virtue in science. Consequently, multiple explanations for the same pattern of results in different situations are something to be avoided. This logic clearly influenced Crowder (1993) when he proposed that it was unreasonable to postulate different explanations for the bow-shaped serial position functions found in the standard episodic immediate free-recall task as well as in long-term and semantic memory tasks. Instead, he proposed that these functions could all be explained in terms of a single underlying mechanism based on position distinctiveness. He used as an example an ingenious semantic memory task that he developed with Roediger (Roediger & Crowder, 1976) in which participants recalled the names of the presidents of the United States and, in some cases, indicated their historical positions. This task yielded a bow-shaped serial position function under free-recall instructions and scoring. The function was even more regular under free position recall instructions and scoring. It seemed remarkable that this task, which was very far removed from the standard episodic immediate free-recall task, could yield a similar serial position function. This finding fascinated us and inspired us to explore the president recall task in greater detail. However, these findings led us to conclude that parsimony may not be possible in this case because there is an alternative, more compelling explanation for the serial position function in the president recall task that does not rely on distinctiveness and is not applicable to

This investigation was supported by U.S. Army Research Institute Contracts DASW01-96-K-0010 and DASW01-99-K-0002 and U.S. Army Research Office Grant DAAG55-98-1-0214. We thank James Kole for his help with data tabulation. We are most indebted to Bob Crowder not only for conducting the groundbreaking research that laid the framework for this study but also for graciously encouraging our research despite the theoretical differences. Bob was an extraordinary scholar, colleague, and friend.

most other memory tasks. In particular, we found that the bow-shaped serial position function for recalling the order of the presidents can be best explained in terms of the frequency of the participants' previous exposure to relevant information about the presidents' terms in office.

In a recent study focused on order memory, we (Healy, Havas, & Parker, 2000) used a reconstruction of order task that was a modified version of Roediger and Crowder's (1976; Crowder, 1993) procedure. We found with this task the typical primacy and recency advantages for the first three and last three presidents, similar to primacy and recency effects found for the standard episodic immediate free-recall task. In addition, we found a novel effect, which we termed a "penultimate" advantage, for the nine presidents preceding those in the recency positions. This penultimate advantage was significantly affected by the age of the participants. The specific pattern of results observed could simply be explained by the hypothesis that participants could better order the presidents who served in office during their lifetimes than earlier presidents because they were more frequently exposed to information about the later presidents' terms in office. It seems unlikely that participant age would affect the shape of the serial position function in the standard episodic immediate free-recall task in the same way as it did in the president reconstruction of order task.

Thus, the president reconstruction of order task yielded a bow-shaped serial position function, but its shape differed from the standard episodic immediate free-recall function to some extent (because of the penultimate effect). Also the function was sensitive to a variable (participant age) that probably does not affect the function in the standard episodic immediate free-recall task in the same way. In contrast, earlier work on serial learning indicated that the serial position functions for that task, when normalized, were the same shape across changes in many different variables (see, e.g., McCrary & Hunter, 1953). Murdock (1960) explained these functions completely in terms of the distinctiveness of the positions. He measured distinctiveness of a position by computing the sum of the differences between the ordinal number of that position and the ordinal number of each of the other positions in the list. He transformed the ordinal numbers into log values, which enabled him to account for the asymmetry of the serial position function.

However, a review of the literature involving other episodic memory tasks yielding bow-shaped serial position functions reveals that these functions, like those for the president reconstruction of order task, differ in shape to some extent from those for the standard episodic immediate free-recall task. This review reveals further that the function for a given task is sensitive to at least one variable that probably does not affect the function in the standard episodic immediate free-recall task. In addition, the literature suggests that distinctiveness of the positions does not provide a fully adequate account of these effects.

As an example, the bow-shaped serial position function in the distractor paradigm for free position recall of a list of four items is perfectly symmetrical, with primacy and recency effects each involving only a single position, and is found only with position scoring, not with scoring based solely on item recall (see, e.g., Bjork & Healy, 1974). The function for this task is explained by the Estes (1972, 1997) perturbation model, and it seems unlikely that an explanation in terms of distinctiveness would be preferable in this case.

Similarly, the bow-shaped serial position function in the digit span task, which involves immediate serial recall, includes a recency effect that typically encompasses only a single item. The shape of this serial position function is sensitive to the modality of the items; the recency effect is found with auditory presentation but not with visual presentation (see, e.g., Crowder & Morton, 1969). Crowder (e.g., 1978) provided an elegant explanation for these effects involving precategorical acoustic storage. Although subsequent studies reveal some problems with this account (see, e.g., Crowder, 1986), it seems unlikely that distinctiveness would provide a better explanation in this case.

For these reasons, it does not seem possible to explain all bow-shaped serial position functions found in memory paradigms with the same underlying mechanism, namely the distinctiveness of the positions. We, therefore, sought in the present study to explore further the hypothesis concerning the alternative explanation for the bow-shaped serial position function in the president reconstruction of order task, that is, the frequency of participants' previous exposure to information relevant to the presidents' terms in office. To provide a further test of this explanation, in the present study, we examined free reconstruction of order for two different lists of items in semantic memory, the U.S. presidents and vice presidents. We chose to compare the lists of presidents and vice presidents for three reasons. First, both lists of items have a precise serial order. Second, the items in both lists vary with respect to the frequency of participants' previous exposure. Third, the frequency of participants' previous exposure to vice presidents should be lower overall than to presidents because of the vice presidents' less prominent office. In our earlier study, we (Healy et al., 2000) compared performance on the president reconstruction of order task with performance on an analogous episodic immediate memory task involving the same stimuli. In the episodic task, participants saw a pseudorandom order of the presidents' names and then were immediately required to reconstruct that order. Although the semantic and episodic tasks both yielded bow-shaped serial position functions, we found differences between these two memory tasks both in the precise shape of the functions and in the overall levels of performance. Specifically, there was a penultimate advantage evident in the semantic task but not in the episodic task, and there was a higher overall level of performance in the semantic task than in the episodic task. Even though we examined normalized and absolute serial position functions in our earlier study, it is possible that the shapes of the serial position functions were affected by the overall levels of performance. In particular, it is possible that the novel penultimate advantage in the president free reconstruction of order task was an artifact of the very high overall level of performance in that task.

As an additional means to test the hypothesis concerning frequency of exposure, as in one of the experiments in our earlier study (Healy et al., 2000, Experiment 4), we included in the present study more a direct measure of the frequency of participants' previous exposure to the items. Specifically, we obtained participants' ratings of their familiarity with each president's and vice president's name. On the basis of our hypothesis, we expected that the level of performance on the reconstruction of order task would be positively correlated with the familiarity ratings. In particular, the familiarity ratings should be higher overall for the presidents' names than for the vice presidents' names, and the familiarity ratings for each list of names should show a bow-shaped serial position function analogous to the function for the reconstruction of order task with that list.

In the present study, we also introduced a third index of performance that should provide insight into the participants' level of categorical knowledge about the names of the presidents and vice presidents. Specifically, prior to providing a familiarity rating for a given name, participants were required to categorize that name according to whether it belonged to a U.S. president, vice president, or both. Because this index reflected participants' previous knowledge, it might also serve as a measure of the frequency of participants' previous exposure to the items, although less directly than would familiarity ratings.

Method

Design and Analyses

Each participant was tested on both reconstruction of order lists (presidents and vice presidents), with the order of lists counterbalanced across participants. The task in each case involved free reconstruction of order of a list of names. The president list included 42 names, and the vice president list included 45 names. For each list, participants ordered the names according to the terms in office. For the analyses, the scores on each set of three consecutive names according to terms in office (e.g., George Washington, John Adams, and Thomas Jefferson for the president list) were averaged together to define a triplet position. There were, thus, 14 triplet positions for the president list and 15 triplet positions for the vice president list. A categorization and familiarity rating task was also included either before or after the reconstruction of order task. There were equal numbers of participants in both orders of the tasks (i.e., reconstruction of order task before or after the categorization and familiarity rating task).

There were three sets of analyses. The first set included separate analyses of the president and vice president lists, one for each of three dependent variables.

The dependent variables were proportion of correct responses on the reconstruction of order task, mean familiarity ratings, and proportion of correct categorization responses. Each analysis consisted of a multifactorial mixed analysis of variance (ANOVA) with task order (reconstruction of order task first or second) and list order (presidents first or vice presidents first) as between-subjects factors and triplet position as the single within-subjects factor. For the president task, there were 14 levels of the within-subjects factor (i.e., 14 triplet positions), and for the vice president task, there were 15 levels. Because of the unequal number of triplet positions for the tasks involving presidents and vice presidents, the president and vice president lists could not be compared directly in this set of analyses.

The second set of analyses was conducted to compare performance on the president and vice president lists. Again, all three dependent variables (reconstruction of order accuracy, familiarity ratings, and categorization accuracy) were examined in different analyses. The data for any individual who served as both a president and a vice president were excluded from this set of analyses (there were 14 individuals who served in both offices). Further, only 14 triplet positions were used, with the vice presidents organized according to the terms in office of the presidents. Each analysis, thus, consisted of a multifactorial repeated measure ANOVA with list (presidents or vice presidents) and triplet position (1–14) as factors.

The third set of analyses involved correlation coefficients. Correlations were computed comparing accuracy on the reconstruction of order task with accuracy on the categorization task, accuracy on the reconstruction of order task with familiarity ratings, and accuracy on the categorization task with familiarity ratings, separately for the presidents and the vice presidents using the full set of data.

Participants

Forty-eight undergraduate college students participated for credit in an introductory psychology course. All were U.S. citizens who were ages 18–23 years ($M = 18.53$ years). Participants were assigned by a fixed rotation to the four counterbalancing conditions, with 12 in each condition.

Materials and Apparatus

At the time of test, each participant received a packet containing the categorization and familiarity rating task as well as the free reconstruction of order task with two lists (presidents and vice presidents). The ordering task for each list included an answer sheet with numbered blanks from 1 to 42 or 1 to 45, depending on the list (presidents or vice presidents, respectively). Also, alphabetical lists of the presidents and vice presidents were constructed. Because Grover Cleveland had two nonconsecutive terms in office, his name appeared twice in the alphabetical list of presidents.

Procedure

The first 24 participants who were tested completed the categorization and familiarity rating task before the reconstruction of order task, whereas the remaining 24 participants completed the reconstruction of order task before the categorization and familiarity rating task. Half of the participants in each of these counterbalancing groups were given the president list for the reconstruction of order task followed by the vice president list, and the other half of the participants were given the two lists for the reconstruction of order task in the opposite order.

The participants were tested in groups ranging from 1 to 18 students. For the categorization and familiarity rating task, participants were given a packet with an instruction page followed by 12 pages including all the names of the presidents and vice presidents in alphabetical order. Below each name, participants were instructed to make a categorization decision by selecting either "president," "vice president," or "both." Below each categorization response was the word "familiarity" and the numbers 1 through 6. Participants were told that for each name listed they should circle a number on the familiarity scale that best indicated how familiar they were with that name ($1 =$ not familiar; $6 =$ most familiar). Participants were also told to respond to one name at a time, not to go back and change any answers already made, to select only one choice for the categorization decision, and to circle only one number on the familiarity rating scale. The participants were reminded of the instructions and the meaning of the rating scale at the top of every page of the packet containing the names of the presidents and vice presidents.

Either before or after completing the categorization and familiarity rating task, participants completed the reconstruction of order task for one of the two lists. They were instructed to recall the presidents or vice presidents according to their terms in office by placing each name next to a number (from 1 to 42 for the presidents and from 1 to 45 for the vice presidents). Participants were given an alphabetical list to help them, and they were instructed not to leave any space unfilled. After participants completed the reconstruction of order task for the first list, they proceeded onto the reconstruction of order task for the second list.

Results

Separate Serial Position Functions

Reconstruction of Order Task

The results are summarized in Figure 9.1 in terms of the absolute proportion of correct responses on the reconstruction of order task as a function of list (presidents or vice presidents) and triplet position.

Performance on the reconstruction of order task was better overall for the president list ($M = .201$) than for the vice president list ($M = .123$), although no

FIGURE 9.1

Absolute proportion of correct responses on the reconstruction of order task for the president and vice president lists as a function of triplet position.

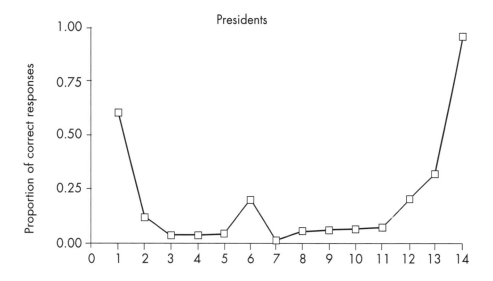

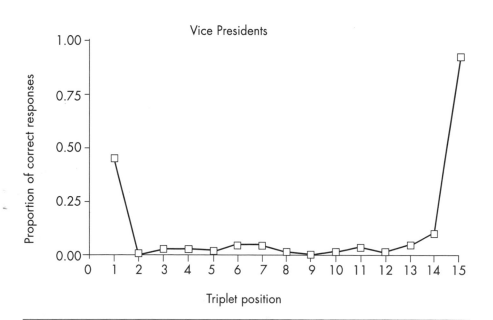

direct statistical comparison was made in this analysis. Performance on the president list varied as a function of triplet position, $F(13, 572) = 108.03$, $MSE = .0328$, $p < .001$, reflecting primacy, penultimate, and recency advantages (and an advantage for the 6th triplet position, which included Lincoln). A similar pattern of performance was found on the vice president list, which also varied as a function of triplet position, $F(14, 616) = 153.01$, $MSE = .0195$, $p < .001$, again reflecting primacy, penultimate, and recency advantages (but no advantage for the 6th triplet position). Note that in the reconstruction of order task the penultimate advantage for the president list extends to the last two triplet positions prior to the recency position (i.e., the 12th and 13th triplet positions), whereas the penultimate advantage for the vice president list extends to only the last triplet position prior to the recency position (i.e., only the 14th triplet position). The same serial position functions were found for both task orders and list orders; the factors of task order and list order did not enter into any significant main effects or interactions in the analyses.

Familiarity Ratings

The results for the familiarity ratings are summarized in Figure 9.2. Familiarity ratings were higher overall for the presidents ($M = 3.571$) than for the vice presidents ($M = 2.369$), although again no direct statistical comparison was made in this analysis. Ratings of the presidents varied as a function of triplet position, $F(13, 572) = 106.72$, $MSE = .5017$, $p < .001$, reflecting primacy, penultimate, and recency advantages (and an advantage for the 6th triplet position, which included Lincoln). A similar pattern of performance was found for the ratings of the vice presidents, which also varied as a function of triplet position, $F(14, 616) = 150.97$, $MSE = .3988$, $p < .001$, reflecting primacy, penultimate, and recency advantages (but no advantage for the 6th triplet position). Note also that the penultimate advantage is much more consistent for the ratings of the presidents than for the ratings of the vice presidents. The same serial position functions were found for both task orders and list orders; the factors of task order and list order did not enter into any significant interactions with serial position in the analyses. The main effect of task order was marginally significant in the analysis of the ratings for presidents, $F(1, 44) = 3.16$, $MSE = 12.5325$, $p = .079$, reflecting the fact that the ratings for participants who gave familiarity ratings first tended to be higher (3.813) than those for participants who gave familiarity ratings after completing the reconstruction of order task (3.328), perhaps because the participants were less confident about their familiarity judgments after being required to order the presidents and vice presidents according to their terms in office.

Categorization Responses

Half of the participants made categorization responses before they performed the reconstruction of order task (which included separate alphabetical lists of presidents

FIGURE 9.2

Mean familiarity ratings for the presidents and vice presidents as a function of triplet position.

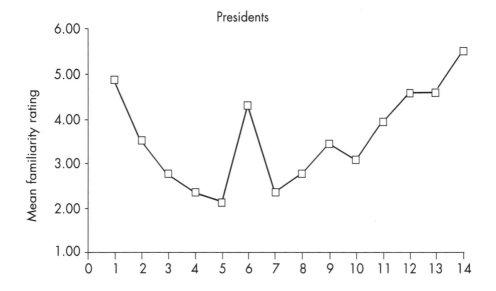

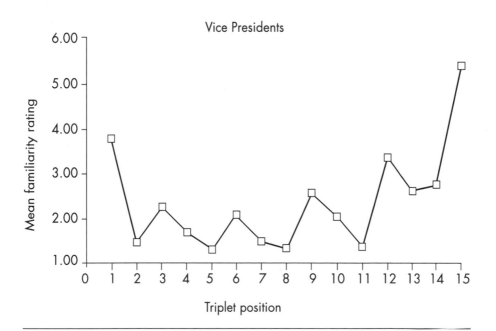

and vice presidents), and the remaining half of the participants made categorization responses after they performed the reconstruction of order task. Because the categorization responses by those participants who performed the reconstruction of order task first were necessarily corrupted by exposure to the separate lists of presidents and vice presidents, our analysis of the categorization responses was restricted to those participants who made categorization responses first. The results for the categorization responses of these participants are summarized in Figure 9.3.

It is interesting to note that categorization responses were more accurate overall for the vice presidents ($M = .653$) than for the presidents ($M = .539$), although again no direct statistical comparison was made in this analysis. This result can easily be explained if participants used the strategy of categorizing any unfamiliar name as belonging to a vice president. Proportions of correct categorization responses of the presidents varied as a function of triplet position, $F(13, 286) = 7.69$, $MSE = .0524$, $p < .001$, although the pattern deviates from the typical bow-shaped function in a number of respects. The proportions of correct categorization responses of the vice presidents also varied as a function of triplet position, $F(14, 308) = 32.61$, $MSE = .0318$, $p < .001$. In this case, the pattern deviates to an even greater extent from the typical bow-shaped function, making it clear that bow-shaped functions are not necessarily found when dealing with these stimuli.

Comparing Serial Position Functions

To compare the presidents and vice presidents directly, we grouped both lists according to the triplet positions of the presidents. Also for this comparison, we removed the data from all 14 individuals who served as both president and vice president.

Reconstruction of Order Task

This comparison for the reconstruction of order task is summarized in Figure 9.4. The proportion of correct responses on the reconstruction of order task was significantly higher overall for the presidents (.243) than for the vice presidents (.102), $F(1, 47) = 134.30$, $MSE = .0498$, $p < .001$. Proportions of correct responses also varied overall as a function of triplet position, $F(13, 611) = 208.67$, $MSE = .0336$, $p < .001$, reflecting primacy, penultimate, and recency advantages. The functions for presidents and those for vice presidents both show all three advantages, but the specific form of the functions differed; the interaction of list and serial position was significant, $F(13, 611) = 45.59$, $MSE = .0294$, $p < .001$. Note that the primacy advantage is larger for presidents than for vice presidents, the penultimate advantage for the president list extends to one more triplet position than does the penultimate advantage for the vice president list, and there is an advantage for the 6th triplet position (which included Lincoln) for the president list but not for the vice president list.

FIGURE 9.3

Proportion of correct categorization responses (including only participants who made categorization responses first) for the presidents and vice presidents as a function of triplet position.

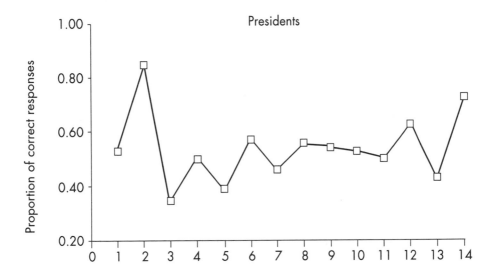

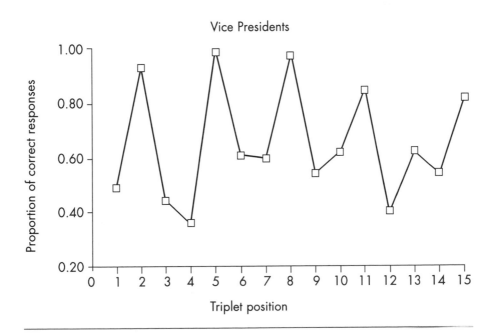

FIGURE 9.4

Absolute proportion of correct responses on the reconstruction of order task as a function of list and triplet position.

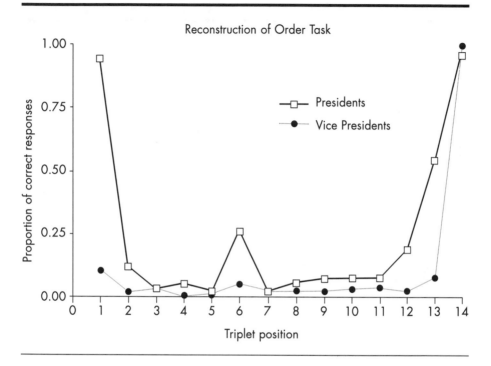

Familiarity Ratings

The comparison of familiarity ratings for presidents and vice presidents is summarized in Figure 9.5. The mean familiarity ratings were significantly higher overall for the presidents (3.705) than for the vice presidents (1.889), $F(1, 47) = 285.20$, $MSE = 3.8841$, $p < .001$. The familiarity ratings also varied overall as a function of triplet position, $F(13, 611) = 163.35$, $MSE = .5807$, $p < .001$, again reflecting primacy, penultimate, and recency advantages. As with the reconstruction of order task, the functions for presidents and those for vice presidents both show all three advantages, but the specific form of the functions differed; the interaction of list and serial position was significant, $F(13, 611) = 40.60$, $MSE = .5983$, $p < .001$. Note that, as also found for the reconstruction of order task, the primacy advantage is larger for presidents than for vice presidents, the penultimate advantage for the president list extends to one more triplet position (Position 11) than does the penultimate advantage for the vice president list (which only included Positions 12 and 13), and there is an advantage for the 6th triplet position (which included Lincoln) for the president list but not for the vice president list.

FIGURE 9.5

Mean familiarity ratings as a function of list and triplet position.

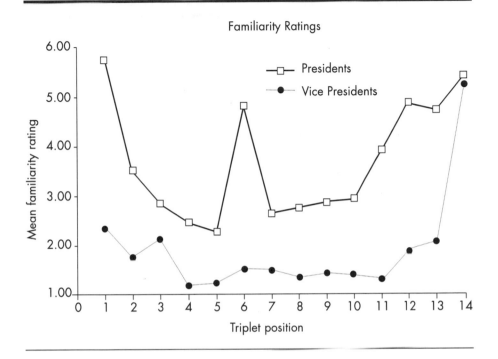

Familiarity Ratings

Categorization Responses

As mentioned earlier, the analysis of the categorization responses was restricted to participants who made categorization responses first. The comparison of categorization responses for presidents and vice presidents is summarized in Figure 9.6. As suggested earlier, categorization responses were more accurate overall for the vice presidents ($M = .857$) than for the presidents ($M = .739$), $F(1, 23) = 8.06$, $MSE = .2928$, $p = .009$. Proportions of correct categorization responses varied overall as a function of triplet position, $F(13, 299) = 4.99$, $MSE = .0701$, $p < .001$, with a pattern that deviates from the typical bow-shaped function in a number of respects. However, the pattern is closer to the typical bowed function for presidents than for vice presidents; the interaction of list and triplet position was significant, $F(13, 299) = 5.48$, $MSE = .0659$, $p < .001$. The finding that the serial position functions deviate from the typical functions underlines the fact that bow-shaped functions are not necessarily found when dealing with these stimuli. In addition, the finding that the overall performance level was higher and that the serial position function was more irregular for the vice presidents than for the presidents can be explained by the hypothesis that participants use the strategy of categorizing any unfamiliar name as a vice president.

FIGURE 9.6

Proportion of correct categorization responses (including only participants who made categorization responses first) as a function of list and triplet position.

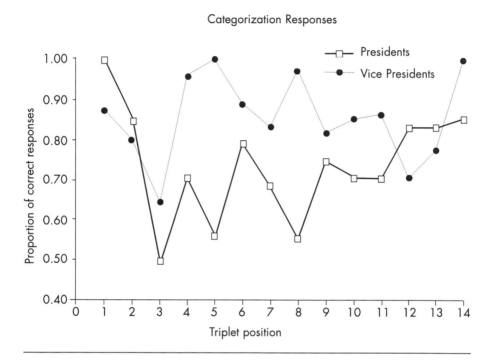

Correlations

The mean proportions of correct responses on the reconstruction of order task for each of the 42 presidents were compared both with the mean familiarity ratings and with the mean proportions of correct categorization responses (in this case only for the 24 participants who made categorization responses before the reconstruction of order task), which were also compared with each other. There was a significant positive correlation between accuracy on the reconstruction of order task and the familiarity ratings, $r(40) = .744, p < .01$. The correlations comparing the reconstruction of order task with the categorization responses, $r(40) = .279, p < .10$, and comparing the familiarity ratings and categorization responses, $r(40) = .370, p < .05$, were much lower and only marginally significant in the former case.

We made similar comparisons for each of the 45 vice presidents. As in the correlational analysis of the presidents, there was a significant positive correlation between accuracy on the reconstruction of order task and the familiarity ratings, $r(43) = .704, p < .01$. The correlation comparing the reconstruction of order task with the categorization responses was close to zero, $r(43) = .006$, but the correlation comparing the familiarity ratings and categorization responses was significantly negative, $r(43) = -.504, p < .01$.

The significant correlations for both presidents and vice presidents between performance on the reconstruction of order task and the familiarity ratings support the hypothesis that frequency of exposure, as indexed by the familiarity ratings, provides a reasonable explanation for performance on the reconstruction of order task. The marginal (for the presidents) and zero (for the vice presidents) correlation between the reconstruction of order task and the categorization responses can be explained by the hypothesis that participants use the strategy of categorizing any unfamiliar name as a vice president. This hypothesis receives further support from the positive correlation between familiarity ratings and categorization responses for the presidents and the corresponding negative correlation for the vice presidents.

General Discussion

In summary, in the present study, we found bow-shaped serial position functions for reconstructing the historical order of both the presidents and vice presidents. Performance for the list of presidents was significantly higher than that for the list of vice presidents. The serial position functions for the two lists had similar shapes, each containing primacy, penultimate, and recency advantages. However, the primacy advantage was larger and the penultimate advantage was more extensive for the president list than for the vice president list, and there was an advantage for the 6th triplet position (which contained Lincoln) for the president list but not for the vice president list. The different overall levels of performance for presidents and vice presidents as well as the specific serial position functions are well explained in terms of the frequency of participants' prior exposure to information relevant to the terms in office of the presidents and vice presidents. In fact, the correlation between proportions of correct responses on the reconstruction of order task and familiarity ratings was over .7 for both presidents and vice presidents. The bow-shaped serial position function and the penultimate advantage previously found for the president list in the reconstruction of order task are, thus, clearly not an artifact of the high level of performance with that list because a lower level of performance, but a similar serial position function, was found for the vice president list. However, it is clear that bow-shaped serial position functions are not necessarily found with these stimuli because the shapes of the serial position functions deviated substantially from the bow shape for the proportion of correct categorization responses.

In our earlier study, we (Healy et al., 2000) found that the penultimate advantage in the reconstruction of order task extended as far as the last three triplet positions prior to the recency advantage. The penultimate advantage extended to only two triplet positions for the presidents in the present experiment and to only one triplet position for the vice presidents. However, in the present experiment (which was conducted during the fall semester of 1998), all of the participants were 18–23 years old, so that they were alive only during the presidencies in the last two triplet positions (i.e., the 13th and 14th) and were very young during the presidencies in the earlier of these two triplet positions. (In fact, the youngest participants were only one year old during Carter's presidency, which is the last presidency in the 13th triplet position.) It seems reasonable to assume that very young children would have some exposure to information about the current or immediately previous presidents but much less about the current or immediately previous vice presidents. Hence, the findings concerning performance in the reconstruction of order task are consistent with the frequency of exposure hypothesis.

The familiarity ratings collected do not directly measure the frequency of previous exposure to relevant information about the presidents' and vice presidents' terms in office. We considered instead asking participants to rate explicitly the frequency of their previous exposure to such order information. However, we decided against that alternative rating task for two reasons. First, we thought that the familiarity rating task would be more straightforward and easier for the participants to understand. Second, the frequency of exposure rating task could be interpreted by the participants as a request to judge how well they could position each president or vice president according to his term in office, especially for participants who completed the reconstruction of order task before the rating task. Thus, the frequency of exposure rating task could be viewed more as a confidence rating for the ability to reconstruct the order of the presidents or vice presidents than as an independent judgment. Finding a correlation between frequency of exposure ratings and performance on the reconstruction of order task would, thus, not be nearly as impressive as the correlation found between the presumably more independent familiarity ratings and the performance on the reconstruction of order task.

Roediger and Crowder (1976; Crowder, 1993) found an advantage for the recall of Lincoln, just as we found in our reconstruction of order task. Specifically, the proportion of correct responses was .458 for Lincoln in our reconstruction of order task. This relatively high level of performance is easily explained in terms of the frequency of participants' previous exposure to information relevant to Lincoln's term in office because the participants' average familiarity rating for Lincoln was 5.479 (out of 6). It is clear that the advantage for Lincoln on the reconstruction of order task cannot be attributed to the distinctiveness of his position because a similar advantage was not found for Lincoln's vice presidents, Hannibal Hamlin and Andrew Johnson (who became president after Lincoln was assassinated). The proportion of correct responses on the reconstruction of order task was only .042 for each of these vice presidents, as would be expected because their mean familiarity ratings were relatively low (1.500 for Hamlin and 3.188 for Johnson).

What is the form of the participants' knowledge that they use in performing the reconstruction of order task? The hypothesis about frequency of exposure to information relevant to the terms in office allows one to predict how well participants will perform on specific items in the reconstruction of order task (e.g., best for the most familiar presidents) but does not specify the form of their knowledge. At this point, it seems appropriate to assume that their knowledge is not based on a single type of order information. Rather, it seems better to assume that there are multiple forms of knowledge, including associations between presidents or vice presidents and the position numbers of their terms in office (e.g., an association between Lincoln and 16), sequential associations between particular presidents or vice presidents (e.g., an association between Nixon and Ford), and other historical facts about the presidents or vice presidents (e.g., the fact that Franklin Roosevelt proposed the New Deal and was president during World War II). Frequency of exposure to order information can, thus, be used to predict how well participants perform in the reconstruction of order task but itself is not the knowledge used by participants. Thus, there is no reason to expect participants to confuse presidents or vice presidents who have similar levels of frequency of exposure to order information or similar familiarity ratings. Only if the order information itself were similar would confusion be expected (e.g., information that an individual with the last name Johnson was a vice president who became a president following an assassination of a famous president might lead participants to confuse the positions of Andrew Johnson and Lyndon Johnson).

Likewise, the distinctiveness account leads to predictions about how well participants will perform on specific items in the reconstruction of order task (e.g., best for the most distinctive positions) but does not specify the form of their knowledge. Similarly, there is no reason to expect participants to confuse positions with similar levels of distinctiveness or else confusions would be expected between primacy and recency positions that are equally distinct.

There is, however, a theory that does specify the form of participants' knowledge about the order of the presidents. To account for the bow-shaped serial position function in a similar task, Brown and Siegler (1991) proposed that participants organize the presidents into three groups consisting of (a) Founding Fathers (Washington through John Quincy Adams), (b) noncontemporary presidents (Jackson through Franklin Roosevelt), and (c) post-World War II presidents (beginning with Truman). The Founding Fathers group and the post-World War II group are both considerably smaller than the middle group of noncontemporary presidents. Brown and Siegler argued that knowledge of group membership would thus yield weaker positional constraints for presidents in the middle group. However, in our earlier study, we (Healy et al., 2000) pointed to four problems with this account. First, it cannot explain our earlier findings concerning the effect of participant age on the penultimate advantage. Second, it cannot explain Roediger and Crowder's (1976; Crowder, 1993) bow-shaped serial position function with their free-recall instructions and scoring. Third, it cannot explain the advantage for Lincoln (who was in the middle group of presidents) found in these tasks. Fourth, it cannot explain the fact that the recency advantage was usually greater than the primacy advantage in these tasks. Thus, the exact form of participants' knowledge underlying these tasks is still unclear.

Although we cannot specify the form of participants' knowledge used for these tasks, we argue that we have gained a better understanding of what leads to superior performance in these tasks. Specifically, we suggest that participants perform well for a given president or vice president on the reconstruction of order task to the extent of the frequency of their prior exposure to information relevant to the individual's term in office. Nevertheless, frequency of exposure to order information cannot account for all the differences we observed in performance levels in the task. A complete account of the serial position functions in the semantic memory reconstruction of order task would have to include other factors, and Crowder's (1993) notion of distinctiveness would undoubtedly be one of them. A model that includes a multitude of factors is not nearly as elegant as one that includes only a single factor. Nevertheless, once again parsimony may not be possible in this case.

References

Bjork, E. L., & Healy, A. F. (1974). Short-term order and item retention. *Journal of Verbal Learning and Verbal Behavior, 13,* 80–97.

Brown, N. R., & Siegler, R. S. (1991). Subjective organization of U.S. presidents. *American Journal of Psychology, 104,* 1–33.

Crowder, R. G. (1978). Mechanisms of auditory backward masking in the stimulus suffix effect. *Psychological Review, 85,* 502–524.

Crowder, R. G. (1986). Auditory and temporal factors in the modality effect. *Journal of Experimental Psychology: Learning, Memory, and Cognition, 12,* 268–278.

Crowder, R. G. (1993). Short-term memory: Where do we stand? *Memory & Cognition, 21,* 142–145.

Crowder, R. G., & Morton, J. (1969). Precategorical acoustic storage (PAS). *Perception & Psychophysics, 5,* 365–373.

Estes, W. K. (1972). An associative basis for coding and organization in memory. In A. W. Melton & E. Martin (Eds.), *Coding processes in human memory* (pp. 161–190). New York: Halsted Press.

Estes, W. K. (1997). Processes of memory loss, recovery, and distortion. *Psychological Review, 104,* 148–169.

Healy, A. F., Havas, D. A., & Parker, J. T. (2000). Comparing serial position effects in semantic and episodic memory using reconstruction of order tasks. *Journal of Memory and Language, 42,* 147–167.

McCrary, J., & Hunter, W. S. (1953). Serial position curves in verbal learning. *Science, 117,* 131–134.

Murdock, B. B., Jr. (1960). The distinctiveness of stimuli. *Psychological Review, 67,* 16–31.

Roediger, H. L., III, & Crowder, R. G. (1976). A serial position effect in recall of United States presidents. *Bulletin of the Psychonomic Society, 8,* 275–278.

CHAPTER 10

The Modality Effect and the Gentle Law of Speech Ascendancy

Protesting the Tyranny of Reified Memory

Michael J. Watkins

It is a high privilege to contribute to this celebration of Robert G. Crowder. Over the last third of the 20th century, few have done as much as Bob to advance the understanding of memory and cognition. His extraordinary powers of critical analysis are attested by a long list of wide-ranging research reports. Of his books, *Principles of Learning and Memory* is the best memory text ever written. In addition, his wit and charm and unassuming manner made him as cherished as anyone I know. This essay is a token of my very high esteem for Bob—a regard I know I share with all who knew him.

My particular purpose in this chapter is to advocate and illustrate a way of thinking about memory that is at variance with contemporary practice. I argue that although memory should, as a fundamentally psychological construct, be conceived in mental or behavioral terms, researchers invariably reify it and so cast it in material terms, either hypothetical or neural. I illustrate the nonnecessity of such reductionism in a report of findings pertaining to the modality effect and specifically to Crowder and Morton's (1969) theory of precategorical acoustic storage (PAS). This theory enjoys the increasingly rare virtue of disprovability and, although still by far the best-known account of the modality effect, it has already generated sufficient contrary evidence to warrant its rejection. As Crowder quipped with uncommon dispassion, the theory of PAS is correct except for the *P, A,* and *S.* Although some readers may find the contrary evidence presented here of some interest in its own right, the conclusions that are drawn from it are consistent with Crowder's verdict. This fact should help allay concerns about their validity and so free the reader to consider the more general conclusion that a genuinely psychological conception of memory can constitute an adequate basis for meaningful research.

Mediationism

Psychology is the science of mind and behavior. Most of the research reported in the mainstream psychology journals is consistent with this definition. But much of the theorizing in which the findings are embedded is not.

The use of nonpsychological theorizing is especially characteristic of cognitive research and flagrantly so of memory research. If psychology is taken as the science of mind,[1] then memory is the having in mind something that is, and is known to be, of the past; if psychology is taken as the science of behavior, then memory is the effect of some prior occurrence on behavior. Either way, the memory experiment involves doing something to subjects and observing its subsequent effect—for example, presenting a list of items and sometime thereafter measuring recall of the items or facilitation in their perception. Such research is authentic psychology. But the way in which the findings are typically discussed is not.

This blunder is rooted in an insistence on reifying memory, on turning it into a thing. The thing is conceptualized as a trace of, or as otherwise created by, whatever is being remembered, and its purpose is to bridge the temporal gap between the occurrence and its recall or other effect. Such hypostatizing in the interest of mediating across time has a history dating from at least as far back as Plato, but since the coming of the cognitive era in the 1960s, it has been elevated to dogma. Two forms of the dogma may be distinguished: artificial intelligence and cognitive neuroscience.

In most contemporary memory theorizing, the mind is mechanized and memory is wrought from hypothetical information-processing machinery. As with cognitive theorizing generally, memory theorizing consists in devising, configuring, or programming this machinery so that it produces the target finding. Sometimes a theory is completely specified and fully capable of simulating the finding. More often, it is a mere schematic, showing how in principle the critical feature of the finding might be produced. Either way, such practice is not psychology. Indeed, it is not even science. Rather, it is engineering, and specifically that branch of engineering having to do with artificial intelligence (M. J. Watkins, 1991). Its goal is not one of seeking psychological truths but one of showing how psychological findings can be simulated. Of course, there is no limit to the number of mechanisms that would, at least in principle, produce a given finding, and any notion of science as a public enterprise notwithstanding, respectability in the fraternity of experimental psychologists requires at least one such hypothetical mechanism (usually styled "model" or, more grandly, "theory") of one's very own. Because even the simplest possible mediationist model of memory is necessarily underdetermined by the operations available to psychology (M. J. Watkins, 1978, 1990), these theories are remarkably durable. Usually the critic has misunderstood, but if need be, a little fine-tuning can safeguard

---

[1]By *mind,* I mean consciousness.

a theory from virtually any brush with data. Consequently, theory evaluation is usually in terms of elegance, although the quest for elegance never threatens the complexity needed to sustain the indulgent thrill of personalized theorizing.

The second approach to reifying memory, cognitive neuroscience, has as its objective the identification of the neurological underpinnings of cognition. Unlike artificial intelligence, this approach is irrefutably scientific. But it is not basic psychology. To presume otherwise is to confuse cognition with its physical substrate (M. J. Watkins, 1990). The objective of cognitive neuroscience is the elucidation not of cognition but of its neural correlates. In this endeavor, psychology serves as handmaiden to natural science and is therefore applied psychology.

The distinction between these two approaches to mediationism is not entirely clean. For example, a simulation model may consist of multiple processors contrived to interconnect in much the same way that neurons do. More generally, a hypothetical information-processing model may serve as a bona fide conjecture of the broad outline of the underlying neurology. But sharp or fuzzy, the distinction is not germane to the present purposes. What is important is that both approaches reify memory. Whether cast as neural tissue or as some purely hypothetical thing, memory is defined as a physical change that endures from the time of occurrence of whatever is being remembered until the time of its effect. Such change is, of course, essential for memory, but it should not be confused with memory. Nor should one be misled by the scientific legitimacy of seeking the nature of this change. The search for the engram surely ranks among the most exciting of all contemporary scientific endeavors, but such science is not psychology. Psychology is the science of mind and behavior, and the physical substrate of memory is neither mind nor behavior. To reduce the mental and the behavioral to the material is thus to reject rather than advance psychology.

An alternative to reifying and mechanizing is to appeal to action at a distance, to interpret the state of affairs at one temporal and spatial location in terms of that at another. Thus, memory for the presentation of a word in a typical experiment can be attributed directly to the prior presentation of the word, without reference to a mediating "trace" or "representation," whether cautiously hypothetical or boldly neural. Unfortunately, this conception of memory is virtually never considered. One reason for this disregard is doubtless a general unease with its scientific status—an impression that it is inadequate, insubstantial, even magical. I consider this impression misguided. As argued elsewhere (M. J. Watkins, 1990), even in the natural sciences the concept of action at a distance has provided adequate underpinnings for a variety of theoretical advances, including Newton's universal law of gravitation.

Also at play here are two unwritten but cardinal rules concerning explanation. The first is that no finding can be reported in mainstream experimental psychology journals without being given an explanation. To the uninitiated, the idea that a finding that eludes explanation is unworthy of report may seem draconian, but in practice it imposes no real hardship because all mechanistic simulations are vested with explanatory power. Thus, any conceivable finding can be "explained" simply by referring to a mechanistic model or, if need be, creating a new one. Put another way, describe any of the indefinite number of mechanisms that could, in principle, produce a given finding, and the finding is explained. Now there's magic!

More draconian is the second rule, whereby an explanation not only can but must be mechanistic. Certainly, an appeal to action at a distance will never do. A corollary of this rule is that if, as I argue, a mechanistic explanation is inherently nonpsychological, then psychology has a problem. The solution to this problem, I believe, lies in the adoption of an alternative explanatory mode. In particular, a given finding can be explained with reference to a general principle or law. By way of illustration, I sometimes find one of the libraries I frequent to be closed and momentarily wonder why, only to realize that it is late on Friday and that on Fridays this library closes early. Thus, the general principle of closing early on Fridays adequately explains each such individual closing, even though the general principle itself remains unexplained.

In the study of memory, this mode of explanation has found use in, for example, the *cue-overload principle,* wherein memory is assumed to be effected by way of cues that are subject to overload. An obvious application of this principle is to the *list length effect*—the finding that the recall of a given item from a list becomes progressively less probable as the number of items in the list increases. The idea here is that the recall of list items occurs, at least to some extent, by way of a "list" cue and that as list length increases, so does the load on this cue; consequently, the efficacy of the cue with respect to a given item decreases. Such a principle can be, and indeed has been (e.g., Raaijmakers & Shiffrin, 1981), incorporated into mechanistic models of reified item memories, but the important point is that it does not have to be.

Although application of the cue-overload principle to the list length effect may appear to be little more than a statement of the effect, it is a more abstract statement, and as such, it suggests links to other effects. For example, the finding that list recall can be enhanced by clustering the list items in a way that brings out their category relationships (Bower, Clark, Lesgold, & Winzenz, 1969) may be attributed to an easing of the load on the list cue through the intuitively plausible assumption that cues corresponding to the various categories are nested between the list cue and the individual items. In similar fashion, the notion of cue overload can be invoked to account for various other memory phenomena, including subjective organization, negative transfer and retroactive interference, the buildup and release of proactive interference, the part-set cuing effect, and the von Restorff effect (see M. J. Watkins, 1979; and O. C. Watkins & Watkins, 1975). What is important for present purposes is that each of these findings can be explained simply by referring it to a single general principle. Of course, the general principle itself remains unexplained, but this is a less disorderly state of affairs than one involving multiple unexplained phenomena.

In the balance of this chapter, my concern is with another such principle, one I call the law of speech ascendancy. It pertains to echoic memory—a topic of research shaped in substantial measure by Bob Crowder.

Echoic Memory and the Gentle Law of Speech Ascendancy

Echoic memory refers to the short-lived but high-fidelity retention of auditory information, much like an echo in the physical world. As Crowder (1976) noted, because auditory information necessarily spans time, echoic memory is essential for auditory perception. For example, speech would surely be incomprehensible if the sound corresponding to each infinitesimal slice of information were entirely lost or reduced to a modality-independent form by the time the next slice arrives. Also, consider the familiar scenario of looking up and dialing a telephone number. On finding the number, I might capitalize on echoic memory by saying it aloud before dialing. If, however, someone speaks before I dial, I may lose echoic memory and so forget the number.

Such beneficial and detrimental effects of echoic memory are well documented in the experimental literature in the form of the modality and suffix effects. The modality effect is the advantage in recall of the last few of a list of verbal items that occurs when the items are presented auditorily rather than visually (Corballis, 1966). Closer to the dialing scenario, the effect also arises when the speech comes not from the experimenter but rather from the subjects' reading aloud visually presented items (Murray, 1965). The *suffix effect* arises when a sequence of auditorily presented items is followed by a nominally irrelevant item. After hearing, say, a random sequence of eight digits, a subject may hear "zero" or the instruction "recall." Although this extra item, or suffix, is fully anticipated by the subject and requires no response, it sharply reduces the chances of recalling the last two or three items of the sequence, thereby converting an auditory pattern of results into more of a visual pattern (Crowder, 1967).

I suggest that these phenomena can be interpreted by way of a simple law. Before I lay down the law, however, consideration should be given to the kind of interpretation that these phenomena currently provide.

It might be thought that echoic memory is, of its very nature, the product of stimulus control, for by definition, it is peculiar to the auditory sensory modality. Such an interpretation would, however, run afoul of the cognitive zeitgeist. With the cognitive revolution, we, the rememberers, were freed from stimulus control and granted such strategic capabilities as selective encoding and organization and rehearsal, to be exercised within the structural constraints of a hypothetical information-processing system. Ever since, memory theorists have taken whatever measures necessary to avoid appeal to stimulus control. Memory phenomena that in a different ethos would be flaunted as compelling demonstrations of the power of the stimulus have been cast in the information-processing mold. There are perhaps no more striking examples of this than the interpretations given to the experimental evidence underpinning echoic memory.

The array of theoretical accounts proffered for echoic memory befits the practice of personalized theorizing but defies succinct review. Fortunately, a comprehensive review of these accounts is not necessary here; it is enough to focus on one. Being both apposite to the occasion of this book and still preeminent in textbook coverage (e.g., Greene, 1992; Neath, 1998), Crowder and Morton's (1969) theory of precategorical acoustic storage serves my purpose nicely. The key innovation of this theory is a store that briefly retains the most recent acoustic information at a low level of analysis. For example, speech is retained in this store at a level of analysis prior to segmentation into the words or higher linguistic units assumed to populate the upper reaches of the information-processing system. To account for the modality effect, the higher order information is said to be supplemented by precategorical information pertaining to the most recent item or items of spoken lists; to account for the suffix effect, this precategorical information is assumed to be substantially overwritten by a spoken suffix.

This phenomenon, echoic memory, would be seen by the uninitiated as manifestly stimulus driven, but nonetheless the specialists have seen fit to reconcile it to a zeitgeist that stresses rememberer over stimulus control. The reconciliation is primarily a matter of marginalizing the phenomenon by consigning it to a modality-specific store at the periphery of the information-processing system. For good measure, echoic memory is assumed, even without the obliterating effect of immediately ensuing speech, to fade rather quickly. In particular, Crowder (1976, p. 65) tentatively suggested a usable life of 2 seconds, and this suggestion has been widely accepted. So it is, then, that advocates of the theory of precategorical acoustic storage assume echoic memory to be (a) fleeting, (b) too far downstream to directly interact with information coming in on the visual or any other sensory channel, and (c) too far downstream to be influenced by meaning.

I am about to report evidence contrary to each of these three assumptions. But first my reason for doing so needs to be made clear. My intent is not primarily one of undermining these assumptions—after all, evidence that does just that is already available in the public record. Rather, my intent is to illustrate a way of thinking about echoic memory that does not resort to reification. Instead of conceiving of echoic memory as grist for an information-processing mill, I cast it in terms of a principle or law. It is important to note that this way of thinking not only can bring order to existing data but, contrary to an opinion often confided to me, also can stimulate pertinent research.

The law is simple and intuitive: Recently heard items tend to ascend and linger in mind. I call it the law of speech ascendancy.[2] In keeping with the probabilistic nature of recall underlying the modality and suffix effects, the law is expressed as

---

[2]The law may extend beyond the realm of speech to audition in general, but the details of any such extension remain largely unexplored.

a mere tendency and so should be considered as gentle and perhaps pliant in character (more akin to "please keep off the grass" than to "thou shalt not kill"). In a similar vein, it seems likely that the laws of mind and behavior form a complex web, so any given phenomenon is likely to fall within the provenance of more than one law. Consequently, not all findings pertaining to echoic memory should be expected to be unequivocally predicted by, or even consistent with, any given law, including the law of speech ascendancy. Nevertheless, this particular law does seem to be respected by most of the more prominent findings in the echoic memory literature.

Rather than trying to relate this law to the entire echoic memory literature, I restrict consideration to the three assumptions that I identified as characterizing Crowder and Morton's (1969) theory of PAS. I further restrict consideration to the expression of these assumptions in the modality effect, although their expression in the suffix effect tells a parallel and no less compelling tale (see, e.g., Bloom, 1999). Some of the research considered here has not previously been reported, so I describe it in detail. To be acceptable for publication in a mainstream experimental psychology journal, this research, like any other memory research, would have to be cast in mechanistic, information-processing terms. This was the case when the research was new (which, for the most part, was about two decades ago), and it is certainly the case in the more entrenched information-processing ethos of today. But to comply with this requirement would be to distort the facts. To the extent that this research was motivated or guided by theory, the theory was nothing more than the law of speech ascendancy. And it is in the context of this law that I describe the research here.

Study 1: Persistence of Echoic Memory

This study addresses the rate of decay of echoic memory for speech in the absence of additional speech. The general assumption of rapid decay serves to constrain stimulus control, which is in keeping with contemporary rememberer-centered theorizing. But it does not jibe with the intuition that gave rise to the law of speech ascendancy; speech sometimes lingers in my mind much longer than 2 seconds. Moreover, there is experimental evidence suggesting that I am not alone in this regard (e.g., Balota & Duchek, 1986; M. J. Watkins & Todres, 1980; O. C. Watkins & Watkins, 1980). Study 1 is comprised of two experiments designed to provide evidence that echoic memory for speech may persist for appreciably longer than even these findings indicate. The underlying idea was that if it derives from echoic memory, then the modality effect can tell about echoic memory persistence. A fuller report can be found in an unpublished master's thesis by Douglas Brems (1984).

Experiment 1

In his first experiment, Brems (1984) presented lists of alternating written and spoken words for free recall. He found a robust modality effect, despite an unusually slow rate of presentation.

Method

Eleven 10-word lists were formed by randomly assigning a set of common bisyllabic words. One list was used for practice, the other 10 for the experiment proper. In the experiment proper, the order of presentation of both the lists and the words within each list was reversed for the second half of the subjects. Modality of presentation alternated from item to item. For odd-numbered subjects, the odd-numbered items of the odd-numbered lists and the even-numbered items of the even-numbered lists were presented visually, and the intervening items were presented auditorily; for the even-numbered subjects, the modalities were reversed.

The words were presented at a rate of one every 15 s, so that presentation of a list took fully 2.5 min. For visual presentation, the words were displayed by way of a slide projector for 2.5 s; for auditory presentation, they were spoken by the experimenter in the presence of a 2.5-s blank screen. As a precaution against an uninformatively high level of performance, five simple arithmetic problems (e.g., $97 - 14 = ?$; $88 + 26 = ?$; $67 + 29 = ?$; $54 - 38 = ?$; $74 - 45 = ?$) were shown immediately after the 2.5 s presentation interval, and the subjects mentally solved as many problems as they could. The last arithmetic display was followed by a row of asterisks, which served as a signal for recall of the words in any order. One minute was allowed for this task. Responses to both the arithmetic task and recall test were written in prepared booklets. After all of the lists had been presented and tested in this way, the subjects were engaged in a brief conversation and then given a surprise grand recall test, in which they were allowed 5 min. to write down as many of the words from all of the lists as they could remember, again without regard to order. The subjects were 20 Rice University undergraduates.

Results

Figure 10.1 summarizes the results in the form of serial position functions. These functions were constructed by unraveling the presentation modalities, so that each curve shows the probability of recall for a given modality at all serial positions. The upper two functions are for the immediate recall test, the lower two for the grand recall test.

The immediate recall data show a strong modality effect spanning the length of the list. Inferential analyses of these data confirm that the main effect of presentation modality was compelling, $F(1, 19) = 118.81$, $p = .000$,[3] as was the interaction between presentation modality and list half, $F(1, 19) = 47.06$, $p = .000$. Specific comparisons indicated that for all except the second serial position, an effect of modality as large or larger than that observed was unlikely ($p < .05$) to have arisen by chance.

As is clear from Figure 10.1, the modality effect did not survive until the grand recall test. This finding is consistent with the presumption that the modality effect

---

[3]All p values have been rounded to the number of places shown.

FIGURE 10.1

Probability of recall for auditorily and visually presented words as a function of within-list position.

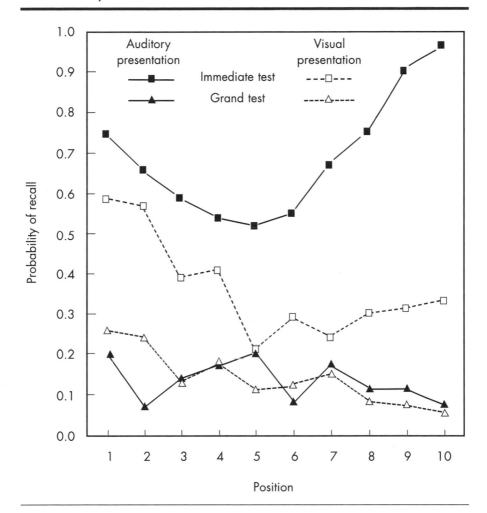

in immediate recall was indeed the product of an echoic memory that can endure for much longer than usually supposed while remaining vulnerable to the effects of subsequent speech.

Experiment 2

If the longevous modality effect observed in Experiment 1 really was the product of echoic memory, then it should diminish if phonological discriminability is reduced through the use of words that sound alike. Certainly, just such a reduction has been observed with a more normal presentation rate (M. J. Watkins, Watkins, & Crowder, 1974). In his second experiment, therefore, Brems (1984) examined the effect of phonological similarity on the modality effect with the 15-s presentation rate used in Experiment 1. For purposes of comparison, he also did the same thing with a 2.5-s presentation rate.

Method

Rate of presentation varied between subjects, being one word every 15 s for half of the subjects and one every 2.5 s for the other half. Presentation modality and phonological similarity were varied within subjects.

Twenty-four sets of 12 monosyllabic rhyming words (e.g., *shot, dot, pot, blot, squat, plot, knot, spot, jot, slot, trot,* and *got*) were formed into two 12 × 12 matrices, with the rhyming sets constituting the rows. From these matrices, four exclusive series of 12-word lists were extracted such that each series consisted of six rhyming lists drawn from six rows of one matrix and six nonrhyming lists drawn from six columns of the other matrix. Each set of lists was presented to a quarter of the subjects of both the slow and fast presentation conditions. Thus, across subjects, each of the 288 words occurred equally often in a rhyming and nonrhyming list for each presentation rate, and no word was presented to a given subject more than once. A 12-word rhyming list and a 12-word nonrhyming list were also formed for use as practice.

Rhyming lists alternated with nonrhyming lists. Because of the potential confusability of spoken monosyllabic words, especially in the rhyming condition, and because neither the theory of precategorical storage nor the law of speech ascendancy implies any effect of using bimodal rather than auditory presentation, what for convenience is called auditory presentation was really bimodal. Thus, all words were shown on the screen for 1.75 s, with alternate words also read aloud by the experimenter. With the .75-s change time, this made for a 2.5-s presentation rate. For the 15.0-s presentation condition, arithmetic problems were shown during the intervals between the word presentations. Counterbalancing measures ensured that for any given subject, half of the rhyming lists and half of the nonrhyming lists began with a visually presented word and the others began with an auditorily presented word; and that across subjects, rhyming and nonrhyming lists were assigned equally often to the odd and even list positions, and for each list auditory and visual presentation were used equally often in the odd and even positions. The procedural details for the 15.0-s presentation condition were the same as for Experiment 1; those for the 2.5-s presentation condition differed only by the omission of the arithmetic task. The procedure ended with a grand recall test, also as described for Experiment 1. The subjects were 64 Rice University undergraduates.

Results

The recall functions are shown in Figure 10.2. The functions for the 2.5-s presentation condition are shown in the upper panels, and those for the 15.0-s presentation

FIGURE 10.2

Probability of recall for auditorily and visually presented phonologically dissimilar and similar words presented at 2.5-s and 15.0-s rates as a function of within-list position.

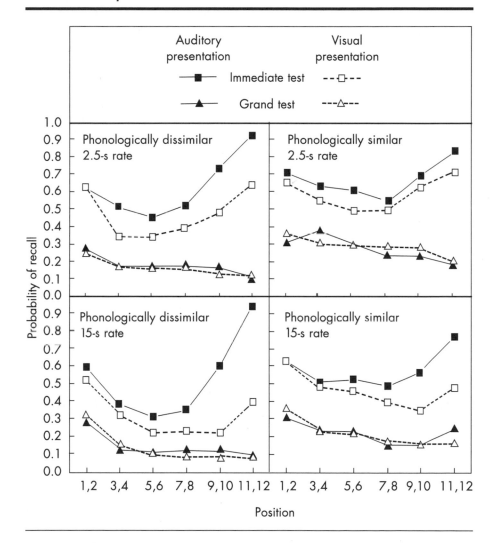

condition in the lower panels; those for the phonologically dissimilar lists are shown in the lefthand panels, and those for the phonologically similar lists in the righthand panels. Consider first the results for the immediate recall test, depicted by the higher two functions within each panel. For the 2.5-s presentation condition, a modality effect occurred for both types of lists but was smaller for the phonologically similar lists. These findings are consistent with previous research (M. J. Watkins et al., 1974). Of more interest, the same pattern held for the 15.0-s presentation condition.

Inferential analyses of the immediate recall data confirmed these observations. Thus, presentation modality interacted with type of list, $F(1, 62) = 21.30$, $p = .000$, but there was no evidence of a second-order interaction among presentation modality, type of list, and presentation rate, $F(1, 62) = 0.34$, $p = .56$. Additionally, there were clear main effects of both presentation modality, $F(1, 62) = 190.80$, $p = .000$, and type of list, $F(1, 62) = 70.81$, $p = .000$, as well as of presentation rate, $F(1, 62) = 9.90$, $p = .003$, and list half, $F(1, 62) = 9.26$, $p = .003$; first-order interactions between presentation modality and list half, $F(1, 62) = 33.40$, $p = .000$, and type of list and list half, $F(1, 62) = 20.74$, $p = .000$; and second-order interactions among presentation modality, type of list, and list half, $F(1, 62) = 10.21$, $p = .002$, and presentation modality, presentation rate, and list half, $F(1, 62) = 10.72$, $p = .002$. Also, there was tentative evidence of interactions between presentation modality and presentation rate, $F(1, 62) = 4.56$, $p = .04$, and presentation rate and list half, $F(1, 62) = 4.16$, $p = .05$. There was no evidence of interactions among type of list and presentation rate, $F(1, 62) = 0.37$, $p = .55$, type of list, presentation rate, and list half, $F(1, 62) = 0.10$, $p = .75$, or presentation modality, type of list, presentation rate, and list half, $F(1, 62) = 0.20$, $p = .66$.

The lower pair of functions within each panel of Figure 10.2 clearly shows that the modality effects had fully dissipated by the grand recall test. In conjunction with the effect of phonological similarity, this finding suggests that the slow-presentation modality effect is, at least in some ways, functionally similar to that arising with a more conventional presentation rate, which in turn supports the intuition that it is the product of echoic memory.

Study 2: Relation Between Echoic and Nonechoic Memory[4]

According to the theory of precategorical acoustic storage, echoic information is retained independently of other sources of immediate memory. A corollary of this assumption is that overall immediate memory capacity is greater for auditory than for visual lists. By contrast, the law of speech ascendancy says not that speech expands the capacity of memory but merely that it tends to ascend and linger in mind. The ascent is considered to be relative to, and at the expense of, nonechoic retention.

The very existence of the modality and suffix effects may appear to clinch the case for the theory of precategorical acoustic storage. Characterized as, respectively, an end-of-list recall advantage for auditory over visual lists and a loss of this advantage on the presentation of a spoken suffix, these effects would appear to accord with

---

[4]The experiments mentioned in this study have been reported (M. J. Watkins, 1984) but not published before.

the theory of precategorical acoustic storage rather than the law of speech ascendancy. But there are reasons for caution. First, to the extent that the mind is susceptible to extraneous thoughts during list presentation, the law of speech ascendancy, too, predicts a higher level of recall for auditory than for visual lists, for according to the law such thoughts would interfere less with auditory items than with visual items. Second, extraneous thoughts aside, the law of speech ascendancy predicts a tendency for the end-of-list modality effect to be offset by a beginning-of-list advantage for visual lists. This is because the early items, which are nonechoic regardless of presentation modality, suffer greater domination from late items if presentation is auditory, for with auditory presentation the last few items are echoic and hence tend to ascend in mind. Although given little attention, such a finding is certainly the rule. Third, introspection suggests that echoic memory preserves item order more faithfully than does nonechoic primary memory, and even if it did not, the mere knowledge that information was echoic tells something about item position, especially in the case of the last few items. It follows that the modality effect should be more dramatic if the recall test calls for position as well as for item information, and this, too, is certainly the case. Fourth, the restriction of the suffix effect to auditory lists may be a problem that is more apparent than real. The pertinent reference is Morton and Holloway (1970), and its title, "Absence of a Cross-Modal 'Suffix Effect' in Short-Term Memory," has proven to be more influential than its findings, which show a clear and statistically convincing auditory suffix effect on the serial recall of a visual list. That this effect was neither as localized nor as large as the effect on auditory lists is in keeping with the law of speech ascendancy because those list items in mind, and hence vulnerable to the suffix, at the conclusion of list presentation would be less likely to be from near the end of the list and less likely to carry position information if presentation were visual than if it were auditory.

Study 2 was designed to provide more direct evidence on the relative merits of the theory of precategorical acoustic storage and the law of speech ascendancy as explanations of the modality effect. The idea was to compare the modality effect obtained with pure auditory and pure visual lists with that obtained with lists of mixed auditory and visual items. Both explanations predict, correctly (Murdock & Walker, 1969), that the effect will be larger with mixed-modality presentation— the theory of PAS because a fixed amount of echoic information will extend over more serial positions when the auditory items are spread out; the law of speech ascendancy because the ascent of the auditory items will be at the expense of the more vulnerable visual items. The predictions differ in detail, however. According to the theory of PAS, the enhancement in the modality effect arises solely because the auditory recency effect is stronger with mixed-modality lists than with pure auditory lists. According to the law of speech ascendancy, by contrast, it arises not only because mixed-modality lists yield a stronger auditory recency effect but also because they yield a correspondingly weaker visual recency effect. The purpose of Experiment 3 was to put these predictions to the test.

Experiment 3

Method

Twenty Rice University undergraduates were presented with 32 lists of 18 familiar bisyllabic words. Any given subject saw on a computer monitor all of the words of one block of eight lists, heard from a tape recorder all of the words of another block, saw the odd-numbered words and heard the even-numbered words of a third block, and heard the odd-numbered words and saw the even-numbered words of the remaining block. The lists were always presented in the same order, but the modalities of the blocks varied between subjects according to a Latin-square design so that, over subjects, each list served equally often in each of the four presentation formats. Whether auditory or visual, word presentation took about 700 ms and occurred at a 1-s onset-to-onset rate.

Immediately after each list, the subjects wrote down the words they recalled. They had been told that they could write the words in any order, but that performance could be maximized by recalling the last few words first. No time limits were imposed.

Results

The key findings are summarized in Figure 10.3. Although the modality effect obtained from the single-modality lists is somewhat larger than expected, it is not as large as that obtained from the mixed-modality lists. Thus, for just the second half of the list, the recall probability for an auditorily presented word exceeded that for a visually presented word by .12 (.52 vs. .40), $t(19) = 6.59$, $p = .000$, for pure lists and by .28 (.61 vs. .33), $t(19) = 11.99$, $p = .000$, for mixed lists; the discrepancy between these modality effects was compelling, $t(19) = 7.12$, $p = .000$. Most important, these same probabilities show that the benefit of a mixed-modality format in the recall of auditory words (.61 − .52 = .09) was largely offset by a cost in the recall of visual words (.40 − .33 = .07), so that the proportion of second-half words recalled was not discernibly different for the pure-list and mixed-list formats (.46 and .47, respectively), $t(19) = 0.91$, $p = .37$.

It is perhaps worth noting the tendency for visual words to be more recallable than auditory words over the first part of the list, a tendency that was fairly convincing for the pure lists, $t(19) = 2.99$, $p = .007$, although not for the mixed lists, $t(19) = 0.93$, $p = .36$. This pattern is entirely in keeping with the law of speech ascendancy because the ascendance in mind of the last few auditory items would be at the expense of earlier auditory items in the case of single-modality lists, but largely at the expense of the last few visual items in the case of mixed-modality lists.

Of other experiments conducted along the lines of Experiment 3, two warrant mention. One involved the free recall of 12-word mixed-modality lists in which

FIGURE 10.3

Probability of recall for auditorily and visually presented words from single- and mixed-modality lists as a function of within-list position.

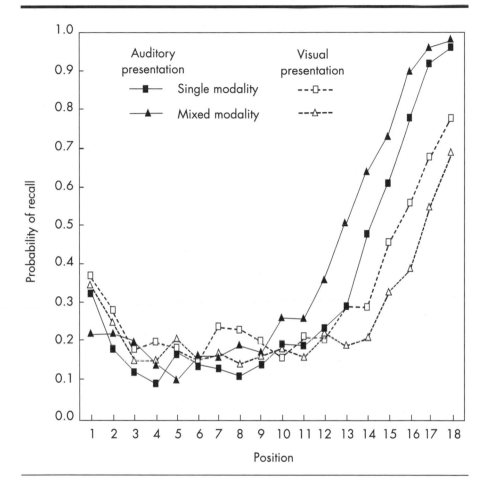

modality was blocked by list half instead of alternating across consecutive positions. Given the findings of Study 1, echoic memory should survive from the first half of the auditory–visual lists through the silent presentation of the second half. If one adopts the assumption of the modal information-processing model of immediate memory that the free recall of the last few items of a list derives primarily from a short-term postcategorical source, then the theory of PAS predicts that level of overall recall will be higher for auditory–visual lists than for visual–auditory lists. This is because immediately after list presentation, the precategorical and postcategorical stores will contain different items in the case of auditory–visual lists but substantially the same items in the case of visual–auditory lists. The prediction was not borne out. Overall recall was identical for the two kinds of list (.53), even though the auditory items had a higher probability of recall than the visual items both in the first half of the list (.53 vs. .30) and in the second (.76 vs. .53). A similar procedure, but with serial rather than free recall, has been used by Greene (1989). When the items have to be recalled in their presentation order, predictions regarding the contents of the postcategorical store are uncertain, but it is of interest to note that Greene's findings were in general accord with ours.

The other experiment warranting mention was designed to address the possibility that the increase in the size of the modality effect obtained by use of mixed-modality lists had more to do with recall order than with the contents of mind. Thus, the echoic items could be recalled first and in the process recent visual items would be lost from mind. An experiment was conducted to check this possibility. In brief, the modality effect was obtained for mixed-modality lists, both when recall was required for all items, as in Experiments 1–3, and when it was required for just the auditory or just the visual items. The subjects did not know how they would be tested until after list presentation, when they were cued with a picture of an ear, an eye, or both an ear and an eye; otherwise, the design and procedural details were much as in Experiment 3. The modality effect was just as large (indeed, trivially larger) with part-list recall than with whole-list recall, implying that the enhancement of the modality effect with mixed-modality lists is not a recall order effect.

Study 3: Modality Effect With Lists of Phrases

According to the theory of PAS, the modality effect derives from the retention of speech at a level of analysis prior to categorization into words. Because this retention is by way of a store of limited capacity, the limits of echoic memory should be in precategorical units. Long ago, as a graduate student, I tested this notion by comparing the modality effects for lists of short (1-syllable) and long (4-syllable) words. Contrary to the theory of PAS, the modality effect was just as large and just as extensive for the long-word lists as for the short-word lists (M. J. Watkins, 1972; see also M. J. Watkins & Watkins, 1973). It should be added that this result does not obtain if the words are unfamiliar to the subjects (Nilsson, 1975; see M. J. Watkins & Watkins, 1975). Given the plausible assumption that the concern of the mind is more with meaning than with sublexical information, these findings are in keeping with the law of speech ascendancy.

This line of reasoning can be taken a step further. Just as echoic memory for word lists seems to be of meaningful words rather than of their precategorical elements, so echoic memory for regular discourse seems to be of meaningful word clusters rather than of individual words. At the very least, this would seem to be true for well-worn phrases and idioms, in which the individual words are either somewhat redundant or else not especially predictive of meaning. Therefore, the modality effect might reasonably be expected to embrace more words if the words are presented not in random order and at an even rate but grouped into distinct phrases. This prediction was tested in Experiment 4.

Experiment 4

Method

Patricia Haertlein, at the time a Rice University undergraduate, and I tested this reasoning by presenting subjects with lists of alternating visually and auditorily presented phrases for free recall. Using dictionaries of catch phrases and idioms and various other sources, we formed a large pool of 3- and 4-word phrases, which we culled to a set of 168 on the basis of both familiarity ratings made by peers of those who would serve as subjects and a requirement that each phrase include a "critical" word not shared by any other phrase in the set. The phrases of this set comprised an average of 3.42 words. Examples are *out of the blue, pure as snow, law of the jungle, bright and early, peace and quiet, fly off the handle, down and out, over the rainbow, no doubt about it,* and *think nothing of it.* The phrases were assembled into 14 12-phrase lists, of which the first 2 were used for practice and the remaining 12 for the experiment proper. For any given subject, the phrases of half of the lists, including one of the practice lists, were stripped to just the critical word. Both word and phrase lists were presented at a rate of one item (word or phrase) every 5 s. Every other item, whether of a word list or phrase list, was displayed in uppercase letters in the center of a computer monitor for 1.5 s, followed by a 3.5-s blank interval. The intervening items were spoken in a clear female voice synchronous with the presentation of a row of asterisks. In the experiment proper, each block of 4 lists included 2 word lists and 2 phrase lists. For 1 word list and 1 phrase list within each block, presentation of the odd-numbered items was auditory and that of the even-numbered items visual; for the other 2 lists, the modalities were reversed. Counterbalancing measures ensured that across subjects, each list appeared in word and phrase forms equally often and that within each of these forms, it was assigned to the two modality orders equally often.

Following each list, the subjects were allowed as much time as they wished to write down in any order as many of the list items as they could remember. After recall of the last list, they were allowed 10 min. for a grand recall test, in which they wrote, again in any order, all of the words and phrases they could remember. The subjects were 24 Rice University undergraduates.

Results

The results are summarized in Figure 10.4. Although their details could be expected to vary merely by virtue of a difference in level of overall performance, the modality effects for word lists (lefthand panel) and phrase lists (righthand panel) were of

FIGURE 10.4

Probability of recall for auditorily and visually presented words and phrases as a function of within-list position.

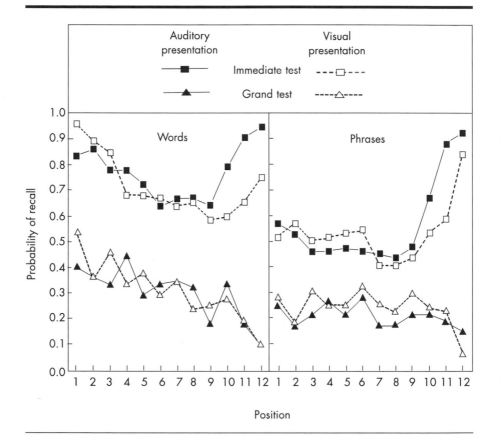

comparable magnitude and spanned about the same number of items, even though each item of the phrase lists comprised 3 or 4 words. Clearly, the modality effect is sensitive to meaning at a level beyond that of individual words.

Inferential analyses of the immediate recall data revealed the lack of a compelling main effect of presentation modality, $F(1, 23) = 1.61, p = .22$, but a clear interaction of presentation modality with list half, $F(1, 23) = 22.87, p = .000$, reflecting a switch from a visual advantage in the first half of the list to an auditory advantage in the second half. Of more particular concern for present purposes, there was no convincing evidence that either the effect of presentation modality or the interaction between presentation modality and list half depended on type of list: For the interaction between presentation modality and type of list, $F(1, 23) = 0.31, p = .55$, and for the second-order interaction between presentation modality, list half, and type of list, $F(1, 23) = 0.00, p = 1.00$. The analysis also showed a clear main effect of type of list, $F(1, 23) = 106.18$, $p < .001$, reflecting a higher level of recall for words than for phrases, and a lack of a main effect of list half, $F(1, 23) = 0.01$, $p < .93$. Finally, the interaction between type of list and list half was convincing, $F(1, 23) = 27.32$, $p = .000$, reflecting a primacy advantage for words and a recency advantage for phrases (cf. Glanzer & Razel, 1974).

The grand recall test showed a tendency for a negative recency effect, especially for the words. Of more concern here is the lack of a clear auditory advantage, even over the recency positions, for either the word or phrase lists. This null effect demonstrates that the auditory recency advantage shown in immediate recall was transient.

Conclusion

These experiments demonstrate that memory can be researched without being reified. Although ordinary in both method and yield, they are apparently extraordinary in having been conceived without reification, without reference to the mechanism of the information-processing conception of memory. Of course, enacting the law of speech ascendancy can be construed as tantamount to affirming one of the more venerable constructs of the information-processing era, namely echoic memory. But claiming that primary memory may take on an echoic character is not the same as invoking echoic traces, stores, or neural tissue. Granted the license of metaphoric extension, echoic memory can be reified and so applied to the material realms of natural science and engineering. But, however fashionable, such a practice should not obscure the fact that, as with primary memory generally (James, 1890), it is the fundamentally mental status of echoic memory that secures it a place within the realm of psychology.

References

Balota, D. A., & Duchek, J. M. (1986). Voice-specific information and the 20-second delayed-suffix effect. *Journal of Experimental Psychology: Learning, Memory, and Cognition, 12,* 509–516.

Bloom, L. C. (1999). *Control and organization in primary memory: Evidence from suffix effects.* Unpublished doctoral dissertation, Rice University, Houston, TX.

Bower, G. H., Clark, M. C., Lesgold, A. M., & Winzenz, D. (1969). Hierarchical retrieval schemes in recall of categorized word lists. *Journal of Verbal Learning and Verbal Behavior, 8,* 501–506.

Brems, D. (1984). *The persistence of echoic memory: Evidence from the effect of presentation modality in immediate and final recall tests.* Unpublished master's thesis, Rice University, Houston, TX.

Corballis, M. C. (1966). Rehearsal and decay in immediate recall of visually and aurally presented items. *Canadian Journal of Psychology, 20,* 43–51.

Crowder, R. G. (1967). Prefix effects in immediate memory. *Canadian Journal of Psychology, 21,* 450–461.

Crowder, R. G. (1976). *Principles of learning and memory.* Hillsdale, NJ: Erlbaum.

Crowder, R. G., & Morton, J. (1969). Precategorical acoustic storage (PAS). *Perception and Psychophysics, 5,* 365–373.

Glanzer, M., & Razel, M. (1974). The size of the unit in short-term storage. *Journal of Verbal Learning and Verbal Behavior, 13,* 114–131.

Greene, R. L. (1989). Immediate serial recall of mixed-modality lists. *Journal of Experimental Psychology: Learning, Memory, and Cognition, 15,* 266–274.

Greene, R. L. (1992). *Human memory: Paradigms and paradoxes.* Hillsdale, NJ: Erlbaum.

James, W. (1890). *Principles of psychology.* New York: Holt.

Morton, J., & Holloway, C. M. (1970). Absence of a cross-modal "suffix effect" in short-term memory. *Quarterly Journal of Experimental Psychology, 22,* 167–176.

Murdock, B. B., & Walker, K. D. (1969). Modality effects in free recall. *Journal of Verbal Learning and Verbal Behavior, 8,* 665–676.

Murray, D. J. (1965). Vocalization of presentation and immediate recall with varying presentation rates. *Quarterly Journal of Experimental Psychology, 13,* 47–56.

Neath, I. (1998). *Human memory: An introduction to research, data, and theory.* Pacific Grove, CA: Brooks/Cole.

Nilsson, L.G. (1975). Locus of the modality effect in free recall: A reply to Watkins. *Journal of Experimental Psychology: Human Learning and Memory, 104,* 13–17.

Raaijmakers, J. G. W., & Shiffrin, R. M. (1981). Search of associative memory. *Psychological Review, 88,* 93–104.

Watkins, M. J. (1972). Locus of the modality effect in free recall. *Journal of Verbal Learning and Verbal Behavior, 11,* 644–688.

Watkins, M. J. (1978). Theoretical issues. In M. M. Gruneberg & P. E. Morris (Eds.), *Aspects of memory* (pp. 40–60). London: Methuen.

Watkins, M. J. (1979). Engrams as cuegrams and forgetting as cue overload: A cueing approach to the structure of memory. In C. R. Puff (Ed.), *Memory organization and structure* (pp. 347–372). New York: Academic Press.

Watkins, M. J. (1984, April). *Short-term memory and the law of auditory ascendancy.* Paper presented to the annual meeting of the Southern Workers in Memory at the Southeastern Psychological Association, New Orleans, LA.

Watkins, M. J. (1990). Mediationism and the obfuscation of memory. *American Psychologist, 45,* 328–335.

Watkins, M. J. (1991). An experimental psychologist's view of cognitive science. In R. G. Lister & H. J. Weingartner (Eds.), *Perspectives in cognitive neuroscience* (pp. 132–144). New York: Oxford University Press.

Watkins, M. J., & Todres, A. K. (1980). Suffix effects manifest and concealed: Further evidence for a 20-second echo. *Journal of Verbal Learning and Verbal Behavior, 19,* 46–53.

Watkins, M. J., & Watkins, O. C. (1973). The postcategorical status of the modality effect in serial recall. *Journal of Experimental Psychology, 99,* 226–230.

Watkins, M. J., & Watkins, O. C. (1975). A categorically postcategorical interpetation of the modality effect: A reply to Nilsson. *Journal of Experimental Psychology: Human Learning and Memory, 1,* 733–735.

Watkins, M. J., Watkins, O. C., & Crowder, R. G. (1974). The modality effect in free and serial recall as a function of phonological similarity. *Journal of Verbal Learning and Verbal Behavior, 13,* 430–447.

Watkins, O. C., & Watkins, M. J. (1975). Buildup of proactive inhibition as a cue-overload effect. *Journal of Experimental Psychology: Human Learning and Memory, 104,* 442–452.

Watkins, O. C., & Watkins, M. J. (1980). The modality effect and echoic persistence. *Journal of Experimental Psychology: General, 109,* 251–278.

CHAPTER 11

Recency and Recovery in Human Memory

Robert A. Bjork

As time passes following a series of to-be-remembered items or events, there is a shift from recency to primacy in the ease of access to the memory representations corresponding to those events or items. Such effects occur on many time scales, across species, and for a variety of to-be-remembered materials. In this chapter, I argue that this shift, with delay, from preferential access to newer memory representations to preferential access to older representations is adaptive; I also argue that such shifts reflect the interplay of certain fundamental storage and retrieval dynamics that characterize human memory.

A chapter on recency and recovery dynamics in human memory is especially appropriate for this volume because Robert Crowder played an early and critical role in the efforts to understand the theoretical implications of recency and primacy effects and changes in those effects over time. He contributed both directly, through his own research and writing—as I attempt to indicate at various points in this chapter—and indirectly, through his students, who have shaped the field of memory research across the past several decades.

Before I move on to an analysis of the shift from recency to primacy with delay, which is the primary focus of this chapter, I need to review the evidence that recency effects reflect retrieval processes in human memory that are backward looking and sensitive to the temporal distinctiveness of to-be-recalled items. Much of the evidence for that conclusion was triggered by the introduction of the continuous-distractor paradigm, which I discuss in the next section.

Continuous-Distractor Paradigm

By accident, William Whitten and I (Whitten & Bjork, 1972, 1977), in a series of experiments on tests as learning events, stumbled across long-term effects of recency

I thank Arthur Glenberg, Ian Neath, and Henry Roediger for insightful comments on this chapter.

in a paradigm we designed to eliminate any such effects. To eliminate both primacy and recency effects, we devised what later came to be called (among other names) the *continuous-distractor paradigm*. We presented pairs of words to be remembered, we instructed the participants to restrict their rehearsal and other mnemonic activities to one pair at a time, and we required the participants to carry out a distracting (rehearsal preventing) arithmetic task before and after each pair. We then delayed the final test of participants' free recall by an additional period of arithmetic activity.

According to then-prevailing views, this procedure should have largely or entirely nullified the rehearsal and short-term-memory dynamics responsible for primacy and recency effects in free recall. Eliminating cumulative rehearsal across the early pairs should have eliminated primacy effects, and the final period of distraction, which was designed to exceed the holding time of short-term memory by a considerable margin, should have eliminated recency effects.

In fact, however, as shown in Figure 11.1, Whitten and I obtained striking effects of recency that extended back in time far beyond the holding-time limits of short-term memory. Our initial experiment included—during the period of distraction following the presentation of a given pair—an embedded overt test on, or covert rehearsal opportunity for, that pair. We entertained the possibility that such test and rehearsal events, which were the actual focus of our first experiment, might have somehow contributed to the long-term recency effects we obtained. In subsequent experiments, however, we were able to show that such effects were also obtained when such test and rehearsal events were eliminated. We also found that such effects did not appear with recognition testing, which suggested that the observed effects reflected retrieval dynamics in the recall of episodic events.

Whitten and I obtained these and other findings with variants of the continuous-distractor paradigm, which led the two of us and a number of other researchers, particularly Robert Crowder, to question not only the standard short-term-memory interpretation of recency effects in free recall but also—especially in Robert Crowder's view—the distinction between short-term and long-term memory. (We also obtained effects of primacy—as shown in Figure 11.1—which were later shown by Glenberg and his collaborators [e.g., Glenberg et al., 1980] to disappear if participants' opportunities and motivation to engage in cumulative rehearsal of successive word pairs were entirely eliminated.)

Recency-Sensitive Retrieval Processes

After initially being puzzled by the long-term recency effects we obtained and after a series of follow-up experiments, we (R. A. Bjork & Whitten, 1974) became convinced that the continuous-distractor paradigm reveals fundamental recency-sensitive retrieval processes—which, we argued, are "obscured by procedural characteristics of typical free-recall experiments" (p. 173). On the basis of our findings, we proposed

FIGURE 11.1

Recall probability as a function of input serial position. From "Recency-Sensitive Retrieval Processes in Long-Term Free Recall," by R. A. Bjork and W. B. Whitten, 1974, Cognitive Psychology, 6, p. 175. Copyright 1974 by Academic Press. Reprinted with permission.

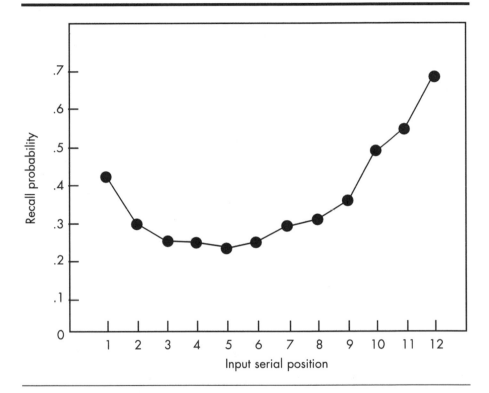

that retrieval of the memory representations resulting from a well-ordered series of episodic events is a backward-looking process that results in preferential access to the most recent of those events.

Recency and the Ratio Rule

More specifically, we (R. A. Bjork & Whitten, 1974) proposed that

> recall following a series of ordered inputs to memory will exhibit long-term recency provided the inputs constitute a well-ordered series. Whether a series is well ordered in time is determined by two requirements: (a) Each input, whether a single item, two items, or a list of items, must be discrete in the sense that any encoding or rehearsal activities are focused on only the current item at any point in time; and (b) the actual temporal separation between adjacent inputs to memory must be at least a certain fraction of the retention interval from the presentation to the recall of those inputs. (p. 184)

The first of those requirements reflects a recognition that processes of interassociation and rehearsal during the study of a series of to-be-remembered items or events can reorder and smear the "input" positions of items or events. That is, the functional recency of a given event or item may not be determined by its nominal recency but, rather, by the point when it was last rehearsed or associated with some later event or item in the series.

The second requirement, and the kind of "Weber–Fechner reasoning" (R. A. Bjork & Whitten, 1974, p. 184) that lies behind it, is a key aspect of the proposal. The basic idea is that retrieval of a series of episodic events, as a kind of backward-looking search of memory, is sensitive to the temporal distinctiveness of the events in the series, but that such distinctiveness is determined by "the ratio of the temporal separation of successive to-be-remembered items (or sets of items) to the temporal delay from those items to the point of recall" (p. 189) rather than by the temporal separation of successive events per se. In other words, analogous to perceptual judgments of various types, whether representations in memory remain temporally distinct depends on their separation relative to the time that has elapsed prior to an effort to recall those events.

The ratio rule implies that recency effects that are present at one point in time disappear with a longer retention interval. In a test of that implication, we (R. A. Bjork & Whitten, 1974) presented four continuous-distractor lists, and we administered an end-of-experiment final free-recall test for all words from all lists—in addition to an end-of-list free-recall test after each list. On the final test, consistent with the ratio rule, within-list recency effects were no longer present, but there were between-list recency effects. That is, at the end of the experiment, the lists themselves constituted a well-ordered series but the word pairs within a list did not because, presumably, the interval separating successive pairs within a list was no longer substantial enough, relative to the increased retention interval, to make those pairs temporally distinct in memory.

It occurred to us (R. A. Bjork & Whitten, 1974) that the list-recency effects we obtained on the end-of-experiment test should also, according to the ratio rule, disappear at long enough retention intervals. When we contacted the participants the next day, unexpectedly from their standpoint, and asked them to free recall as many of the words from the studied lists as they could, the list-recency effects we had observed at the end of the experimental session were no longer in evidence. Our findings prompted us (R. A. Bjork & Whitten, 1974) to comment that "extended to its limit, the [ratio rule] implies that independent of time scale, recency effects that obtain at the conclusion of an ordered series of inputs to memory should disappear given that recall is delayed sufficiently" (p. 188).

Crowder's Elaboration of the Ratio-Rule Argument

Robert Crowder—in his 1976 textbook *Principles of Learning and Memory,* a masterwork of elegant writing and scholarship that became the basic text for graduate courses in human memory for the next 10–15 years—provided an especially clear and compelling characterization of the temporal-distinctiveness (ratio-rule) model William Whitten and I proposed. He also pointed out, in detail, the important implications of such temporal-distinctiveness mechanisms, not only for the understanding of recency effects but also for the distinction (or the lack thereof) between short-term and long-term memory and for the dynamics of proactive and retroactive interference. Because his analysis was so clear and provocative, and because his text, in addition to being the standard graduate text in human memory, also served as an indispensable resource for memory researchers, his arguments had a large impact on the field, triggering additional empirical and theoretical research on the role of temporal distinctiveness.

Crowder (1976) summarized his argument with the following passage; his telephone-pole analogy, which I italicized, captures the ratio-rule idea in a particularly concrete and compelling way.

It is now time to examine in detail the alternative recency mechanism proposed by Bjork & Whitten. . . . There are several steps to the argument. First, they note that there is no long-term (or short-term, for that matter) effect of recency when testing occurs by recognition rather than recall for their experimental conditions. . . . This finding permits the conclusion that the source of recency is located at the retrieval stage rather than at acquisition or during storage. The second part of the argument is a loose assumption that, somehow at retrieval, the subject looks back toward his memories for the recent past much as, when we are moving through space, we can look back over the most recent objects we have passed. The temporal-spatial parallel is too convenient to resist following further: *The items in a memory list, being presented at a constant rate, pass by with the same regularity as do telephone poles when one is on a moving train. The crucial assumption is that just as each telephone pole in the receding distance becomes less and less distinctive from its neighbors, likewise each item in the memory list becomes less distinctive from the other list items as the presentation episode recedes into the past.*

The third assumption of the alternative theory of recency has to do with how discriminability of equally spaced events is related to the passage of time. . . . Although two events that occur 2 sec apart do not ever change their objective separation, we seem to perceive them in a way that later, say a full hour later, these two events are perceived subjectively to have occurred at the same time. One possibility for an index of discriminability is an application of Weber's law stating that the necessary change in stimulus energy for a change in perceived intensity is a constant fraction of the baseline intensity. . . . This would hold that the amount of time by which two adjacent memories would need to be separated in order to be discriminable would be a constant fraction of the distance back, in time, of the younger memory. . . . *In terms of our telephone poles receding in space, the further one is from the two poles, the more widely spaced they must be in order to look separate.*

These assumptions permit a theory of recency that holds up under every situation where recency is found, unlike the possibilities we have considered. (pp. 461–462, emphasis added)

Crowder saw R. A. Bjork and Whitten's (1974) findings, and the temporal-distinctive-ness model, as a challenge to concept of primary (short-term) memory;

that is, to the prevailing idea that there exists a primary-memory component of human memory that differs in fundamental ways from the long-term component of human memory. He pointed out that "to an extraordinary degree the concept of primary memory has been tied to the recency effect in free recall" (Crowder, 1976, p. 170), but that the temporal-distinctiveness model provided an account of "the original recency effect with conventional procedures, the removal of this effect by a distractor task after the last item and its restoration by the Bjork and Whitten manipulation" (pp. 172–173). The argument is that with conventional (immediate) free-recall procedures the last few list items, even without being separated by a distractor activity of some kind, are temporally distinct at the start of the recall process, but that they become indistinct if recall is delayed, even by 30 s or so, which accounts for the findings of Postman and Phillips (1965), Glanzer and Cunitz (1966), and other researchers, including R. A. Bjork and Whitten (1974). With the continuous-distractor procedure, recency effects survive such a delay because the greater temporal separation of successive list items keeps them temporally distinct for a longer period of time.

Crowder's basic argument, which he voiced more vigorously in subsequent publications, was that if a single mechanism could explain both short-term and long-term effects of recency there might not be a need for the concept of a separate short-term (primary) memory. In his subsequent analysis of another procedure used to study short-term-memory phenomena, the Brown–Peterson paradigm, he made similar arguments.

"Using an analogy with depth perception, and recalling the similar argument made in Chapter 6 to understand the data of Bjork and Whitten (1974)," Crowder (1976) continued,

> we see why performance deteriorates during the retention interval of any particular trial in the Brown–Peterson situation: When the stimulus has just been presented (that is, at an early retention interval) its own age in storage is just a tiny fraction of the ages of traces from other, previous items; there is a big differential in time between the correct item and potential interfering items, enhancing their temporal discriminability. However, after some time spent performing the distractor activity the various traces, correct and incorrect, have all receded toward the past and have become less distinct as they all recede into the distance. (p. 211)

After reviewing the body of research on the Brown–Peterson paradigm, and considering four other hypotheses that had been offered to explain the observed buildup of proactive interference across Brown–Peterson trials, Crowder (1976) concluded that the retrieval-discriminability hypothesis is consistent "with the evidence that we have used to reject, one by one, the other four hypotheses" (p. 213).

Generality of Long-Term Recency and the Ratio Rule

R. A. Bjork and Whitten (1974) speculated that their findings might reveal a fundamental law of sorts governing the retrieval of episodic events—independent of time scale and type of event. Robert Crowder not only endorsed that speculation but also pointed to even broader implications of the temporal-distinctiveness (ratio-rule) idea. It was other researchers, however, who gathered evidence that long-term recency was indeed general, provided certain conditions were met, and that the ratio rule, to a first approximation, accounted for the presence or absence of recency effects over a great range of temporal intervals. The following are some of those findings.

1. Alan Baddeley and his collaborators reported two naturalistic studies in which pronounced long-term recency effects were obtained over intervals of weeks and months. Baddeley and Hitch (1977) asked rugby players to recall the names of the teams they had played during the many weeks of the Rugby Union competition. They found a pronounced and long-term recency effect. Pinto and Baddeley (1991) examined participants' memory for parking locations. In one experiment, they surreptitiously recorded where their colleagues at the Applied Psychology Unit (APU) in Cambridge, England, had parked on arriving at the APU in the morning. They then tested each colleague's ability to remember where he or she had parked his or her car during the preceding 25 working days or so. In a second experiment, Pinto and Baddeley examined how well individuals who had visited the APU only once or twice (to serve as experimental participants) could remember—after delays that ranged from 2 to 6 weeks—where they had parked in the APU lot. As in the case of memory for rugby games, memory for parking locations exhibited recency effects extending back across days and weeks.

2. Rigorous and convincing support for the ratio rule was provided by Glenberg and his colleagues (Glenberg, Bradley, Kraus, & Renzaglia, 1983; Glenberg et al., 1980) and by Hitch, Rejman, and Turner (1980, reported by Baddeley, 1986). Both groups of researchers, using somewhat different procedures, covaried the interpresentation interval (IPI) between successive items in a list and the retention interval (RetI) from the last item to the test for recall of the list. In each case, the size of the recency effect obtained was fit well by a linear function of the log of the IPI:RetI ratio. Glenberg and his collaborators were able to show that the ratio rule not only gave a good account of the findings for IPIs of 4, 12, and 36 s and RetIs of 12, 36, and 72 s but also gave a good account for IPIs of 5 min., 20 min., 1 day, and 7 days, and RetIs of 40 min., 1 day, and 14 days. Pinto and Baddeley (1991), in their study of participants' memory for parking locations, also found support for the ratio rule. For those participants who parked twice in the APU parking lot, either 2 weeks and 4 weeks earlier or 4 weeks and 6 weeks earlier, the percentage of correct recall of given parking location was again fit well by a linear function of the log of ratio of the IPI (interparking, in this case) and RetI.

3. Watkins and Peynircioglu (1983) were able to demonstrate that participants' memories for interleaved events from three different categories exhibited pronounced recency across the events in each category. That is, they obtained three recency effects at the same time, each of which extended back in time far beyond the reach of short-term memory. The participants in Watkins and Peynircioglu's experiment were presented multiple lists, each of which consisted of the 15 members of a single category or the 45 members of three different categories. In the three-category case, the members of a first category were presented in list positions 1, 4, . . ., 43; the members of a second category in list positions 2, 5, . . ., 44; and the members of the third category in positions 3, 6, . . ., 45. After each single-category list, the category name was presented as a cue to participants to free recall the 15 members of that list. After each triple-category list, the names of the three categories were presented in succession as a cue to participants to free recall, in turn, as many members of each category as they could.

Watkins and Peynircioglu (1983) made the categories of to-be-remembered events distinct from each other, which they suggested is an essential part of their procedure, and they also structured the categories so that participants had to make some kind of active response when a member of a category was presented. Thus, in the "favorites" category, for example, the experimenter inquired as to a participant's favorite kind of pet, hobby, and so forth, which the participant then had to write down and remember. Other examples were the "drawings" category in which participants heard the name of an item, such as an umbrella or house, and had to quickly draw a simple sketch of that item, and the "sounds" category in which segments of sounds taken from sound-effect recordings, such as the sound of an owl, had to be identified and remembered. On average, the members of the to-be-remembered categories were presented about one every 10 seconds.

The results from the Watkins and Peynircioglu's (1983) three-category conditions are shown in Figure 11.2. As is apparent from the figure, there were pronounced recency effects across the 15 members of each category—effects that were comparable, in fact, to the recency effects obtained for the single-category lists. Because the members of the three categories were interleaved, the recency effects across the last 7 members or so of each category, as shown in Figure 11.2, actually extended back about 21 list positions from the end of a three-category list. Apparently, and consistent with ratio-rule arguments, the substantial interval between successive members of a given category—which was created by the presentations of one member from each of the other two categories—was sufficient to

FIGURE 11.2

Proportion category-cued free recall as a function of cuing order and within-category input serial position and for each set of presentation positions within the full list. From "Three Recency Effects at the Same Time," by M. J. Watkins and Z. F. Peynircioglu, 1983, Journal of Verbal Learning and Verbal Behavior, 22, p. 383. Copyright 1983 by Academic Press. Reprinted with permission.

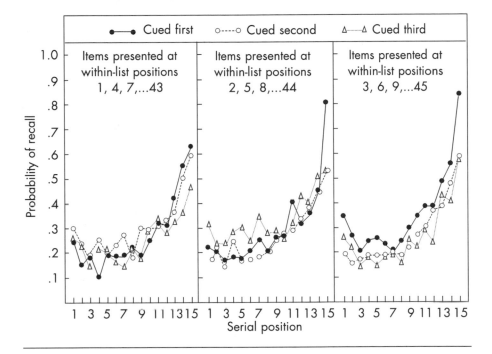

make the last 7 members or so of each category temporally distinct at the time of recall.

4. Finally, Wright, Santiago, Sands, Kendrick, and Cook (1985) demonstrated that recency effects consistent with ratio-rule arguments could be obtained not only on many time scales and for many types of to-be-remembered materials but also across species. Using a memory-search paradigm that was adapted for pigeons, monkeys, and humans, Wright et al. found strikingly similar recency effects for all three species, which then disappeared if the memory probe following a given list was delayed.

Temporal Distinctiveness, Retention Functions, and the Passage of Time

One thrust of the ratio-rule analyses summarized above, and more broadly the role of temporal distinctiveness in determining level of recall, is that elapsed time per se plays little or no role in forgetting. Because forgetting functions, as typically measured and plotted, show an orderly decrease in performance with the passage of time, it is tempting to conclude that passage of time is the cause of forgetting. In Robert Crowder's (1976) words,

> intuitively, the most obvious aspect of forgetting is that we recall more and more poorly with the passage of time. It is quite natural in light of this intuition to suppose that memories fade because of the lapse of time since learning. Thorndike (1914) formalized this reasoning in his "law of disuse," which maintained that although use of habits leads to strengthening of them, the passage of time without practice, that is, disuse, weakened them. (p. 218)

Crowder went on, however, to point out that intuition and Thorndike's "law" are misguided, as McGeoch (1932), who "is generally credited with having buried the law of disuse, or decay theory, as the same idea is often called" (Crowder, 1976, p. 218), was the first to demonstrate. On the basis of both logic and empirical findings, McGeoch argued that the passage of time per se was unsatisfying and inadequate as a theoretical mechanism. He argued that rust, for example, is correlated with, but not caused by, the passage of time. McGeoch's most convincing arguments derived from evidence that degree of forgetting across a fixed retention interval could vary greatly, depending on what happened in that interval, and that under some conditions recall can increase with the passage of time.

The ratio-rule findings summarized above provide additional evidence that conditions exist where memory performance increases, rather than decreases, with retention interval. Increasing the activity and time between two successive to-be-remembered events—which, all other things being equal, also increases the retention interval to the first of those events—improves access to and, hence, recall of that event.

A compelling example of the importance of temporal distinctiveness and of the irrelevance of the passage of time was provided by Glenberg and Swanson (1986). They presented each of four pairs of to-be-remembered words auditorily. In a control condition, corresponding to the standard continuous-distractor procedure, there was a 4-s distraction period before each word pair and 10 s of distraction between the last pair and a free-recall test for the word pairs. In a second condition everything was the same, except for one crucial difference: 40 s of distraction rather than 4 s separated the first and second word pairs. In that condition, then, the retention interval for the first pair consisted of 58 s of distraction (plus the brief times necessary to present the second, third, and fourth pairs), whereas that same interval in the control condition included 22 s of distraction, nearly a three to one difference. The outcome, however, was superior recall of the first word pair in the condition with the much longer interval between the first and second word pairs (58% vs. 32%).

In the next section, I focus on another finding—the shift from recency to primacy with delay—that also illustrates, among other things, that recall performance for certain items can increase, not decrease, as they become less recent.

Shift From Recency to Primacy With Delay

On many time scales, for multiple types of events or materials, there is a shift from recency to primacy as the retention interval from the end of a list to a test of some kind increases. In the immediate free recall of a list of words, for example, recency effects are larger than primacy effects (e.g., Murdock, 1962), but that pattern is transient: On a test of final free recall, administered after several lists have been presented and tested (Craik, 1970) or not tested (R. A. Bjork, 1975), it is the early items in each list that are the best recalled and the final items in each list may even exhibit negative recency.

Such a shift occurs at the list level as well. As mentioned earlier, on an end-of-session test for all items from all lists studied during that session, the items in the recent lists are the best recalled, but that advantage is absent if recall is tested again at a 24-hour delay (R. A. Bjork & Whitten, 1974). In an experiment by Bower and Reitman (1972), in which participants learned each of five lists through a particular mnemonic method (the peg-word system), a pronounced list recency effect on an end-of-session test changed to a primacy effect across the five lists when recall was again tested after a week's delay.

A shift from recency to primacy—on a much shorter time scale—is also evident with probe (memory-search) procedures. If a list of items is presented one item at a time and then followed by a test item ("probe"), with the participant's task being to say whether the test item did or did not occur in the preceding list, there is recency at short probe delays, but primacy at longer delays (see, e.g., Knoedler, Hellwig, & Neath, 1999; Neath, 1993; and Wright et al., 1985). In fact, if the probe item matches the first item in the list, there is often an absolute increase in correct responding with delay of the probe. That is, as the retention interval increases, performance on the earliest list members increases and does not decrease.

In the learning of competing lists or habits, there is also a shift toward primacy with delay. Earlier learned habits or responses become relatively—and sometimes absolutely—more accessible with a delay, whereas later learned (competing) habits or responses become less accessible. Such a pattern is very general. It occurs in verbal-learning tasks, such as the classic A–B, A–D paired-associates list-learning paradigm, where the second to-be-learned list involves the same stimulus members as in the first list, but requires that a new response be learned to each stimulus (see Postman, 1971, for a thorough review of the spontaneous-recovery literature prior to that time; and see Wheeler, 1995, for a re-examination of recovery phenomena in verbal learning). In the clinical treatment of fears, where new, more adaptive, behaviors are learned to fearful stimuli, it is also common for there to be a gradual return of fear after treatment has concluded (see, e.g., Lang, Craske, & Bjork, 1999). There are motor skills examples as well: It is common knowledge among coaches and skilled athletes that earlier learned swings, styles, and techniques that have been replaced can often recover or reappear over time.

There are also, of course, compelling examples of such recovery in the animal-learning literature. Spontaneous recovery—in the form of a recovery, over time, of a learned response after the apparent complete extinction of that response—was first demonstrated in research on animals and dates back at least as far as the work of Pavlov (1927). Counterconditioning procedures in research on animals, which can be viewed as analogous to the A–B, A–D verbal learning paradigm, can also yield a recovery of first-learned response with time. The results of an experiment by Bouton and Peck (1992), shown in Figure 11.3, provide a good example. In a first phase of Bouton and Peck's experiment, rats were exposed to a tone followed by shock until the tone reliably elicited shock-appropriate anticipatory behavior. In a second—counterconditioning—phase, the tone was paired with food until the tone elicited food-appropriate behavior reliably. There was then a test phase, either 1 day or 28 days after the tone–food conditioning. As is apparent from Figure 11.3, the tone tended to trigger food-appropriate behavior after a 1-day retention interval, but when the testing was delayed by 28 days, the tone elicited more shock-appropriate behavior than it did food-appropriate behavior. Again, with a delay there was a shift in access toward the earlier learned behavior.

Regression as a Fundamental Property of Human Memory

The generality of such laboratory findings—across paradigms, time scales, and even species—coupled with observational and anecdotal parallels in everyday living has led me to argue elsewhere that a kind of regression process is a fundamental property of human memory (see, e.g., R. A. Bjork, 1978; and R. A. Bjork & Bjork, 1992). In the myriad instances where everyday living requires that one update procedural or declarative memory representations (by learning to operate a new car, e.g., or by learning a new tennis serve, a new married name of a friend, a new or updated computer program, or a new list in a memory experiment), one creates a competition among stored representations. At the end of the new learning, it is the more recent of those representations that is most accessible, but with the passage of time—and disuse of either representation—there is a loss of access to the more recent representation and an increase in access to the earlier representation. That is, over time, access to competing memory representations regresses toward the older of those representations.

Training personnel in sports and military contexts tend to be aware, in a general way, of such regression. In military contexts, individuals who have been apparently well trained in new procedures and equipment are at risk over time of taking actions appropriate to the old procedures or equipment, particularly under stress. Elite athletes tend to be aware that a layoff can lead to the return of old habits—which, depending on the situation, can have desirable or undesirable consequences, such as when a recent slump in performance is attributable to recently acquired bad habits and techniques.

FIGURE 11.3

Percentage of food-appropriate or shock-appropriate behavior in response to a tone sounded 1 day or 28 days after tone–food training. The tone–food training was preceded by tone–shock training. From "Spontaneous Recovery in Cross-Motivational Transfer (Counterconditioning)," by M. E. Bouton and C. A. Peck, 1992, Animal Learning and Behavior, 20, p. 316. Copyright 1992 by the Psychonomic Society. Adapted with permission.

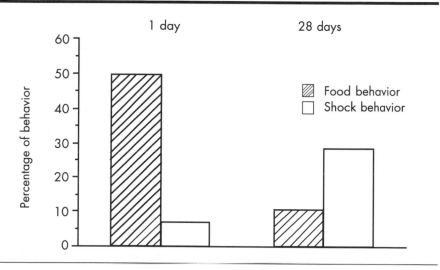

Such regression may also play a role in certain metacognitive assessments, such as estimates of how much a person or place has changed. As I emphasized elsewhere (R. A. Bjork, 1978),

> we are often surprised at how much a child had grown up, a friend has aged, or a town has changed since the last time one saw that child, friend, or town. Children do grow up, of course, friends do age, and towns do change, but a subjective judgment of such changes based on the difference between a regressed memory representation and the current state of the child, friend, or town will overestimate the actual changes. (p. 250)

Memory Regression as a Theoretical Problem

Understanding the process dynamics of regression and recovery phenomena poses a formidable theoretical problem. It is absolute recovery of the earlier of two competing representations, however, not its relative recovery, that is difficult to explain. Recovery of the earlier of two competing representations—relative to the more recent of those representations—is understandable, given the negatively accelerated form of forgetting functions. Jost (1897) may have been the first to make this point (in the first of the two "laws" he proposed): "If two associations are now of equal strength but different ages, the older one will lose strength more slowly with the passage of time" (as translated by Woodworth & Schlossberg, 1954, p. 730). Miller and Stevenson (1936) may have been the first to point out that the negatively accelerated character of forgetting over time provided a natural account of why first-learned responses recover relative to competing second-learned responses.

Absolute recovery of the first of two representations—as time and events pass following the learning of a more recent and competing representation—is much more difficult to understand. Intuitively, as mentioned earlier, one does not expect one's access to memory representations to improve over time. Absolute recovery, however, also poses a puzzle for formal theories as well as for memory researchers' intuitions, especially given that—empirically—access to first-learned responses and information can recover to the point that it exceeds access to second-learned responses and information (see Wheeler, 1995, for a similar argument).

Without some added assumptions, for example, temporal-distinctiveness mechanisms—including the ratio rule, Glenberg's (1987) "search-set" elaboration and extension of distinctiveness, and the "dimensional distinctiveness" model of Neath and his collaborators (e.g., Knoedler et al., 1999; Neath, 1993; Neath & Crowder, 1990)—cannot explain why access to the first of two competing representations should increase with delay, exceeding, eventually, access to the second, more recent, of those representations. Such ideas provide a natural explanation for why the advantage of second-learned representation over the first-learned representation should dissipate with delay and disuse, but they do not provide a mechanism to explain why access to the first representation should increase with delay—to the point where it dominates access to the more recently learned representation. In the next section I present a new interpretation of absolute recovery and an empirical test of that interpretation.

Absolute Recovery: A Possible Explanation

As Postman, Stark, and Fraser (1968) emphasized in the case of learning successive lists of paired associates, especially when those lists bear an A–B, A–D relationship— and I emphasized more broadly (R. A. Bjork, 1989)—learning new responses requires inhibiting old responses. In the case of the A–B, A–D paradigm, once A–D learning begins, the task at hand is to give the appropriate D responses, which requires not giving the earlier B responses. To the extent that the B responses come to mind during the learning of the A–D list, they need to be inhibited or suppressed.

That basic fact, viewed in the context of the "new theory of disuse" that Elizabeth Bjork and I proposed (R. A. Bjork & Bjork, 1992), suggests an explanation for why first-learned responses may recover with time, even to the point that they may dominate competing second-learned responses. The basic idea is that the need to inhibit first-list responses during second-list learning results in decreasing the retrieval strength (current accessibility) of those responses but may increase, not decrease, the storage strength (learning) of those responses.

Retrieval and Storage Strengths of First-Learned and Second-Learned Responses

In the new theory of disuse, Elizabeth Bjork and I assumed (R. A. Bjork & Bjork, 1992) that memory representations are double indexed in memory—by their current "retrieval strength" (how accessible or active they are) and their "storage strength" (how well learned or interassociated with other memory representations they are). Storage strength is assumed to accumulate as a consequence of study or practice and, once accumulated, is permanent. Retrieval strength, however, which completely determines the probability of being able to access a given stored representation, is volatile. It is assumed to increase as a consequence of study or practice but to decrease as a consequence of study or practice of competing responses or behaviors. Our theory is a "new" theory of disuse because, in contrast to Thorndike's (1914) original law of disuse, it is access to learned representation (retrieval strength) that is lost over a period of disuse, not the representation per se (storage strength).

In distinguishing between storage strength and retrieval strength, the theory resurrects a distinction that was common among learning theorists of an earlier era. The distinction is essentially the same, for example, as Hull's (1943) distinction between habit strength and momentary excitatory potential or Estes's (1955) distinction between habit strength and response strength. The distinction also corresponds, in a general way, to the time-honored distinction between learning and performance, a distinction necessitated by a range of findings from research on both humans and animals: What one observes is performance; what one is often trying to infer is learning. Storage strength and retrieval strength also correspond, roughly, to Tulving's distinction between the availability and accessibility of memory representations (see, e.g., Tulving & Pearlstone, 1966).

What is new about the theory are the assumptions governing how the current storage and retrieval strengths of a representation influence (a) the increments in the storage strength of that representation that result from study or practice and (b) the increments and decrements, respectively, in the retrieval strength of that representation that result from study or practice of that representation or competing representations. The assumptions of special pertinence to an analysis of recovery phenomena are the following:

Assumption 1. Storage strength serves to enhance the gain and retard the loss of retrieval strength. That is, access to representations in memory, as indexed by retrieval strength, is lost more slowly with disuse—and regained more rapidly given study or practice— the higher that representation's current storage strength.

Assumption 2.   The higher the current retrieval strength of a representation, the smaller the increments in both storage strength and retrieval strength that result from study or practice of that representation. Thus, somewhat surprisingly, the more accessible a representation, the smaller the increment in storage strength (learning) that results from additional study or practice of that representation. Put differently, conditions that result in forgetting (loss of retrieval strength) also create opportunities for additional learning (i.e., increments in storage strength).

As applied to a situation such as the A–B, A–D paradigm, where new learning updates or replaces old learning, the hypothesis is that the elicitation of first-list responses during second-list learning, and the need to suppress those responses, has differing consequence for the storage and retrieval strengths of those responses. More specifically, the active suppression of those responses is assumed to decrease their retrieval strength, but the elicitation process is assumed to increase the storage strength of those responses. As a consequence, by the end of second-list learning, first-list responses have lower retrieval strength than second-list responses but higher storage strength. The retrieval strength of second-list responses therefore is lost more rapidly than the retrieval strength of first-list responses, leading, perhaps, to a crossover in dominance as retention interval increases.

A Test of the Explanation

An experiment by Liu, Bjork, and Wickens (1999) was designed, in part, as a test of the foregoing conjecture. After being asked to study a first list of words, participants were then instructed to either forget or remember that list. In the forget-instruction condition, the participants were told that the first list had been presented for practice, that it should be forgotten, and that the upcoming list was the actual list to remember. In the remember-instruction condition, the participants were told that they should continue to remember the first list and that they should try to also remember the second, upcoming, list. In both conditions, a second list was then presented for study. Following the second list, half the participants in each group were asked to relearn list 1, which was then presented for study. The remaining participants in each group were presented a third list to learn. In all cases there was then a 5-min. filled retention interval after which the participants were asked to recall list 1 or list 2, but not both. The design and procedure are summarized in Figure 11.4.

Prior research on directed forgetting demonstrates that one consequence of an instruction to forget a first list is enhanced recall of the second (to-be-remembered list) list—compared with a corresponding remember-instruction condition. Recall of the first list, however, when participants are unexpectedly asked to recall that list, is impaired relative to a remember-cue condition. Liu et al. (1999) expected that same pattern of results for the condition in which recall of list 1 or list 2 was

FIGURE 11.4

Sequence of events in the relearning and no relearning conditions. From **Costs and Benefits of Directed Forgetting,** *by X. Liu, R. A. Bjork, and T. W. Wickens, November 1999, paper presented at the meeting of the Psychonomic Society, Los Angeles, CA. Reprinted with permission.*

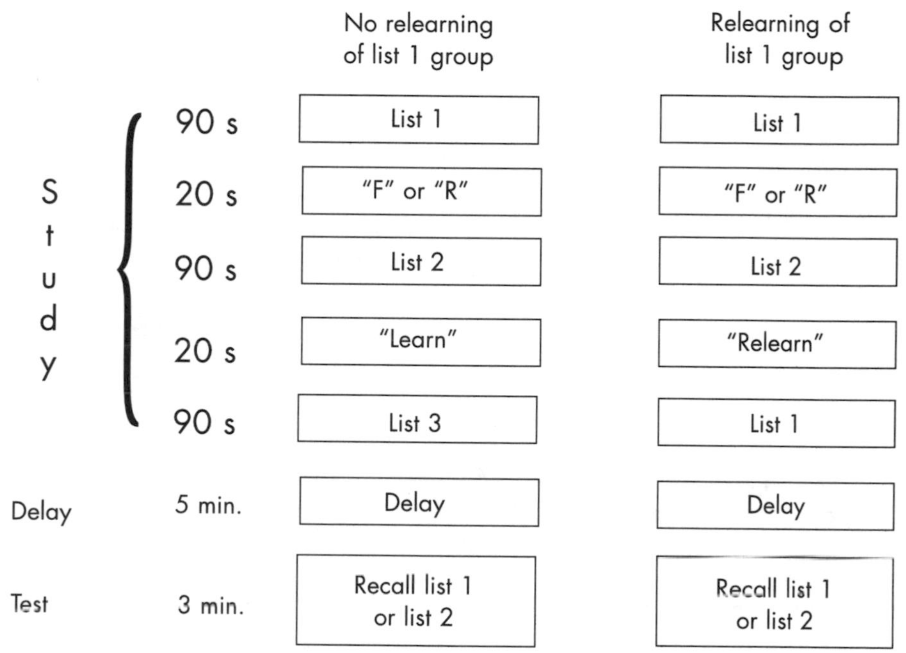

		No relearning of list 1 group	Relearning of list 1 group
	90 s	List 1	List 1
S	20 s	"F" or "R"	"F" or "R"
t u	90 s	List 2	List 2
d y	20 s	"Learn"	"Relearn"
	90 s	List 3	List 1
Delay	5 min.	Delay	Delay
Test	3 min.	Recall list 1 or list 2	Recall list 1 or list 2

delayed by the learning of a third list. That condition served as a control condition for the relearn-list-1 condition, which is the condition of primary interest.

In the condition where list 1 was relearned, the key consideration, from the perspective of the new theory of disuse, is the status of list 1 at the time of its relearning. Multiple findings from research on directed forgetting, such as unimpaired recognition of first-list to-be-forgotten items, support a conclusion that the encoding (storage strength) of first-list items is not affected by an instruction to forget those items (see, e.g., E. L. Bjork & Bjork, 1996; E. L. Bjork, Bjork, & Anderson, 1998). Instead, it is retrieval access to the first-list episode that is inhibited. At the time list 1 is relearned, then, its storage strength in the forget-instruction condition should be comparable to its storage strength in the remember-instruction condition, but its retrieval strength should be lower.

As a consequence of that pattern—that is, equal storage strength but lower retrieval strength—the new theory of disuse predicts that the relearning of list 1 should be more effective in the forget-instruction condition than in the remember-instruction condition. Such a prediction follows because increments in both storage strength and retrieval strength are assumed to be larger the lower the current retrieval strength (see Assumption 2). After relearning, then, list 1 in the forget-instruction condition should possess higher storage strength than list 1 in the remember-instruction condition and its disadvantage in retrieval strength should be narrowed. Given that combination, there should then be a slower rate of loss of retrieval strength across the final retention interval because storage strength acts to retard the loss of retrieval strength (see Assumption 1).

It follows from such reasoning that the final recall of list 1 in the forget condition should exhibit enhanced recovery versus the final recall of list 1 in the remember condition. It also follows that list 2 should retain its advantage in the forget-list-1 condition because that advantage results from more efficient encoding of list-2 items. Overall, such arguments lead to the counterintuitive prediction that total recall in the relearning condition, summed across list 1 and list 2, should be better when participants had earlier been instructed to forget list 1.

The results of Liu et al.'s (1999) experiment are shown in Figure 11.5. As predicted, list 1 shows enhanced recovery in the relearning condition, to the point

FIGURE 11.5

Percentage of free recall of words from list 1 or list 2 as a function of whether participants had been instructed to remember or forget list 2 and whether list 1 was or was not relearned after the presentation of list 2. Data from Liu et al. (1999).

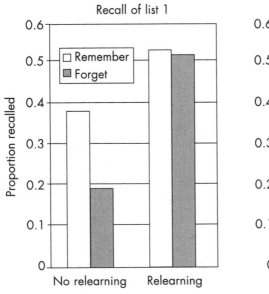
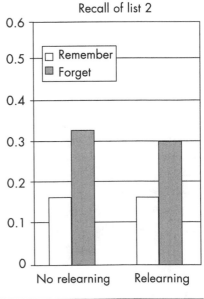

that it is recalled as well in the forget condition as in the remember condition, and list 2 retains its advantage in the forget-instruction condition. In contrast, in the control condition, in which there was no relearning of list 1, recall of lists 1 and 2 exhibits the standard pattern: enhanced recall of list 2 and impaired recall of list 1.

Concluding Comments

The results obtained by Liu et al. (1999) provide preliminary support for the proposition that recovery phenomena reflect an interplay of encoding (storage) strength and current accessibility (retrieval strength), the latter of which is volatile and subject to competitive dynamics. Whether that view holds up under more direct and rigorous testing remains to be seen.

If the shift from recency to primacy with delay—that is, memory regression— is as fundamental a property of human memory as I argue, then one might ask What, if anything, might be useful or adaptive about such a shift? My own conjecture is that the recency and recovery dynamics I sketched in this chapter result, statistically, in enhanced access to the skills and knowledge one tends to need. In general, such dynamics result in information and procedures from the recent past being the most accessible in the near future. On a statistical basis, given the characteristics of everyday work and living, that tends to be the information one most needs. If there is a long period of disuse, however, the statistics seem different. The fact that there has not been a need for recent information and procedures may signal changes that mean that older, typically better learned, information and procedures are once again relevant. Were one to spend a year in England, for example, it would be useful if— in driving a car—recent (England-appropriate) information and procedures were more accessible than less recent (U.S.-appropriate) information and procedures. But what might a period of disuse of England-appropriate procedures tend to mean? Probably that the less recent U.S.-appropriate procedures and habits are once more what are needed, meaning that a regression to less recently learned procedures and habits would definitely be adaptive.

As an evolutionary argument, the preceding driving-in-England example may be less than convincing. It is not difficult, however, to think of other examples that might have evolutionary significance. Suppose, for example, that a location long used for hunting or foraging were to become dangerous, owing to the presence of a predator, a contaminated food supply, or another reason. On the short term, it would clearly be adaptive to avoid that area, that is, to have access to relevant memories that encourage avoiding that area, but it may well be nonadaptive to avoid that region permanently. After a period of disuse, a recovery of access to memories and habits that would once again encourage hunting or foraging in that area is likely to be adaptive.

Viewed more broadly, my conjecture as to what might be useful or adaptive about a shift from recency to primacy with delay is consistent with Anderson's argument that human cognitive processes may have evolved to be a solution, perhaps optimal, to the information-processing demands posed by the environment (Anderson, 1990; Anderson & Milson, 1989). One aspect of Anderson's (1990) argument, based in part on the similarities in use statistics for library borrowings and file accessing, is that "there [may be] 'universals' in information retrieval that may transcend device and generalize to human memory" (p. 49).

Pursing the library analogy, consider the likely future-use statistics for a book that has been borrowed n times, all in the last couple months, versus another book that has been borrowed n times, but with the borrowings distributed across the past year. Anderson did not report the exact statistics of interest, but it seems clear that in the near future, it is the first of those books that is the more likely to be needed (i.e., signed out). Suppose, though, that there is a period of disuse for both books— that is, that neither book is signed out for a month or so. It then seems likely that the second book, the one with the longer history of use, is the more likely to be needed (borrowed).

Whether such statistics-of-use arguments can withstand scrutiny and additional empirical analyses remains to be seen. What is clear at this point is what Robert Crowder was probably the first to see—that temporal distinctiveness and changes in such distinctiveness with time play a critical role in the retrieval and interference dynamics that characterize human memory.

References

Anderson, J. R. (1990). *The adaptive character of thought.* Hillsdale, NJ: Erlbaum.

Anderson, J. R., & Milson, R. (1989). Human memory: An adaptive perspective. *Psychological Review, 96,* 703–719.

Baddeley, A. D. (1986). *Working memory.* New York: Oxford University Press.

Baddeley, A. D., & Hitch, G. J. (1977). Recency re-examined. In S. Dornic (Ed.), *Attention and performance VI* (pp. 647–667). Hillsdale, NJ: Erlbaum.

Bjork, E. L., & Bjork, R. A. (1996). Continuing influences of to-be-forgotten information. *Consciousness and Cognition, 5,* 176–196.

Bjork, E. L., Bjork, R. A., & Anderson, M. C. (1998). Varieties of goal-directed forgetting. In J. M. Golding & C. MacLeod (Eds.), *Intentional forgetting: Interdisciplinary approaches* (pp. 103–137). Hillsdale, NJ: Erlbaum.

Bjork, R. A. (1975). Retrieval as a memory modifier. In R. L. Solso (Ed.), *Information processing and cognition: The Loyola Symposium* (pp. 123–144). Hillsdale, NJ: Erlbaum.

Bjork, R. A. (1978). The updating of human memory. In G. H. Bower (Ed.), *The psychology of learning and motivation* (Vol. 12, pp. 235–259). New York: Academic Press.

Bjork, R. A. (1989). Retrieval inhibition as an adaptive mechanism in human memory. In H. L. Roediger & F. I. M. Craik (Eds.), *Varieties of memory and consciousness: Essays in honour of Endel Tulving* (pp. 309–330). Hillsdale, NJ: Erlbaum.

Bjork, R. A., & Bjork, E. L. (1992). A new theory of disuse and an old theory of stimulus fluctuation. In A. Healy, S. Kosslyn, & R. Shiffrin (Eds.), *From learning processes to cognitive processes: Essays in honor of William K. Estes* (Vol. 2, pp. 35 67). Hillsdale, NJ: Erlbaum.

Bjork, R. A., & Whitten, W. B. (1974). Recency-sensitive retrieval processes in long-term free recall. *Cognitive Psychology, 6,* 173–189.

Bouton, M. E., & Peck, C. A. (1992). Spontaneous recovery in cross-motivational transfer (counterconditioning). *Animal Learning and Behavior, 20,* 313–321.

Bower, G. H., & Reitman, J. S. (1972). Mnemonic elaboration in multilist learning. *Journal of Verbal Learning and Verbal Behavior, 11,* 478–485.

Craik, F. I. M. (1970). The fate of primary memory items in free recall. *Journal of Verbal Learning and Verbal Behavior, 9,* 143–148.

Crowder, R. G. (1976). *Principles of learning and memory.* Hillsdale, NJ: Erlbaum.

Estes, W. K. (1955). Statistical theory of spontaneous recovery and regression. *Psychological Review, 62,* 145–154.

Glanzer, M., & Cunitz, A. R. (1966). Two storage mechanisms in free recall. *Journal of Verbal Learning and Verbal Behavior, 5,* 351–360.

Glenberg, A. M. (1987). Temporal context and recency. In D. S. Gorfein & R. R. Hoffman (Eds.), *Memory and cognitive processes: The Ebbinghaus Centennial Conference* (pp. 173–190). Hillsdale, NJ: Erlbaum.

Glenberg, A. M., Bradley, M. M., Kraus, T. A., & Renzaglia, G. J. (1983). Studies of the long-term recency effect: Support for a contextually guided retrieval hypothesis. *Journal of Experimental Psychology: Learning, Memory, and Cognition, 9,* 231–255.

Glenberg, A. M., Bradley, M. M., Stevenson, J. A., Kraus, T. A., Tkachuck, M. J., Gretz, A. L., Fish, J. H., & Turpin, B. N. (1980). A two-process account of long-term serial position effects. *Journal of Experimental Psychology: Human Learning and Memory, 6,* 355–369.

Glenberg, A. M., & Swanson, N. (1986). A temporal distinctiveness theory of recency and modality effects. *Journal of Experimental Psychology: Learning, Memory, and Cognition, 12,* 3–15.

Hitch, G. J., Rejman, M. J., & Turner, M. C. (1980, July). *A new perspective on the recency effect.* Paper presented at the meeting of the Experimental Psychology Society, Cambridge, England.

Hull, C. L. (1943). *The principles of behavior.* New York: Appelton-Century-Crofts.

Jost, A. (1897). Die assoziationfestigkeit in ihrer abhangigheit von der verteiling der wiederholungen. *Zeitschrist für Psychologie, 14,* 436–472.

Knoedler, A. J., Hellwig, K. A., & Neath, I. (1999). The shift from recency to primacy with increasing delay. *Journal of Experimental Psychology: Learning, Memory, and Cognition, 25,* 474–487.

Lang, A. J., Craske, M. G., & Bjork, R. A. (1999). Implications of a new theory of disuse for the treatment of emotional disorders. *Clinical Psychology: Science and Practice, 6,* 80–94.

Liu, X., Bjork, R. A., & Wickens, T. W. (1999, November). *Costs and benefits of directed forgetting.* Paper presented at the meeting of the Psychonomic Society, Los Angeles, CA.

McGeoch, J. A. (1932). Forgetting and the law of disuse. *Psychological Review, 39,* 352–370.

Miller, N. E., & Stevenson, S. S. (1936). Agitated behavior of rats during experimental extinction and a curve of spontaneous recovery. *Journal of Comparative Psychology, 21,* 205–231.

Murdock, B. B., Jr. (1962). The serial position effect of free recall. *Journal of Experimental Psychology, 64,* 488.

Neath, I. (1993). Distinctiveness and serial position effects in recognition. *Memory & Cognition, 21,* 256–263.

Neath, I., & Crowder, R. G. (1990). Schedules of presentation and temporal distinctiveness in human memory. *Journal of Experimental Psychology: Learning, Memory, and Cognition, 16,* 316–327.

Pavlov, I. P. (1927). *Conditioned reflexes: An investigation of the physiological activity of the cerebral cortex.* London: Oxford University Press.

Pinto, A. da C., & Baddeley, A. D. (1991). Where did you park your car? Analysis of a naturalistic long-term recency effect. *European Journal of Cognitive Psychology, 3,* 297–313.

Postman, L. (1971). Transfer, interference, and forgetting. In J. W. Kling & L. A. Riggs (Eds.), *Woodworth and Schlossberg's experimental psychology* (3rd ed., pp. 1019–1132). New York: Holt, Rinehart, & Winston.

Postman, L., & Phillips, L. (1965). Short-term temporal changes in free recall. *Quarterly Journal of Experimental Psychology, 17,* 132–138.

Postman, L., Stark, K., & Fraser, J. (1968). Temporal changes in interference. *Journal of Verbal Learning and Verbal Behavior, 7,* 672–694.

Thorndike, E. L. (1914). *The psychology of learning.* New York: Teachers College.

Tulving, E., & Pearlstone, Z. (1966). Availability versus accessibility of information in memory for words. *Journal of Verbal Learning and Verbal Behavior, 5,* 381–391.

Watkins, M. J., & Peynircioglu, Z. F. (1983). Three recency effects at the same time. *Journal of Verbal Learning and Verbal Behavior, 22,* 375–384.

Wheeler, M. A. (1995). Improvement in recall over time without repeated testing: Spontaneous recovery revisited. *Journal of Experimental Psychology: Learning, Memory, and Cognition, 21,* 173–184.

Whitten, W. B., & Bjork, R. A. (1972, April). *Test events as learning trials: The importance of being imperfect.* Paper presented at the meeting of the Midwestern Mathematical Psychology Association, Bloomington, IN.

Whitten, W. B., & Bjork, R. A. (1977). Learning from tests: The effects of spacing. *Journal of Verbal Learning and Verbal Behavior, 16,* 465–478.

Woodworth, R. S., & Schlossberg, H. (1954). *Experimental psychology* (2nd ed.). New York: Holt.

Wright, A. A., Santiago, H. C., Sands, S. F., Kendrick, D. F., & Cook, R. G. (1985, July 19). Memory processing of lists by pigeons, monkeys, and people. *Science, 229,* 287–289.

CHAPTER 12

Modality Specificity in Cognition

The Case of Touch

Roberta L. Klatzky

Susan J. Lederman

A fundamental theme in Bob Crowder's research is the critical relationship between perception and cognition. Bob's early work, for example, compares serial position functions that followed auditory and visual presentation to trace the effect of perceptual representations on high-level memory processes. A secondary theme is that perception means more than vision. Much of Bob's work is in the domain of audition, where his research is eclectic enough to encompass word perception and music. No doubt these themes have influenced many researchers, ourselves included.

In keeping with Bob's work, we focus this chapter on the relationship between perception and cognition within a sensory modality that has been relatively neglected from a cognitive perspective, namely, the modality of touch. We began our work at a time when most people, formally or informally, considered touch to be little more than an inferior version of vision. In fact, researchers have rarely considered systems other than vision when discussing object recognition and other relatively high-level aspects of perceptual–cognitive processing. Yet our initial fascination with this modality has only deepened as we have jointly pursued, for almost 20 years, a program on cognitive aspects of touch. The results of one of these initial studies on haptic object recognition (Klatzky, Lederman, & Metzger, 1985) clearly highlight the fact that the haptic system engages in highly complex information processing. Subsequent work reveals, we believe, not only fundamental aspects of the domain of touch but more general insights into how the sensory modality with which one encounters the world affects the way it is represented in memory and thought.

The Haptic System

Let us back up a bit to describe the minimally understood—at least by most cognitive psychologists—modality of touch. The word *touch* is an encompassing one, which generically refers to sensory processes initiated by receptors underneath the skin's surface. Following Loomis and Lederman (1986), we divide touch into two broad subdomains. One is *cutaneous,* which relies on receptors in the layers of skin and directly underlying tissue. The other is *kinesthesis,* which involves receptors in muscles, tendons, and joints. This latter subdomain comes into play, in particular, when touching involves actively moving the limbs. Perception by the combination of the two subdomains is referred to as haptic perception or, more familiarly, "haptics."

Within the cutaneous and kinesthetic systems are varied sets of receptors that transduce different kinds of stimulation and give rise to distinct perceptual responses. In this way, the haptic system is similar to vision, which even as early as the retina comprises functionally and phenomenologically distinct subsystems such as form and motion. Cutaneous receptors include four distinct types of mechanoreceptors that respond to different aspects of mechanical stimulation on the skin. The classes of mechanoreceptors represent a dichotomous partitioning on each of two properties: the size of the receptive field and the rate of adaptation to continuous static stimulation. Thus, some receptors have large receptive fields and adapt rapidly; others have small receptive fields and adapt slowly; and so on. Both populations of rapidly adapting units respond well to temporal information (vibration) but not so well to a static spatial pattern. In contrast, the slowly adapting units with small receptive fields process spatial pattern well but temporal information not so well. In addition to the mechanoreceptors, other kinds of skin sensors include thermoreceptors that code cool and warm temperatures and heat flow between the skin and touched surface.

The implication of this cataloguing of cutaneous sensing is that different receptors, by virtue of their specialized responses, pick up different properties of the world. For example, the purr of a cat can be felt and heard, and it is most likely felt by rapidly adapting mechanoreceptors called "Pacinian corpuscles." Lying deep within the skin and receiving vibrations that emanate from skin sites, these receptors have poor spatial resolution. Different are the slowly adapting, small-receptive-field receptors that mediate pattern perception from the skin, which are used to read Braille.

Relative to the knowledge of the cutaneous mechanoreceptors, little is known about the perceptual properties delivered by the receptor populations in muscles, tendons, and joints. Clearly, however, knowledge of limb position and ability to judge the outcome of motor commands rely extensively on these receptors. Note that we say extensively but not exclusively. For example, the visual system certainly codes limb position and movement, and skin stretch—a cutaneous signal—may be a cue to joint angle.

Haptically Perceived Properties

So far we have kept our discussion of touch close to the sensory level. So how do people arrive at the knowledge of properties of the world, and, ultimately, how do they form memories of events in it? In simple form, the answer is that stimulation of the skin by mechanical or other means ultimately gives rise to a perception of the properties of objects and events in the world. Within the domain of haptic perception as in other sensory modalities, many properties can be perceived. In the case of visual object perception, one can talk about perceiving an object's color, shape, and size, for example. Arguably, touch is equally diverse in the information it delivers about objects, such as texture, hardness, apparent temperature, weight, shape, and volume.

The diversity of haptic receptors would, by itself, give rise to distinct properties when one encounters the world through touch. Rapidly adapting receptors tell about vibration; slowly adapting receptors tell about the spatially distributed pattern of pressure on the skin to various degrees of resolution; thermoreceptors tell about heat flow between skin and objects, which is directly related to the material from which they are made.

But there is another source of perceptual diversity. It arises from the fact that the haptic system is coupled with the ability to move one's limbs and explore the world. When one contacts a fixed surface, one can apply minimal force to maintain contact, push on it, or rub it. When one encounters a freestanding object, one can further lift it, apply forces, mold fingers to it, and sense the consequences. These myriad ways of interacting with the world produce greatly varied perceptual experiences, even when stimulating the same underlying receptor populations.

In our joint research program, we have described the coupling between actions on the world and perceptual experience by identifying a set of "exploratory procedures" (Lederman & Klatzky, 1987). An exploratory procedure is a stereotyped movement that has consequences for perception by affecting how haptic receptors are stimulated. The movement is stereotyped not so much in the particular effectors involved or in the motion of joints but in the consequences of the movement for the interaction between the explorer and the explored object. Consider, for example, an exploratory procedure that we (Lederman & Klatzky, 1987) called "lateral motion." This pattern of exploration leads to relative transverse movement between the skin and the surface of an object. One might achieve lateral motion by rubbing a surface with one's finger, toe, or, for that matter, with one's tongue. What matters is that there is motion between the skin and the surface in a transverse direction. Repeated pushing against an object is not lateral motion, although it involves motion. Static transverse force that does not yield motion (e.g., because the force is too weak relative to the coefficient of friction) is not lateral motion either.

Lateral motion is a particular exploratory procedure, and it is highly effective at delivering information about a particular object property, namely, surface texture. (We include, under the label of texture, a variety of subproperties, e.g., roughness or slipperiness.) Texture perception is facilitated by lateral motion because it enhances the responses of slowly adapting mechanoreceptors (Johnson & Lamb, 1981). Other exploratory procedures are effective at delivering information about different object properties. For example, *static contact,* use of a large hand surface with little molding to the object, is associated with perceiving the apparent warmth of a surface, presumably because the thermal signal summates over the skin (Kenshalo, 1984). *Enclosing,* molding to an object, is associated with gross shape or size. *Contour following,* running one's fingers along changing concavities and convexities of an object's envelope, is used to obtain precise shape.

We have verified the pairing of object properties and exploratory procedures through a variety of methods. For example, we (Lederman & Klatzky, 1987) observed the procedures people freely use to explore objects when performing a match-to-sample task with a targeted property, such as roughness. We also forced people to explore with procedure x while matching to a sample on property y and determined which $x-y$ pairings produced the most accurate or rapid performance.

Active movement, as manifested in exploratory procedures, expands on what the haptic receptor populations convey about the properties of objects. When stimulated by movement in different ways, the same receptors can tell different stories. For example, the slowly adapting, high-resolution receptors can tell about the pattern of an embossed surface that is held without motion against the skin, but they can also tell about surface roughness when the skin is rubbed across an object (Hsaio, Johnson, & Twombly, 1993).

Exploratory procedures, although they provide a means for expanding what one knows about the world through touch, are also gatekeepers of a sort. In some cases, one needs to use the necessary procedure to get certain information about the world. In other cases, using a procedure that is merely sufficient does not fully shut out information about an object property, but it delivers less of it. For example, contour following is necessary to achieve accurate performance in tasks such as fine shape discrimination and categorization. For another example, the lateral motion procedure can deliver information about the apparent temperature of an object, but greater accuracy and more accurate performance in thermal discrimination tasks occur if the object is held in a static fashion, without movement.

Haptic and Visual Properties

From its earliest stages, vision is directed to extracting information about object contours. It progresses from edges to representations of primitive shapes and volumes at specific sizes. Our own work, along with that of many others, points to a sharp contrast between haptic and visual perception of geometric properties, such as size and shape. The haptic coding of two-dimensional shape, in particular, requires slow exploration and is not very accurate. Conversely, some properties are unlikely to be available with visual cues. For example, it is difficult to judge the apparent temperature of an object visually, except as it is inferred from categorizing the object's material, or in extreme cases as it is signaled by the object's color.

These differences in the modalities are highlighted in a simple experiment in which Klatzky, Lederman, and Matula (1993) asked how people would explore objects when they could see them. The researchers asked their participants to compare pairs of objects on particular dimensions: Which is larger? Which is heavier? and so forth. They found that when comparing objects with respect to shape and size, participants looked at the objects and touched them only to bring them closer to their eyes. This was true whether the discriminations were easy or difficult. In contrast, for difficult discriminations of weight, texture, and hardness, participants felt the objects, using exploratory procedures that were appropriate given the to-be-compared property.

These results clearly indicate that people know what modality they should use to perceive a particular object property and that they use vision for geometric properties and touch for material properties. We referred to these tendencies as a *modality-encoding bias*. That is, there is a bias to differentially encode a property with vision or touch, presumably because of a lifetime history of success and failure with those modalities.

Implications for Representation of Perceived Objects

The first part of this chapter was intended to provide a brief introduction to haptic perception. In the context of a festschrift honoring a renowned cognitive psychologist, it might be considered a preamble. We now turn from perception through touch to an intrinsically cognitive topic, namely, the representation of the world that is achieved through perceptual processes. Our concern is with representation of the proximal, tangible world that people encounter through touch and how it relates to representation of the distally sensed world of vision. Representational differences reflect, not surprisingly, the differences between the sensory modalities with respect to the accessibility of object properties and resulting modality bias.

Some time ago, along with Catherine Reed, we (Klatzky, Lederman, & Reed, 1987) suggested the following "gedanken" experiment:

> First, think of the attributes you would expect to see if you were *looking* at a cat. You would probably first think of the visible parts (e.g., four legs, tail, whiskers), perhaps imagining their particular shape or size. Next, suppose you were *touching* a cat without being able to see it. Which attributes now come to mind? You would be likely to think of the softness of the cat's fur, the warmth of its body, or its movement as it breathed. (p. 356, emphasis original)

This thought experiment suggests that the salience of the properties of an object changes not only in perception but in imagination and cognition, according to the modality that is emphasized in processing.

Thought experiments being insufficient, the same group (Klatzky et al., 1987) also conducted an empirical study designed to show that people's operative representations of objects could be altered by calling their attention to different sensory modalities. They created the following situation: Participants were touching, and sometimes seeing, the objects. The researchers "called attention to" vision or touch in various ways: limiting sensory experience, using instructions to concentrate on sensations in a modality, and controlling the way that people touched the objects. Seeking a task that could be used to examine people's cognitive representation of objects, they decided on similarity-based sorting. Judging similarity goes beyond perceptual discrimination. The task requires people to think about what attributes of the objects are important, thus interrogating their consciously accessible representation.

The participants sorted 81 tangible, freestanding objects. The objects were designed so that they were factorial combinations of four properties: shape, size, hardness, and surface texture. There were three levels of each property, and the properties were matched with respect to discriminability of the levels within them. The objects were waferlike forms in which shape varied in two dimensions. There were ovals, hourglass shapes, and clover shapes; thickness was constant, unless the object was soft and deformed by force. The participant's task was to place the objects into bins, so that objects in a common bin were similar to one another. The number of bins was limited, so that the participant had to combine objects within a bin, even though they varied with respect to some of the properties.

As an example of this variation, when there were three bins, if the participant chose to sort by similarity of shape (placing ovals in one bin, hourglasses in another, etc.), he or she would have to combine objects in a common bin that varied in size, roughness, and hardness. A measure of the extent to which objects in the same bin had a particular property (e.g., shape) in common was an index of the salience of that property for determining similarity. The researchers anticipated that the salience index of different properties would vary, as attention was called to vision or touch.

More specifically, they tested the following conditions: In an unbiased-touch condition, the participant could feel the objects but never saw them. Similarity was defined simply by saying that similar objects "go together," with no more specific instructions. In a touch-biased condition, the participant could again feel the objects but not see them; in addition, similarity was defined for the participant as based on how the objects felt. In a visual-imagery condition, again the participant had touch but not vision, but this time similarity was defined as based on how the objects would look if they could be seen. Finally, a touch-with-vision condition allowed participants to see and touch the objects, and similarity was not specifically defined. In these four conditions, no constraint was placed on how the objects should be explored. Two additional conditions were similar to the unbiased-touch and visual-imagery conditions just described but with the additional constraint that the participant had to explore the object with two hands.

The results show clearly that the salience index was affected by the attentional manipulations. Figure 12.1 (left panel) shows the salience index (as a proportion

FIGURE 12.1

Salience index for shape, texture, and hardness (left) and for shape and material under four different instructions (right). Visual imagery = 0 in far right graph. The left panel is from "There's More to Touch Than Meets the Eye: The Salience of Object Attributes for Haptics With and Without Vision," by R. L. Klatzky, S. J. Lederman, and C. Reed, 1987, Journal of Experimental Psychology: General, 116, p. 362. Copyright 1987 by the American Psychological Association. Reprinted with permission. The right panel is from "Cognitive Salience of Haptic Object Properties: Role of Modality-Encoding Bias," by S. J. Lederman, C. Summers, and R. L. Klatzky, 1996, Perception, 25, p. 991. Copyright 1996 by Pion Limited, London. Reprinted with permission.

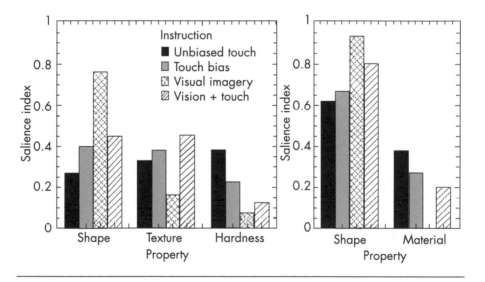

of the maximum possible value) for the properties of shape, texture, and hardness. (Shown are data for the three-bin sort condition, the most natural one to perform given three levels on each property.) Shape was most salient when vision was present or with visual-imagery instructions. Texture and hardness were more salient in the haptic conditions than with visual-imagery instructions. Hardness was also more salient in the haptic conditions than when vision was present. Texture, however, became salient when participants saw the stimuli; this is not surprising because there were strong visual cues to texture. Thus, there was a tendency for attention to haptics to foster salience of material and attention to vision (real or imagined) to foster salience of geometry.

These patterns of salience were highly correlated with procedures used to explore the objects. In the unbiased and touch-biased conditions, where material properties of texture and hardness were salient, exploration took the form of procedures associated with those properties. When visual imagery was used, contour following became more frequent. This procedure requires stabilizing the object while its contours are explored. With the imposition of a two-handed exploration, where one hand stabilizes while the other explores, shape became virtually the only property used for sorting under visual-imagery instructions. It is interesting to note that haptic exploration simply dropped out when vision was present, as Klatzky et al. (1993) found in the study of visually guided exploration described previously. With vision available, people sorted merely by looking at the objects and then primarily used shape and texture.

In short, instructions that motivate people to think about different sensory modalities both change the way they explore objects haptically and change the properties that become salient as they judge object similarity. These changes in property salience presumably reflect differences in the operative representation of the objects within systems that are not just perceptual but cognitive.

We argue that focusing attention on a perceptual modality changes the internal representation of objects and, as a result, alters patterns of information seeking. That is, attention to a modality may directly make certain object properties salient, which in turn leads to associated patterns of exploration. The resulting exploratory procedures deliver modality-appropriate object properties, commensurate with their gatekeeping function. It is also possible that attention to a modality invokes the most relevant exploratory procedures and that the resulting perception of associated properties shapes the internal representation. Both mechanisms may exist.

The hypothesis that modality bias, based on long-term experience, can directly guide representation was tested in a further experiment (Lederman, Summers, & Klatzky, 1996). To address this question, the researchers repeated the similarity sorting task but with objects that were not matched with respect to the discriminability of various properties. The objects were spheres or cubes in two sizes and two materials, pine or aluminum, for a total of eight. All of the properties could readily be discriminated by simply grasping and holding the objects; no specialized exploration was needed. If previously obtained patterns of modality-specific sorting were obtained with this stimulus set, this would suggest that the bases for similarity are driven by the modality directly, without mediation by specialized exploration and restricted perception of object properties.

Given that participants grasp and lift the objects without specialized haptic exploration, a factor that might dictate the salience of properties is their perceptual discriminability when grasped and lifted. With the experimental stimuli, tests of speeded sorting, without vision, into the two levels of each property—and two properties correlated with material, namely, weight and apparent temperature—revealed that size and shape were more quickly discriminated than were the material properties. This pattern of discriminability, favoring geometric properties, should work against the previous pattern of findings with respect to similarity-based sorting, where material properties were most salient under haptically biased and unbiased sorting without vision. If the perceptual discriminability of the particular properties in the stimulus set governs the cognitive representation of similarity, participants would be expected to separate objects that differ in size and shape more than they do objects of different material; instructions should not moderate this tendency. If experience with a modality is important, unbiased and touch-biased instruction conditions would foster the salience of material.

In fact, this latter result is what Lederman et al. (1996) found. Figure 12.1 (right panel) shows the salience scores for shape and material, relative to the maximum possible, under each instructional condition (two-bin sorting). Shape was the dominant basis for sorting overall, as would be predicted by the fact that the geometric properties were more discriminable than the material properties. However, instructions moderated the salience of properties. Shape was particularly salient when participants had vision or visual-imagery instructions, whereas the salience of material was greatest when participants sorted by touch alone, without visual bias. It is important to note that this greater emphasis on material under haptic encoding occurred even though participants did not overtly use specialized haptic exploratory procedures that would favor the perception of material properties.

We described evidence that the representation of touched objects is different from that of seen or visually imagined objects when the objects are physically present. Moreover, differences in representation directly reflect modality-specific biases. It is not the case that representations must be dominated by bottom-up processing, reflecting the relative discriminability of object properties within a given sensory modality. Cognitive processes that emphasize a given modality can impose patterns of information seeking; in doing so they determine what properties of the physical world are available for perception and ultimate representation.

Implications for Representation of Remembered and Imagined Objects

What if objects were not physically present and were only imagined or retrieved as representations from memory? Are modality biases still evident? We have conducted two sets of work related to this question.

In one study, we (Lederman & Klatzky, 1990) asked how people's representations of common object categories in memory might change when different sensory modalities were emphasized. Specifically, we wished to know what properties of an object would be salient if people thought about categorizing it by touch alone. It is well known that an object's shape and part structure constitute the primary basis for assigning it to a category at the basic or most commonly named level (Rosch, 1978; Tversky & Hemenway, 1984). However, researchers of studies demonstrating the prominence of shape in categorical definition have tended to assume that vision is an operative modality. Our concern was with the properties that would be associated with an object's category when it was not seen but, rather, encountered haptically.

Accordingly, we (Lederman & Klatzky, 1990, Experiment 1) asked participants to list from a closed set those properties that would be most diagnostic of a named object if it were to be identified by touch. That is, we asked what properties would be used to verify the object's category—for example, its size, shape, weight, or hardness. The names of the objects were designated at each of two levels: the basic level (e.g., bread) and a more specific subordinate level (e.g., stale bread). Participants ranked the properties they thought would be diagnostic for the named object in order of importance. From these rankings, we computed a weighted frequency for each property (i.e., frequency with which property was listed, weighted by rank). Figure 12.2 shows the weighted frequency for each property, averaged across objects, when the objects were named at the basic and subordinate levels.

We initially selected a pool of objects for which we thought a priori that a variety of properties might be relevant to the categorization at the subordinate level (e.g., for stale bread, hardness). Our predictions were confirmed: When the objects were named at the subordinate level, there were some for which a material property like texture was most diagnostic (highest mean weighted frequency) and others for which a geometric property like shape was most diagnostic. We found further that when the same objects were named at the basic level, shape became the most highly weighted basis for categorization—but texture was also frequently cited as diagnostic, in contrast to previous findings. Thus, asking participants to focus on touch altered, to some extent, the distribution of object properties with respect to diagnosticity at the basic and subordinate levels.

A further study (Lederman & Klatzky, 1990, Experiment 2) in which people were given physical instantiations of each object and asked whether it matched a given name (basic or subordinate) shows that the people's exploration was directly related to the most diagnostic property. For example, if hardness was highly diagnostic to the named category, according to the previously obtained norms, there was a tendency to apply pressure to the object to verify its identity. The same object was explored differently, depending on whether it was to be judged at the basic or subordinate level, given that the level of categorization altered the properties that were diagnostic.

A second line of research dealing with modality bias, in the absence of physical contact with objects, focuses on the nature of haptic imagery. In stark contrast to the voluminous literature on visual imagery, little is known about imagery associated with touch. One finding about visual imagery is that it tends to be used when people answer spatial questions that are novel but drops out when there is a factual representation that can deal with the same question (Jolicoeur & Kosslyn, 1985). Klatzky, Lederman, and Matula (1991) investigated whether people would use haptic imagery for difficult judgments about objects' material properties, when a factual answer was unlikely to be available. The study was similar to the one described

FIGURE 12.2

Mean weighted frequencies for object properties at basic and subordinate levels of classification. The properties are hardness (Hard), part motion, shape, size, temperature (Temp), texture (Text), weight (Wt), and nature of parts of the object (Part). From "Haptic Classification of Common Objects: Knowledge-Driven Exploration," by S. J. Lederman and R. L. Klatzky, 1990, Cognitive Psychology, 22, p. 432. Copyright 1990 by Academic Press Inc. Reprinted with permission.

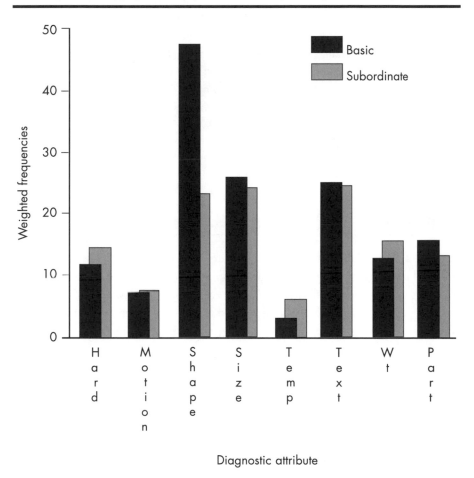

Diagnostic attribute

above in which real objects were used: Participants indicated which of two objects was harder, heavier, and so forth. However, in this study, the objects were named rather than physically presented.

The researchers (Klatzky et al., 1991) found that when the judgments were difficult (e.g., Which is heavier, a baseball or a can of soup?), participants tended to report having a visual image in which their hand physically interacted with the objects. Moreover, within that image, the hand frequently executed the specific exploratory procedure that was associated with the judged property. For example, when judging relative weight, participants often imagined lifting and hefting the objects.

For these difficult judgments of material properties, then, imagined haptic exploration occurred but within the phenomenological experience of a visual image. In contrast, for difficult judgments of imagined geometric properties, namely, size and shape complexity, visual imagery also often occurred but without the phenomenon of the hand being present in the image.

We can only speculate, but this suggests the existence of a cognitive system in which imagined exploration takes place, delivering haptic properties that are analogous to the spatial properties that could be obtained by visual imagination. Yet it seems that a strong phenomenological experience, when haptic imagery occurs, is of a concomitant visual image. Perhaps the close relationship between haptic and visual imagery takes advantage of cortical sites that respond to perceptual tasks in both modalities (e.g., Sathian, Zangaladzu, Hoffman, & Grafton, 1997).

Conclusion

We have attempted to demonstrate that research in perception can illuminate general issues of cognitive representation and function. The research that we have reviewed indicates that the information-processing specialization of sensory modalities plays an important role not only in object perception but in representation and cognitive processes such as categorization, when objects are physically present or when they are remembered or imagined.

The modality with which an object is perceived understandably affects what one ultimately knows and remembers about the object. Differences between vision and touch in perceptual capabilities give rise to different percepts, even of the same object. Beyond modality-specific tendencies in the perception of a physically present object, the evocation of a particular modality can bias an object's internal representation in memory and thought. The operation of such modality-specific biases is not unlike the way in which semantic context can shape the interpretation and recollection of language and events. But these biases are rooted in past perceptual experience.

Particularly among cognitive psychologists, touch is an unusual perceptual modality on which to focus. We find touch fascinating and hope that we have been persuasive in making it so. We intend our examples to remind readers of something that Bob Crowder told us long ago: Issues of perception and memory are inextricably intertwined, and study of the two in tandem can enrich one's understanding of both domains.

References

Hsaio, S., Johnson, K. O., & Twombly, I. A. (1993). Roughness coding in the somatosensory system. *Acta Psychologica, 84*, 53–67.

Johnson, K. O., & Lamb, G. D. (1981). Neural mechanisms of spatial tactile discrimination: Neural patterns evoked by Braille-like dot patterns in the monkey. *Journal of Physiology, 310*, 117–144.

Jolicoeur, P., & Kosslyn, S. M. (1985). Is time to scan visual images due to demand characteristics? *Memory & Cognition, 13*, 320–332.

Kenshalo, D. R. (1984). Cutaneous temperature sensitivity. In W. W. Dawson & J. M. Enouch (Eds.), *Foundations of sensory science* (pp. 419–464). Berlin: Springer-Verlag.

Klatzky, R. L., Lederman, S. J., & Matula, D. E. (1991). Imagined haptic exploration in judgments of object properties. *Journal of Experimental Psychology: Human Learning, Memory, and Cognition, 17*, 314–322.

Klatzky, R. L., Lederman, S. J., & Matula, D. E. (1993). Haptic exploration in the presence of vision. *Journal of Experimental Psychology: Human Perception and Performance, 19*, 726–743.

Klatzky, R., Lederman, S., & Metzger, V. (1985). Identifying objects by touch: An "expert system." *Perception and Psychophysics, 37*, 299–302.

Klatzky, R. L., Lederman, S. J., & Reed, C. (1987). There's more to touch than meets the eye: The salience of object attributes for haptics with and without vision. *Journal of Experimental Psychology: General, 116*, 356–369.

Lederman, S. J., & Klatzky, R. L. (1987). Hand movements: A window into haptic object recognition. *Cognitive Psychology, 19*, 342–368.

Lederman, S. J., & Klatzky, R. L. (1990). Haptic classification of common objects: Knowledge-driven exploration. *Cognitive Psychology, 22*, 421–459.

Lederman, S. J., Summers, C., & Klatzky, R. L. (1996). Cognitive salience of haptic object properties: Role of modality-encoding bias. *Perception, 25*, 983–998.

Loomis, J., & Lederman, S. (1986). Tactual perception. In K. Boff, L. Kaufman, & J. Thomas (Eds.), *Handbook of human perception and performance* (pp. 1–41). New York: Wiley.

Rosch, E. (1978). Principles of categorization. In E. Rosch & B. Lloyd (Eds.), *Cognition and categorization* (pp. 27–48). Hillsdale, NJ: Erlbaum.

Sathian, K., Zangaladzu, A., Hoffman, J. M., & Grafton, S. T. (1997). Feeling with the mind's eye. *NeuroReport, 8*, 3877–3881.

Tversky, B., & Hemenway, K. (1984). Objects, parts, and categories. *Journal of Experimental Psychology: General, 113*, 169–193.

CHAPTER 13

The Irrelevant Sound Effect Is Not Always the Same as the Irrelevant Speech Effect

Ian Neath

Aimée M. Surprenant

B ob Crowder characterized his own research as belonging to the domain of "auditory cognition" but confessed to an occasional excursion into "mainstream" memory research. His publications focus on disentangling memory for sensory quality from memory for verbal descriptions of events, and he explored these issues in a variety of paradigms. One particular line of his research concerns the difference between speech and nonspeech stimuli in various auditory tasks. As a general rule, memory effects involving speech are qualitatively different than those with nonspeech stimuli. There is one area of research, however, where speech and nonspeech stimuli appear to have identical rather than different effects. In this chapter, we report three experiments that examine this apparently anomalous finding.

The Irrelevant–Unattended Speech–Sound Effect

The empirical result of interest is that immediate serial recall of verbal sequences is impaired when list presentation is accompanied by irrelevant auditory stimuli compared with quiet presentation (Colle & Welsh, 1976; Salamé & Baddeley, 1982). Although there are an increasingly large number of researchers who have examined this finding, it is still poorly understood; even its appellation is subject to debate, with different researchers using different terms. Some researchers have called it the "irrelevant speech effect" (Neath, Surprenant, & LeCompte, 1998; Surprenant, LeCompte, & Neath, 2000; Surprenant, Neath, & LeCompte, 1999), others have

The authors wish to thank Angela Bruens, Kirsten Hartwig, Ericka King, Jennifer Moeller, and Melissa Winkler for their assistance with data collection. A coauthored chapter was deemed appropriate because we were both graduate students of Bob Crowder and somehow both of us ended up in the wilds of Indiana. Order of authorship is based solely on when the dissertation was completed.

called it the "unattended speech effect" (Hanley & Broadbent, 1987; Salamé & Baddeley, 1982), and still others have called it the "irrelevant sound effect" (Beaman & Jones, 1998; Macken, Tremblay, Alford, & Jones, 1999). The fundamental difference concerns whether the effect differs as a function of the type of irrelevant auditory item, speech or nonspeech.

A recent review by Neath (2000) summarizes the irrelevant speech effect literature as follows:

> The irrelevant speech effect is independent of the intensity of the irrelevant items when the to-be-remembered items are visual; is observed regardless of the presentation modality of the to-be-remembered items; is equivalent whether the irrelevant speech occurs during presentation or after presentation; is independent of the phonological similarity between the to-be-remembered items and the irrelevant items; is independent of the semantic similarity between the to-be-remembered items and the irrelevant items; can be obtained with nonwords; can be obtained with nonspeech, although the effect may be smaller than for speech and may have different properties; can be found on at least some tasks that appear not to involve serial recall, serial rehearsal, or serial processing; and can be found for unvarying and repeated stimuli, although the effects are smaller than for varying or changing stimuli. (p. 405)

In the typical irrelevant speech experiment, the participant sees a list of items presented visually either in quiet or accompanied by some irrelevant speech and is then asked to recall the items in their original presentation order. Whereas the majority of early researchers used speech tokens as the irrelevant material (Colle & Welsh, 1976; Salamé & Baddeley, 1982), more recent studies demonstrate that nonspeech tokens such as tones also produce reliable decrements (Jones & Macken, 1993; LeCompte, 1994; LeCompte, Neely, & Wilson, 1997; Tremblay & Jones, 1998). Although both speech and nonspeech stimuli produce a decrement in recall, it is unclear whether the type of irrelevant information—speech or nonspeech—is important: In many studies, researchers have found no difference between irrelevant speech and irrelevant sounds, but some do. One reason for this lack of consensus is that most researchers have examined only main effects, comparing reductions in overall performance. However, the apparent equivalence often seen is not good evidence that the decrements arise from the same cause. For example, a fly buzzing around the head of a participant during list presentation would also probably reduce overall levels of recall, but one may not want to conclude that this "irrelevant fly effect" is the same as one caused by irrelevant speech.

Speech Versus Nonspeech

One might expect differences between speech and nonspeech stimuli based on a variety of empirical findings. For example, general principles of interference—such as the Skaggs–Robinson hypothesis (McGeoch, 1942)—lead to the prediction that tones and speech tokens should not interfere with each other. The speech perception literature is replete with differences between the perception of tones and speech (Liberman, 1996). Even the gentle law of speech ascendancy, that recently heard speech items tend to ascend and linger in mind, might admit that speech and nonspeech could differ (see M. J. Watkins, chapter 10, this volume).

We focus most, however, on two related results, the modality effect and the suffix effect (for reviews, see Crowder, 1976; and Neath, 1998). Conrad and Hull (1968) asked participants to read a list of items either silently or out loud and then recall the items in order. The first item was recalled accurately (the primacy effect), but recall levels systematically decreased through the rest of the list. The final item in the read silently condition was correctly recalled in order only about 20% of the time compared with 80% accuracy when the final item was read aloud. This modality effect—the advantage of the final item when presentation is auditory compared with visual—occurs only when the to-be-remembered items are speech. The magnitude of the modality effect decreases the further from speech one gets, with mouthed and lip-read stimuli producing intermediate effects and tones and other nonspeech tokens producing little effect.

The modality effect can be abolished if the list is followed by a speech item, a so-called stimulus suffix (Crowder, 1967; Dallett, 1965). In a suffix effect experiment, the participant is told that the same irrelevant item occurs at the end of every list and is asked either to ignore the suffix or to treat the suffix as a sign that the serial recall test is about to begin. When the suffix is a speech token, the modality effect is eliminated; that is, performance on the final item is greatly reduced with little or no effect on other list items. When the suffix is not a speech token (i.e., a buzzer, a pure tone), memory for the final item is unimpaired. For example, Crowder (1972) found that recall of the final item was approximately 90% correct when the list was followed by a nonspeech token compared with approximately 30% correct when the suffix was a speech token.

Although there are many physical differences between speech and nonspeech stimuli, the physical nature of the item may not be all that important; instead, it may be that the interpretation of an ambiguous token can also determine whether it acts like a speech or nonspeech item (Ayres, Jonides, Reitman, Egan, & Howard, 1979). For example, Neath, Surprenant, and Crowder (1993) conducted a suffix experiment in which one group of participants were led to believe that one of the suffixes, the onomatopoeic English word *baa*, was produced by a human, whereas a second group was led to believe that it was produced by an actual sheep.[1] Recall

---

[1] We would like to take this opportunity to correct an error reported in the original article. We defined *baa* as the "noise a contented sheep makes" (Neath et al., 1993, p. 699). A colleague at Purdue has since informed us that contented sheep do not, as a rule, make noises; it is only discontented sheep that produce *baa*. Indeed, the literature suggests that the more distressed a sheep, the more vocalizations are heard (e.g., Orgeur et al., 1998). We regret the error.

of the final item was greatly impaired when participants thought the suffix was speech but was unaffected when participants thought the suffix was produced by an animal. Thus, the exact same physical token can have two different effects depending on whether it is interpreted and processed as speech or nonspeech.

Three Theories, Three Predictions

The question of whether speech tokens have qualitatively different effects than nonspeech tokens has important theoretical implications. There are three different explanations of the effects of irrelevant auditory stimuli on memory. Each theory makes different predictions about the effects of irrelevant tones, irrelevant speech, and a method of presenting irrelevant stimuli not yet mentioned, articulatory suppression. When participants engage in articulatory suppression, they repeatedly say an irrelevant word, such as *the* or *cola*, out loud over and over (Murray, 1968). Working memory (Baddeley, 1986, 1992) views all three manipulations—articulatory suppression, irrelevant speech, and irrelevant tones—as different from one another; the object-oriented episodic record (O-OER) model (Jones, 1993) views all three manipulations as being similar; and the feature model (Nairne, 1990; Neath, 1999, 2000) views irrelevant speech and articulatory suppression as similar but irrelevant nonspeech as different. We consider each in turn.

The working memory framework (Baddeley, 1986, 1992) distinguishes between a phonological store and an articulatory control process, which together make up the articulatory loop. Speech-based information is registered in the phonological store either through subvocalization using the articulatory control process or through obligatory direct registration on hearing spoken material. According to this view, the disruption seen when articulatory suppression accompanies list presentation occurs because the concurrent articulation occupies the articulatory control process and prevents subvocal rehearsal. Irrelevant speech, in contrast, does not interfere with rehearsal. The impairment seen when irrelevant speech accompanies list presentation occurs because phonological information from the irrelevant stimuli enters the phonological store and interferes with the phonological representation of the to-be-remembered items. Irrelevant tones neither interfere with rehearsal nor can they enter the phonological store.

According to the working memory framework, then, the locus of the irrelevant speech effect is the phonological store. Irrelevant tones cannot enter this store, so the locus of this effect must lie elsewhere. One possibility may be that irrelevant tones create a dual-task situation: The extra attention or resources necessary to ignore the tones detracts from resources available in processing the to-be-remembered items. Although articulatory suppression could lead to some interference in the phonological store—the items the participant produces are auditory speech tokens and, when heard, would have obligatory access—the major effects occur due to disruption of the articulatory control process and rehearsal.

The O-OER model (Jones, 1993; Jones & Macken, 1993) assumes that both visual and auditory items are represented using amodal, abstract representations called *objects*. Objects are created by the same processes used in perception, most important, those dealing with segmentation. The different modalities are indicated through streaming, where items or events are assigned to either the same or a different source. According to this view, irrelevant speech, irrelevant tones, and articulatory suppression all produce functionally equivalent objects because of the amodal nature of objects (Macken & Jones, 1995; Macken et al., 1999). Order information is encoded using pointers that are associated with individual objects. The formation of a pointer is a probabilistic process and, once formed, its strength decays over time. Errors in recall occur when pointers from a different stream of objects interfere with a different set of pointers. To the extent that articulatory suppression, irrelevant speech, and irrelevant tones each produce multiple objects, all three should produce impairment in recall. Because the locus of all three effects is the same, all three manipulations should produce similar results.

The feature model (Nairne, 1988, 1990) assumes that items are represented using two kinds of features, those coding modality-specific information (modality-dependent features) and those coding information that is the same regardless of the presentation modality (modality-independent features). The disruption seen when either articulatory suppression or irrelevant speech accompanies list presentation is due to feature adoption, the process by which some modality-independent features of the irrelevant stimuli are incorporated into the representation of the to-be-remembered items (Neath, 1999, 2000). This reduces the probability of correctly matching the degraded trace in primary memory with the appropriate item in secondary memory (see also Murray, Rowan, & Smith, 1988, for a similar idea). Irrelevant tones should not usually result in feature adoption because it is unlikely that modality-independent features that arise from processing a tone would interfere with the modality-independent features that arise from processing a speech token. Instead, as in the working memory account, irrelevant tones reduce performance by creating a dual-task situation.

The current experiments were designed to investigate the similarities and differences among articulatory suppression, irrelevant speech, and irrelevant tones. If all three have similar effects, then that is support for Jones's O-OER model. If all three have different effects, then that is support for Baddeley's working memory. If articulatory suppression and irrelevant speech have similar effects and irrelevant tones have a different effect, then that is support for Nairne's feature model.

Experiment 1

The phonological similarity effect refers to the finding that lists of words that rhyme (e.g., stain, vain, grain, lane) are recalled in order less well than comparable lists of words that do not rhyme (Conrad, 1964). It has long been known that articulatory suppression eliminates the phonological similarity effect for visually presented items but not for auditory items (Murray, 1968; Peterson & Johnson, 1971). Previous studies also show that irrelevant speech eliminates the phonological similarity effect for visually presented items (Colle & Welsh, 1976). Recently, Surprenant et al. (1999) demonstrated that the phonological similarity effect remains for auditory items in the presence of irrelevant speech, just as it does for articulatory suppression. Experiment 1 was designed to see whether irrelevant tones would eliminate the phonological similarity effect for visual items just like articulatory suppression and irrelevant speech.

Method

Participants

Eighty Purdue University undergraduates volunteered to participate in exchange for credit in introductory psychology courses. All identified themselves as native speakers of American English, reported normal hearing, and were arbitrarily assigned to one of four conditions.

Stimuli

The to-be-remembered items are shown in Exhibit 13.1. Ten lists of eight similar-sounding words were drawn from Nairne and Kelley (1999). Each list was used three times, with the words presented in a different random order each time to form the stimuli for the similar condition. For the dissimilar condition, 8 words were drawn at random from these lists with the constraints that only 1 item could occur from a given list and that no word could appear more than four times in dissimilar lists during the course of the experiment. The irrelevant speech was the word *teatime* pronounced by a male voice and digitized at 22 kHz. The irrelevant tone was

EXHIBIT 13.1

Stimuli used in Nairne and Kelley's (1999) Experiment 1

stair scare glare spare rare chair fair share
wheat neat beat treat meat sheet seat heat
stain vain grain lane plain chain rain train
sock flock knock clock lock block rock stock
float goat bloat quote coat boat vote note
lace brace ace trace grace pace base race
rail jail tail trail fail male sale mail
rake bake cake stake wake snake lake break
stole pole bowl coal roll soul hole goal
chip lip slip whip tip strip ship trip

designed to approximate the temporal and frequency characteristics of the word. There were, thus, two sine-wave tones, the one for *tea* slightly higher in frequency and shorter in duration than the one for *time*. Both the speech and nonspeech stimuli were recorded onto cassette tapes.

Design

Phonological similarity was a within-subjects factor, and presentation condition (quiet, irrelevant tones, irrelevant speech, articulatory suppression) was a between-subjects factor.

Procedure

Participants were tested individually. Each sat in front of an Apple Macintosh LC or IIci computer. The participants in the irrelevant tones and irrelevant speech conditions wore headphones through which the irrelevant tones and speech were delivered. All participants were informed that they would see a list of words and would be tested on how accurately they could remember the presentation order. Participants in the articulatory suppression condition were asked to say *teatime* out loud over and over during list presentation. They were to begin articulating when they saw the warning signal and they could stop when they saw the test. An experimenter remained in the room to ensure compliance with the instructions. For participants in the irrelevant tones and irrelevant speech conditions, the irrelevant stimuli began prior to the onset of the first list and played continuously until the end of the experiment.

A visual signal (five asterisks) was shown 2 s prior to the onset of the list. All stimuli were shown in 18-point Geneva typeface in the center of the screen for 1 s with each item appearing immediately after the offset of the previous item. Fifteen seconds were allowed for the serial reconstruction of order test. The eight list items were shown, in alphabetical order, in the center of the screen, and the participant was asked to use the mouse and click on the words in the order in which they were presented. The words remained on the screen all the time, and there was no feedback given to the participant about which words had been selected or whether the words selected were correct. There was one practice trial, in which the stimuli were eight color names; regardless of the experimental condition, the practice list was presented with no irrelevant stimuli and no articulatory suppression.

Results and Discussion

The results of Experiment 1 are shown in Figure 13.1. All three manipulations of irrelevant information reduced overall performance relative to the quiet condition, with slightly worse performance in the articulatory suppression condition. The

FIGURE 13.1

The proportion of words correctly recalled in order as a function of phonological similarity and type of irrelevant information in Experiment 1. Error bars show the standard error of the mean. Art. supp. = articulatory suppression.

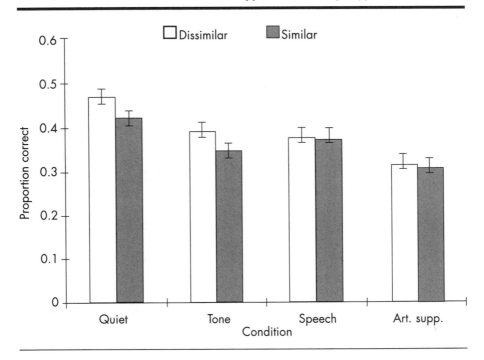

phonological similarity effect evident in the quiet condition was eliminated by both articulatory suppression and irrelevant speech. The irrelevant tones left the phonological similarity effect intact.

A 4-conditions (quiet, irrelevant tones, irrelevant speech, articulatory suppression) × 2-phonological similarity (dissimilar, similar) ANOVA yielded reliable main effects of both condition, $F(3, 76) = 8.88$, $MSE = .014$, $p < .01$, and phonological similarity, $F(1, 76) = 12.87$, $MSE = .002$, $p < .01$. The interaction was marginally reliable, $F(3, 76) = 2.55$, $MSE = .003$, $p = .06$. All three manipulations of irrelevant information reduced performance relative to the quiet condition (LSD test with an alpha level of .05). Overall recall in the irrelevant tones and irrelevant speech conditions did not differ, whereas recall in the articulatory suppression condition was lower than in all other conditions.

Secondary analyses examined the differences in recall of the similar and dissimilar items within each condition. In the quiet condition, the proportion of dissimilar words correctly recalled in order was .471 compared with .424 similar words, $F(1, 19) = 10.67$, $MSE = .002$, $p < .01$. In the irrelevant tones condition, there was also a reliable phonological similarity effect: The proportion of dissimilar words recalled in order was .393 compared with .347 for similar words, $F(1, 19) = 8.11$, $MSE = .002$, $p < .05$. In the irrelevant speech condition, there was no evidence of a phonological similarity effect: The proportion of dissimilar items recalled was .377 compared with .372 for similar words, $F(1, 19) < 1$. In the articulatory suppression condition, the proportion of dissimilar words correctly recalled in order was .313 compared with .306 for similar words, $F(1, 19) < 1$.

Irrelevant tones, irrelevant speech, and articulatory suppression all reduced overall level of recall compared with the quiet condition. Moreover, there was no difference in the level of impairment caused by the irrelevant tones and the irrelevant speech. However, only irrelevant speech eliminated the phonological similarity effect; irrelevant tones left the effect intact. The results are consistent with the idea that irrelevant tones create a dual-task setting and reduce overall levels of recall. Irrelevant speech and articulatory suppression also create a dual-task setting, and thus reduce overall levels of recall, but they also remove whatever advantage the dissimilar items enjoyed over the similar. Performance is slightly worse in the articulatory suppression condition due to the extra task demands of active vocalization.

Experiment 2

For Experiment 2, a different independent variable was used. The word length effect is the finding that a list of long words (words that take longer to pronounce) is recalled less well than a list of short words; articulatory suppression eliminates the word length effect (Baddeley, Lewis, & Vallar, 1984; Baddeley, Thomson, & Buchanan, 1975). Neath et al. (1998) reported an experiment that compared the effects of articulatory suppression with those of irrelevant speech and tones on the word length effect. Both articulatory suppression and irrelevant speech eliminated the word length effect, whereas the irrelevant tones manipulation did not. They did not make much of this difference between irrelevant tones and irrelevant speech at the time, merely noting that the "results suggest an important distinction between the irrelevant tone effect and the irrelevant speech effect" (p. 348). This supposition that irrelevant tones and irrelevant speech have different effects has received further empirical support from Experiment 1 above. Nonetheless, given that this aspect of Neath et al.'s data was not originally predicted, Experiment 2 was designed as a replication.

Method

Participants

Eighty different Purdue University undergraduates volunteered to participate in exchange for credit in introductory psychology courses. All identified themselves as native speakers of American English and reported normal hearing, and each was arbitrarily assigned to 1 of 4 conditions.

Stimuli

The to-be-remembered items were 80 long and 80 short words taken from a pool assembled by LaPointe and Engle (1990). Each word appeared three times during the course of the experiment. The irrelevant speech and irrelevant tone stimuli were the same as in Experiment 1.

Design

Word length was a within-subjects factor, and presentation condition (quiet, irrelevant tones, irrelevant speech, articulatory suppression) was a between-subjects factor.

Procedure

All aspects of the procedure were the same as in Experiment 1.

Results and Discussion

As Figure 13.2 shows, there is a reliable word length effect in the quiet condition, which is eliminated in the articulatory suppression condition. All 3 noise conditions lowered overall performance relative to the quiet condition. There is a reliable word length effect in the irrelevant tones condition and no word length effect in the irrelevant speech condition.

A 4-condition (quiet, irrelevant tones, irrelevant speech, articulatory suppression) × 2-word length (short, long) ANOVA yielded reliable main effects of both condition, $F(3, 76) = 8.39$, $MSE = .014$, $p < .01$, and word length, $F(1, 76) = 20.97$, $MSE = .003$, $p < .01$, and a reliable interaction, $F(3, 76) = 3.96$, $MSE = .003$, $p < .05$. All three manipulations of irrelevant information reduced performance relative to the quiet condition (LSD test with an alpha level of .05). Overall recall in the irrelevant tones and irrelevant speech conditions did not differ, whereas recall in the articulatory suppression condition was lower than in all other conditions except for the irrelevant tones.

Secondary analyses examined recall of short and long items within each condition. In the quiet condition, the proportion of short words correctly recalled in order was .502 compared with .429 for long words, $F(1, 19) = 18.65$, $MSE = .003$, $p < .01$. In the irrelevant tones condition, there was also a reliable word length effect: The proportion of short words recalled in order was .411 compared with .343 for long words, $F(1, 19) = 17.85$, $MSE = .003$, $p < .01$. In the irrelevant speech condition, there was no evidence of a word length effect: The proportion of short items recalled was .397 compared with .390 for long words, $F(1, 19) < 1$. In the articulatory suppression condition, the proportion of short words correctly

FIGURE 13.2

The proportion of words correctly recalled in order as a function of word length and type of irrelevant information in Experiment 2. Error bars show the standard error of the mean. Art. supp. = articulatory suppression.

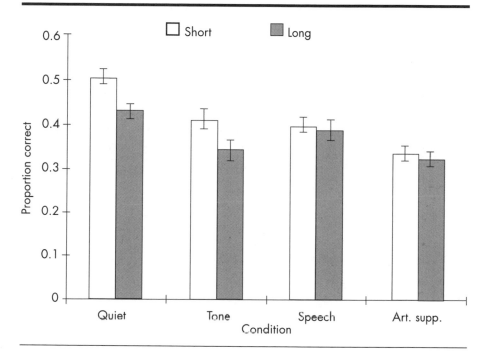

recalled in order was .340 compared with .327 for long words, $F(1, 19) = 1.04$, $MSE = .002, p > .25$.

Irrelevant tones, irrelevant speech, and articulatory suppression all reduced the overall level of recall compared with the quiet condition. Moreover, there was no difference in the level of impairment caused by the irrelevant tones and the irrelevant speech. However, only irrelevant speech eliminated the word length effect; irrelevant tones left the effect intact. There are now three instances in which irrelevant speech has a qualitatively different effect than irrelevant tones, Experiments 1 and 2 here and Experiment 1 of Neath et al. (1998). In this respect, irrelevant speech functions like articulatory suppression, whereas irrelevant tones do not. We view the effect of irrelevant tones as reducing overall levels of performance by creating a dual-task situation. Irrelevant speech and articulatory suppression also create a dual-task setting, but they also remove whatever advantage the short (or dissimilar) items enjoyed over the long (or similar) items. Both irrelevant speech and irrelevant tones, then, lower overall performance but irrelevant speech also selectively impairs the short items.

Experiment 3

Thus far, we have intentionally emphasized the difference between speech and nonspeech stimuli as if they were dichotomous categories. A more precise statement, however, is that speech and nonspeech stimuli tend to be processed differently, and it is the result of this processing that drives the two effects. It is possible to produce ambiguous nonspeech stimuli that are interpreted as speech (Ayres et al., 1979) and to produce ambiguous speech stimuli that are interpreted as nonspeech (Neath et al., 1993). Experiment 3 was designed to see whether the same physical token can sometimes produce an irrelevant tones effect and other times produce an irrelevant speech effect. In this experiment, the same onomatopoeic token *baa* used by Neath et al. (1993) was used as the irrelevant auditory token. Half of the participants were informed that the token was produced by a sheep and half were informed that the token was produced by a human. The question of interest is Which interpretation, if any, affects the word length effect?

Method

Participants

Forty different Purdue University undergraduates volunteered to participate in exchange for credit in introductory psychology courses. All identified themselves as native speakers of American English and were arbitrarily assigned to one of two conditions.

Stimuli

The stimuli were the same short and long items used in Experiment 2. The same digitized sound used by Neath et al. (1993) was recorded onto a cassette tape that was used in both the "human" and "animal" conditions.

Design

Word length was a within-subjects variable, and presentation condition (irrelevant human *baa,* irrelevant animal *baa*) was a between-subjects variable.

Procedure

The procedure was identical to the irrelevant tones and irrelevant speech conditions in Experiment 1, with the following exceptions. Each research assistant was separately briefed. For those testing participants in the human condition, one of the authors demonstrated production of the sheeplike sound. For those testing participants in the animal condition, the authors emphasized that the sheep sound had been obtained from a sound effects collection. The irrelevant sound or speech began prior to the first list and continued nonstop until the end of the experiment.

Results and Discussion

As can be seen in Figure 13.3, when the ambiguous token was interpreted as speech, the word length effect was statistically eliminated; when the ambiguous token was interpreted as nonspeech, the word length effect remained.

The results of a 2-presentation condition (human sheep, animal sheep) $\times$ 2-word length (short, long) ANOVA support the above conclusions. There was no main effect of presentation condition, $F(1, 38) = 1.85, MSE = .03, p > .15$, although

FIGURE 13.3

The proportion of words correctly recalled in order as function of word length and type of irrelevant information in Experiment 3. Error bars show the standard error of the mean.

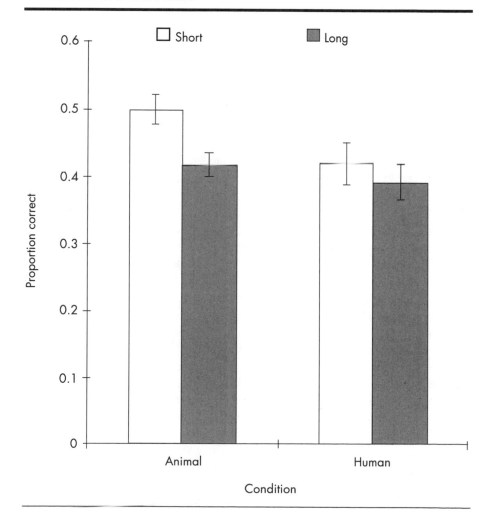

it appeared as though more words were correctly recalled in order in the animal group than in the human group (.457 vs. .405, respectively). There was a main effect of word length, $F(1, 38) = 16.52$, $MSE = .004$, $p < .01$, and there was also a reliable interaction, $F(1, 38) = 4.13$, $MSE = .004$, $p < .05$.

Secondary analyses examined the differences in recall of short and long items within each condition. In the human *baa* condition, there was little evidence of a word length effect: The proportion of short words correctly recalled in order was .419 compared with .391 for long words, $F(1, 19) = 1.98$, $MSE = .004$, $p > .15$. In the animal condition, there was a reliable word length effect: The proportion of short words correctly recalled in order was .499 compared with 416 for long words, $F(1, 19) = 19.48$, $MSE = .004$, $p < .01$. When perceived as speech, the *baa* reduced the word length effect; when perceived as an animal sound, the *baa* left the word length effect intact.

General Discussion

Consistent with several decades of research, the results of the experiments reported here show that speech tokens can have qualitatively different effects on memory than auditory nonspeech tokens. Although both irrelevant speech and irrelevant tones have a similar overall detrimental effect on recall, only the irrelevant speech stimuli interfered selectively with the to-be-remembered items.

The working memory model, the O-OER model, and the feature model all made different predictions. Working memory predicted that all three manipulations would have different effects, whereas the results show that irrelevant speech is similar to articulatory suppression in that both manipulations reduce or eliminate the phonological similarity effect and the word length effect. The O-OER model predicted that all three manipulations would have similar effects, whereas the results show that irrelevant tones have a different effect than irrelevant speech or articulatory suppression. The feature model predicted the similarity between irrelevant speech and articulatory suppression and the difference between the speech and nonspeech.

According to the feature model, only articulatory suppression and irrelevant speech—not irrelevant tones—give rise to feature adoption. To make this process clearer, consider an analogy between the features in the feature model and pixels on a television set. By itself, a particular pixel gives no information about the represented item, but in conjunction with other pixels, the image is fully specified. Moreover, even if a relatively large number of pixels are broken, the image can often be successfully identified. The same is true of features. Feature adoption is similar to when the signal from a particular television station—for example, Channel 2— suffers interference from a signal from a competing station, Channel 3. Some of the individual pixels represent information from Channel 2 and some from Channel 3. To continue the analogy, irrelevant speech and articulatory suppression are like competing television signals, whereas irrelevant tones are like a radio signal.

The general idea is that irrelevant noise, whether speech or nonspeech or produced or heard, has the potential for creating a dual-task setting. To the extent that ignoring the noises or separating the signal from the noise requires some effort, overall performance is lower—an idea similar to one proposed in the speech perception literature (Rabbitt, 1968; Surprenant, 1999). Consistent with this general idea, irrelevant speech has its largest effect during presentation and little effect on retrieval (Jones & Macken, 1993), the same result observed in more traditional dual-task settings (Craik, Govoni, Naveh-Benjamin, & Anderson, 1996). One reason for the reduced effect at test may be that retrieval is a far more automatic process than those processes that occur during encoding (e.g., Logan, 1991). Note that this dual-task interpretation could readily be incorporated into the working memory framework, as suggested above.

In addition to creating a dual-task setting, irrelevant stimuli can lead to feature adoption when the irrelevant stimuli are similar to the to-be-remembered items. Feature adoption can selectively remove the advantage enjoyed by the better-recalled stimuli. For example, the dissimilar items in Experiment 1 have some of their unique features interfered with and thus the probability of successful redintegration is reduced. This leaves them functionally equivalent to the similar items. The short items in Experiments 2 and 3 are less complex than the long items (see Neath & Nairne, 1995). The adoption of some features from the irrelevant items renders them more difficult to redintegrate, again resulting in a functional equivalence with the long items. The major difference between irrelevant speech and articulatory suppression is that more effort is required to actively produce irrelevant noises than to merely listen to them. Evidence consistent with this interpretation includes the finding of slightly worse memory when active vocalization is required compared with listening to someone else vocalizing (Crowder, 1970), and this pattern is evident in the results of Experiments 1 and 2 here.

Although there are clear differences between speech and nonspeech stimuli on memory, we do not wish to imply a dichotomy. First, Experiment 3 makes the crucial point that whether an item is a speech or a nonspeech token may not be as important as how the participant processes the item. As in the suffix studies of Ayres et al. (1979) and Neath et al. (1993), the same physical token was processed differently depending on the participant's expectations. A second reason is that not all speech stimuli function as speech stimuli. By this, we refer to the many differences observed between different types of speech tokens (Surprenant & Neath, 1996). For example, the modality effect is attenuated when short vowels are used rather than long vowels (Crowder, 1973) or when lists of consonant-contrasting stimuli are used rather than vowel-contrasting stimuli (Crowder, 1975).

Conclusion

Nairne (chapter 15, this volume) demonstrates how the feature model embodies the same functional analysis of immediate memory that Crowder and Morton (1969) proposed. First, remembering depends on cues and, in the case of immediate memory, these are typically the remnants of the original processing. In precategorical acoustic storage (PAS), these are "echoes" of the original sensory event, whereas in the feature model, these are the degraded items themselves in primary memory. Second, the utility of these cues depends on how well they help discriminate between competitor items. If all the items sound similar (e.g., pair, pare, pear), a phonological cue is less useful than if the items are dissimilar sounding (e.g., grape, peach, pear).

The research reported here continues the examination of modality-specific interference. From its first formulation in PAS, the idea has become more general, being expressed now as "processing-appropriate interference"—the flip side of transfer-appropriate processing (Crowder, 1993). The specific interference patterns we report are entirely consistent with this view. The three experiments reported here show how the these basic principles of memory developed by Bob Crowder 30 years ago are still applicable and continue to generate predictions.

References

Ayres, T. J., Jonides, J., Reitman, J. S., Egan, J. C., & Howard, D. A. (1979). Differing suffix effects for the same physical suffix. *Journal of Experimental Psychology: Human Learning and Memory, 5,* 315–321.

Baddeley, A. D. (1986). *Working memory.* New York: Oxford University Press.

Baddeley, A. D. (1992). Is working memory working? *Quarterly Journal of Experimental Psychology, 44A,* 1–31.

Baddeley, A. D., Lewis, V. J., & Vallar, G. (1984). Exploring the articulatory loop. *Quarterly Journal of Experimental Psychology, 36,* 233–252.

Baddeley, A. D., Thomson, N., & Buchanan, M. (1975). Word length and the structure of short-term memory. *Journal of Verbal Learning and Verbal Behavior, 14,* 575–589.

Beaman, C. P., & Jones, D. M. (1998). Irrelevant sound disrupts order information in free recall as in serial recall. *Quarterly Journal of Experimental Psychology, 51A,* 615–636.

Colle, H. A., & Welsh, A. (1976). Acoustic masking in primary memory. *Journal of Verbal Learning and Verbal Behavior, 15,* 17–32.

Conrad, R. (1964). Acoustic confusions in immediate memory. *British Journal of Psychology, 55,* 75–84.

Conrad, R., & Hull, A. J. (1968). Input modality and the serial position curve in short-term memory. *Psychonomic Science, 10,* 135–136.

Craik, F. I. M., Govoni, R., Naveh-Benjamin, M., & Anderson, N. D. (1996). The effects of divided attention on encoding and retrieval processes in human memory. *Journal of Experimental Psychology: General, 125,* 159–180.

Crowder, R. G. (1967). Prefix effects in immediate memory. *Canadian Journal of Psychology, 21,* 450–461.

Crowder, R. G. (1970). The role of one's own voice in immediate memory. *Cognitive Psychology, 1,* 157–178.

Crowder, R. G. (1972). Visual and auditory memory. In J. F. Kavanagh & I. G. Mattingly (Eds.), *Language by ear and eye: The relation between speech and learning to read.* Cambridge, MA: MIT Press.

Crowder, R. G. (1973). Precategorical acoustic storage for vowels of short and long duration. *Perception qnd Psychophysics, 13,* 502–506.

Crowder, R. G. (1975). Inferential problems in echoic memory. In P. M. A. Rabbit & S. Dornic (Eds.), *Attention and performance V* (pp. 218–229). London: Academic Press.

Crowder, R. G. (1976). *Principles of learning and memory.* Hillsdale, NJ: Erlbaum.

Crowder, R. G. (1993). Systems and principles in memory theory: Another critique of pure memory. In A. F. Collins, S. E. Gathercole, M. A. Conway, & P. E. Morris (Eds.), *Theories of memory* (pp. 139–161). Hove, England: Erlbaum.

Crowder, R. G., & Morton, J. (1969). Precategorical acoustic storage (PAS). *Perception and Psychophysics, 5,* 365–373.

Dallett, K. (1965). "Primary memory": The effects of redundancy upon digit repetition. *Psychonomic Science, 3,* 237–238.

Hanley, J. R., & Broadbent, C. (1987). The effect of unattended speech on serial recall following auditory presentation. *British Journal of Psychology, 78,* 287–297.

Jones, D. M. (1993). Objects, streams, and threads of auditory attention. In A. Baddeley & L. Weiskrantz (Eds.), *Attention: Selection, awareness, and control* (pp. 87–104). Oxford, England: Oxford University Press.

Jones, D. M., & Macken, W. J. (1993). Irrelevant tones produce an irrelevant speech effect: Implications for phonological coding in working memory. *Journal of Experimental Psychology: Learning, Memory, and Cognition, 19,* 369–381.

LaPointe, L. B., & Engle, R. W. (1990). Simple and complex word spans as measures of working memory capacity. *Journal of Experimental Psychology: Learning, Memory, and Cognition, 16,* 1118–1133.

LeCompte, D. C. (1994). Extending the irrelevant speech effect beyond serial recall. *Journal of Experimental Psychology: Learning, Memory, and Cognition, 20,* 1396–1408.

LeCompte, D. C., Neely, C. B., & Wilson, J. R. (1997). Irrelevant speech and irrelevant tones: The relative importance of speech to the irrelevant speech effect. *Journal of Experimental Psychology: Learning, Memory, and Cognition, 23,* 472–483.

Liberman, A. M. (1996). *Speech: A special code.* Cambridge, MA: MIT Press.

Logan, G. D. (1991). Automaticity and memory. In W. E. Hockley & S. Lewandowsky (Eds.), *Relating theory and data: Essays on human memory in honor of Bennet B. Murdock* (pp. 347–366). Hillsdale, NJ: Erlbaum.

Macken, W. J., & Jones, D. M. (1995). Functional characteristics of the inner voice and the inner ear: Single or double agency? *Journal of Experimental Psychology: Learning, Memory, and Cognition, 21,* 436–448.

Macken, W. J., Tremblay, S., Alford, D., & Jones, D. M. (1999). Attentional selectivity in short-term memory: Similarity of process, not similarity of content, determines disruption. *International Journal of Psychology, 34,* 322–327.

McGeoch, J. A. (1942). *The psychology of human learning.* New York: Longmans, Green.

Murray, D. J. (1968). Articulation and acoustic confusability in short-term memory. *Journal of Experimental Psychology, 78,* 679–684.

Murray, D. J., Rowan, A. J., & Smith, K. H. (1988). The effect of articulatory suppression on short-term recognition. *Canadian Journal of Psychology, 42,* 424–436.

Nairne, J. S. (1988). A framework for interpreting recency effects in immediate serial recall. *Memory & Cognition, 16,* 343–352.

Nairne, J. S. (1990). A feature model of immediate memory. *Memory & Cognition, 18,* 251–269.

Nairne, J. S., & Kelley, M. R. (1999). Reversing the phonological similarity effect. *Memory & Cognition, 27,* 45–53.

Neath, I. (1998). *Human memory: An introduction to research, data, and theory.* Pacific Grove, CA: Brooks/Cole.

Neath, I. (1999). Modelling the effects of irrelevant speech on order information. *International Journal of Psychology, 34,* 410–418.

Neath, I. (2000). Modeling the effects of irrelevant speech on memory. *Psychonomic Bulletin and Review, 7,* 403–423.

Neath, I., & Nairne, J. S. (1995). Word-length effects in immediate memory: Overwriting trace decay theory. *Psychonomic Bulletin and Review, 2,* 429–441.

Neath, I., Surprenant, A. M., & Crowder, R. G. (1993). The context dependent stimulus suffix effect. *Journal of Experimental Psychology: Learning, Memory, and Cognition, 19,* 698–703.

Neath, I., Surprenant, A. M., & LeCompte, D. C. (1998). Irrelevant speech eliminates the word length effect. *Memory & Cognition, 26,* 343–354.

Orgeur, P., Mavric, N., Yvore, P. Bernard, S., Nowak, R., Schaal, B., & Levy, F. (1998). Artificial weaning in sheep: Consequences on behavioural, hormonal and immuno-pathological indicators of welfare. *Applied Animal Behaviour Science, 58,* 87–103.

Peterson, L. R., & Johnson, S. T. (1971). Some effects of minimizing articulation on short-term retention. *Journal of Verbal Learning and Verbal Behavior, 10,* 346–354.

Rabbitt, P. M. A. (1968). Channel capacity, intelligibility and immediate memory. *Quarterly Journal of Experimental Psychology, 20,* 241–248.

Salamé, P., & Baddeley, A. D. (1982). Disruption of short-term memory by unattended speech: Implications for the structure of working memory. *Journal of Verbal Learning and Verbal Behavior, 21,* 150–164.

Surprenant, A. M. (1999). Effects of noise on memory for spoken syllables. *International Journal of Psychology, 34,* 328–333.

Surprenant, A. M., LeCompte, D. C., & Neath, I. (2000). Manipulations of irrelevant information: Suffix effects under articulatory suppression and irrelevant speech. *Quarterly Journal of Experimental Psychology, 53A,* 325–348.

Surprenant, A. M., & Neath, I. (1996). The relation between discriminability and memory for vowels, consonants, and silent-center vowels. *Memory & Cognition, 24,* 356–366.

Surprenant, A. M., Neath, I., & LeCompte, D. C. (1999). Irrelevant speech, phonological similarity, and presentation modality. *Memory, 7,* 405–420.

Tremblay, S., & Jones, D. M. (1998). Role of habituation in the irrelevant sound effect: Evidence from the effects of token set size and rate of transition. *Journal of Experimental Psychology: Learning, Memory, and Cognition, 24,* 659–671.

CHAPTER 14

Repetition Effects in Immediate Memory in the Absence of Repetition

Robert L. Greene

erhaps one of Bob Crowder's less notable claims to fame is that he helped introduce contemporary psychology to the Ranschburg effect and the response-prefix effect. Insofar as neither one of these phenomena occupied a particularly prominent place in psychological research in the 1990s, it is a temptation not to place too much importance on this fact. Still, recently there seems to be a reawakening of interest in at least the Ranschburg effect (see Henson, 1998), with some authors (e.g., Fagot & Pashler, 1995) claiming that this effect is related to perceptual inhibition of repeated stimuli (i.e., repetition blindness). I argue here that the Ranschburg and prefix effects still hold considerable potential for shedding light on immediate memory. In fact, one of Bob Crowder's articles (Crowder, 1968b), in which he used response prefixes as a way of studying the Ranschburg effect, seems to present something of a challenge to contemporary understanding of immediate recall. That article, and my attempts to replicate and extend it, is the focus of this chapter.

The Ranschburg Effect

First, I need to introduce the background of the Ranschburg effect. This phenomenon defies some of the casual generalizations about memory. Two of the most basic principles in human memory are that repetition improves remembering and that the magnitude of this improvement increases as a function of the spacing between repetitions. These principles apply well to most situations in delayed memory testing. However, in immediate recall, repetition of an item in a sequence may hurt memory span for that sequence. I first use one of my own experiments as an example of how one might study this effect. Participants are shown a series. Each series consists of eight consonants shown one at a time on a computer screen at a rate of one item per second. Immediately after the presentation of the last item, the participant is cued to recall the items in order by typing them into the computer. This process continues until the participant has gone through many lists (in the case of the experiments presented here, typically around 100).

In the control condition, each item is presented once on the list. However, in other conditions, there is a repetition, with an item occurring at two different positions. Figure 14.1 presents a convenient comparison of the control condition with a condition where an item occurred in the second and fifth serial positions. The dependent variable is the probability of recalling an item in its correct position. Note that the two conditions yield similar patterns of recall. The one point where the curves diverge is at the fifth position, where there is a clear decrement in recall of the second occurrence of the repeated item relative to the control condition.

Crowder and Melton (1965) carried out a preliminary investigation showing that item repetition can sometimes impair and sometimes improve recall. A more comprehensive analysis was carried out by Crowder (1968a), who compared immediate serial recall of control lists containing no repetitions with recall of lists containing all possible arrangements of a single repeated item. Crowder found that when a repeated item occupies two immediately adjacent positions, recall of the items at

FIGURE 14.1

Proportion of items recalled in the correct position in a typical Ranschburg-effect experiment for control condition with no repeated items and repeat condition with a repeated item occurring at positions 2 and 5.

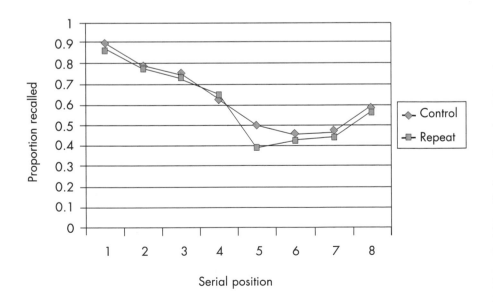

both positions improves, relative to the control condition. However, if the two occurrences are spaced apart (ideally with two or more items between the occurrences of the repeated item), recall is impaired. This decrement is only found in recall of the second occurrence, with recall of the first occurrence unimpaired. This decrement in recall of the second occurrence of a repeated item is now generally referred to as the "Ranschburg effect." According to Crowder's data, this effect is greatest when there are exactly two other items separating the occurrences of the repeated item.

Hinrichs, Mewaldt, and Redding (1973) offered a guessing-strategy account of the Ranschburg effect. This account assumes that participants deliberately try to avoid giving the same stimulus as a response at two different points on the list; in other words, when participants are unsure as to which item occurred at a particular position, they avoid guessing one that they recalled. Such a strategy is usually beneficial because most list positions contain nonrepeated items. However, it reduces the probability of getting the second occurrence of a repeated item correct. Some evidence supports such an account. Instructions not to guess reduce the magnitude of the effect (Greene, 1991; Henson, 1998; Walsh & Schwartz, 1977). No Ranschburg effect is found when participants are given tests that do not require emission of an item twice, such as recognition of the whole list (Wolf & Jahnke, 1968) or probed recall of single items (Jahnke, 1970). When list items are taken from a large vocabulary so that there is little chance of guessing an item correctly in the control condition, no Ranschburg effect is found (Hinrichs et al., 1973; Jahnke, 1974). To explain the finding that recall is improved when an item is recalled at two adjacent positions, one must add the additional assumption that a participant is likely to encode the fact that there was a repetition when an item occurs twice in a row and, therefore, avoids using a no-repetition-guessing strategy.

Elsewhere, I endorsed this guessing-strategy account of the Ranschburg effect (Greene, 1991). However, I have always been aware that there is one article containing results that are only accommodated poorly by this account, namely, Crowder's (1968b).

Crowder's Experiments

Crowder's (1968b) article is in many respects a logical outgrowth of his previous research in response-prefix effects. For example, Crowder (1967) carried out a series of experiments in which participants were required to say a particular stimulus between presentation of a list and recall. Although this stimulus (the response prefix) was the same on every trial, it still had a substantial negative effect on recall; indeed, the magnitude of the effect was about the same as if the list length had been increased by one. It did not matter whether or not the response prefix came from the same semantic category as the list items. However, the magnitude of this response-prefix impairment appeared to be greater when the prefix also occurred as a member of the list. No serial position curves were reported here, and no attempt was made to determine which list items were affected by the response prefix when it matched one of the list items.

Crowder (1968b) carried out a pair of experiments in which participants were asked to emit a response prefix that may also occur on a list. His first experiment is the most straightforward. Participants went through 128 trials in which they heard a list of eight consonants played on a tape recorder at a rate of 500 ms each; the consonants were always a random permutation of the set *BFHKNRTX.* Immediately after presentation of the list, the participant had to say a particular letter (i.e., the response prefix) and then had to recall the eight-letter list in order. In one block of trials, the response prefix was *L,* a letter that was not used on any of the lists; Crowder called this the *exclusive* condition. In another block, the response prefix was one of the letters also used in the list; this was called the *inclusive* condition. For all lists within a block, the response prefix was always the same, so there was presumably little memory load involved in remembering which prefix to emit.

The order of the two blocks was counterbalanced between participants. Crowder found that the exclusive condition led to greater recall than the inclusive condition. He then compared the exclusive condition with the eight subconditions of the inclusive block (i.e., the first subcondition is when the prefix matched the first list item, the second is when it matched the second list item, and so on, through all eight positions). The only one of these comparisons that was statistically significant was when there were two other items separating the prefix and the item it matched (i.e., the prefix matched the third list item). Crowder noted a parallel with the Ranschburg effect, where the greatest decrement in recall was found when two other items separated the occurrences of a repeated item. He suggested that this impairment in recall when the recall of two other items intervened between the prefix and its twin was a sort of Ranschburg effect without repetition on the study list.

If one accepts the claim that the decrement in recall caused when a response prefix is included on the study list reflects the same processes as the conventional Ranschburg effect, then one has a hard time fitting it into the biased-guessing account that has been applied to this effect. Perhaps the critical fact underlying acceptance of this account as an explanation of the Ranschburg effect is that a strategy whereby people avoid guessing items that they have already recalled is rational under most circumstances. That is, say that one truly has no idea what item occupies a particular position in the second half of a list. As long as the items come from a rather small set (and the Ranschburg effect is not found if they do not), under the conditions in which these experiments are usually done, one has a much higher probability of guessing the item correctly if one emits an item that one has not already recalled as opposed to an item one has.

However, such reasoning does not apply to the Crowder (1968b) study at all. First, no items are repeated on the list, so the whole idea of essentially betting against an intralist repetition does not apply. Of course, one could assume that participants (for some inexplicable reason) decide that their chance of guessing an item correctly is higher if they avoid using the prefix letter as a recall response. However, insofar as the prefix occurs on every list in the inclusive condition, such a guessing strategy would appear rather irrational. One might think that perhaps people do not realize until after having some experience with the inclusive condition that the response prefix is occurring in every list. However, such a hypothesis would lead one to predict that the prefix decrement found would shrink over the course of the experiment, and Crowder found no evidence of such a pattern. Of course, one does not discard a reasonable theory simply because there is one inconvenient result. However, it does seem as if Crowder's (1968b) results are worth following up, even if nobody has done so for the past few decades.

Experiment 1

My first priority was to replicate the results of Crowder (1968b). The only major change in procedure that I followed was to intermix inclusive and exclusive lists randomly rather than blocking the conditions, as done in the Crowder study. (Randomly intermixing the conditions seemed more analogous to the standard Ranschburg-effect experiments, where control and repetition lists are typically intermixed.) In all of the experiments here, the participants were students meeting a requirement for the introductory psychology class. In Experiment 1, 18 participants were tested. They were given a particular letter and were told that they would have to begin each recall test by saying and typing it. They then went through 90 test trials. On each trial, they saw a random permutation of eight letters from the set *BFHKLNRTX,* all shown one at a time at a 500-ms rate on a computer screen. Participants had to read each letter aloud as it was being shown. Then, they had to emit a letter as a response prefix. The response prefix was the same letter on all trials for each participant, and it always was one of the nine letters that were possible list items; the particular letter used was counterbalanced across participants. Immediately after emitting the response prefix, participants had to recall the eight list items in order. Emission of the prefix and recall of the list items were carried out in the same way. Participants had to type in the response while saying it aloud, with the response vanishing from the screen as soon as it was typed. As soon as the last response was typed, the next list began, until all 90 trials were completed.

There were essentially nine different conditions, all intermixed. One condition was the exclusive condition, in which the response prefix did not occur on the list. The other eight conditions were all inclusive conditions, in which the prefix could occur at any of the eight list positions. Each condition was tested on 10 lists. On each list, eight of the possible nine letters were used; across lists, each letter was omitted from exactly 10 of the study lists, so that use of a particular letter as a response prefix was completely uninformative as to whether it would occur on the list. Participants were informed of this design and the stimulus set at the beginning of the experiment.

The first question to ask is whether the inclusive and exclusive conditions differed at all: Is a response prefix more disruptive if it is included on a list than if it is excluded? The results are shown in Figure 14.2, which compares recall at each position in the exclusive condition with the mean recall for the inclusive conditions. Note that there is no particularly striking pattern: The inclusive condition is higher at some points, and the exclusive condition is higher at some points. There is no generalization possible such as the following: "Inclusion of the prefix on the study list impairs recall."

A different way of examining the data is to focus directly on recall for list items that match the response prefix. To do this, I made up a new serial position curve for the inclusive condition. The first position corresponds to recall of the first item on lists where the first item matches the response prefix. The second position corresponds to recall of the second item on lists where that item matches the prefix. Thus, I made up a serial position curve where each point corresponds to the probability of recall when an item at that position matches the response prefix. I plotted the proportion recalled in Figure 14.3 against recall at each position in the exclusive condition. The results replicate those reported by Crowder (1968b): Recall of an item that matches the response prefix is inhibited overall, with the magnitude

FIGURE 14.2

Proportion recalled in the exclusive condition and the combined inclusive conditions in Experiment 1.

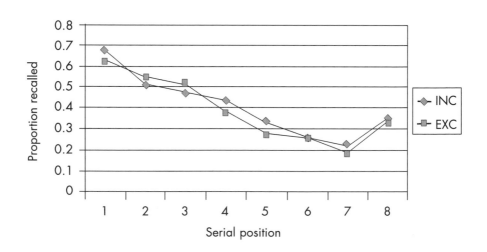

FIGURE 14.3

Proportion recalled in Experiment 1 for the exclusive and inclusive conditions. The inclusive curve consists of the probability of recalling an item at each position when that item was identical to the response prefix.

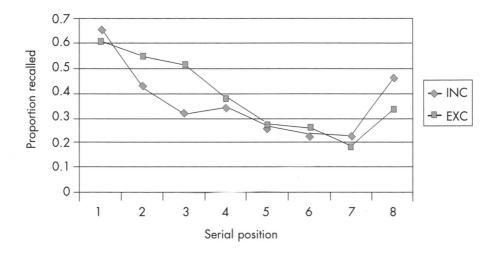

of this inhibition being greatest at the third position. Note, however, that at the beginning and end of the list, recall is facilitated when the item matches the response prefix. (For those who are interested, if one carries out significance tests using a .05 criterion at each position, the exclusive advantages at the second, third, and fourth positions are statistically significant by t tests, as are the inclusive advantages at the first and eighth positions; in any case, the replicability of this pattern across experiments proves to be the most convincing evidence for its validity.)

Figure 14.3 really captures the essence of what happened in this experiment. Here (and in the other experiments), there were no statistically significant differences between the inclusive and exclusive conditions at positions other than those containing the item that matched the response prefix in the inclusive condition. For example, when the inclusive condition has a prefix matching the third item in the list, the only position where the inclusive and exclusive conditions differed significantly was the third position. Thus, Figure 14.3 portrays the ways in which the inclusive and exclusive conditions may differ.

What I have here is a clear parallel with the Ranschburg effect. When a response prefix and an identical item occur consecutively, recall is facilitated, just as consecutive intraserial repetition facilitates recall. Note that the consecutive pattern occurs both at the last position (where the presentation of the last item is immediately followed by emission of the prefix) and at the first position (where emission of the prefix is immediately followed by recall of the last item).

Experiment 2

One of the hallmarks of the biased-guessing explanation of the Ranschburg effect is that it supposedly represents a rational decision on the part of the participant. The probability of guessing an item typically is higher if items already recalled are excluded. However, such reasoning does not apply to this experiment. There are no repeated items, and the identity of the response prefix is completely uninformative as to the items included on the list. In any case, little item information was required either in Experiment 1 (where the eight items always came from the same set of nine consonants) or in the Crowder (1968b) study, where lists were all permutations of a set of eight consonants. Still, one straightforward way of reconciling these data with the guessing approach came to mind. When people emit a consonant as a prefix, perhaps they increase the probability that they will mistakenly believe that they had emitted that consonant as a to-be-recalled item. To make things a little more concrete, say that the letter R was the prefix for a specific participant and that R was also the third letter on a specific list. The participant emits R as the prefix. Then, when it is time to recall the third list item, the participant mistakenly believes that R had been already recalled as a list item. Because no items were repeated on the study list, the participant decides to try some other item at the third position. The end result is a failure to recall a list item that matched the prefix, but this failure is caused not by a mistake in memory for the item but rather by a mistake in memory for when the response prefix had been emitted. Such a mistake would be easy to imagine in the Crowder (1968b) study, where recall was entirely spoken. Similarly, in Experiment 1 here, the computer cleared after each input so that there was no external record of the various responses.

To eliminate the possibility that this sort of response-monitoring confusion underlies the effect, all of the responses were kept on the screen during recall in Experiment 2. The procedure of presentation of the study lists for each of the 18 participants was the same as in Experiment 1. However, after the last item had disappeared from the screen, the words "type in and say your letter" appeared on the screen. The participant then had to type in and say the response prefix. The computer then printed "recall the list items," and the participant had to type in the list items while saying each aloud. All input by each participant (both the prefix and the recalled items) stayed on the screen until the last item was input. The experimenter encouraged each participant to look at the screen during recall and to use the information there to improve performance.

The results are shown in Figure 14.4. The data are plotted in the same way as in Figure 14.3 for Experiment 1; that is, recall in the exclusive condition is plotted

FIGURE 14.4

Proportion recalled in Experiment 2 for the exclusive and inclusive conditions. The inclusive curve consists of the probability of recalling an item at each position when that item was identical to the response prefix.

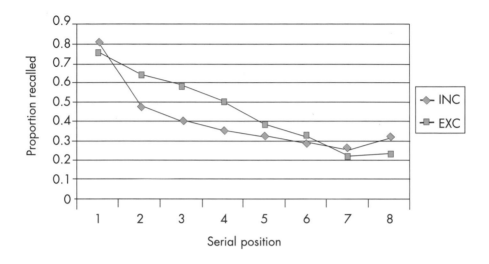

along with recall in the inclusive condition at each position when that item matched the response prefix. The first question to ask is whether supplying information during recall had any effect on performance. It clearly did. The level of recall is markedly higher in Experiment 2 than Experiment 1. Somewhat surprisingly, the shape of the serial position curve was also different in Experiment 2 than Experiment 1. Although participants had to read each item aloud as it was being presented, a circumstance that should lead to marked recency effects in serial recall (Crowder, 1970), there was only a small rise at the end of the list. Why providing participants with a visible record of their recall should reduce recency effects appears somewhat mysterious. Indeed, one could have predicted that by making it easy for people to see what items they had already recalled, this manipulation should help narrow the possible items at the last position and thereby enhance recency effects. Possibly, this shrinking of the recency effect resulted from the participants becoming too slow and deliberate as they worked their way through the list, so that this constant checking of already recalled items became a sort of distractor task that reduced the recency effect (cf. Postman & Phillips, 1965).

In any event, even though supplying participants with a record of their response activities clearly influenced their behavior, the results shown in Figure 14.4 make clear that it did not eliminate (or even noticeably reduce) the difference between the inclusive and exclusive conditions. As in Experiment 1, recall at interior positions is inhibited if the item matches the response prefix (with the exclusive condition being significantly higher than the inclusive condition by matched t tests at the second, third, fourth, and fifth positions), but performance is enhanced at the beginning and end of a list when the item matches the prefix (with a significant inclusive advantage at the first and last positions). This makes the sort of response-confusion account that I have been considering seem less attractive: Even though I made it presumably much less likely that participants would mistake their emission of the prefix with the recall of an item, the differences between the inclusive and exclusive conditions remained.

Experiment 3

One unfortunate aspect of serial recall is that it typically confounds input serial position with output position. That is, when one finds that the effect of condition interacts with serial position, one cannot be sure whether it is input position or output position that is critical. One way to disentangle these factors is to require recall in a different order than the input order. The most straightforward way to do this is to ask participants for backward recall. The procedure was exactly the same as in Experiment 1, with the exception that the 18 participants were required to type and say the items in backward order.

The results are shown in Figure 14.5. As one expects to find with backward recall, the serial position curve displays a large recency effect with only a slight primacy effect. However, for my purposes, the most striking finding is that there is not a significant advantage for the exclusive condition over the inclusive condition at any serial position. In other words, by switching the order of recall from forward to backward, one could reduce or eliminate the exclusive advantage found at some positions.

Experiment 4

The results of Experiment 3 are not completely convincing as a demonstration that an exclusive advantage is eliminated in backward recall. There are small exclusive advantages still found at several interior positions; moreover, the overall level of performance is low, especially in the critical interior positions, so one cannot rule out the possibility that a floor effect may be obscuring the expected advantage for the exclusive conditions. One way to get around that is to use shorter lists. In Experiment 4, participants were tested on lists of six items. The items on each list came from the set *BFHKRTX*, and recall was always preceded by a response prefix. Fourteen participants were asked for forward recall of the entire list, whereas 14 others were asked for backward recall.

FIGURE 14.5

Proportion recalled in Experiment 3 for the exclusive and inclusive conditions. The inclusive curve consists of the probability of recalling an item at each position when that item was identical to the response prefix.

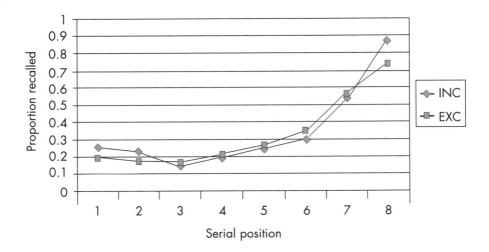

The forward-recall group was included in this experiment to ensure that one could find, using lists of six items, results analogous to those found in Experiments 1 and 2. The results from the forward-recall group are shown in Figure 14.6. If anything, use of six-item lists, which moves performance at all positions far from the floor, magnified the differences between the conditions. There is a clear advantage for the exclusive conditions at the interior positions and for the inclusive condition at the first and last positions. The differences at each position were statistically significant.

The results from the backward-recall group are presented in Figure 14.7 and show a different pattern. There is no advantage for the exclusive condition. Instead, there is an advantage for the inclusive condition at every position, although this advantage is only significant at the first and last positions.

General Discussion

The initial inspiration for these experiments was Crowder's (1968b) demonstration that emission of a response prefix could impair recall of a list item that is identical to the prefix. Crowder noted that this finding paralleled the typical Ranschburg

FIGURE 14.6

Proportion recalled in the forward-recall group in Experiment 4 for the exclusive and inclusive conditions. The inclusive curve consists of the probability of recalling an item at each position when that item was identical to the response prefix.

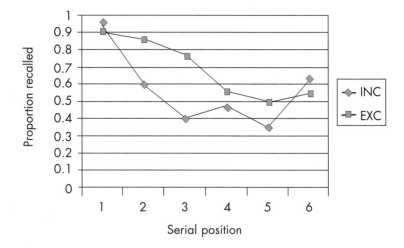

effect, where recall of the second occurrence of an item on a list was disrupted. The results reported here support Crowder's interpretation. When an item is identical to the response prefix, and when other (especially two) items separate emission of the prefix and recall of the item, recall of the item is impaired. Just as in typical Ranschburg procedures, when the presentation or recall of an item is immediately adjacent to the response prefix, recall of the item is facilitated.

First, I take these two findings separately. A popular interpretation of the Ranschburg effect is that it reflects participants' realization that they could maximize their chances of guessing correctly if they avoided using already recalled items as guesses. Such an interpretation seems less likely to be applicable here or in Crowder's (1968b) study. There are no repeated items here, and it was made clear to participants that the identity of the prefix was uninformative as to the makeup of the list; indeed, Crowder's lists always involved permutations of the same eight letters so no list-specific item information was required at all. The results of Experiment 2 make it appear unlikely that the inhibition caused by the prefix was due to a confusion between emission of the prefix and recall of the list items. It appears that the results found here (and possibly the typical Ranschburg effect as well) could better be

FIGURE 14.7

Proportion recalled in the backward-recall group in Experiment 4 for the exclusive and inclusive conditions. The inclusive curve consists of the probability of recalling an item at each position when that item was identical to the response prefix.

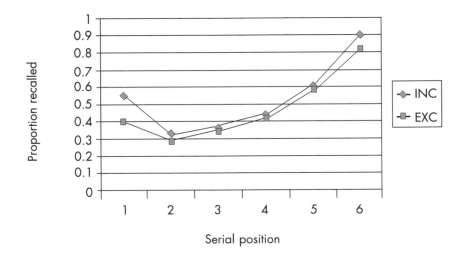

found by an involuntary short-lived inhibition process, whereby emission of a response reduces the probability that the response will be emitted again.

Why is recall facilitated when an item at a terminal position matches the prefix? It has been common for authors to speculate that recall at the beginning and end of a list involves somewhat different processes than recall of interior items. For example, Ebenholtz (1972) argued that recall at the beginning and end positions is based on associations of the items with some sort of positional representation, whereas recall at interior positions is based primarily on interitem associations. Typically, it is assumed that the context is somehow used to cue recall of the first and last item. Some such argument is necessary to explain recall of the first item because no other items had been recalled and therefore interitem associations could not be used. Although not logically necessary, contextual associations have often been seen as playing a role in recall of terminal items as well (e.g., Glenberg & Swanson, 1986). As always, the notion of context is somewhat undefined. Still, one would think that emission of a response prefix would be a component of the context. A prefix should be a particularly good reminder for an item that is identical to it. Therefore, the prefix serves as an effective retrieval cue for itself, and this more than compensates for whatever inhibition may result from having to emit the same response twice.

The other notable finding is that no inhibitory effect is found when participants have to recall the items in backward order. Logically, it would seem that people should be able to use the same processes in forward and backward recall, but evidence is accumulating that this is not true. Li and Lewandowsky (1995) reviewed a body of evidence that although interitem associations may be used for forward recall, backward recall largely depends on the use of a visual–spatial representation of the input material. The experiments reported here are uninformative as to the different processes underlying forward and backward recall, but the existence of this functional dissociation supports the general idea that different processes are used for forward and backward recall.

In short, the experiments reported here, along with the Crowder (1968b) study, support three conclusions. The first is that emission of a response can lead to a (probably involuntary) inhibition process, whereby repetition of that response becomes less likely to occur. A second conclusion is that recall of terminal and interior items is likely to be based on different processes, as one finds different patterns for items matching a response prefix depending on where in the list an item occurs. Finally, the results suggest that forward recall and backward recall are likely to involve different processes.

The concept of inhibition is one that has a long history in experimental psychology but declined in influence for many years beginning in the 1960s. The past decade has shown a noticeable increase in interest in inhibitory processes, although this interest has chiefly been concerned with inhibitory processes in long-term memory (see Anderson & Neely, 1996, for a review). Experiments such as these illustrate the point that for a complete understanding of immediate memory, one also needs to take inhibition into account.

References

Anderson, M. C., & Neely, J. H. (1996). Interference and inhibition in memory retrieval. In E. L. Bjork & R. A. Bjork (Eds.), *Memory* (pp. 237–313). San Diego, CA: Academic Press.

Crowder, R. G. (1967). Prefix effects in immediate memory. *Canadian Journal of Psychology, 21,* 450–461.

Crowder, R. G. (1968a). Intraserial repetition effects in immediate memory. *Journal of Verbal Learning and Verbal Behavior, 7,* 446–451.

Crowder, R. G. (1968b). Repetition effects in immediate memory when there are no repeated elements in the stimuli. *Journal of Experimental Psychology, 78,* 605–609.

Crowder, R. G. (1970). The role of one's own voice in immediate memory. *Cognitive Psychology, 1,* 157–178.

Crowder, R. G., & Melton, A. W. (1965). The Ranschburg phenomenon: Failures of immediate recall correlated with repetition of elements within a stimulus. *Psychonomic Science, 2,* 295–296.

Ebenholtz, S. M. (1972). Serial learning and dimensional organization. In G. H. Bower (Ed.), *The psychology of learning and motivation* (Vol. 5, pp. 267–314). New York: Academic Press.

Fagot, C., & Pashler, H. (1995). Repetition blindness: Perception or memory failure? *Journal of Experimental Psychology: Human Perception and Performance, 21,* 275–292.

Glenberg, A. M., & Swanson, N. G. (1986). A temporal distinctiveness theory of recency and modality effects. *Journal of Experimental Psychology: Learning, Memory, and Cognition, 12,* 3–15.

Greene, R. L. (1991). The Ranschburg effect: The role of guessing strategies. *Memory & Cognition, 19,* 313–317.

Henson, R. N. A. (1998). Item repetition in short-term memory: Ranschburg repeated. *Journal of Experimental Psychology: Learning, Memory, and Cognition, 24,* 1162–1181.

Hinrichs, J. V., Mewaldt, S. P., & Redding, J. (1973). The Ranschburg effect: Repetition and guessing factors in short-term memory. *Journal of Verbal Learning and Verbal Behavior, 12,* 64–75.

Jahnke, J. C. (1970). Probed recall of strings that contain repeated elements. *Journal of Verbal Learning and Verbal Behavior, 9,* 450–455.

Jahnke, J. C. (1974). Restrictions on the Ranschburg effect. *Journal of Experimental Psychology, 103,* 183–185.

Li, S., & Lewandowsky, S. (1995). Forward and backward recall: Different retrieval processes. *Journal of Experimental Psychology: Learning, Memory, and Cognition, 21,* 837–847.

Postman, L., & Phillips, L. W. (1965). Short-term temporal changes in free recall. *Quarterly Journal of Experimental Psychology, 17,* 132–138.

Walsh, M. F., & Schwartz, M. (1977). The Ranschburg effect: Tests of the guessing-bias and proactive interference hypotheses. *Journal of Verbal Learning and Verbal Behavior, 16,* 55–68.

Wolf, T. M., & Jahnke, J. C. (1968). The effects of intraserial repetition on short-term recognition and recall. *Journal of Experimental Psychology, 77,* 572–580.

CHAPTER 15

A Functional Analysis of Primary Memory

James S. Nairne

It is ironic that Bob Crowder, trained in the functionalist tradition, was perhaps best known as the cocreator of a structural memory store known as precategorical acoustic storage (PAS). PAS was proposed by Crowder and Morton (1969) as an auditory analog to visual sensory memory (e.g., Sperling, 1960) and, like most memory stores, is defined by fixed mnemonic characteristics. Information registered in PAS is assumed to be (a) acoustic, (b) precategorical or prelinguistic, (c) subject to loss from rapid decay or overwriting, and (d) constrained by capacity limitations (only one or two sequential auditory signals can be stored). There are hints throughout Crowder's writings that he was never completely comfortable with the structural aspects of PAS (e.g., Crowder, 1983), but the theory was embraced by a memory community eager for the proposal of multiple memory stores.

One of the appealing qualities of the PAS model is its compelling account of two benchmark short-term memory phenomena: the modality effect and the suffix effect. The modality effect is the recency advantage, usually restricted to the last one or two items, that one sees for lists presented aloud; the auditory advantage can be eliminated—the suffix effect—by the addition of a redundant spoken item, such as the word *recall*, at the end of the list. Both effects are explained by assuming that lingering acoustic information, residing in PAS, can act as an additional source of information about the identity of list items. Only recency is affected because PAS is limited in capacity; the suffix, acting as if it is an additional list item, interferes with the contents of PAS, eliminating the recency boost.

By the mid-1980s, in a number of empirical studies, researchers had established that the PAS model, as envisioned by Crowder and Morton (1969), cannot be correct. For example, studies show that nonauditory stimuli (mouthed or lipread) can produce serial position curves that mimic the modality and suffix effects (Campbell & Dodd, 1980; Nairne & Walters, 1983); the suffix effect was discovered to be sensitive in some circumstances to postcategorical dimensions (Ayres, Jonides, Reitman, Egan, & Howard, 1979; Neath, Surprenant, & Crowder, 1993) and to last over intervals far exceeding those proposed in the original model (Watkins & Watkins, 1980). To his credit, Crowder accepted the failure of PAS and even championed it as an

283

achievement of sorts; among other things, he argued, it demonstrated that the model had been specified enough to be falsified (Crowder, 1983).

Although the demise of PAS may seem disheartening to those who have followed Crowder's career, it is important to resist that temptation. If one ignores the structuralist aspects of PAS—the idea that it represents some kind of specialized sensory memory system—and attends instead to the functional analysis, much of what Crowder had to say about PAS still rings true. In fact, I argue that Crowder's functional analysis of PAS provides an excellent conceptualization not of sensory memory but of primary memory as a whole. Two ideas are central to this functional analysis: (a) remembering is driven by cues, remnants of processing, rather than by stored "items," and (b) the mnemonic value of these cues depends on their discriminability.

I briefly show how these key assumptions are implemented in a general model of primary memory called the "feature model" (Nairne, 1988, 1990), and I describe how the model accounts for some classic data from Crowder on the immediate recall of homophones. My main focus, however, is on the critical role that discriminability plays in the functional analysis: Successful remembering, rather than depending on a passive matching of encoding and retrieval conditions, is controlled by how well the conditions of retrieval uniquely specify or predict target information. Although appeals to discriminability have a long history in memory theory, through concepts such as distinctiveness and cue overload, theorists often consider discriminability only as an afterthought; instead the majority of attention is placed—incorrectly I argue—on the absolute match between the encoded trace and the conditions present during retrieval. This last point has implications that extend beyond the study of primary memory, as I discuss in the latter part of this chapter.

Function of Precategorical Acoustic Storage

At the heart of any functional analysis is an adaptive question: What is X for? In the case of PAS, the lingering acoustic information was assumed to provide additional information about the last one or two list items—in the form of raw sensory energy. The contents of PAS were potentially useful because they enabled the participant to give the last one or two items a kind of once-over prior to recall. He or she could compare the lingering echoic information with the categorized memory for the last item, residing in primary memory, and use the former to correct the latter (Crowder, 1976). The comparison process was never specified in any formal detail, but it was assumed that (a) it probably occurred during the pause between the end of the list and the beginning of recall, and (b) its main purpose was to help the participant resolve uncertainty about the identity of recency items.

The precategorical nature of the information stored in PAS is a key element of the theory. The echo, according to Crowder (1978), was "functionally uncorrelated with the whole semantic-episodic system" (p. 74), which meant that by itself it could not be directly recalled as a familiar linguistic item. PAS served merely as a repository for "cues," or remnants of processing, that by themselves lacked meaning. In contrast, primary memory was the storage location for categorized items and the ultimate source for immediate recall. Performance improved with auditory presentation because the participant had two sources of information about the final list items—the precategorical echo in PAS and the categorized "item" circulating in primary memory. But the former was useful only as a check and played no role in the production of an actual recall response.

Because PAS contained only raw stimulus energy rather than categorized items, Crowder correctly anticipated that acoustic input would not lead to recall benefits under all circumstances. The echo would aid performance, Crowder argued, if and only if it provided discriminative information about one or more of the list items. Consider a case in which a participant has received a list of five digits for immediate recall (8–3–6–4–9) and there is a lingering echoic trace (na^yn) for the last item on the list. In this instance, any comparison that the participant makes between the echoic trace and the contents of primary memory is apt to be useful because the echo uniquely predicts one of the list items (nine); consequently, one would expect better recall of that item compared with the visual case where the corresponding sensory energy is subject to more rapid decay or interference.

Now consider a different scenario in which the participant has been given a list of homophones (write–right–rite) presented visually (to allow for identification) along with concurrent auditory input. Because of the auditory presentation, there should still be an echoic trace in PAS for the last list item (ra^yt), but the acoustic information is nondiscriminative—it is consistent with all of the list items and does not uniquely predict any one of them. There is still an echo, providing for a "richer" absolute representation, but the echo provides no discriminative information about item identity. Under these conditions, Crowder predicted, there should be no modality effect—concurrent auditory presentation should not improve recency performance relative to silently presented lists.

Crowder (1978) confirmed this prediction in a series of experiments in which he explored the recall of phonologically uniform lists. Participants were given lists containing only homophones (write–right–rite; pare–pair–pear), presented visually on a screen, and were asked to read each word either aloud or silently when it appeared. The task was immediate serial recall, which required the participants to recall the items in order, beginning with the first item presented and ending with the last. Not surprisingly, Crowder found that errors increased over serial position but, most important, there was no evidence for enhanced recency. In fact, in this instance there was actually better overall performance for the input presented silently. Crowder (1978) argued that these data provide strong support for the precategorical hypothesis: The mnemonic record in PAS is raw, prelinguistic, and useful only to the extent that it uniquely predicts a meaningful list item.

The Feature Model

It is best to separate Crowder's analysis of the echo, and its ultimate usefulness, from Crowder and Morton's (1969) other assumptions about the architecture of PAS. The structural aspects of PAS—assumptions about decay and capacity, for example—have not withstood the test of time, but the functional analysis described in the preceding section turned out to be a prescient characterization of memory. The idea that one uses the remnants of prior processing as cues for reconstructing the past, rather than as items to be recalled, remains popular and is reflected in many current memory models. Theorists often now appeal to redintegration processes, during which cues in primary memory are used to help decide on an appropriate candidate for recall or recognition (e.g., Lewandowsky, 1999; Schweickert, 1993). Less overt attention is typically given to the role of discriminability in these models, although it, too, flows from the machinery of most redintegration assumptions. To demonstrate, in this section I show how the "deep structure" of Crowder's functional analysis is implemented in a particular model of primary memory—the feature model (Nairne, 1988, 1990).

The feature model is one of primary memory, not sensory memory, but it shares two important assumptions with Crowder's characterization of PAS: First, as a storage device, primary memory is simply a repository for cues that can be used for reconstructing the immediate past. No items are represented—only features that by themselves are not recallable. Second, the contents of primary memory, rather than leading to direct recall, benefit performance if and only if they provide discriminative information about a possible recall candidate. Observable recall, and presumably the subjective internal experience as well, is the product of a cue-driven redintegration process. The collection of features is interpreted or deblurred, and the end result is the recalled item.

Notice that this characterization of primary memory differs from the traditional view where categorized items are assumed to "sit" in some special state of enhanced availability (e.g., Atkinson & Shiffrin, 1971; Baddeley, 1986). In the feature model encoded traces are stored in secondary memory, but what sits in primary memory trace is simply a fragile copy, or remnant, of the encoded secondary memory trace.[1] As a consequence, it is not possible for the participant to recall (or "dump") an item directly out of a storage buffer (e.g., Atkinson & Shiffrin, 1971) or out of a time-limited rehearsal loop (Baddeley, 1986); instead, the participant simply uses the

---

[1]In both PAS and the feature model, transient memory traces consist only of patterns of information that must be interpreted before recall. However, all information in PAS is precategorical; in the feature model, the primary memory trace is a record of encoding and contains sets of features that are "meaningful" in the sense that they are by-products of categorization—but, again, these features do not constitute a recallable item.

processing record, along with any other externally provided cues, in an attempt to reconstruct what occurred moments before. In the feature model, as in most current long-term memory models, all remembering is cue driven regardless of the time scales involved.

The feature model gets its name from the fact that memory traces in the model, regardless of where they are stored, consist of ordered features (represented in vectors). These features come in two varieties: modality dependent and modality independent. Modality-dependent features represent the presentation conditions and are assumed to consist of both intraitem (e.g., modality, language) and extraitem (e.g., room cues) attributes. Modality-independent features are "independent" of presentation conditions, meaning they generally are the same, regardless of presentation conditions; they are assumed to result from and reflect the processes of categorization (e.g., elements of a verbal label, semantic or imaginal elements). The distinction between modality-dependent and modality-independent features is important because it enables the model to handle modality-specific effects, such as the modality effect and the suffix effect.

The Deblurring Process

At the point of recall, the participant analyzes the processing records left in primary memory in an effort to decide on an appropriate recall candidate. Primary memory traces are inherently blurry because of interference from subsequently occurring material, so what remains is almost always a degraded version of the original encoding. A given primary memory trace is interpreted by comparing it with a collection of "intact" traces in secondary memory (contained in the secondary memory search set). This deblurring process is similarity based, which means that the probability that a particular item from secondary memory will be sampled as a recall candidate depends on its similarity to the primary memory trace that is being interpreted. More formally, the probability of sampling (P_s) is stated as

$$P_s[(SM(j) \ / \ PM(i)] \ = \ \frac{s(i, j)}{\Sigma s(i, k)} , \tag{1}$$

where $s(i, j)$ represents the computed similarity between primary memory trace, $PM(i)$, and secondary memory trace, $SM(j)$. On the basis of the work of Shepard and others (Nosofsky, 1986; Shepard, 1987), similarity is defined by the distance between two trace vectors in some psychological space. In the feature model, distance is calculated by simply adding the number of mismatched features across the primary and secondary memory vectors and dividing by the number of compared features. That is,

$$d(i, j) \ = \ \frac{\Sigma M(k)}{N} , \tag{2}$$

where the index of mismatches, $M(k)$, is incremented by one if feature position

$x(i, k)$ does not match feature position $x(j, k)$. The distance measure is then related to similarity in the manner described by Shepard (1987):

$$s(i, j) = e^{-d(i, j)}. \tag{3}$$

Figure 15.1 shows an example of how the deblurring process works. Assume there is a degraded trace in primary memory, containing seven features, but only the middle three features are interpretable. To decide on an appropriate recall response, the degraded trace is compared with possible recall candidates in the secondary memory search set, represented here by the three intact traces on the second line. First, the "distance" between the primary memory trace and each of the intact traces is calculated; features are compared position by position and the number of mismatching features is summed and divided by the total number of features. Distance is then transformed into similarity through the application of Equation 3. At this point, there is a certain probability that any member of the search set will be selected, or sampled, based on a ratio of similarities. For example, the probability that the second intact item will be sampled is equal to the similarity between the primary memory trace and this second item divided by the sum of the similarities between the primary memory trace and all of the members of the search set.

There are other assumptions in the feature model—for example, regarding the overwriting of features and output probabilities—that have no direct bearing on this chapter. I showed in detail elsewhere how the feature model handles modality and suffix-related effects (Nairne, 1990; see also Neath, 1998). Briefly, the auditory recency advantage is due to residual modality-dependent features. Modality-

FIGURE 15.1

Schematic representation of redintegration in the feature model.

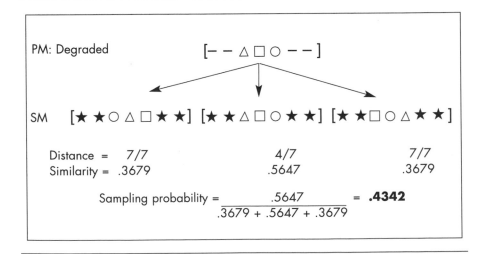

dependent features are given more weight when items are presented aloud, for reasons outlined in Nairne (1988), and they generally help to specify the correct list item.[2] However, the intrinsic qualities of any individual feature, or group of features, do not ultimately control performance. As I show below, what matters is the discriminability of those features, as argued by Crowder (1978) in his functional analysis of PAS.

Discriminability of Features

Once redintegration is assigned a central role, then predicted recall obviously depends on the specific assumptions that are made about the deblurring process. In the case of the feature model, as described above, redintegration is controlled by a similarity-based sampling rule (i.e., a choice axiom). This means that a particular primary memory trace is likely to be interpreted correctly only if its features specify the appropriate item in the secondary memory search set. In the example shown in Figure 15.1, notice that the degraded primary memory trace is most similar to the second intact item—there are the fewest number of mismatches—and this item, in fact, is the item with the largest sampling probability.

At face value, this suggests that the match between the primary memory trace and its true representation in secondary memory is probably the main controller of performance; this is, of course, a commonly accepted "principle" among memory theorists, namely, that performance benefits vary directly as a function of the match, or overlap, between the cue and target trace—as encoded (e.g., Roediger & Guynn, 1996; Tulving, 1983). However, as Crowder (1978) showed in his analysis of phonologically uniform lists, improving the match does not, by fiat, lead to improvements in performance. For homophones presented aloud, the residual echoic information for the last list item improves the cue–target match, at least compared with the cue–target match for visual items, but there is no gain in recall performance. It is not the cue–target match that is important, but whether the cues uniquely specify the target to the exclusion of other recall possibilities.

These ideas about the discriminability of features are developed more formally in Figure 15.2, which shows how sampling probabilities in the feature model can change with an overall improvement in the cue–target match. The top half of the figure shows the sampling calculations for the retrieval scenario presented in Figure 15.1; the bottom half of the figure shows what happens when the cue–target match improves by virtue of an "intact" primary memory trace. In this case, the three missing features in the degraded trace (represented by dashed lines in the top row)

---

[2]Here there are few, if any, differences between PAS and the feature model. Modality-dependent features are essentially "precategorical" in the sense that they faithfully represent the presentation conditions (although see Nairne, 1988).

FIGURE 15.2

Redintegration in the feature model for a partially degraded trace (top) and redintegration when the same trace is presented intact (bottom). There is no increase in the sampling probability even though the absolute cue–target match has improved.

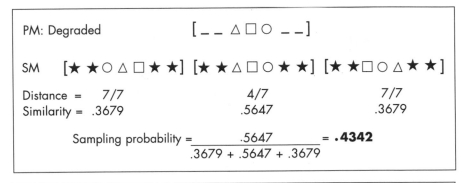

have been restored, revealing that the primary memory record is actually a copy of the second item in the secondary memory search set. There are no longer any mismatches between the primary memory trace and the correct target, leading to a calculated similarity of 1.0.

However, notice there is no increase in the actual sampling probabilities. The probability of correctly sampling the second item when the primary trace is intact is equal to the sampling probability found when over half of the primary memory trace's features have degraded. The reason, of course, is that the restored features (each represented by a filled star) are shared by all the members of the secondary memory search set. These particular features are nondiscriminative—they are consistent with all of the list items and provide no unique information. This example roughly models Crowder's (1978) phonologically uniform list experiment, in which added residual acoustic information failed to lead to a performance gain; in that case, the additional cue information (the acoustic record [ra�53t]), as in Figure

15.2, failed to uniquely specify any of the list items (write–right–rite). Crowder (1978) found no evidence for an auditory advantage despite the fact that presumably there was residual auditory information for the last item on the list. Again, providing additional cue information—that is, improving the match—helps memory if and only if the information is discriminative.

It is worth pausing briefly to note that the situation depicted in Figure 15.2 is not clouded by concerns about the difference between a nominal and functional cue–target match. Tulving (1983) argued persuasively that one must consider the compatibility between the trace and the cue as encoded rather than as the nominal cue–target match. Thus, increasing the physical similarity between encoding and retrieval conditions is not sufficient; one also needs to increase the functional similarity between encoded cues and target traces. This is not a problem in Figure 15.2 because the comparisons are occurring between encoded features in sets of memory traces. In the feature model, even when the cue is not a remnant of prior list processing (e.g., an extralist cue), the retrieval comparisons are made between encoded features in primary memory and candidate sets in secondary memory. Thus, even when there is an increase in the functional cue–target match (e.g., Figure 15.2) there need not be an increase in overall recall performance.

Role of the Encoding–Retrieval Match

The retrieval assumptions of the feature model, especially target sampling based on a choice axiom, are not particularly controversial. Many long-term memory models use a similar approach (e.g., Raaijmakers & Shiffrin, 1980), as do many models of categorization (Nosofsky, 1986) and many connectionist models (McClelland & Rumelhart, 1986). However, by stressing the retrieval *value* of features, or cues, the feature model undercuts the idea that it is primarily the match, or compatibility, between encoded cues and traces that controls remembering. Of course, the latter idea is commonplace in the memory literature, often appearing in the form of general memory "principles" such as encoding specificity or transfer-appropriate processing (Roediger & Guynn, 1996; Tulving, 1983).[3]

It may be true that in most instances improving the encoding–retrieval match improves performance. For example, in the feature model, sampling probabilities increase with the encoding–retrieval match as long as the additional matching features are not shared by the other competitors in the search set. Again, however, it is the

---

[3]The principle of transfer-appropriate processing usually refers to the match between the processing activities engaged during encoding and retrieval (e.g., Roediger & Guynn, 1996). Thus, in common usage, it is treated as transfer-similar processing rather than as transfer-appropriate processing. One could use the term transfer-appropriate processing to mean any processing that appropriately specifies the correct target item.

predictability of the features that actually controls performance, not the number of matching features. Increasing cue–target overlap simply increases the chances that features may come into play that uniquely specify the correct target. As Crowder's (1978) phonologically uniform list experiment and the example in Figure 15.2 show, performance does not necessarily improve as the cue becomes more similar to the encoded target trace.

In fact, it is easy to conceive of situations where an increase in the functional match between a cue and a target trace might lead to lower subsequent memory performance. Correct performance in the feature model depends on selecting the appropriate item from a pool of competitors; performance therefore depends not only on the nature of the competitors but also on the total number of competitors in the set. Increasing the cue–target match potentially lowers performance anytime added cue information "recruits" additional members into the secondary memory search set. The overall size of the competitor set is reflected in the denominator of Equation 1, so sampling probabilities decrease as the size of the search set increases. This is the mechanism in the feature model (and in other models as well) that produces list-length effects (Strong, 1912).

As shown in Figure 15.3, the idea that added features might increase the size of the search set is not farfetched. Imagine that the composition of the secondary memory search set is determined by the presence of any feature overlap between a primary and secondary memory trace. In the top half of Figure 15.3, the search set consists of only three items, those items that contain at least one of the three interpretable features contained in the primary memory trace. In the bottom half of the figure, showing the intact version of the primary memory trace, the size of the search set has increased by two items because those items contain features present in the intact version of the trace. These features are nondiscriminative—they do not uniquely specify a trace—and the presence of the additional competitors lowers the overall sampling probability for the correct item. Thus, in this particular case, increasing the functional cue–target match hurts the chances of successful remembering.[4]

Tying memory performance exclusively to the match between an encoded cue and an isolated memory trace is somewhat analogous to claiming that time is the underlying cause of forgetting. Time is correlated with forgetting, just as the match is typically correlated with remembering, but neither plays a truly causal role. It is easy to find examples demonstrating how memory decreases, stays the same, or increases with the passage of time (e.g., McGeoch, 1932). As just discussed, the

---

[4]There are, of course, many examples in the memory literature where increasing the nominal match between a retrieval cue and a presented item is associated with lower performance (e.g., recognition failure of recallable words, part-set cueing inhibition). These effects are typically interpreted as arising from a poor functional cue–target match. I argue that increases in the functional cue–target match can lead to lower performance as well.

FIGURE 15.3

Schematic showing how an improvement in the cue–target match can lead to a lowering of performance. In the bottom panel, presentation of the intact trace "recruits" additional members into the secondary memory search set, lowering sampling probability.

same can be said for increases in the overlap between cues and targets—performance may increase, stay the same, or decrease. The passage of time is not a sufficient condition for observing forgetting; similarly, increasing the compatibility between a cue and target is not sufficient for improving memory. What matters is the extent to which the conditions of retrieval uniquely specify or predict the to-be-remembered target.

Rejoinders

Does this mean that principles such as encoding specificity or transfer-appropriate processing are wrong? Although I cannot offer a resounding "yes," it does seem clear that statements about the benefits of cue-trace compatibility need to be qualified in a major way. In fairness, most memory theorists acknowledge that factors other than the cue–target match are important to performance (e.g., Eysenck, 1979; Jacoby & Craik, 1979; Roediger & Guynn, 1996; Tulving, 1983). The principle of cue overload, for example, is really a statement about the distinctiveness of cues: The more information associated with a retrieval cue, the less likely that any given piece of information will be retrieved (Watkins & Watkins, 1975).

There may also be situations in which the match between a cue and a target trace is both necessary and sufficient to predict mnemonic performance. Some kinds of recognition judgments, for example, could be based on a global index of familiarity that increases or decreases with the match between the retrieval cue and information stored in memory (e.g., Gillund & Shiffrin, 1984; Hintzman, 1988; Murdock, 1982). Models that rely on a measure of global familiarity have the additional advantage that they can easily account for why and how false recognitions increase or decrease with changes in the structure of retrieval cues (e.g., Arndt & Hirshman, 1998). The feature model, and the matching examples that I consider here, are diagnostic of situations in which the intent is to recover a particular stored item from among a set of competitors. Not all retrieval environments require this kind of specificity.

One might also argue that any processing record, regardless of the encoding task, is essentially unique at some level because it is created at a particular moment in time. It is unlikely that multiple memory traces can be created simultaneously, so any given stored trace contains idiosyncratic contextual elements. It follows, then, that increasing the match between the cue and the target trace will at some point tap these key elements, improving memory performance. But even here, and ignoring the difficulties surrounding the task of improving compatibility in this way, the benefit to performance lies not in the match but in the presence of predictive features. Memory performance is enhanced because the retrieval cue contains features that uniquely specify one target trace to the exclusion of others.

The Legacy of Crowder's Functional Analysis

Although Bob Crowder may have been widely known for developing and promoting a structural memory system—PAS—he never really strayed far from his functionalist roots. Even with PAS, a deep structure—a functional analysis—rises above the structuralist assumptions that eventually fell victim to the rigors of empirical testing. Key to Crowder's analysis are two important proposals: (a) Remembering is driven by cues, remnants of prior processing, that are not themselves recallable items, and (b) the mnemonic value of these cues depends on their discriminability.

I have argued in this chapter that both of these assumptions play a prominent role in modern conceptualizations of memory. In the case of primary memory, in particular, the traditional idea that items sit in a special state of availability, allowing for a kind of direct retrieval, has been replaced by an emphasis on redintegration. What is stored in primary memory is information that can be used to help reconstruct the immediate past, not items per se that can be directly dumped out of buffers or articulatory loops. Similar ideas are characteristic of long-term memory models that assume, of course, that all remembering is cue driven. Crowder's analysis of the content of PAS, and the role it plays in remembering, thus stands as a prescient accounting of the way memory operates.

The second key assumption of the functional analysis is the emphasis on the discriminability of mnemonic information. What matters to remembering is not the presence of cues that match the features encoded in the target trace but rather the predictability of those cues. The feature model was used to show how these ideas about discriminability could be formally implemented; it was found that increasing the functional match between the primary memory trace and its copy in secondary memory can increase, decrease, or have no effect on correct memory performance. Stressing the discriminability of cues, rather than the encoding-retrieval match, may constrain some widely accepted principles of remembering—such as the encoding-specificity principle. Increasing the match between encoding and retrieval may lead to enhancements in remembering, but only to the extent that distinctive, predictive cues come into play.

References

Arndt, J., & Hirshman, E. (1998). True and false recognition in MINVERA2: Explanations from a global matching perspective. *Journal of Memory and Language, 39,* 371–391.

Atkinson, R. C., & Shiffrin, R. M. (1971). The control of short-term memory. *Scientific American, 225,* 82–90.

Ayres, T. J., Jonides, J., Reitman, J. S., Egan, J. C., & Howard, D. A. (1979). Differing suffix effects for the same physical suffix. *Journal of Experimental Psychology: Human Learning and Memory, 5,* 315–321.

Baddeley, A. D. (1986). *Working memory.* Oxford: Oxford University Press.

Campbell, R., & Dodd, B. (1980). Hearing by eye. *Quarterly Journal of Experimental Psychology, 32,* 85–99.

Crowder, R. G. (1976). *Principles of learning and memory.* Hillsdale, NJ: Erlbaum.

Crowder, R. G. (1978). Memory for phonologically uniform lists. *Journal of Verbal Learning and Verbal Behavior, 17,* 73–89.

Crowder, R. G. (1983). The purity of auditory memory. *Philosophical Transactions of the Royal Society of London, B.382,* 251–265.

Crowder, R. G., & Morton, J. (1969). Precategorical acoustic storage (PAS). *Perception & Psychophysics, 5,* 365–373.

Eysenck, M. W. (1979). Depth, elaboration, and distinctiveness. In L. S. Cermak & F. I. M. Craik (Eds.), *Levels of processing in human memory* (pp. 89–118). Hillsdale, NJ: Erlbaum.

Gillund, G., & Shiffrin, R. M. (1984). A retrieval model for both recognition and recall. *Psychological Review, 91,* 1–67.

Hintzman, D. L. (1988). Judgments of frequency and recognition memory in a multiple-trace memory model. *Psychological Review, 95,* 528–551.

Jacoby, L. L., & Craik, F. I. M. (1979). Effects of elaboration of processing at encoding and retrieval: Trace distinctiveness and recovery of initial context. In L. S. Cermak & F. I. M. Craik (Eds.), *Levels of processing in human memory* (pp. 1–21). Hillsdale, NJ: Erlbaum.

Lewandowsky, S. (1999). Redintegration and response suppression in serial recall: A dynamic network model. *International Journal of Psychology, 34,* 434–446.

McClelland, J. L., & Rumelhart, D. E. (1986). *Parallel distributed processing: Explorations in the microstructure of cognition* (Vol. 1). Cambridge, MA: MIT Press.

McGeoch, J. A. (1932). Forgetting and the law of disuse. *Psychological Review, 39,* 352–370.

Murdock, B. B., Jr. (1982). A theory for the storage and retrieval of item and associative information. *Psychological Review, 89,* 609–626.

Nairne, J. S. (1988). A framework for interpreting recency effects in immediate serial recall. *Memory & Cognition, 16,* 343–352.

Nairne, J. S. (1990). A feature model of immediate memory. *Memory & Cognition, 18,* 251–269.

Nairne, J. S., & Walters, V. L. (1983). Silent mouthing produces modality- and suffix-like effects. *Journal of Verbal Learning and Verbal Behavior, 22,* 475–483.

Neath, I. (1998). *Human memory: An introduction to research, data, and theory.* Pacific Grove, CA: Brooks/Cole.

Neath, I., Surprenant, A. M., & Crowder, R. G. (1993). The context-dependent stimulus-suffix effect. *Journal of Experimental Psychology: Learning, Memory, and Cognition, 19,* 698–703.

Nosofsky, R. M. (1986). Attention, similarity, and the identification–categorization relationship. *Journal of Experimental Psychology: General, 115,* 39–57.

Raaijmakers, J. G. W., & Shiffrin, R. M. (1980). Search of associative memory. *Psychological Review, 95,* 93–134.

Roediger, H. L., III, & Guynn, M. J. (1996). Retrieval processes. In E. L. Bjork & R. A. Bjork (Eds.), *Memory* (pp. 197–236). New York: Academic Press.

Schweickert, R. (1993). A multinomial processing tree model for degradation and redintegration in immediate recall. *Memory & Cognition, 21,* 168–175.

Shepard, R. N. (1987). Toward a universal law of generalization for psychological science. *Science, 237,* 1317–1323.

Sperling, G. (1960). The information available in brief visual presentations. *Psychological Monographs, 74*(11, Whole No. 498).

Strong, E. K., Jr. (1912). The effect of length of series upon recognition memory. *Psychological Review, 19,* 447–462.

Tulving, E. (1983). *Elements of episodic memory.* New York: Oxford University Press.

Watkins, O. C., & Watkins, M. J. (1975). Buildup of proactive inhibition as a cue-overload effect. *Journal of Experimental Psychology: Human Learning and Memory, 104,* 442–452.

Watkins, O. C., & Watkins, M. J. (1980). The modality effect and echoic persistence. *Journal of Experimental Psychology: General, 109,* 251–278.

CHAPTER 16

What Is Working Memory Capacity?

Randall W. Engle

obert Crowder's 1983 article "The Demise of Short-Term Memory" influenced me on the questions that led to the research and ideas I discuss in this chapter. In that article, Crowder questioned the need for a separate short-term memory (STM) and pointed out that research has not established that STM is necessary for successful cognitive functioning. Furthermore, I make the case that working memory (WM) should be considered a system consisting of temporarily activated long-term memories and controlled attention, which is important in maintaining activation. The maintaining of the activation of a representation is generally unnecessary but becomes particularly important in the face of proactive interference. Both of these issues are discussed at length by Crowder in his 1983 article. Crowder also discussed the role of individual differences in drawing conclusions about the existence of a short-term store; that approach is pivotal to the conclusions I draw here.

Research following Baddeley and Hitch (1974) and Daneman and Carpenter (1980) shows that the broader concept of WM is important to higher order cognition. Furthermore, complex WM tasks "work" in the sense that they predict performance on a variety of cognitive tasks. However, the nature of individual differences in WM is still unclear.

The research I describe in this chapter is directed at two general questions. The first is "What is WM capacity?" That is, what mechanisms account for the covariation between a variety of WM tasks, on the one hand, and tasks of higher level cognition, such as reading comprehension and reasoning, on the other hand? The second question is "What do the results of studies on individual differences in WM capacity tell us about the nature of WM in general?" The conclusions that I draw are based largely on individual differences studies, but studies using dual-task methods were also helpful to me. For example, a relatively safe generalization is that individuals with high WM capacity who are performing a task while concurrently performing

This work was supported by Grants F49620-93-1-0336 and F49620-97-1041 from the Air Force Office of Scientific Research. I thank Michael Kane, Zach Hambrick, Tabitha Payne, Rebekah Smith, and Kate Bleckley for their comments on this chapter.

an attention-demanding secondary task perform similarly to individuals with low WM capacity (Kane & Engle, 2000; Rosen & Engle, 1997). The evidence for my conclusions comes from a variety of memory and attention paradigms, which increase the generality of the results and give convergent validity to the ideas. My interest in these questions was initially directed at relatively molecular issues about the importance of temporarily active memory. However, pursuit of answers to the two questions described above led me to questions of intelligence and attention and the brain structures underlying those constructs.

Measures of Working Memory Capacity

Although numerous tasks have been used over the years to measure WM capacity, I describe only the three tasks that I use most often: reading span, operation span, and counting span. These tasks all work in the sense that performance on them reliably predicts performance on a range of ecologically relevant cognitive tasks, suggesting that they reflect something about WM that is fundamentally important to cognition. Furthermore, the tasks appear to reflect a common construct because they account for similar variance, all load on the same factor in a factor analysis, and all fit a relatively tight latent variable in a structural equation analysis (Engle, Tuholski, Laughlin, & Conway, 1999).

The reading span was the first task used to study WM capacity and its relationship with reading comprehension. Daneman and Carpenter (1980) asked participants to read sets of sentences and recall the last word of each sentence. My lab generally used a modified version of this task to avoid concerns that individual differences in comprehension of the sentences lead to differences in ability to generate or reconstruct the words on the basis of the gist of the sentence rather than recall them. In my version, participants read aloud sentences shown centered on a computer monitor while trying to remember unrelated words printed at the end of each sentence. The set of words recalled typically varies from two to seven. For example, Exhibit 16.1 presents three sentences—participants see one sentence at a time, read the sentence aloud, and then read aloud the word in capital letters. At that point, the experimenter presses a key causing the next sentence to be presented. After the last sentence in each set, a set of question marks cues the recall of the words shown

EXHIBIT 16.1

Example of a reading span trial

For many years, my family and friends have been working on the farm. *SPOT*
Because the room was stuffy, Bob went outside for some fresh air. *TRAIL*
We were 50 miles out at sea before we lost sight of the land. *BAND*

in capitals. To ensure that a participant takes the sentence reading task seriously, after recall of the words he or she answers a question about one of the sentences from the set.

The operation span task was developed to be similar in format to the reading span but to involve reading per se only in the broadest sense (Turner & Engle, 1989). Participants see individual operation–word strings (see Exhibit 16.2) centered on the monitor of the computer. They read aloud and solve the math problems, each of which is followed by a word; after a set of such operation–word strings, they recall the words. For example, in the following set size of three strings, the participant reads aloud "Is $(8/4) - 1 = 1$?" and answer *yes* if the equation is correct or *no* if the equation is incorrect; then the participant reads aloud the word *bear*. After hearing *bear,* the experimenter presses a key, resulting in the presentation of the next string. This procedure allows adequate time for each individual to process the operation and word but serves to reduce the time for rehearsal.[1] After the last operation–word string in the set (in this case, the third string), the participant sees a set of question marks centered on the screen, which is the cue to write down the words in order.

The counting span task used is a form of a task first used by Case, Kurland, and Goldberg (1982). In my version of the task, the experimenter initiates the presentation of the first display of the type shown in Exhibit 16.3. Each display consists of 3–9 dark blue circles, 1–9 dark blue squares, and 1–5 light blue circles, all randomly arranged (without overlap) on the monitor. Participants count the number of dark blue circles aloud and repeat the digit corresponding to the final tally. For example, if the display contains three dark blue circles, the participant says aloud "1–2–3–3." When the "3" is repeated, the experimenter presses the key that causes the immediate presentation of the next display, and the participant begins to count immediately. After up to eight displays, a cue occurs for the participant to recall in order the digits corresponding to the number of targets on each display. It should be noted that the memory component of this task is essentially a digit

EXHIBIT 16.2

Example of an operation span trial

Is $(8/4) - 1 = 1$? *bear*
Is $(6 \times 2) - 2 = 10$? *Dad*
Is $(10 \times 2) - 6 = 12$? *beans*

---

[1]An interesting question is the extent to which individual differences in rehearsal lead to the predictive nature of these tasks. In a recent study, Kandi Jo Turley (1998) demonstrated that a procedure that equated rehearsal on the task led to an increase in correlation between operation span and reading comprehension.

EXHIBIT 16.3

Example of a single counting span display

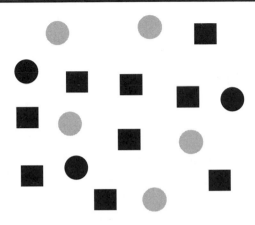

span task, with the counting of objects interleaved with the "presentation" of the digits to be recalled.

These tasks and many others of similar form clearly reflect some fundamental aspect of cognition. Scores on these tasks can predict a range of cognitive functions, including reading and listening comprehension (Daneman & Carpenter, 1980), language comprehension (King & Just, 1991), following directions (Engle, Carullo, & Collins, 1991), vocabulary learning (Daneman & Green, 1986), note taking (Kiewra & Benton, 1988), writing (Benton, Kraft, Glover, & Plake, 1984), reasoning (Barrouillet, 1996; Kyllonen & Christal, 1990), bridge playing (Clarkson-Smith & Hartley, 1990), and computer-language learning (Shute, 1991).

Why Do Working Memory Tasks Work?

These WM capacity tasks were originally thought to work because they reflected the level of skill in performing the processing component of the task, which, in turn, determined the residual available storage capacity. However, it is now known that beyond a minimal level, individual differences on the processing portion of the task are relatively unimportant to the covariation of these tasks with higher order tasks. Engle, Cantor, and Carullo (1992) measured the time it took participants to solve equations in the operation span task and to read the sentences in the reading span task. If skill or expertise on the processing portion of the task is an important factor in the relationship to higher level tasks, then covarying the time to solve the arithmetic string and to read the sentences out of the correlation between span and higher order cognition should lead to an elimination of or at least a reduction in that correlation. However, the WM span–reading comprehension correlation was not reduced by partialling out the estimates of processing expertise, suggesting that skill on the processing component is not the critical factor in whether a task works.

Conway and Engle (1996) used a different approach to the same question. They pretested participants on operation strings representing 15 levels of difficulty. Then each participant received operation spans with the operations adjusted to equate difficulty of the arithmetic across participants. Each participant performed three different operation spans created with strings that they had performed correctly at the 75%, 85%, and 95% accuracy level in the pretest. If individual differences on the processing component of the complex span task was what accounted for the relationship between the span score and higher order cognition, then matching participants on processing should have eliminated or at least statistically reduced the correlation. However, this manipulation did not reduce the span–comprehension correlation; in fact, it rose slightly. Thus, it does not appear that the complex span tasks reflect individual differences in skills or expertise that are common to those skills used in performing the higher level tasks. But what do they reflect that causes them to work?

I believe that I can safely draw several generalizations about these tasks. The tasks that reliably work in predicting higher level cognition are, at base, dual tasks. The operation span task involves solving equations and trying to remember words. The reading span involves reading sentences and trying to remember words. The counting span involves controlled counting and trying to remember digits. One or both of the components of the tasks require controlled processing. One component involves retention of some information (the individual words or digits in the emerging list) over a delay that is filled with distraction (typically the so-called processing portion of the task). In this sense, the tasks are similar to the Brown–Peterson procedure with a fixed delay, and the tasks may work well because they reflect the participants' ability to do the mental work necessary to resist the effects of interference from one trial to the next and across sets. Note that I am not suggesting that WM capacity reflects differential vulnerability to interference per se (cf. Hasher & Zacks, 1988) but that people differ in the ability to do the mental work necessary to resist interference. I have more to say on this issue later.

The term *capacity,* as used in discussions of STM, often conjures up images of a fixed number of items (e.g., 7 ± 2). However, my sense is that WM capacity is not about a limitation in number of items in some limited set of metaphorical bins but is instead about limitations in the ability to use controlled processing to maintain information in an active, quickly retrievable state. Thus, I can talk about WM capacity as being important in retention of a single representation, such as a goal or the status of a changing variable, just as well as how many representations can be maintained. WM capacity is not about storage and processing but is about retention over a period in which there is distraction or shift of attention away from the stored information. The need for this quick accessibility is particularly salient when there is interference from competing information. WM capacity is not directly about memory—it is about attention. WM capacity is about memory only indirectly. WM capacity is about attention in the service of memory. Greater WM capacity means that more items can be maintained in the focus of attention, but it also means that information can more effectively be blocked from the focus of attention.

I think that helping one deal with the effects of interference is one of the primary functions of WM. The reality is that without the effects of interference, most of the information one knows and needs to function in the world could be retrieved from long-term memory sufficiently quickly to perform even complex cognitive functions. Keppel and Underwood (1962) found that the Brown–Peterson retention function does not hold for the first or even second trial in an experiment, and this finding should be informative to us. Crowder (1983) certainly found it informative. The effects that are generally attributed to STM or to active memory are likely to be observed only when the effects of interference force one to maintain information in an active state. It is in those conditions in which WM capacity is important and in which individual differences manifest themselves.

Negative Priming

Larger WM capacity leads to better ability to block information from the active state either by increased attention to task-relevant information or to active suppression of potentially intrusive task-irrelevant information. For example, Engle, Conway, Tuholski, and Shisler (1995) demonstrated that the negative priming effect was eliminated by a secondary load task. Participants were shown two slightly overlapping letters, one green and one red, and asked to name the green one as rapidly as possible. When the green letter had been the red letter on the previous trial, participants were slower to name the letter, a result known as the *negative priming effect*. One interpretation of this phenomenon is that when faced with two competing action schemas such as saying both letters, one suppresses the weaker one, which makes one slower to say the corresponding letter on the next trial. When participants in the Engle et al. study performed this task while trying to remember a list of words, the negative priming effect was eliminated. Conway, Tuholski, Shisler, and Engle (2000) conducted a negative priming study with individuals classified as high or low in WM capacity.[2] Conway et al. observed that only high-WM participants showed the negative priming effect. Furthermore, their negative priming effect was eliminated when they also tried to remember either a list of words or a list of irregular shapes. Those with low spans did not show the negative priming effect with or without load.

---

[2]In this study and the other studies I discuss throughout the chapter, high- and low-WM participants were classified as such by scoring in the upper and lower quartile, respectively, on the operation span task.

My interpretation is that suppression of competing information requires attention-demanding mental work and that participants with high WM have superior capability to suppress competing intrusions.

Proactive Interference

Rosen and Engle (1998) reached a similar conclusion using a different procedure. Participants learned three paired-associate lists in which they were shown one word and were to say aloud a different word as a response. Rosen and Engle measured the time to make the oral response to the cue and response accuracy. In one experiment, the instructions emphasized accuracy, and they anticipated that participants would vary in speed of responding. The experimental participants learned three 12-item lists with the same 12 cue words for every list. Thus, participants might learn *bird–bath* as 1 of 12 items for list 1 and *bird–dawn* for list 2 and relearn *bird–bath* for list 3. Participants with high and low WM took a similar number of trials to learn list 1, supporting the idea that they were not different when performing in the absence of interference. However, on list 2, participants with low spans made many more errors than did those with high spans, specifically, intrusions of the responses from list 1. For list 3, participants simply relearned list 1. If those with high spans actively suppressed the responses from list 1 during the learning of list 2, then they would be slower to give *bath* in response to *bird* than would the control participants, who learned *bird–bath* for the first time in list 3. Not only did we find that participants with high WM were slower than the control participants to make responses on list 3, those with high spans were also slower to give *bath* as a response to *bird* on list 3 than they were themselves on list 1. Those with low spans were actually faster to make list 3 responses than were the control participants. Rosen and Engle found that those with low WM showed greater effects of proactive interference as evidenced by the greater number of intrusions from list 1. Our interpretation was that during the learning of list 2, high-WM participants were better equipped to do the necessary mental work required to suppress the response *bath* to the cue word *bird* so that they could give the weaker *dawn* as a correct response. However, that came back to haunt those with high spans when *bath* was needed again in list 3 because, for them, retrieval of *bath* was much slower.

Kane and Engle (2000) conducted a set of experiments using a modification of the Wickens, Born, and Allen (1963) paradigm that supported the idea that resisting interference is a result of processes requiring executive attention. Participants had three trials in which they saw 10 words to recall, performed a rehearsal preventative task for 16 s, and then tried to recall the 10 words. Participants with high and low spans were nearly identical in recall of list 1 at about 60%, which is well below ceiling. However, those with low spans showed steeper declines in recall over trials than did those with high spans, reflecting greater proactive interference (PI) for those with the low spans. When participants performed a secondary load task at either encoding or retrieval, the PI function for those with high spans looked just like that of those with low spans where PI function was unaffected by load. Therefore, the finding that those with high spans were hurt by divided attention suggests that under normal conditions, participants were actually using attentional control to combat the effects of PI. In contrast, the lack of a load effect on PI for those with low spans suggests that participants do not normally allocate attention to resist interference.

WM, STM, and General Fluid Intelligence

My argument is that individual differences in WM capacity correspond to individual differences in a construct similar to the supervisory attention system proposed by Shallice and Burgess (1993) and that this is critical for dealing with interference, potentially distracting information, or both. So what is the evidence for this claim? One source of evidence comes from a regression study by Engle et al. (1999) directed at Cowan's (1995) distinction between STM and WM. Cowan assumed that STM is a subset of WM. STM is a storage component consisting of those memory units active above some baseline, whereas WM refers to a system consisting of the storage component plus an attention component. I submit that all WM and STM tasks reflect elements of both constructs. Conceptually, variance shared between WM tasks and STM tasks should reflect the STM component and the extent to which executive attention is required in the STM tasks. Therefore, the variance left over in WM, that is, the residual in WM tasks after removal of variance common to the two types of tasks, should reflect an estimate of the role of controlled or supervisory attention. Of course, that residual would be a conservative estimate of the attention component because even the common variance removed would likely include some variance attributable to capability for controlled processing on the STM tasks as well.

Engle et al. (1999) also addressed questions about the relationship between STM, WM, and general fluid intelligence (Horn & Cattell, 1967). A connection has been made between STM and intelligence (Bachelder & Denny, 1977), between WM capacity and intelligence (Kyllonen & Christal, 1990), and between controlled processing and intelligence (Duncan, 1995). By Cowan's (1995) logic, one should be able test among those three possibilities to the extent that latent constructs for STM, WM, and controlled attention can be isolated.

Engle et al. (1999) asked three questions:

1. Do WM tasks reflect the same underlying construct?
2. Do WM capacity tasks measure something different from traditional STM tasks and, if so, what makes them different?
3. What is the relationship between these constructs and general fluid intelligence?

Participants performed 14 different tasks, but those germane to the three questions were the three WM tasks I described above, the three simple span tasks thought to reflect STM, and the two measures of general fluid intelligence that I used as my criteria for higher order cognition. Factor analyses show that the three WM tasks I described above loaded on one factor and that the three STM tasks loaded on a different factor. A structural equation analysis shows that whereas the WM and STM constructs were highly correlated, a model with separate constructs for WM and STM fit the data significantly better than a model with a single construct for WM and STM.

Although the latent variables for both WM and STM correlated with the latent variable for fluid intelligence, that does not tell the source of the relationships. If my logic is correct, one should be able to determine whether STM has a relationship with intelligence separate from that of WM or whether the relationship is driven by controlled attention. By that logic, removal of the variance common to the WM and STM constructs would leave a residual from WM that reflects controlled attention. The model that results from this common factor removal is shown in Figure 16.1. The boxes reflect manifest variables or specific tasks, and the numbers and arrows pointing to those boxes reflect task-specific error variance. The circles represent latent variables (i.e., hypothetical constructs), and the numbers and arrows between rectangles and circles and between circles reflect standardized regression coefficients. Solid lines reflect significant links and dotted lines reflect nonsignificant links.

When the variance common to the WM and STM latent variables was removed, the correlation between the residual remaining from the WM variable and the construct for general fluid intelligence was substantial and significant (.49). However, the residual from the STM variable, which by my logic should include only error, did not significantly correlate with intelligence. Although measures of WM capacity are certainly not pure, these results are consistent with the idea that the latent variable resulting from those tasks reflects a mechanism one might think of as executive attention and that that mechanism is strongly related to general fluid intelligence.

Antisaccade Task

Shallice and Burgess (1993) proposed that the supervisory attention system (SAS) comes into play whenever the action schema generated by the relatively automatic contention scheduling system conflicts with the goals of the current task. Thus, if the automatically elicited response in a given situation does not fit with the current goals for the situation, SAS leads to increased activation of the more appropriate action and that can lead to inhibition of the inappropriate action.

The antisaccade task is almost perfectly suited to model this feature of the SAS. In that task, the participant must respond to information presented to either side

FIGURE 16.1

Path model for relationship among STM, WM, and gF. STM = short-term memory; WM = working memory; gF = general fluid intelligence; OSPAN = operation span; RSPAN = reading span; CSPAN = counting span; BSPAN = backward span; FSPAND = forward span with dissimilar words; FSPSANS = forward span with similar sounding words; RAVENS = Ravens Standard Progressive Matrices Test; CATTELL = Cattell Fair Test of Intelligence; * = significant path. From "Working Memory, Short-Term Memory, and General Fluid Intelligence: A Latent Variable Approach," by R. W. Engle, S. W. Tuholski, J. E. Laughlin, & A. R. A. Conway, 1999, Journal of Experimental Psychology: General, 128, p. 324. Copyright 1999 by the American Psychological Association. Reprinted with permission.

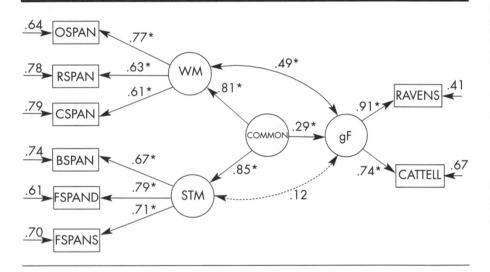

of a display. However, just before the information is presented, a cue of some type occurs to the opposite side of the display. The relationship is perfectly lawful; the cue always predicts that the target information will occur on the opposite side of the display. However, the cue is designed to naturally capture the participants' attention, so the prepotent tendency is to shift gaze to the wrong side of the display. Optimal performance in the task requires that this tendency be blocked. As a control, most experiments also include a prosaccade condition in which the cue occurs on the same side of the display as the subsequent target. Thus, the prepotent tendency to look at the flashing cue facilitates processing of the target when it occurs in the prosaccade condition but hurts performance in the antisaccade condition. Roberts, Hager, and Heron (1994) showed that performance in the prosaccade condition was not hurt when the participants also performed a concurrent memory load task. However, performance in the antisaccade task was substantially hurt by the load task. Participants who were also performing an attention-demanding concurrent task were much more likely to shift their eyes to the cue and then not be able to do sufficient processing of the target when it occurred on the opposite side of the display.

If my logic about individual differences in WM capacity corresponding to differences in the executive attention is correct, then we should see a relationship between performance on measures of WM capacity and performance on the antisaccade task. Specifically, participants with high and low WM will not differ on the prosaccade condition. However, whereas both groups would be worse on the antisaccade condition, participants with low WM span would be hurt much more by the need to maintain the goal to look opposite to the cue and to block the prepotent response to look in the direction of the cue. Kane, Bleckley, Conway, and Engle (in press) performed two studies to test this prediction. In the first study, participants with high and low spans were tested in prosaccade and antisaccade conditions. A trial began with a central fixation that persisted for a period of 200–2,200 ms and was followed by a blinking " = ," which was displayed 11.33° of visual angle randomly to the left or right of center for a total of 250 ms. In the prosaccade condition, that cue was followed by presentation of a B, P, or R in the space immediately above the " = ." The letter was displayed for 100 ms and then masked until the response. Participants were to press one of three keys indicating the identity of the letter. In the antisaccade condition, the letter and mask were displayed 11.33° of visual angle from the fixation point to the side opposite the cue. Saccade condition was a within-subjects variable with half the participants doing the block of prosaccade first and half doing the antisaccade first.

There was a three-way interaction of WM group, saccade condition, and order of saccade condition; we examined each of the saccade conditions performed first. Figure 16.2 shows the time to identify the letters for the saccade condition performed first, and one sees that the predictions were supported. Participants with high and low WM did not differ in the prosaccade condition but, although both were slowed in the antisaccade condition, those with low WM were slowed substantially more. The three-way interaction mentioned above reflects the fact that, whereas participants with high WM were relatively unaffected by order of task, participants with low spans who performed antisaccade first were significantly slowed to perform prosaccade later. That is, once they had adjusted to the antisaccade condition and were moderately successful in blocking the prepotent tendency to look in the direction of the misleading cue, they persisted in that tendency even when it was maladaptive to do so in the prosaccade condition. This is similar to what is referred to as perseveration behavior in individuals with frontal-lobe damage and represents another one of many instances in which the pattern of performance for participants with low WM and patients with frontal-lobe damage is similar (Engle & Oransky, 1999).

In the second study, participants' eye movements were monitored during performance of an extended set of antisaccade trials. As with the first study, those with

FIGURE 16.2

Response time in the letter task as a function of span group and saccade condition. ProSacc = prosaccade task; AntiSacc = antisaccade task.

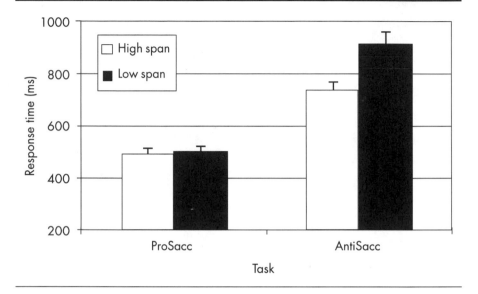

low WM were substantially slower to perform the letter identification than were those with high spans. The eye movement data in Figure 16.3 show that those with low spans were much more likely to follow their reflexive predisposition and look in the direction of the cue. Increasingly over trials, they were slower to make the initial saccade.

After 10 blocks of antisaccade trials, participants were presented with a block of prosaccade trials with explicit instructions that the letter would now be presented in the same location as the cue, so they should look in that direction when the cue occurred. They also had a block of practice trials on prosaccade. In spite of those elaborate instructions and the practice trials, both low- and high-span participants made a substantial number of errors on the initial saccades in the prosaccade condition by looking away from the cue. However, those with low WM made more saccades in the wrong direction (mean proportion errors = .28) than did those with high spans (mean proportion errors = .20). Further, the initial saccades for those with low spans, both correct and incorrect, were slower. In fact, those with low spans were as slow to initiate prosaccades as they were to make antisaccades in the previous block. This was not true for those with high spans. Thus, participants with low WM appear to have greater difficulty establishing and maintaining a set to behave in opposition to a prepotent response, but they also have greater difficulty abandoning that set when the task changes, even when it changes so that the formerly prepotent response is now appropriate.

FIGURE 16.3

Proportion of initial eye movements to the misleading cue in the antisaccade condition as a function of span group and block of trials.

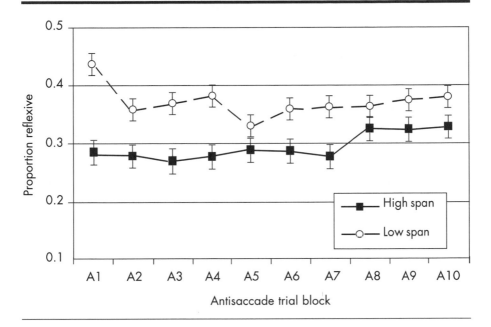

The data from the Kane et al. (in press) experiments would not be predicted from any view that WM is limited in number of items that can be stored at any given moment. The results also are not predicted by any view that individual differences in WM capacity reflect abilities and skills specific to the span tasks used to measure them or that the pertinent attentional resources are domain specific (Shah & Miyake, 1996). The data, however, are consistent with a view that the underlying construct responsible for the relationship between measures of WM capacity and higher order cognitive tasks is a domain-free executive attention system similar to that described by Shallice and Burgess (1993). Whereas individuals possessing different WM capacities show differences in number of items stored in a variety of memory tasks, this is a result of differing ability to maintain and inhibit information, particularly in the face of distraction and proactive and retroactive interference.

Stroop Task

The beauty of this view is that it leads one to consider situations that other views would not think of as involving WM: situations that require maintenance of a single crucial goal or production in WM. If that goal or production must compete with a preternaturally stronger goal that happens to be inappropriate for the current task or if the task environment elicits a strong response tendency that is inappropriate for current conditions, then one should see lawful differences between participants with high and low WM on that task. Furthermore, even participants with high WM should suffer on that task if they perform the task under the load of another task that also demands executive attention.

The Stroop task is one situation in which a strong predisposition to make a task-inappropriate response—saying the word—can hurt performance on the task, which is to say the color of the ink in which the word is printed. My view predicts that performance on the Stroop task should rely on executive attention to maintain the goal of saying the name of the color of the letters even when the word elicits a stronger response tendency to say the name of the word. Maintaining the appropriate goal in a highly active state should be particularly difficult when some of the trials are congruent, that is, the ink color and the word correspond. It is likely easier to maintain the goal if no congruent trials are presented, which is often the case in neuropsychological administration of the task. In such cases, the immediate demands of the task serve to continually remind the participants about the goal to block the word and to say the ink color. However, it should be harder to maintain the goal in active memory if the environment or context presents many trials on which performance can be successful without the necessity to maintain the goal to block the tendency to say the word. If maintaining the goal in active memory requires mental work, and participants with high WM are better equipped to do that work, then they should be more likely to maintain the goal in active memory in such conditions. Moreover, by manipulating such a contextual variable, one can test whether individual differences in WM capacity result from a relatively pure and invariant inhibitory capability or whether inhibition varies with the need to maintain the task goal. If WM capacity simply reflects differences in ability to inhibit information (Hasher & Zacks, 1988), then span differences would occur in all Stroop contexts; but if goal maintenance is critical (O'Reilly, Braver, & Cohen, 1999), then span differences may only be observed when goal maintenance is difficult.

Kane and Engle (2000) conducted a study in which high- and low-span participants named the color of the print for strings of random letters (*jkm, fdtmq,* etc.) and color names (red, blue, or green) that were printed in the colors red, blue, or green. The percentage of trials on which the color name and word name matched or were congruent was 0%, 50%, or 75% and was a between-subjects variable. In the 0% condition, goal maintenance should be easiest because no trials present matching ink color and words, and in 75% congruent trials, maintenance should be most difficult because the word name can be used to speak the color of the ink on the vast majority of trials. Kane et al. (in press) found that time to name the color did not differ between high- and low-span participants, but the number of errors differed substantially. As can be seen in Figure 16.4, although both groups showed increased errors as the proportion of congruent trials increased, high- and

FIGURE 16.4

Percentage of errors in the Stroop task as a function of span group and percentage of congruent trials.

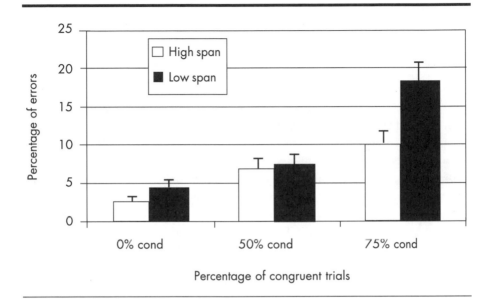

Percentage of congruent trials

low-WM participants did not differ in errors with 0% or 50% congruent trials. It was only when 75% of the trials were congruent that high- and low-WM subjects differed in number of errors, with low-span participants making almost twice as many errors as high-span participants. Thus, high- and low-span differences do not represent overall inhibition differences in all situations but only when the context makes it difficult to maintain the appropriate task goal.

Dichotic Listening Task

Yet another attention task in which WM capacity has been shown to be important is the venerable dichotic listening task. Conway, Cowan, and Bunting (in press) had high- and low-WM participants shadow unrelated words in one ear while ignoring unrelated words spoken to the other ear. The experimenters had recorded the participant's first name before the experiment, and the name occurred as a word in the ignored message after 4 min. and again after 5 min. The question was whether participants would report hearing their name at the end of the study. I argue that participants with high WM will be better at blocking the distracting information and therefore less likely to report hearing their name than low spans. Conway et al. found that high- and low-span participants were equivalent in performance on the shadowing task on trials preceding their names. However, although only 20%

of participants with high spans reported hearing their name, 65% of those with low spans reported hearing their name. Again, the conclusion is that those with low spans are less capable of doing the mental work necessary to block the distracting information.

Conclusion

I have presented an argument that tasks of WM capacity reflect a common construct, that that construct is fundamentally important to higher order cognition, that it is distinguishable from a construct for STM, and that it is at least related to, if not isomorphic to, general fluid abilities and executive attention. I have further argued that one particularly important function of the WM system is for keeping information quickly retrievable and usable under conditions in which there is interference from information that is strongly elicited by task context but that nevertheless would lead to a response inappropriate for the current task. I have described the results of several studies showing that individual differences in WM capacity are important in tasks that would not seem to rely on the number of things a person could remember but that would rely on the ability to keep one piece of information highly active. WM capacity is not about memory per se; it is about individual differences in executive attention.

References

Bachelder, B. L., & Denny, M. R. (1977). A theory of intelligence: II. The role of span in a variety of intelligence tasks. *Intelligence, 1,* 237–256.

Baddeley, A. D., & Hitch, G. (1974). Working memory. In G. A. Bower (Ed.), *The psychology of learning and motivation* (Vol. 8, pp. 47–89). New York: Academic Press.

Barrouillet, P. (1996). Transitive inferences from set-inclusion relations and working memory. *Journal of Experimental Psychology: Learning, Memory, and Cognition, 22,* 1408–1422.

Benton, S. L., Kraft, R. G., Glover, J. A., & Plake, B. S. (1984). Cognitive capacity differences among writers. *Journal of Educational Psychology, 76,* 820–834.

Case, R., Kurland, M. D., & Goldberg, J. (1982). Operational efficiency and the growth of short-term memory span. *Journal of Experimental Child Psychology, 33,* 386–404.

Clarkson–Smith, L., & Hartley, A. A. (1990). The game of bridge as an exercise in working memory and reasoning. *Journal of Gerontology, 45,* P233–P238.

Conway, A. R. A., Cowan, N., & Bunting, M. F. (in press). The cocktail party phenomenon revisited: The importance of working memory capacity. *Psychonomics Bulletin and Review.*

Conway, A. R. A., & Engle, R. W. (1996). Individual differences in working memory capacity: More evidence for a general capacity theory. *Memory, 4,* 577–590.

Conway, A. R. A., Tuholski, S. W., Shisler, R. J., & Engle, R. W. (2000). The effect of memory load on negative priming: An individual differences investigation. *Memory & Cognition, 27,* 1042–1050.

Cowan, N. (1995). *Attention and memory: An integrated framework.* Oxford, England: Oxford University Press.

Crowder, R. G. (1983). The demise of short-term memory. *Acta Psychologica, 50,* 291–323.

Daneman, M., & Carpenter, P. A. (1980). Individual differences in working memory and reading. *Journal of Verbal Learning and Verbal Behavior, 19,* 450–466.

Daneman, M., & Green, I. (1986). Individual differences in comprehending and producing words in context. *Journal of Memory and Language, 25,* 1–18.

Duncan, J. (1995). Attention, intelligence, and the frontal lobes. In M. Gazzaniga (Ed.), *The cognitive neurosciences* (pp. 721–733). Cambridge, MA: MIT Press.

Engle, R. W., Cantor, J., & Carullo, J. J. (1992). Individual differences in working memory and comprehension: A test of four hypotheses. *Journal of Experimental Psychology: Learning, Memory, and Cognition, 18,* 972–992.

Engle, R. W., Carullo, J. J., & Collins, K. W. (1991). Individual differences in working memory for comprehension and following directions. *Journal of Educational Research, 84,* 253–262.

Engle, R. W., Conway, A. R. A., Tuholski, S. W., & Shisler, R. J. (1995). A resource account of inhibition. *Psychological Science, 6,* 122–125.

Engle, R. W., & Oransky, N. (1999). Multi-store versus dynamic models of temporary storage in memory. In R. J. Sternberg (Ed.), *The nature of cognition* (pp. 518–555). Cambridge, MA: MIT Press.

Engle, R. W., Tuholski, S. W., Laughlin, J. E., & Conway, A. R. A. (1999). Working memory, short-term memory, and general fluid intelligence: A latent variable approach. *Journal of Experimental Psychology: General, 128,* 309–331.

Hasher, L., & Zacks, R. T. (1988). Working memory, comprehension, and aging: A review and a new view. In G. H. Bower (Ed.), *The psychology of learning and motivation: Advances in research and theory* (Vol. 22, pp. 193–225). San Diego, CA: Academic Press.

Horn, J. L., & Cattell, R. B. (1967). Age differences in fluid and crystallized intelligence. *Acta Psychologica, 26,* 107–129.

Kane, M. J., Bleckley, M. K., Conway, A. R. A., & Engle, R. W. (in press). A controlled-attention view of working memory capacity. *Journal of Experimental Psychology: General.*

Kane, M. J., & Engle, R. W. (2000). Working memory capacity, proactive interference, and divided attention: Limits on long-term memory retrieval. *Journal of Experimental Psychology: Learning, Memory, and Cognition, 26,* 336–358.

Keppel, G., & Underwood, B. J. (1962). Proactive inhibition in short-term retention of single items. *Journal of Verbal Learning and Verbal Behavior, 1,* 153–161.

Kiewra, K. A., & Benton, S. L. (1988). The relationship between information processing ability and notetaking. *Contemporary Educational Psychology, 13,* 33–44.

King, J., & Just, M. A. (1991). Individual differences in syntactic processing: The role of working memory. *Journal of Memory and Language, 30,* 580–602.

Kyllonen, P. C., & Christal, R. E. (1990). Reasoning ability is (little more than) working-memory capacity? *Intelligence, 14,* 389–433.

O'Reilly, R. C., Braver, T. S., & Cohen, J. D. (1999). A biological based computational model of working memory. In A. Miyake & P. Shah (Eds.), *Models of working memory* (pp. 375–411). Cambridge, England: Cambridge University Press.

Roberts, R. J., Jr., Hager, L. D., & Heron, C. (1994). Prefrontal cognitive processes: Working memory and inhibition in the antisaccade task. *Journal of Experimental Psychology: General, 123,* 374–393.

Rosen, V. M., & Engle, R. W. (1997). The role of working memory capacity in retrieval. *Journal of Experimental Psychology: General, 126,* 211–227.

Rosen, V. M., & Engle, R. W. (1998). Working memory capacity and suppression. *Journal of Memory and Language, 39,* 418–439.

Shah, P., & Miyake, A. (1996). The separability of working memory resources for spatial thinking and language processing: An individual differences approach. *Journal of Experimental Psychology: General, 125,* 4–27.

Shallice, T., & Burgess, P. W. (1993). Supervisory control of thought and action. In A. D. Baddeley & L. Weiskrantz (Eds.), *Attention: Selection, awareness and control: A tribute to Donald Broadbent* (pp. 171–187). Oxford, England: Oxford University Press.

Shute, V. J. (1991). Who is likely to acquire programming skills? *Journal of Educational Computing Research, 7,* 1–24.

Turley, K. J. (1998). *Strategies and working memory capacity.* Unpublished manuscript, Idaho State University, Pocatello.

Turner, M. L., & Engle, R. W. (1989). Is working memory capacity task dependent? *Journal of Memory and Language, 28,* 127–154.

Wickens, D. D., Born, D. G., & Allen, C. K. (1963). Proactive inhibition and item similarity in short-term memory. *Journal of Verbal Learning and Verbal Behavior, 2,* 440–445.

CHAPTER 17

The Ravages of Absolute and Relative Amounts of Time on Memory

Nelson Cowan

Scott Saults

Lara Nugent

obert Crowder was one of those rare scientists who delighted in clear evidence, perhaps more than almost anything else. The first interchange between the first author and Crowder occurred when Nelson Cowan submitted an article to *Psychological Bulletin* (Cowan, 1984), for which Crowder was a reviewer (who always signed his reviews, being willing to be held accountable for his opinions). In the process of responding to one of the reviewers' concerns, Cowan asked Crowder for individual-participant data from a study conducted a few years earlier (Crowder, 1982), so that the results could be modeled. Crowder not only complied but was delighted that he had been asked. He said that this was the first time that anyone had asked for his original data and that he was proud to say he found it in good order in his filing cabinet. Many other researchers also would have complied with the request, but ask yourself, How many would have seemed delighted at the request as opposed to being a little apprehensive about how the evidence might be used? This is a strong indication of character in science. Also indicative of this was Crowder's striking intellectual honesty mixed with good humor, as, for example, in one article (Crowder, 1983) in which he lamented that another investigator had used a title that he otherwise would have liked to use for his own article. In this chapter, we seek to emulate Robert Crowder in his courageous path where he was among the first to repudiate his own earlier, well-received theory about sensory memory (e.g., Crowder & Morton, 1969) in light of evidence that he found contradictory (e.g., Crowder, 1989, 1993).

This work was completed with funding from the National Institutes of Health Grant R01 HD-21338. The authors thank Emily Elliott for her comments.

Immediate Memory and Its Loss: Definition of the Problem

William James (1890) distinguished between one's current thoughts (*primary memory*) and one's mental storehouse of knowledge (*secondary memory*). A natural distinction that one can draw between these types of memory is that there is a limit in how long a particular thought can remain in primary memory. Many empirical studies have led to suggestions of an upper limit of about 30 s for primary-memory information, unless it is refreshed through rehearsal. As James noted, one also can observe a kind of memory mechanism that temporarily preserves the sensory information from all stimuli, even the ones that observers ignore but could turn their attention to quickly. It has often been suggested that this kind of sensory memory is also limited to about 30 s or less. (For reviews of the literature, see Cowan, 1988, 1995.) One might define *immediate memory* as temporarily held information including both conscious primary memory and any other transient information source, such as sensory memory, available to primary memory.

The typical finding of a gradual decrease in average performance in immediate-memory tasks as the retention interval increases, reaching an asymptote within about 30 s, can be termed *memory decay*. One might suggest that the concept of memory decay is on a priori grounds unreasonable because time itself cannot cause a loss of information; processes taking place during that time must cause the loss, and these processes can be altered. We note that this type of objection has not stopped the concept of decay from being respectable in other areas of science. The prototypical case is radioactive decay. A radioactive material usually loses half of its radioactivity over a fixed time period X, which depends on the nature of the material. Even in the case of radioactivity, though, time itself is not an ultimate, unchanging causal factor. If a material is accelerated to nearly the speed of light, its rate of loss of radioactivity (and every other temporal process) slows down as measured by a stationary clock. Thus, even in this case, one must specify the conditions before decay can be described. This situation seems similar to the use of the term *decay* to describe the loss of information from immediate memory at a certain rate under ordinary circumstances, although various factors can modify it. In both cases, the term can be used only with the conditions specified.

A more general question that can be investigated with less theoretical baggage is whether there is an effect of the absolute duration of the retention interval on memory or whether, instead, only relative amounts of time between stimuli make a difference. Researchers of several recent studies have discussed this issue explicitly (Cowan, Saults, & Nugent, 1997; Cowan, Wood, Nugent, & Treisman, 1997; Nairne, Neath, Serra, & Byun, 1997), but it still remains unresolved. On the one hand, some classic results suggest that the relative distribution of time periods among the stimuli is so important that the absolute duration of the retention interval may not matter (e.g., Bjork & Whitten, 1974; Keppel & Underwood, 1962). On the other hand, one easily can imagine that there are some inevitable temporal limits to the ability of an active neural cell assembly (Hebb, 1949) to retain information, such as cellular fatigue or neural noise that eventually destroys the essential pattern carrying the information. This chapter focuses on the question of whether the absolute duration of the retention interval can be shown to be important for primary memory.

A "Brief History of Time" in Memory Research

The decay concept was popular early on in cognitive psychology (e.g., Broadbent, 1958; Brown, 1958, 1959; Glanzer & Cunitz, 1966; Peterson & Peterson, 1959) because of studies showing that memory was lost across a retention interval of some seconds filled with distracting information. The use of the concepts of decay and memory loss as a function of an absolute amount of time has continued into recent times in cognitive psychology, to account for apparently time-limited memory (e.g., Baddeley, 1986; Koppenaal & Glanzer, 1990; Towse, Hitch, & Hutton, 1998), and in cognitive neuroscience, to explain the loss of information about unattended stimuli automatically saved in the brain (Näätänen, 1992; Sams, Hari, Rif, & Knuutila, 1993).

Also for a very long time, there has been a reaction against these absolute time concepts. This reaction might be traced back to John McGeoch (1932) at the University of Missouri and his successor Art Melton (1963). After Bjork and Whitten (1974) and Keppel and Underwood (1962), probably no one has argued against the decay principle as effectively as Robert Crowder (1989, 1993), who was a student of Art Melton. The persuasiveness of Crowder's arguments is evident in the fact that many of his students and close colleagues also have argued, in various ways, against the notion of decay. These include, among others, Art Glenberg (e.g., Glenberg & Swanson, 1986), Allison Marks (Marks & Crowder, 1997), Jim Nairne (e.g., Nairne et al., 1997), Ian Neath (e.g., Neath & Crowder, 1990; Neath & Nairne, 1995), Robert Greene (e.g., Greene, 1986; Thapar & Greene, 1993), and Henry Roediger (e.g., Roediger, Knight, & Kantowitz, 1977).

The difficulty in measuring effects of time per se on memory has always been that one must rule out effects of three sources of interference: *retroactive,* interference from subsequent items; *concurrent,* interference from concurrent items; and *proactive,* interference from previous items. Also memory loss over time cannot be observed to its fullest extent unless covert rehearsal is blocked because rehearsal can refresh items in memory (Baddeley, 1986). However, most attempts to block rehearsal use materials meant to serve as distracting tasks, and these, unfortunately, can impose retroactive interference. A few studies block rehearsal in ways that may allow forgetting to be observed in the absence of important retroactive interference (Cowan, Lichty, & Grove, 1990; Eriksen & Johnson, 1964; Keller, Cowan, & Saults, 1995;

Reitman, 1974; Watkins, Watkins, Craik, & Mazuryk, 1973; Wingfield & Byrnes, 1972). Of course, concurrent interference is the easiest to avoid, simply by presenting only one stimulus at a time.

The most difficult type of interference to avoid is probably proactive interference. Although one can refrain from presenting items concurrent to a target item or during its retention interval, it is impossible to refrain from presenting items before a particular target item. In one study, Baddeley and Scott (1971) practically did so by presenting only one trial per participant, although one can question whether they still imposed retroactive interference. The question, then, is typically how to measure proactive interference. The assumption of nondecay theorists has been that if all types of interference could be taken into account, there would be no more variance left to be explained by decay. It is this issue that we re-examine in this chapter.

Research Strategies for Assessing Decay

Given the strong bias that most of us as researchers have toward confirmation of our own theories, it makes a great deal of sense to try to counteract that bias by attempting to disprove our working hypothesis (Platt, 1964). Robert Crowder previously adopted a viewpoint in which decay was important, inasmuch as he demonstrated aspects of forgetting in auditory memory that, at first, were explained according to a decaying auditory sensory memory trace (e.g., Crowder, 1982; Crowder & Morton, 1969). In this light, it has been deeply scientific for Crowder and his colleagues to be willing to disconfirm their own theories. Specifically, they asked whether they could account for all of the phenomena in the short-term memory literature without making use of *decay* and to explore and embrace concepts other than decay that could account for the data, thus attempting to disconfirm Crowder's own earlier conclusions.

More recently, our laboratory operated from a framework in which decay (or, let us say, "the absolute duration of the retention interval") appeared to play a critical role. Several articles from our laboratory have provided evidence suggesting that decay could be an important principle, despite the doubts that others have expressed (e.g., Cowan et al., 1992; Cowan, Nugent, Elliott, & Geer, 2000; Cowan, Wood, & Borne, 1994; Cowan, Wood, et al., 1997). Therefore, in emulation of Crowder's scientific approach, it behooves us to look hard for evidence against the principle of decay. It is not feasible to prove that something does not exist (in this case, that decay does not occur), but a way to go about this in practical terms would be to look hard for problems with the evidence that supposedly favors decay. That is the task that we take on in this chapter. It leads to somewhat different research than the tack of looking for evidence in favor of principles other than decay and therefore complements the existing literature.

Decay or Proactive Interference? New Evidence From a Two-Tone Comparison Task

Cowan, Saults, et al. (1997) presented pairs of 200-ms-long tones on every trial, with a 1%, 2%, or 3% difference between the frequencies of the two tones. Twenty-eight participants were tested, and on the basis of a pretest, each was assigned to the 1%, 2%, or 3% tone difference condition. This was done to achieve a relatively uniform, sensitive level of performance across participants. The tone memory task was to decide whether the second tone was higher or lower in pitch than the first tone in a pair. Two time intervals were varied: the time between tones within a pair on a trial or interstimulus interval (ISI), which could be 1.5, 3, 6, or 12 s, and the time between pairs of tones or interpair interval (IPI), which could be 3, 6, 12, or 24 s. Each possible combination of these two intervals occurred equally often. Following pretest and practice trials, there were 256 tone comparison trials per participant. Each trial included the following phases: (a) a yellow background monitor display during which a silent distracting task was carried out (in which the left or right arrow keys were pressed in a nonrepeating sequence to signify the directions of movement of a small icon on the screen), starting as soon as the response to the previous trial was completed and continuing for the duration of the IPI; (b) a blue background display with the word *listen* printed in a large font, beginning 250 ms before the first tone in a pair and continuing throughout the ISI and during the presentation of the second tone in the pair; and (c) a green background with a response display, during which the participant could use the arrow keys to indicate that the second tone was "higher" or "lower" in pitch than the first. This display ended when the response was made (with a 2-s limit for responses). Absence of a response within the time limit counted as incorrect. After the fixed, 2-s response period, the participant returned immediately to the silent task.

Performance was examined not only as a function of the ISI but also as a function of the ratio between the immediately preceding IPI and the current ISI. The results are shown in Figure 17.1. Each data line reflects data from one particular IPI:ISI ratio. If one compares vertically the data points present at any one ISI, the effect of the IPI:ISI ratio can be seen in that points on different ratio lines differ from one another systematically. If one looks at the function across ISIs shown by any one ratio line, this indicates the effect of ISI with the IPI:ISI ratio held constant. In an analysis of variance (ANOVA) of the data with IPI and ISI as factors, both main effects were significant ($p < .02$ or smaller), but the interaction was not. In separate one-way ANOVAs of the data restricted to a single IPI:ISI ratio per ANOVA, there were still significant effects of the ISI for the 2:1 ratio and the 1:1 ratio ($p < .04$ or better), the only two ratios that included at least three data means and included data at the 12-s ISI, where the strongest forgetting occurred. These results show that although there appear to be effects of distinctiveness (the IPI:ISI ratio

FIGURE 17.1

Proportion correct tone comparisons as a function of ISI between tones in a pair (x axis) and the ratio between IPI and ISI (graph parameter). ISI = interstimulus interval; IPI = interpair interval. Redrawn from "The Role of Absolute and Relative Amounts of Time in Forgetting Within Immediate Memory: The Case of Tone Pitch Comparisons," by N. Cowan, J. S. Saults, and L. D. Nugent, 1997, Psychonomic Bulletin and Review, 4, p. 395. Reprinted with permission.

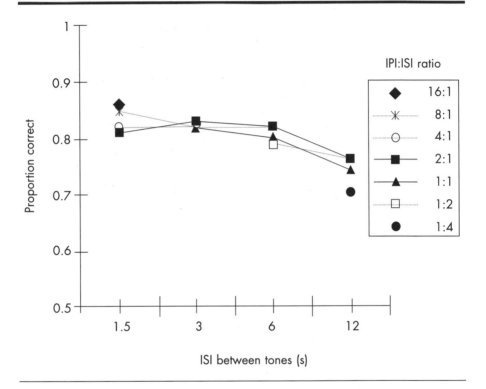

effects), they cannot totally account for the effects of ISI, given that ISI effects are found even with the ratio held constant. This appeared to provide strong support for a theory that included memory decay across ISIs.

Gordon Brown (personal communication, November 16, 1998) emphasized something that we had vaguely thought but had not previously been sufficiently motivated to pursue—that the ratio we measured captured only part of the distinctiveness mechanism. To capture the entire mechanism, we would have to measure back in time at least to the beginning of the experiment to find out how distinct an item was from all previous items in the experiment. We did not track the stimulus lags back that far because there would be no clear way to analyze the information. However, we did what we could. We had recorded not only the IPI preceding a stimulus but also the ISI within the previous tone pair and the IPI preceding that.

In other words, for a particular Trial n, we knew an $IPI(n-1)/ISI(n-1)/IPI(n)/ISI(n)$ timing sequence. To clarify this notation, $ISI(n-1)$ is the time between tones in the previous trial and $ISI(n)$ is the time between tones in the current trial. $IPI(n-1)$ and $IPI(n)$ are the periods preceding these two trials, respectively. This elaborate categorization of trials results in 256 possible timing sequences, with an occurrence randomly determined rather than counterbalanced. On the average, each of these 256 possible sequences occurred in only one trial per participant, and some participants had no data for some of these sequences.

We nevertheless found the data, pooled across participants, to be interesting. Out of 256 trial types contributing to 64 forgetting functions, we narrowed our approach by asking the following question: If we look at the trials in which the distinctiveness of the current trial's tones was as high as possible, based on the $IPI(n-1)$, $ISI(n-1)$, and $IPI(n)$ intervals, would we still find forgetting as a function of the $ISI(n)$ interval? Before this question can be addressed, we must reach an operational definition of "distinctiveness."

Two different distinctiveness theories seemed plausible. In a *pair distinctiveness* theory, what is important is how tones are grouped. For example, if the first tone in Trial n is closer in time to the second tone in the previous trial (Trial $n-1$) than it is to the second tone in the current trial (Trial n), then perceptual grouping may lead to the wrong comparison. According to this theory, the best distinctiveness and least forgetting across $ISI(n)$ should occur when both IPIs are long but when the preceding ISI, namely, $ISI(n-1)$, is short. Under that circumstance, it is least likely that the tones from Trial $n-1$ will be incorrectly separated from one another in the perceptual grouping process and the second one incorrectly grouped with the tones of the current trial, Trial n.

In a *tone distinctiveness* theory, the grouping of tones is not considered. It is simply assumed that it is the previous tones, not their grouping, that interfere with memory for the tones of the current trial. According to this theory, the best distinctiveness and least forgetting across $ISI(n)$ should occur when $IPI(n-1)$, $ISI(n-1)$, and $IPI(n)$ all are long, so that the tones of previous trials are as far from the tones of the current trial as possible.

These theories can be shown graphically as follows: Consider three trials in a row with tones A1 and A2 on Trial A, B1 and B2 on Trial B, and C1 and C2 on Trial C. Then the distinctiveness of the tones on Trial C can be classified as follows with respect to the prior intervals, with more rapid forgetting across the C1–C2 interval when distinctiveness is low. High distinctiveness on Trial C occurs, according to the pair distinctiveness theory, when tones from a trial are grouped together well, as illustrated below:

. . .A2. . . . . .B1. .B2. . . . . .C1. . ., etc.

Low distinctiveness on Trial C occurs, according to the pair distinctiveness theory, when the tones are temporally grouped across trials, not within a trial:

...A2. .B1................B2. .C1..., etc.

High distinctiveness on Trial C occurs, according to the tone distinctiveness theory, when prior tones are maximally far from C1 in time, as follows:

...A2...............B1...............B2...............C1..., etc.

Finally, low distinctiveness on Trial C occurs, according to the tone distinctiveness theory, when prior tones are temporally close to C1:

...A2. .B1. .B2. .C1..., etc.

Some relevant results can be seen in Figures 17.2–17.4. The top panel of Figure 17.2 shows data for trials with the highest level of distinctiveness according to the pair distinctiveness theory. The error bars show standard errors of the mean; no ordinary inferential statistics can be run given that pooled data were used and the contribution of particular participants differed across ISIs. There appears to have been forgetting across ISIs even under these high-distinctiveness conditions. However, it was not a gradual, regular sort of forgetting. Instead, memory was maintained across the first three ISIs and apparently plummeted in the longest ISI. This is not what would be expected according to a decay principle and instead could reflect a higher level type of distinctiveness that we have not been able to define (perhaps related to attentional vigilance given the length of this longest ISI). The bottom panel of Figure 17.2 serves as a manipulation check, showing that there was memory loss in the trials in which distinctiveness was as low as possible according to this theory.

One way to quantify memory loss is to accept the shortest available ISI as a preloss baseline and to express the amount of loss as a percentage of the possible amount of loss between the shortest ISI and the longest. For the top panel of Figure 17.2, the loss across retention intervals was $.88 - .66 = .28$. Because chance level is .50 in this task, the possible loss was $.88 - .50 = .38$ and the percentage of the possible amount was $100 \times (.28/.38) = 74\%$. In the bottom panel of the figure, forgetting was 50% of the possible amount.

The top panel of Figure 17.3 shows the data for the highest level of distinctiveness according to the tone distinctiveness theory. Here there is no tangible evidence of decay (0% of possible). The bottom panel of the figure shows the lowest level of distinctiveness, in which observable memory loss (56% of possible) is again evident.

The top panel of Figure 17.3 suggests that there may be no memory loss when the tones of the current trial are as distinct from previous tones as possible. However, we also found that even a small departure from the maximal distinctiveness conditions already allowed observable forgetting. Two examples of this appear in Figure 17.4. For the top panel of Figure 17.4, we attempted to obtain more stable means by collapsing data across levels of IPI($n - 1$) to produce 16 forgetting functions rather than 64. It was possible to get means for these 16 forgetting functions on an individual-participant basis and then average across these means. The top panel of

FIGURE 17.2

Proportion correct for trials in which the conditions for tone memory were best (top panel) or worst (bottom panel) according to pair distinctiveness theory. IPI = interpair interval; ISI = interstimulus interval. Data are pooled across individuals. Error bars reflect the standard error of the mean. Derived from the data set of Cowan, Saults, and Nugent (1997).

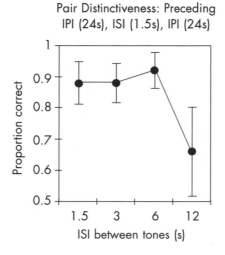

Pair Distinctiveness: Preceding
IPI (24s), ISI (1.5s), IPI (24s)

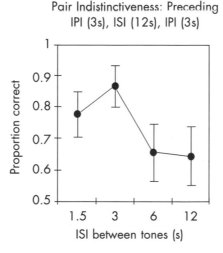

Pair Indistinctiveness: Preceding
IPI (3s), ISI (12s), IPI (3s)

Figure 17.4 shows the forgetting curve, out of 16, with the highest distinctiveness according to the tone distinctiveness theory. One can see that there was observable forgetting (31% of possible). Forgetting is seen in all but 2 of the 16 functions, and

FIGURE 17.3

Proportion correct for trials in which conditions for tone memory were best (top panel) or worst (bottom panel) according to tone distinctiveness theory. IPI = interpair interval; ISI = interstimulus interval. Data are pooled across individuals. Error bars reflect the standard error of the mean. Derived from the data set of Cowan, Saults, and Nugent (1997).

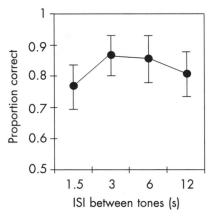

Tone Distinctiveness: Preceding
IPI (24s), ISI (12s), IPI (24s)

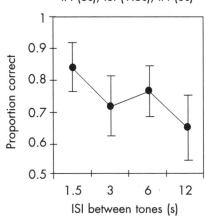

Tone Indistinctiveness: Preceding
IPI (3s), ISI (1.5s), IPI (3s)

we cannot find a principled way to account for the 2 that show no forgetting: trials with ISI($n-1$) = 1.5 s and IPI(n) = 6 s, and trials with ISI($n-1$) = 6 s and IPI(n) = 12 s.

FIGURE 17.4

Proportion correct for trials in which conditions for tone memory were relatively good, not best, according to tone distinctiveness theory. IPI = interpair interval; ISI = interstimulus interval. Top panel: Grand means based on means from each participant, collapsed across the preceding trial's IPI, for the longest possible values of the preceding trial's ISI and the current trial's IPI. Bottom panel: Trials in which one of three preceding intervals (preceding trial's IPI, preceding trial's ISI, and current trial's IPI) is the second longest possible and the other two intervals are as long as possible according to the experimental design. Error bars reflect the standard error of the mean. Derived from the data set of Cowan, Saults, and Nugent (1997).

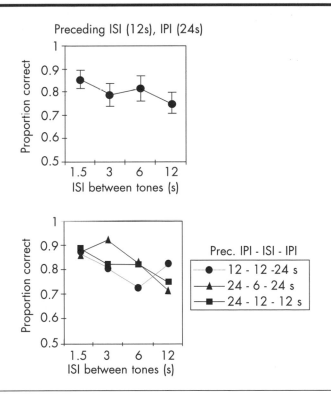

The bottom panel of Figure 17.4 returns to the more detailed data set involving 64 forgetting functions and shows the ones in which just one interval was one value removed from what would be needed for maximal distinctiveness as shown in the top panel of Figure 17.3. This bottom panel of Figure 17.4 shows once more that when the amount of distinctiveness is just a little bit lower than our maximum, there is forgetting (14%, 42%, and 34% of the possible forgetting for the top, middle, and bottom lines on the legend, respectively).

There are at least two possible interpretations of all of these results. First, the data could suggest that a variety of conditions can cause the tones that are to be compared to lose distinctiveness but that conditions have to be just right (as in the top panel of Figure 17.3) to provide sufficient distinctiveness to prevent forgetting across the ISIs between the tones to be compared. Second, alternatively, the absence of observable forgetting in the top panel of Figure 17.3 could reflect testing error given the random way in which these trials were distributed across participants. Either way, the present data provide no clear evidence for the importance of the absolute amount of time in recall, that is, for decay. All of the forgetting that we see could have to do with the loss of distinctiveness. This is true also of the vast two-stimulus comparison literature, which basically has ignored distinctiveness issues. This preliminary investigation should be taken as an impetus for more systematic studies of forgetting with proactive, concurrent, and retroactive interference all minimized.

Concluding Observations

We have failed to find clear evidence of decay in a situation that has often been viewed as one of the simplest paradigm cases for decay, namely in two-tone comparisons (Cowan, 1984). Nevertheless, one caution is in order. It is possible that all of the studies that deal with factors of distinctiveness, including this one, allow for some rehearsal of the stimuli. Some researchers of memory for unattended stimuli have attempted to eliminate retroactive interference (e.g., Cowan et al., 1990; Eriksen & Johnson, 1964) but have not manipulated factors that affect distinctiveness. Possibly, in the future, their procedures will show forgetting that will not go away no matter how distinct the stimuli are. Thus, we do not yet rule out decay as a memory mechanism but have not found clear evidence for it either.

The fact that this difficulty has remained unnoticed until now in such a vast literature can be taken as a caution for other procedures also. In particular, one must look very carefully to make sure that retroactive interference does not sneak in where it is thought not to be. One illustration of this concern occurs in the findings of Cowan, Kanevsky, Nugent, Saults, and Hismjatullina (2000). They attempted to study the effects of response delay on performance in a situation in which rehearsal would be blocked without extra interference being introduced. Participants saw lists of seven digits at irregular intervals. The first three interdigit intervals could be either 0.5 s or 2.0 s, as could the second three interdigit intervals. This resulted in lists with four varieties of stimulus timing: short–short, short–long, long–short, and long–long (although there were other, filler trials that were not analyzed). Half of the participants were simply to recall the digits in each list aloud, at any pace that was preferred, whereas the remaining participants were to recall the list aloud using the same timing that was present in the stimulus list. We hoped that participants who were to repeat the timing would not be able to rehearse (at least when the timing was irregular) because rehearsal would interfere with memory of the timing. We expected that in the absence of rehearsal for participants in this group, a long lag between digits in the spoken response would allow more forgetting of the remaining digits.

Initially, we were delighted because the results were as predicted. For the participants who were to recall the list at any speed that they wished, there was little difference between the presentation timing conditions. In contrast, for the participants who were to recall the list in the presented timing, performance for the long–short trials was markedly inferior to performance in the other three timing conditions. We supposed that memory for not-yet-recalled digits was lost during long interdigit intervals early in the response. Our opinion changed, however, after we conducted a detailed analysis of the timing of responses. Although the onset-to-onset intervals in the responses were exactly as we had expected, participants did not produce long intervals totally by interleaving silent periods between words as we had hoped. The silent periods did vary as was hoped but there also were significant differences in the durations of digits in the responses for different timing conditions. When a participant was supposed to produce a word followed by a long delay, the mean duration of the word itself within the response was longer than when a participant was supposed to produce a word followed by a short delay. Moreover, a regression analysis indicated that the duration of words in the responses accounted for performance levels better than the duration of silent periods in the responses. (This, by the way, is different from our studies of individual differences in list recall, in which it has been the silent periods between words rather than the words themselves that correlate best with recall; see, e.g., Cowan et al., 1998; and Hulme, Newton, Cowan, Stuart, & Brown, 1999.) Retroactive interference rather than decay could account for these new results.

Memory decay could be viewed as a hypothesis that is vague because it fails to state the actual cause of forgetting. Cowan, Saults, et al. (1997) articulated four slightly different possible definitions of memory decay. However, the issue that is most basic is whether the absolute amount of time, and not just the relative timing of stimuli, is relevant for recall. We suggest that it is now important to search for possible effects of the absolute amount of time on forgetting of unattended and attended stimuli. In the realm of attended stimuli, no clear evidence of decay has emerged in, lo, these many years.

Epilogue: A Decadent Song

As a lighthearted tribute to Robert Crowder's theoretical interests, Cowan approximated the singing of the following song at Crowder's festschrift, just before the introduction of the final conference speaker, Robert Bjork.

To the tune of "New York, New York":
I'm tracking my lags / I'm leaving Decay / I want to be a part of it—/ New Bjork[1]
New Bjork! / If I can't find Decay here, / I can't find it anywhere! / It's up to you /
New Bjork, New Bjork!

---

[1]See Bjork and Whitten (1974).

References

Baddeley, A. D. (1986). *Working memory* (Oxford Psychology Series No. 11). Oxford, England: Clarendon Press.

Baddeley, A. D., & Scott, D. (1971). Short-term forgetting in the absence of proactive inhibition. *Quarterly Journal of Experimental Psychology, 23,* 275–283.

Bjork, R. A., & Whitten, W. B. (1974). Recency-sensitive retrieval processes in long-term free recall. *Cognitive Psychology, 6,* 173–189.

Broadbent, D. E. (1958). *Perception and communication.* London: Pergamon Press.

Brown, J. (1958). Some tests of the decay theory of immediate memory. *Quarterly Journal of Experimental Psychology, 10,* 12–21.

Brown, J. (1959). Information, redundancy and decay of the memory trace. In *The mechanisation of thought processes* (National Physical Laboratory Symposium, No. 10, Vol. 2, pp. 729–752). London, UK: Her Majesty's Stationery Office.

Cowan, N. (1984). On short and long auditory stores. *Psychological Bulletin, 96,* 341–370.

Cowan, N. (1988). Evolving conceptions of memory storage, selective attention, and their mutual constraints within the human information processing system. *Psychological Bulletin, 104,* 163–191.

Cowan, N. (1995). *Attention and memory: An integrated framework* (Oxford Psychology Series No. 26). New York: Oxford University Press.

Cowan, N., Day, L., Saults, J. S., Keller, T. A., Johnson, T., & Flores, L. (1992). The role of verbal output time in the effects of word length on immediate memory. *Journal of Memory and Language, 31,* 1–17.

Cowan, N., Kanevsky, A., Nugent, L. D., Saults, J. S., & Hismjatullina, A. (2000). *Response lags and word lengths in verbal serial recall.* Manuscript in preparation, University of Missouri—Columbia.

Cowan, N., Lichty, W., & Grove, T. R. (1990). Properties of memory for unattended spoken syllables. *Journal of Experimental Psychology: Learning, Memory, and Cognition, 16,* 258–269.

Cowan, N., Nugent, L. D., Elliott, E. M., & Geer, T. (2000). Is there a temporal basis of the word length effect? A response to Service (1998). *Quarterly Journal of Experimental Psychology, 53A,* 666–670.

Cowan, N., Saults, J. S., & Nugent, L. D. (1997). The role of absolute and relative amounts of time in forgetting within immediate memory: The case of tone pitch comparisons. *Psychonomic Bulletin and Review, 4,* 393–397.

Cowan, N., Wood, N. L., & Borne, D. N. (1994). Reconfirmation of the short-term storage concept. *Psychological Science, 5,* 103–106.

Cowan, N., Wood, N. L., Nugent, L. D., & Treisman, M. (1997). There are two word length effects in verbal short-term memory: Opposed effects of duration and complexity. *Psychological Science, 8,* 290–295.

Cowan, N., Wood, N. L., Wood, P. K., Keller, T. A., Nugent, L. D., & Keller, C. V. (1998). Two separate verbal processing rates contributing to short-term memory span. *Journal of Experimental Psychology: General, 127,* 141–160.

Crowder, R. G. (1982). Decay of auditory memory in vowel discrimination. *Journal of Experimental Psychology: Learning, Memory, and Cognition, 8,* 153–162.

Crowder, R. G. (1983). The purity of auditory memory. *Philosophical Transactions of the Royal Society of London, B 302,* 251–265.

Crowder, R.G. (1989). Modularity and dissociations in memory systems. In H. L. Roediger & F. I. M. Craik (Eds.), *Varieties of memory and consciousness: Essays in Honor of Endel Tulving* (pp. 271–294). Hillsdale, NJ: Erlbaum.

Crowder, R. G. (1993). Short-term memory: Where do we stand? *Memory & Cognition, 21,* 142–145.

Crowder, R. G., & Morton, J. (1969). Precategorical acoustic storage. *Perception and Psychophysics, 5,* 365–373.

Eriksen, C. W., & Johnson, H. J. (1964). Storage and decay characteristics of nonattended auditory stimuli. *Journal of Experimental Psychology, 68,* 28–36.

Glanzer, M., & Cunitz, A. R. (1966). Two storage mechanisms in free recall. *Journal of Verbal Learning and Verbal Behavior, 5,* 351–360.

Glenberg, A. M., & Swanson, N. G. (1986). A temporal distinctiveness theory of recency and modality effects. *Journal of Experimental Psychology: Learning, Memory, and Cognition, 12,* 3–15.

Greene, R. L. (1986). A common basis for recency effects in immediate and delayed recall. *Journal of Experimental Psychology: Learning, Memory, and Cognition, 12,* 413–418.

Hebb, D. O. (1949). *Organization of behavior.* New York: Wiley.

Hulme, C., Newton, P., Cowan, N., Stuart, G., & Brown, G. (1999). Think before you speak: Pause, memory search and trace redintegration processes in verbal memory span. *Journal of Experimental Psychology: Learning, Memory, and Cognition, 25,* 447–463.

James, W. (1890). *The principles of psychology.* New York: Holt.

Keller, T. A., Cowan, N., & Saults, J. S. (1995). Can auditory memory for tone pitch be rehearsed? *Journal of Experimental Psychology: Learning, Memory, and Cognition, 21,* 635–645.

Keppel, G., & Underwood, B. J. (1962). Proactive inhibition in short-term retention of single items. *Journal of Verbal Learning and Verbal Behavior, 1,* 153–161.

Koppenaal, L., & Glanzer, M. (1990). An examination of the continuous distractor task and the "long-term recency effect." *Memory & Cognition, 18,* 183–195.

Marks, A., & Crowder, R. G. (1997). Temporal distinctiveness and modality. *Journal of Experimental Psychology: Learning, Memory, and Cognition, 23,* 164–180.

McGeoch, J. A. (1932). Forgetting and the law of disuse. *Psychological Review, 39,* 352–370.

Melton, A. W. (1963). Implications of short-term memory for a general theory of memory. *Journal of Verbal Learning and Verbal Behavior, 2,* 1–21.

Näätänen, R. (1992). *Attention and brain function.* Hillsdale, NJ: Erlbaum.

Nairne, J. S., Neath, I., Serra, M., & Byun, E. (1997). Positional distinctiveness and the ratio rule in free recall. *Journal of Memory and Language, 37,* 155–166.

Neath, I., & Crowder, R. G. (1990). Schedules of presentation and temporal distinctiveness in human memory. *Journal of Experimental Psychology: Learning, Memory, and Cognition, 16,* 316–327.

Neath, I., & Nairne, J. S. (1995). Word-length effects in immediate memory: Overwriting trace decay. *Psychonomic Bulletin and Review, 2,* 429–441.

Peterson, L. R., & Peterson, M. J. (1959). Short-term retention of individual verbal items. *Journal of Experimental Psychology, 58,* 193–198.

Platt, J. R. (1964). Strong inference. *Science, 146,* 347–353.

Reitman, J. S. (1974). Without surreptitious rehearsal, information in short-term memory decays. *Journal of Verbal Learning and Verbal Behavior, 13,* 365–377.

Roediger, H. L., III, Knight, J. L., & Kantowitz, B. H. (1977). Inferring decay in short-term memory: The issue of capacity. *Memory & Cognition, 5,* 167–176.

Sams, M., Hari, R., Rif, J., & Knuutila, J. (1993). The human auditory sensory memory trace persists about 10 s: Neuromagnetic evidence. *Journal of Cognitive Neuroscience, 5,* 363–370.

Thapar, A., & Greene, R. L. (1993). Evidence against a short-term-store account of long-term recency effects. *Memory & Cognition, 21,* 329–337.

Towse, J. N., Hitch, G. J., & Hutton, U. (1998). A reevaluation of working memory capacity in children. *Journal of Memory and Language, 39,* 195–217.

Watkins, M. J., Watkins, O. C., Craik, F. I. M., & Mazuryk, G. (1973). Effect of nonverbal distraction of short-term storage. *Journal of Experimental Psychology, 101,* 296–300.

Wingfield, A., & Byrnes, D. L. (1972). Decay of information in short-term memory. *Science, 176,* 690–692.

CHAPTER 18

Neuropsychology of Verbal Working Memory

Ins and Outs of Phonological and Lexical–Semantic Retention

Randi C. Martin

Monica L. Freedman

In putting this chapter together, we looked back over some articles by Bob Crowder to see if there were connections between his theoretical positions and the views that have grown out of the research in our lab. One date stood out when perusing his work. In 1982, he wrote "The Demise of Short-Term Memory." This was the year that I (Martin) started studying short-term memory (STM) deficits. In this chapter, we hope to aid in the resuscitation of the study of STM, particularly with regard to its role in language processing. Although Crowder's article does call into question many of the grounds for distinguishing STM and long-term memory (LTM), he included some statements that are highly relevant to issues that we have examined. He stated that "deep down many of us believe that the main role of short-term memory must surely be in the perception and comprehension of language" (Crowder, 1982, p. 309) and that "the role of short-term memory may really be in deciphering syntax" (p. 316). In this chapter, we discuss the relation of STM and language processing, concentrating more on language production than on comprehension.

Crowder's (1993) more recent writings emphasize what he termed a "procedural-ist" view in which there is no need for postulating memory stores and no need to make a distinction between STM and LTM. Instead, persisting activity in neural structures that carry out processing in different domains could account for what is termed STM, and the repeated presentation of items would activate the same pattern of neural activity, resulting in long-term learning, similar to Hebb's (1949) hypothesis

This research was supported by National Institutes of Health Grant DC-00218 to Randi C. Martin at Rice University. The authors wish to acknowledge Michael Katz for collaboration on several of the projects described and Jessica Mejia, Frank Tamborello, and Ann-Marie Lobo for assistance in transcribing many of the patient testing sessions.

of reverberating cell assemblies. In Hebb's view, the simultaneous presentation of multiple stimuli results in the firing of an assembly of cells, and the activation reverberates for some time after the stimuli are removed. If the same stimuli are repeatedly presented, the same cell assembly is activated. Over time, structural changes occur that facilitate the transmission among the components of the cell assembly. The reverberation could be seen as an instantiation of STM and the necessity of this reverberation for structural changes to occur as implying that reverberation in STM is a necessary component of the formation of long-term memories.

This approach eschews the notion of memory stores that are dedicated to retaining different types of memories. Crowder (1993) argued that this proceduralist position was consistent with brain function. However, there are findings from neurological cases that support a distinction between STM and LTM. As known, classic amnesia patients can perform normally on STM tasks, including list and sentence recall, and they can carry on a coherent conversation that presumably draws on STM resources of some type. However, they perform abysmally on LTM tests—for instance, showing virtually no recall of the coherent conversation that they engaged in a short while earlier (e.g., see Milner, 1966; and Milner, Corkin, & Teuber, 1968). The neuropsychological cases that we have concentrated on in our research show the opposite side of this dissociation. These patients may do extremely poorly on traditional STM tasks, perhaps having a memory span of only one or two items. Yet their long-term memories may be intact. For instance, they may show normal performance on memory for stories (see Romani & Martin, 1999, for a contrast between an STM patient and three amnesia patients).

Although we argue that some distinction between STM and LTM is required to accommodate the neuropsychological data, there are some points of agreement between Crowder's proceduralist view and our approach. In our view of working memory, there is a close relation between language processing and short-term retention. In fact, we see verbal STM as tied to the different types of representations that are involved in language processing. Both language processing and verbal STM activate phonological, lexical, and semantic representations from long-term representations in semantic memory. However, we claimed that some separation between processing and storage needs to be maintained (R. C. Martin, Lesch, & Bartha, 1999).

As shown in Figure 18.1 (R. C. Martin et al., 1999), language processing is supported by interactive activation of representations in the long-term knowledge store (on the left side). During word recognition, acoustic information is mapped onto a phonological form, which then accesses a lexical form, which then activates a semantic representation. In word production, activation begins at the semantic level, which then activates a lexical representation, which then activates its phonological representation, which is used to guide articulation. When a person hears and repeats a word list, both perception and production are involved. The long-term knowledge store feeds into and receives feedback from separable buffers that support retention

FIGURE 18.1

Model of short-term memory incorporating separate lexical–semantic and phonological buffers, and a separation of input and output phonology. From "Independence of Input and Output Phonology in Word Processing and Short-Term Memory," by R. C. Martin, M. F. Lesch, and M. C. Bartha, 1999, Journal of Memory and Language, 40, p. 8. Copyright 1999 by Academic Press. Adapted with permission.

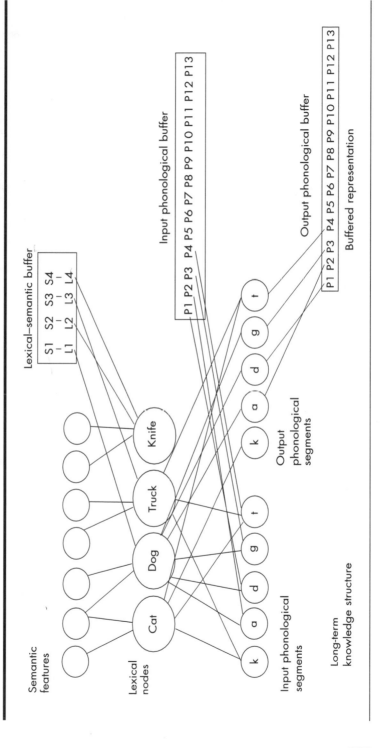

of lexical–semantic and phonological information (on the right side). These buffers have limited capacity and can be selectively damaged such that the representations contained therein undergo overly rapid decay or show greater than normal effects of interference from other items in the buffer. Some models (e.g., N. Martin & Saffran, 1997) take a similar approach but instead argue that persisting activation in the knowledge representations is all that is needed to account for STM.

Most of the evidence that led us to this approach has come from the study of patients with brain damage who have STM deficits that appear to be due to the disruption of either phonological or semantic retention. All of the patients that we included in our studies were screened to show a normal level of accuracy on tests assessing single-word comprehension and production. Thus, we did not look at patients who had major disruptions of the lexical knowledge store but at those who had difficulty with the retention of verbal information. Because of these patients' good single-word processing, their STM deficits cannot be attributed to a disruption of the knowledge store (e.g., R. C. Martin & Lesch, 1996; R. C. Martin, Shelton, & Yaffee, 1994).

All the patients had reduced verbal STM spans, on the order of 1–2 items. The dissociation between phonological and semantic retention was established by the examination of the influence of phonological versus semantic variables on retention. Measures of phonological retention include the phonological similarity effect and word length effect in span, where absence of these effects indicates reduced phonological retention. Other phonological retention measures are nonword span and performance on a rhyme probe task (a series of words is heard followed by a probe word, and the participant must decide if the probe word rhymes with any of the words in the list). Semantic STM measures include the difference in span for words versus nonwords, imageability effect in span, and performance on a category probe (similar to the rhyme probe, but patients must judge whether the probe word is in the same category as any of the preceding items).

Patients with phonological retention deficits show normal effects of semantic variables but an absence of effects of phonological variables, whereas patients with semantic retention deficits show the reverse. In the model, the patients with semantic STM deficits have difficulty maintaining information in the lexical–semantic buffer, and patients with the phonological STM deficits have difficulty maintaining information in the phonological buffer. There also appears to be some anatomical distinction between those patients with phonological and semantic retention deficits. As reported in the neuropsychological literature, patients who have deficits in phonological retention appear to have a common area of overlap in their lesions in the inferior parietal region—Brodmann's area 40 (Shallice & Vallar, 1990; Vallar & Papagno, 1995). There is much less information on the localization of lesions in patients with semantic retention deficits. However, our data (R. C. Martin & Lesch, 1996; Romani & Martin, 1999) and results from a few patients tested at Temple University (N. Martin & Saffran, 1997) suggest that the region of overlap has a more anterior localization, involving frontal language areas.

Recent evidence from our lab and others suggests that the model needs to be complicated further. Specifically, the model should include separable phonological representations for input and output and separable buffers for maintaining these two types of information (see Figure 18.1). This is not the first time this separation has been proposed; in fact, Shallice and Butterworth (1977) made such a suggestion more than 2 decades ago. However, the position has been controversial (see N. Martin & Saffran, 1992). In establishing the distinction between input and output phonology, two lines of evidence have been used. First, dissociations between performance on tasks tapping input versus output phonological retention have been observed. Allport (1984) and Romani (1992) have demonstrated that a patient might show poor list recall, which requires speech output, but do much better on recognition tasks that presumably tap input retention, such as a digit-matching span task during which the patient hears two lists of digits (e.g., 5349; 5394). The opposite dissociation has been demonstrated in a somewhat more indirect form. Specifically, patients with reduced spans and poor retention of phonological information on input STM tasks may show normal speech production (R. C. Martin et al., 1994; Shallice & Butterworth, 1977). This normal production includes normal sentence length, grammatical complexity, and normal pausing and hesitations. Under the assumption that a phonological buffer is needed to plan speech production, the good language production for these patients suggests that the output buffer is preserved despite the severe restriction in the input buffer.

A second line of evidence has come from a patient, M. S.,[1] who is unimpaired in speech perception but has difficulty specifically in retrieving output phonological representations (R. C. Martin et al., 1999). Thus, M. S., unlike our other patients, did show a major disruption in lexical knowledge. Because of the direct connection between the knowledge representations shown in Figure 18.1 and storage of these representations, this patient's difficulty in retrieving output phonology has direct consequences for his STM performance. Details of this case are provided in R. C. Martin et al. (1999), but some facts relevant to the separation of input and output phonology are summarized below.

Output Phonological Buffer Deficit Due to Anomia: The Case of M. S.

M. S.'s brain damage affected mainly the left hemisphere and resulted in language deficits but a remarkable sparing of other cognitive functions. M. S.'s picture naming is reduced, particularly for low-frequency words. He scored only 10 on the Boston

---

[1]M. S. is a 29-year-old man who contracted herpes encephalitis in 1993. MRI scan and EEG recording suggested left temporal damage.

Naming Test (Kaplan, Goodglass, & Weintraub, 1983), where the mean for control participants his age is 55.86 (SD = 2.86). In picture naming, he often produces circumlocutions. For example, for the target "chimney," he responded

> I think this one starts with a "C." It's the stuff that are on the top of a house that you put, if you, if it gets real cold you can put a, uh, you can cut a tree down and catch it on fire inside your house. But, they, uh, the heat comes in, but the, the bad smelling stuff that can knock you out and kill you goes outside of your house. I can't remember what it's called. I don't remember what it starts with.

His spontaneous speech also exhibits many word-finding attempts.

In verbal list recall, M. S. showed a striking pattern of a normal level of performance for nonwords but a below-normal level for words. His word list recall shows patterns like those shown in single-word production. He showed a large effect of word frequency on recall and produced circumlocutions in recalling lists. For example, for the target list "lobster castle bagpipe," M. S. said "'losser'—the thing you eat, the place where kings go in, it comes from the place where men dress like women" (demonstrates use). In contrast to his poor list recall, he showed an excellent level of performance on all input STM tasks in which he did not have to produce any output. These tasks required him to make yes–no decisions about the order or identity of list items and included such tasks as digit-matching span, rhyme probe, order recognition, and nonword probe tasks. He performed at or above the normal mean on all these tasks (R. C. Martin et al., 1999).

It was hypothesized that M. S. has difficulty not with the output buffer per se but rather with activating output phonological representations from lexical–semantic representations (R. C. Martin et al., 1999). In the model in Figure 18.1, the connections between lexical–semantic representations and output phonological representations have been damaged, which has a greater impact on his production of low- than high-frequency words in both naming and list recall. His normal level of performance on nonword list recall implies that the input and output buffers are preserved and that he can translate directly between input and output phonological representations. For word list recall, there is evidence that input phonological representations are activated and maintained normally. However, he did not show the boost in performance compared with nonwords that is shown by normal participants because they receive activation both from direct translation from the input phonological representations and from activation flowing from lexical–semantic representations. It is this activation from lexical–semantic representations to output phonological representations that is missing for M. S. Thus, this patient's reduced performance on the memory-span tasks for word lists derives from a lexical processing disorder, which would be predicted by our model. It should be emphasized, however, that other patients have been reported in the literature who did not have disruptions of word production yet who showed evidence of reduced output phonological buffers (e.g., Romani, 1992).

Semantic STM Deficit: Comprehension Versus Production

In much of the research carried out in our lab, we have examined the relation between STM and syntactic and semantic aspects of sentence processing. It has been repeatedly reported, contrary to Crowder's (1982) hypothesis that the main role of STM may be in deciphering syntax, that patients with restricted memory spans may yet show good comprehension of syntactically complex sentences (for reviews, see Caplan & Waters, 1999; and R. C. Martin, 1993). Consequently, our recent work on sentence processing has been concentrated more on semantically loaded sentences and the relation of STM to the comprehension and production of these sentences.

As summarized earlier, the evidence suggests that there are separate capacities for retaining input and output phonological information. The question addressed in the remainder of this chapter is whether this distinction between input and output buffers applies to the semantic level as well. In previous work, R. C. Martin and Romani (1994) and R. C. Martin (1995) have demonstrated that patients who show semantic retention deficits on memory-span tasks perform poorly on sentence comprehension when they have to maintain several lexical–semantic representations prior to their integration into higher level propositional representations. These researchers used a sentence anomaly task with auditorily presented sentences. The number of adjectives before or after a noun or the number of nouns before or after a verb was manipulated. For example, the "before" condition with adjectives used anomalous sentences, such as "The rusty, old, red swimsuit . . ." or "The rusty swimsuit. . . ." The "after" condition used anomalous sentences of the form "The swimsuit was old, red, and rusty . . ." or "The swimsuit was rusty. . . ." Matching sensible sentences were also presented (i.e., substituting *pail* for *swimsuit*). A similar manipulation was used for the sentences that manipulated the number of nouns. For example, a before sentence with three nouns was "The cloth, the vase, and the mirror cracked . . .," and the matching after sentence was "The movers cracked the mirror, the vase, and the cloth." R. C. Martin and Romani (1994) reasoned that in the before conditions, integration of lexical–semantic information was delayed because the meaning of an adjective had to be maintained until it could be integrated with a noun, and the meaning of a noun had to be maintained until it could be integrated with the verb (i.e., integrated in terms of its thematic role with respect to the verb). In the after conditions, integration was immediate.

R. C. Martin and Romani (1994) and R. Martin (1995) have shown that two patients (A. B. and M. L.)[2] with semantic STM deficits performed poorly in the before

---

[2]A. B. is a 76-year-old man who suffered a left-frontal hematoma in 1979. CT scan after surgery revealed low-density regions in the posterolateral left frontal lobe and in the adjacent anterior parietal lobe. M. L. is a 55-year-old man who suffered a left-hemisphere cardiovascular accident in 1990. CT scan indicated an infarction involving the left-frontal and parietal operculum, with atrophy in the left temporal operculum and mild diffuse atrophy.

condition when two or three words had to be maintained prior to integration. They made a large number of errors and showed a large effect of the distance manipulation (the number of nouns or adjectives that had to be maintained prior to integration). In fact, both performed near chance levels at distances of two and three words in the before condition, about 37–40% errors for each patient in these conditions where 50% would be chance, compared with 10–15% errors at a distance of one word. In contrast, in the after condition, they made many fewer errors overall and showed little effect of the number of nouns or adjectives. Patient E. A.,[3] with a phonological retention deficit, showed, like normal participants, a small main effect of before and after, doing slightly worse in the before condition. However, she did not show the interaction between before and after sentence type and distance shown by the patients with semantic retention deficits.

In the present research, we investigated whether patients with semantic retention deficits would show similar deficits in language production. That is, we wished to determine if the constructions that caused them difficulty in comprehension— noun phrases with several prenominal adjectives and subject–noun phrases with more than one noun—would cause difficulties in production. These patients, unlike the patients with phonological STM deficits, do have difficulties in spontaneous speech production. Their speech rate is slow, and they produce a reduced amount of content information in their noun and verb phrase productions, as measured by the quantitative analysis of speech production (Saffran, Berndt, & Schwartz, 1989).

Noun Phrase Production: The Case of E. A. Versus M. L. and A. B.

The first task examined patients' ability to produce simple adjective–noun (AN) and adjective–adjective–noun (AAN) phrases. In this task, patients were asked to describe pictures—first producing single adjectives and nouns and then producing phrases.

Method

Materials

Pictures of three different objects were constructed that varied on three different dimensions (e.g., hair: long vs. short, blonde vs. black, straight vs. curly). These pictures were presented on a computer using the PsyScope program (Cohen, MacWhinney, Flatt, & Provost, 1993).

---

[3]E. A. is a 66-year-old woman who suffered a left-hemisphere stroke in 1975, involving the left-temporal and parietal lobes, and including the primary auditory cortex, Wernicke's area, and the superior and inferior parietal lobules.

Design and Procedure

First patients saw labeled pictures showing the different dimensions of the pictures to familiarize them with the words they would use in the experiment. Next they completed 10 trials naming only the nouns (hair, curtain, or leaf) and 10 trials naming only the adjectives. The adjectives were elicited by showing two pictures side by side that were identical except for one relevant dimension (e.g., long straight black hair vs. short straight black hair). One picture was highlighted to indicate which adjective should be produced (e.g., long).

In the second part, participants were asked to produce AN phrases (e.g., long hair). These phrases were elicited using the same format as the adjective productions, but participants were instructed to produce an AN phrase to describe the highlighted picture. They were given 2 practice trials to ensure that they understood the procedure and then 10 test trials. Finally, participants completed 10 trials in which they were asked to produce AAN phrases (e.g., long, curly hair). These phrases were elicited by showing three pictures. The target picture was highlighted, and the other pictures differed from the target on only one of the relevant dimensions (e.g., short blond hair [target] shown with long blond hair and short black hair).

Results

As shown in Table 18.1, patient E. A. with a phonological STM deficit performed normally on the noun phrase production task, whereas the two patients with semantic retention deficits performed well on single noun and adjective production but poorly on the AN combinations. These patients struggled to produce a phrase of the appropriate type, often producing pieces of it separately. For example, for the target

TABLE 18.1

Patient Performance on Noun Phrase Production Task

PARTICIPANT	ADJ	N	AN	AAN
Control (n = 6)	100	88	92	77
		(93)	(97)	(82)
Phonological STM				
E. A.	100	90	90	70
			(100)	(80)
Semantic STM				
A. B.	100	100	30	0
M. L.	100	100	20	10
			(80)	(40)

Note.   Numbers in parentheses are the percentage correct after self-correction. ADJ = adjective; N = noun; AN = adjective–noun; AAN = adjective–adjective–noun; STM = short-term memory deficit.

"small leaf" A. B. responded, "It's a leaf. It's small." In the case of M. L., he often worked his way up to the appropriate phrase. For example, when trying to produce the target "small, rough leaf," M. L. responded with "small . . . small . . . rough, rough leaf . . . small, rough leaf." These patients' difficulties in producing simple phrases, together with their difficulty in understanding the sentences with two or three adjectives before a noun, suggest that the same semantic retention buffer that is used in comprehension is used in production.

Production by Phrasal Fragments

Our subsequent work has investigated further the types of sentence constructions that cause difficulties for these semantic STM patients in production. In these investigations, we have been using a model of production that assumes that production proceeds incrementally (de Smedt, 1996; LaPointe & Dell, 1989; Smith & Wheeldon, 1999). A conceptual representation may be developed that spans an entire clause. However, planning at a grammatical level proceeds in a phrase-by-phrase fashion in terms of both grammatical structure and semantic representation. We have also assumed what we have termed the "lexical head" principle. That is, in planning these phrases, the speaker has to have accessed the lexical–semantic representation for the head of the phrase and all words that precede it in the phrase before beginning articulation. If this view is correct, then we might expect that these patients might do better if they were asked to produce the same information as in the AN phrases in a sentence form—for example, to say "the leaf is green" or "the leaf is small and green." In "the leaf is green," there is only one noun in the subject–noun phrase and only one adjective in the adjective phrase following the copula. In "the leaf is small and green," there are now two adjectives in the adjective phrase, so that may begin to cause difficulties.

Method

Materials

Similar to the previous experiment, pictures of three different objects were used that each varied on three different dimensions.

Design and Procedure

The procedure was similar to that described in the previous study. However, there were 18 items in each section, and the single noun and single adjective portions were each repeated three times to ensure that participants were well practiced in producing the single nouns and adjectives prior to attempting the phrases. Furthermore, the training procedure for the AN and AAN conditions was extended to include two examples and six practice trials before the 18 test trials. Patients were tested in two sessions separated by at least 2 weeks in which they produced the noun phrase versions (adjectives before) in one session and the sentence versions in another (adjectives after).

Results

In this study, we have so far tested M. L. and a new patient, G. R.,[4] who also shows a lexical–semantic retention deficit on memory-span tasks. The results are shown in Table 18.2. Both patients did improve in the sentence versions. Their performance was more accurate and they produced more fluent productions with fewer hesitations in the sentence versions. It should be noted, though, that although their performance in the sentence versions was generally fluent and in the correct form, they did make errors in choosing the wrong adjective.

Production of Syntactically Complex Sentences

We have also looked at these patients' ability to produce more complex grammatical constructions, reasoning that they might be able to produce complex sentences if the amount of semantic information in each phrase was limited. In one task, we looked at their ability to produce one-clause active and passive sentences (e.g., "The rabbit chased the monkey" or "The monkey was chased by the rabbit") and in a second looked at their ability to produce relative clause sentences where the clause was either active or passive in form (e.g., "That's the rabbit that chased the monkey," or "That's the monkey that was chased by the rabbit"). All of these sentence types

TABLE 18.2

Noun Phrase Production

	AN		AAN	
PATIENT	**ADJ. BEFORE**	**ADJ. AFTER**	**ADJ. BEFORE**	**ADJ. AFTER**
	Percentage of responses correct on first attempt			
M. L.	78	89	22	39
G. R.	44	89	33	44
	Percentage of responses with pause or initiation delay			
M. L.			77	3
G. R.			55	10

Note. AN = adjective–noun; AAN = adjective–adjective–noun; ADJ. = adjective.

---

[4]G. R. is a 54-year-old man who suffered a stroke in 1989. CT scan revealed a large frontoparietal temporal wedge-shaped middle-cerebral-artery distribution stroke.

allow for production in a phrase-by-phrase fashion in which each phrase has at most one content word. That is, even though the verb phrase might contain more than one content word, the verb is the head of the phrase, and according to the lexical-head principle, only the verb and words preceding it in the same phrase have to be represented in a semantic form prior to phonological encoding.

Method

Materials

Eight different stuffed animals were used to act out scenes described by the patients.

Design and Procedure

Before producing the sentences, patients were familiarized with the animal names and the actions (chase, kick, push, and tickle) that would be used. The experimenter first named each animal and demonstrated each action for the patient. Then the patient named each animal and each action three times.

In the first part of the experiment, patients produced three sets of sentences: blocked active, blocked passive, and mixed active and passive. So that the patients would understand the kinds of constructions we wanted, they received 7 practice trials with feedback before each blocked set and 8 practice trials before the mixed set. There were 16 test trials in each of the blocked sets and 24 test trials in the mixed set. The experimenter acted out a brief scene with the animals, and each patient was asked to describe what occurred, beginning the sentence with the animal pointed to by the experimenter (to elicit passive vs. active sentences). The active and passive blocks always preceded the mixed block.

For the relative clause sentences, we used the following procedure similar to one that had been developed originally to use with children (Hamburger & Crain, 1984). The same type of scene was acted out, but there were two animals of one kind and one animal of another kind present. One of the animals of the pair acted on or was acted on by the other animal. The experimenter pointed to that animal, and the patients were instructed to describe what had occurred, beginning each sentence with "That's the . . ." to invoke a relative clause construction. (For example, if there were two frogs and one bear, and one of the frogs kicked the bear, the experimenter would point to that frog, and the target response would be "That's the frog that kicked the bear.") Again, several training trials with feedback were given for each block, and the active relative clause block and the passive relative clause block preceded the mixed block.

Results

Table 18.3 compares the results for three tasks, all of which required production of three content words—the AAN phrases, the active and passive sentences, and the

TABLE 18.3

Comparison of Tasks Requiring Production of Three Content Words

PATIENT	AAN PHRASES	ONE-CLAUSE SENTENCES			RELATIVE-CLAUSE SENTENCES		
		ACTIVE	PASSIVE	MIXED	ACTIVE	PASSIVE	MIXED
M. L.							
Initial	22	75	81	63	100	88	50
Final	44	81	100	92	100	100	96
G. R.							
Initial	33	94	94	54			
Final	39	94	94	71			

relative clause sentences. M. L. performed much better on producing the syntactically more complex sentences in the active–passive and relative clause sentences than he did on the AAN phrases. The difference in performance between first correct and last correct on the two complex sentence types was not due to the same kind of lexical searching and reiteration of successively longer content phrases that we saw in the AAN phrases. Instead, many of his initially incorrect utterances were ones in which he incorrectly began with a passive form and then self-corrected to the active form. For example, for the target "That's the rabbit that chased the dog," M. L. responded, "It was the, uh, rabbit that was chased the dog. It was the rabbit that chased the dog." This occurred when he had produced a passive sentence on the previous trial. Therefore, he seemed to perseverate on the syntactic form from the previous trial, but only for passives. He would realize that this form was incorrect and begin again.

Patient G. R. also performed better on the active and passive single clause sentences than on the AAN phrases, although the difference was not as dramatic as for M. L., in the mixed condition. Like M. L., he tended to perseverate on the passive form having produced this form correctly on a previous trial.[5]

Moving Pictures: Simple Versus Complex Initial Noun Phrases

In one final study, a reaction time measure was used to assess the production of sentences with either a simple or complex initial noun phrase (R. C. Martin, Vu, &

---

[5]G. R. has not completed the relative clause sentences because of a reluctance on his part to complete any further tasks involving these stuffed animals. It is not clear whether he finds the task too difficult or perhaps demeaning. Future testing should try to elicit similar productions from G. R. but using a different paradigm, such as computerized pictures, which he does not seem to mind.

Miller, 2000). In the comprehension test, two patients with semantic STM deficits, A. B. and M. L., had difficulty understanding sentences in which a complex noun phrase occurred before the verb. Thus, this study was designed to investigate whether they would have difficulty producing similar constructions. The materials in this production task were based on a study by Smith and Wheeldon (1999) that tests the phrase-by-phrase production model. In this study, participants produced sentences that began with either a simple or complex noun phrase. Sentences with a simple noun phrase in the subject position had a complex noun phrase in the predicate, and sentences with a complex noun phrase in the subject position had a simple noun phrase in the predicate. Thus, the sentences were matched in overall length and number of content words to be expressed. Some example sentences included

- Simple–complex: The cat moves above the knife and the finger.
  Complex–simple: The cat and the knife move below the finger.

Across several experiments, Smith and Wheeldon found that participants were about 70–100 ms slower in initiating the complex–simple sentences than the simple–complex sentences. These results support the phrase-by-phrase production model in suggesting that the participants plan both nouns in the complex–simple condition before beginning their utterance.

Method

Participants

In addition to M. L., 10 age-matched control patients were tested.

Materials

Forty-eight simple object line drawings were used in all of the trials. In each critical trial, three objects were displayed in an animated scene in which two objects moved in one direction (up or down) and the third moved in the opposite direction. There were also filler trials in which all of the objects moved in the same direction, and participants were asked to produce sentences like "They all moved left." These were included to introduce some variety into the syntactic constructions that participants were to produce. There were 128 critical trials and 128 filler trials presented in a random order in a session.

Design and Procedure

Participants were shown labeled pictures of all the objects to be used to familiarize them with the names. Then they completed a set of practice trials to learn the types of sentence constructions they were asked to produce. Participants saw a fixation point followed by moving picture displays of three objects. Participants were asked to describe the pictures beginning with the left-most object. For the critical trials, two pictures moved in one direction and one moved in the other. For the control participants, the pictures disappeared from the screen immediately after the participants began their responses. However, for patient M. L., the pictures disappeared 500 ms after he began his utterance as pretesting suggested that he would make too large a proportion of errors if the pictures disappeared immediately.[6] Latency from the onset of the picture display to the beginning of the response was measured for each trial. Because of his high error rate, M. L. was tested on these materials twice with over 2 weeks separating the administrations, and the data were averaged across the two sessions.

Results

In replication of Smith and Wheeldon's (1999) findings from college-age participants, these older controls also showed longer onset latencies for the complex–simple sentences than for the simple–complex sentences. The 86-ms effect was within the range of effects they reported.

The only patient with semantic STM deficits that has been tested so far is patient M. L. As can be seen in Table 18.4, his onset latencies were much slower than were those of the control participants, even in the simple initial noun phrase condition. However, he showed a large effect of the complex versus simple manipulation with a 1,621-ms delay for the complex as compared with the simple condition—an effect about 20 times the size of the control participants' effect and 11 times larger than the largest effect shown by any of the control participants. Thus, there was evidence

TABLE 18.4

Sentence Production Onset Latencies

	REACTION TIME (IN MS)	% ERROR
Age-matched controls (n = 10)		
Simple–complex	1,530	11
Complex–simple	1,626	11
Difference	86*	0
Patient M. L.		
Simple–complex	3,135	45[a]
Complex–simple	4,756	44[a]
Difference	1,621*	−1[a]

Note.   Reaction time range for control participants was −17 to 142. [a]Wrong name, missing name, reversal. *p < .01.

---

[6]A small number of control patients have been tested with this 500-ms latency for removal of the pictures and their results are the same as for the control participants reported here.

that M. L. had great difficulty in producing an utterance in which two nouns had to be produced in the initial noun phrase. The results indicate that M. L. has difficulty maintaining more than one lexical–semantic representation simultaneously during the planning of production. Again, the findings are consistent with the notion that the same lexical–semantic buffer is used in production and comprehension.

The other striking result for M. L. is that he made many errors in both conditions. That is, in this timed production task, in which the pictures disappeared 500 ms after the onset of his production, he made many errors in omitting one of the content words or in substituting a different word for one of the targets. As M. L. is highly accurate in single-picture naming (98% correct on a test where the mean for control participants is 97%), this high error rate cannot be attributed simply to difficulty in naming pictures. Exactly what aspect of the task is causing this great difficulty remains to be determined. Most of his errors were the omission of the final noun, and thus it is likely that M. L. simply forgot the last picture to be produced by the time he reached it in his sentence production. If so, then modifying the procedure so that the pictures remain on the screen longer should reduce his error rate.

Discussion

To summarize the findings, we presented evidence supporting the contention that there are separable buffers for retaining input and output phonological representations. We also presented evidence that there appears to be one buffer that supports lexical–semantic retention in comprehension and production. Patients with a semantic retention deficit had difficulties with the same sentence constructions in production and comprehension—that is, difficulties with noun phrases with several adjectives preceding a noun and difficulties when the initial noun phrase of a sentence contained two nouns as opposed to one. However, their production was improved on more syntactically complex sentences when there was only one content word in a phrase or when the head of a phrase was the first content word in that phrase. We have argued that these data support a model of production in which semantic and syntactic planning proceed in a phrase-by-phrase fashion with phonological production awaiting retrieval of the semantic representation of the head of a phrase. Thus, having content words distributed among different phrases mitigates the difficulty these patients have in maintaining several semantic representations simultaneously.

In general, the results are consistent with the multiple components view of verbal working memory that we have advocated in the past. That is, these results support the distinction between separable capacities for semantic and phonological retention and, within phonological retention, for separate capacities for the retention of input and output representations. Our view is that these capacities are closely linked to language processing and exist to support language production and comprehension. In other domains, such as pictorial or spatial processing, there are presumably different levels of representation and storage buffers dedicated to maintaining these representations.

Now we provide some incautious speculation about the neuroanatomical localization of retention buffers for language. As discussed in the introduction, our view on STM is procedural in the sense that the products of language processing at different levels are the representations that are maintained in STM. However, along with McClelland, McNaughton, and O'Reilly (1995) we suggest that persisting activation within these various knowledge structures is not sufficient for maintaining the activation of multiple representations. Instead, these activated knowledge representations need to be linked to other brain regions in some type of reverberatory circuit that serves to keep the representations activated. Evidence from primates suggests that prefrontal brain areas may be necessary in the maintenance of activation in posterior visual or auditory processing areas for performing a task across a delay (Goldman-Rakic, 1987). In humans, temporal brain areas appear to be involved in semantic and phonological processing (e.g., see McCarthy & Warrington, 1990; Patterson, Graham, & Hodges, 1994). However, again there appear to be separate brain areas involved in maintaining phonological and semantic activation. The inferior parietal lobe appears to be involved in maintaining input phonological representations (Vallar & Papagno, 1995) and the inferior frontal gyrus in maintaining semantic representations. The latter suggestion comes from neuroimaging studies that demonstrate activation in the dorsolateral prefrontal cortex in tasks involving the manipulation of semantic representations (Fiez, 1997; Petersen, Fox, Posner, Mintun, & Raichle, 1989) and from the frontal involvement in the patients that we identified with semantic STM deficits. For maintaining output phonological representations, we have no direct evidence at present regarding localization, although some frontal language area seems likely here as well.

In conclusion, although the model in Figure 18.1 appears complicated, we would argue that all of these different components are necessary to accommodate all the findings. In contrast to a purely proceduralist view, we maintain that although processing and storage are closely linked, a separation between processing and storage components is required, and such a separation provides a better fit to findings related to brain function.

References

Allport, D. A. (1984). Auditory verbal short-term memory and conduction aphasia. In H. Bouma & D. G. Bouwhuis (Eds.), *Attention and performance X: Control and language processes* (pp. 351–364). Hillsdale, NJ: Erlbaum.

Caplan, D., & Waters, G. (1999). Verbal working memory and sentence comprehension. *Behavioral and Brain Sciences, 22,* 77–126.

Cohen, J. D., MacWhinney, B., Flatt, M., & Provost, J. (1993). PsyScope: A new graphic interactive environment for designing psychology experiments. *Behavioral Research Methods, Instruments, and Computers, 25,* 257–271.

Crowder, R. G. (1982). The demise of short-term memory. *Acta Psychologica, 50,* 291–323.

Crowder, R. G. (1993). Systems and principles in memory theory: Another critique of pure memory. In A. F. Collins, S. E. Gathercole, M. A. Conway, & P. E. Morris (Eds.), *Theories of memory* (pp. 139–161). Hove, England: Erlbaum.

de Smedt, K. (1996). Computational models of incremental grammatical encoding. In T. Dijkstra & K. de Smedt (Eds.), *Computational psycholinguistics: AI and connectionist models of human language processing* (pp. 279–307). London: Taylor & Francis.

Fiez, J. (1997). Phonology, semantics, and the role of the left inferior prefrontal cortex. *Human Brain Mapping, 5,* 79–83.

Goldman-Rakic, P. S. (1987). Circuit basis of a cognitive function in non-human primates. In S. M. Stahl & S. D. Iversen (Eds.), *Cognitive neurochemistry* (pp. 90–110). Oxford, England: Oxford University Press.

Hamburger, H., & Crain, S. (1984). Acquisition of cognitive compiling. *Cognition, 17,* 85–136.

Hebb, D. O. (1949). *The organization of behavior: A neuropsychological theory.* New York: Wiley.

Kaplan, E., Goodglass, H., & Weintraub, S. (1983). *Boston Naming Test.* Philadelphia: Lee & Febiger.

LaPointe, S. G., & Dell, G. (1989). A synthesis of some recent work in sentence production. In G. N. Carlson & M. K. Tanenhaus (Eds.), *Linguistic structure in language processing* (pp. 107–156). Boston: Kluwer Academic.

Martin, N., & Saffran, E. M. (1992). A computational account of deep dyslexia: Evidence from a single case study. *Brain and Language, 43,* 240–274.

Martin, N., & Saffran, E. M. (1997). Language and auditory–verbal short-term memory impairments: Evidence for common underlying processes. *Cognitive Neuropsychology, 14,* 641–682.

Martin, R. C. (1993). Short-term memory and sentence processing: Evidence from neuropsychology. *Memory & Cognition, 21,* 176–183.

Martin, R. (1995, November). *A multiple capacities view of working memory in language.* Paper presented at the annual meeting of the Psychonomic Society, Los Angeles, CA.

Martin, R. C., & Lesch, M. F. (1996). Associations and dissociations between language impairment and list recall: Implications for models of STM. In S. E. Gathercole (Ed.), *Models of short-term memory* (pp. 149–178). East Sussex, England: Psychology Press.

Martin, R. C., Lesch, M. F., & Bartha, M. C. (1999). Independence of input and output phonology in word processing and short-term memory. *Journal of Memory and Language, 40,* 1–27.

Martin, R. C., & Romani, C. (1994). Verbal working memory and sentence comprehension: A multiple-components view. *Neuropsychology, 8,* 506–523.

Martin, R. C., Shelton, J., & Yaffee, L. S. (1994). Language processing and working memory: Neuropsychological evidence for separate phonological and semantic capacities. *Journal of Memory and Language, 33,* 83–111.

Martin, R. C., Vu, H., & Miller, M. (2000, November). *Working memory and language production.* Poster presented at the annual meeting of the Psychonomic Society, New Orleans, LA.

McCarthy, R., & Warrington, E. (1990). *Cognitive neuropsychology: A clinical introduction.* San Diego, CA: Academic Press.

McClelland, J. L., McNaughton, B. L., & O'Reilly, R. C. (1995). Why there are complementary learning systems in the hippocampus and neocortex: Insights from the successes and failures of connectionist models of learning and memory. *Psychological Review, 102,* 419–437.

Milner, B. (1966). Amnesia following operation on the temporal lobes. In C. Whitty & O. Zangwill (Eds.), *Amnesia* (pp. 109–133). London: Butterworth.

Milner, B., Corkin, S., & Teuber, H. L. (1968). Further analysis of the hippocampal amnesic syndrome: 14 year follow-up study of H. M. *Neuropsychologica, 6,* 215–234.

Patterson, K., Graham, N., & Hodges, J. R. (1994). The impact of semantic memory loss on phonological representations. *Journal of Cognitive Neuroscience, 6,* 57–69.

Petersen, S., Fox, P., Posner, M., Mintun, M., & Raichle, M. (1989). Positron emission tomographic studies of the cortical anatomy of single-word processing. *Nature, 331,* 585–589.

Romani, C. (1992). Are there distinct input and output buffers? Evidence from an aphasic patient with an impaired output buffer. *Language and Cognitive Processes, 7,* 131–162.

Romani, C., & Martin, R. (1999). A deficit in the short-term retention of lexical–semantic information: Forgetting words but remembering a story. *Journal of Experimental Psychology: General, 128,* 56–77.

Saffran, E. M., Berndt, R. S., & Schwartz, M. F. (1989). The quantitative analysis of a grammatic production: Procedure and data. *Brain and Language, 37,* 440–479.

Shallice, T., & Butterworth, B. (1977). Short-term memory impairment and spontaneous speech. *Neuropsychologia, 15,* 729–735.

Shallice, T., & Vallar, G. (1990). The impairment of auditory–verbal short-term storage. In G. Vallar & T. Shallice (Eds.), *Neuropsychological impairments of short-term memory* (pp. 11–53). Cambridge, England: Cambridge University Press.

Smith, M., & Wheeldon, L. (1999). High level processing scope in spoken sentence production. *Cognition, 73*(3), 205–246.

Vallar, G., & Papagno, C. (1995). Neuropsychological impairments of short-term memory. In A. D. Baddeley, B. A. Wilson, & F. Watts (Eds.), *Handbook of memory disorders* (pp. 135–165). Chichester, England: Wiley.

CHAPTER 19

What Language Needs From Memory (and Vice Versa)

Arthur M. Glenberg

I have spent half of my career studying memory (as exemplified by Crowder's 1976 seminal book *Principles of Learning and Memory*) and the other half studying reading and language comprehension (as in Crowder and Wagner's 1992 concise and cogent *The Psychology of Reading: An Introduction*). Now it is time to put the two areas together, and in fact they belong together, as Crowder's contributions to the field already demonstrate. Understanding and producing language depends on memory at every stage: recognizing phonemes and words, grammatical knowledge, word meanings, and world knowledge used to construct mental models. Similarly, given that many memory paradigms are based on verbal–linguistic stimuli, an understanding of language should contribute to the understanding of memory processes. One goal of this chapter is to lay out how the two research areas can interact to their mutual benefit. A second goal is to demonstrate how recently discovered phenomena in the language domain argue for a particular kind of memory representation and to ask memory researchers for help in figuring out how to study and model those representations.

I begin with a discussion of meaning because memory and language come together naturally in this domain. Language is designed to convey meaning, and meaning plays an important role in memory by contributing to memory phenomena, such as depth of processing–conceptually driven processing, organizational processing, and distinctiveness. The discussion of meaning is framed by two new phenomena related to the linguistic combination of ideas. These phenomena demonstrate how theories based on abstract, amodal, arbitrary symbols, that is, standard propositional–semantic network–feature theories, fall short of capturing meaning. Then I describe an alternative account of meaning based on the notion of embodied cognition (Barsalou, 1999; Glenberg, 1997; Lakoff, 1987) and apply this general frame-

This work was supported in part by a grant from the University of Wisconsin—Madison Graduate School Research Committee, Project 990288.

work to linguistic meaning through a specific hypothesis, the *indexical hypothesis* (Glenberg & Robertson, 1999, 2000). This hypothesis requires a particular type of memory representation, a perceptual symbol. In contrast to abstract symbols, perceptual symbols are representations with flesh and blood. Many informal memory theories deal with perceptual-like representations (e.g., images), but formal theories, those theories that seem to carry the most weight in cognitive psychology, do not. Finally, I suggest how the indexical hypothesis helps explain memory phenomena based on meaningful processing, and I appeal to the creativity and skill of memory theorists for help in modeling these phenomena.

Meaning and Combination of Ideas: Two New Phenomena

Much of meaning seems to require the combination of ideas. To start, consider the domain of learning: Learning often results from extending ideas (i.e., world knowledge) by combining them. For example, Glenberg and Robertson (1999) studied the combination of ideas in learning to use a compass and map to identify landmarks. Of course, most of the participants in their study were familiar with components of a compass (e.g., the magnetic needle) and a map (e.g., that north is at the top). Nonetheless, learning to use the compass and map together was a challenge. Of course, the same is true in learning about a new computer or learning algebra after learning the basic operations of addition, subtraction, and so forth. A second domain in which the combination of ideas is paramount is reading for comprehension. As an example, most people know about roads and forests and mountains. What makes reading a travelogue enjoyable and informative is combining those ideas to introduce people to new lands. Third, a combination of ideas is of the utmost importance in the social domain. One may know a person well, but when one learns of that person's relationship with another person, the combination may generate a new set of social obligations.

Psychologists have developed a variety of ways to account for combinations of ideas. There are theories based on associations, grammar, propositions, networks, and convolutions. I argue, however, that none of these approaches are adequate because none can be used to distinguish between novel combinations that are nonsensical and novel combinations that make sense. People, however, can make that distinction almost effortlessly. Consider the following scenario and the three possible continuations: afforded + related, afforded, and nonafforded.

> **Scenario**: Phil was trying to get a barbecue going early in the morning for a tailgate party before the football game. He got dizzy from blowing on the coals, but they still weren't burning well.
> *Afforded + Related*: Phil grabbed a *bellows* and used it to fan the *fire*.
> *Afforded*: Phil grabbed a *map* and used it to fan the *fire*.
> *Nonafforded*: Phil grabbed a *rock* and used it to fan the *fire*.

The afforded + related sentence (using bellows) seems to make a lot of sense. So does the sentence using a map. But why does a rock not work? Note that all three continuations are grammatical. All three follow traditional selectional restrictions (e.g., the actor must be an animate noun). All three are easy to break into propositions. Nonetheless, when asked to rate the sensibility of the sentences on a scale of 1–7 (Glenberg & Robertson, 2000), participants found the afforded sentence (mean rating = 4.6) to be almost as sensible as the afforded + related sentence (6.3), whereas the nonafforded sentence was clearly unacceptable (1.2).

One might propose that "world knowledge" (i.e., associations) is used to discriminate between sensible and nonsense. That is, one has the knowledge of what a map or a rock can be used for and what they cannot be used for. In some way, that must be correct, but the sort of world knowledge incorporated into cognitive theories is not sufficient to discriminate between sensible and nonsense continuations. That is, in cognitive theories, world knowledge is conceptualized as prestored associations, propositions, or facts, such as "bellows are used to fan fires," "maps are used to find your way," and "rocks are heavy." There are three reasons why this sort of world knowledge does not help for these examples.

First, in making up the scenarios, we (Glenberg & Robertson, 2000) intentionally tried to come up with novel situations in which people would not have had direct experience (world knowledge). Have you ever used a map to fan a fire? Or in another scenario, a character uses an upright vacuum cleaner as a coat rack. Who does that? Second, we were able to demonstrate using the latent semantic analysis (LSA; Landauer & Dumais, 1997) procedure that the important concepts in the afforded sentence (*map, fire*) are just as unrelated as the important concepts in the nonafforded sentence (*rock, fire*).[1] That is, the program demonstrates that prior learning or associations are unlikely to distinguish between using a map to fan a fire and using a rock to fan a fire. Finally, if reasoning from prestored propositions was used to distinguish between the conditions, then there should be a substantial effect on reading time when comparing the afforded condition to the afforded + related condition. In the afforded + related condition, people should be able to retrieve directly "bellows are used to fan fires." But direct retrieval is unlikely in the afforded condition. Instead, people might begin by retrieving from memory facts about maps and fires and then reason that "maps are often made of folded paper," "folded paper

---

[1] The LSA computer program is given thousands of texts. From the texts, it forms a matrix with rows corresponding to individual words and columns corresponding to the texts. The cells of the matrix are filled with the count of the number of times a word appears in a text. After some preprocessing, the matrix is subjected to a singular value decomposition that computes some 300–400 important dimensions, and each word is given a score on each dimension, forming a vector for the word. Finally, one can compute the cosine between two vectors. When the cosine is near 1.0, it indicates that the words tend to occur in similar contexts; when the cosine is near 0.0, it indicates that the words appear in orthogonal contexts.

is often stiff enough to wave," "waving stiff paper is equivalent to fanning."[2] Both the retrieval processes and the inference processes should add to reading time, but in fact, there was no reliable difference in reading time between the afforded + related and afforded sentences.

So although people can distinguish between sensible novel combinations (using a map to fan a fire) and nonsense (using a rock to fan a fire), the task eludes cognitive theories of combination based on grammar, propositions, or world (associative) knowledge. How do people do it? As I describe in more detail later, knowledge of objects, such as maps and rocks, seems to include the *affordances* of those objects: how human beings can interact with them. Furthermore, one can determine whether or not affordances can be combined (or meshed) to accomplish goals, such as fanning a fire. Because the affordances of a rock (i.e., the set of possible human interactions with a rock) cannot be meshed with the actions of waving to accomplish the goal of fanning the fire, the sentence is judged as nonsensical. Why can the standard theories not handle this discrimination? I discuss that shortly, but first consider a second demonstration of combination of ideas that also causes trouble for the standard theories.

In English, one can create verbs out of nouns. In fact, these denominal verbs are very frequent (Clark & Clark, 1979)—consider such verbs as *to bicycle, to hammer, to bottle*, and so forth. One can also create these denominal verbs on the fly, and most of the time people understand them with alacrity. Two such examples from Clark and Clark are "The newsboy porched the newspaper" and "My sister Houdini'd her way out of the closet." Nonetheless, innovative denominal verbs do not always make sense. When does the combination of nouns and context make sense?

Consider the nonafforded and the afforded versions of the following passage (the innovative denominal verb appears in the last sentence):

Nonafforded: Sebastian was perusing the latest issue of *Newsweek*. He became disturbed as he read an article about rising rates of home invasions in his vicinity. Sebastian decided to follow the advice of a security expert quoted in the magazine by purchasing a home security alarm. The salesman at the electronics store thought Sebastian was insane when he insisted on having the alarm installed that very day but agreed when Sebastian threatened to terminate the sale. The alarm woke Sebastian when it began buzzing one evening. He recognized his opportunity. He magazined it.

Afforded: Sebastian was perusing the latest issue of *Newsweek* when he was disturbed by a most annoying buzzing noise. He looked around the room to determine the

---

[2]Laying out the needed propositions like this reveals another problem, namely, propositional theory requires just the right propositions at just the right time. How likely is it that people have encoded anything such as "folded paper is often stiff enough to wave" or "waving stiff paper is equivalent to fanning?"

source of this disturbance and saw that a fly was patrolling the vicinity. Its incessant buzzing was making Sebastian insane. He had no choice but to terminate with extreme prejudice. So, he rolled up his *Newsweek* and waited patiently. When the fly came to rest on the coffee table in front of Sebastian, he recognized his opportunity. He magazined it.

The verb *to magazine* seems a bit bizarre in the nonafforded context. In the afforded context, however, it reads almost as smoothly as *to bicycle* and certainly as smoothly as *Houdini'd*. The participants in the experiment (Glenberg & Robertson, 2000) felt similarly. In the afforded context, people rated the critical sentence as much more sensible (4.02 out of 7) than in the nonafforded context (2.06) or when it was presented out of context (2.69). Glenberg and Robertson also had participants try to paraphrase the critical sentence, and they examined the proportion of paraphrases consistent with the intended meaning in the afforded context. In the afforded context, 96% of the paraphrases were consistent with the intended meaning. The participants were less successful in the nonafforded context (32%) and when the sentences were presented out of context (37%).

How did people come to this new meaning? One thing is for certain: They were not depending exclusively on previously encoded information because the innovative verbs were literally invented for this experiment. Thus, any theory that supposes that meaning comes from a lexicon will be severely embarrassed by these data because *to magazine* is not in anyone's lexicon. What appears to be happening is that people consider the affordances of a magazine and whether those affordances can be meshed with the goal (i.e., to squash the fly).

Meaning: Abstract Symbol Point of View

In this section, I demonstrate why standard accounts of meaning are inadequate in general and why they fail to account for the two phenomena (regarding combination of ideas) just discussed. The exposition may remind some of the debates in the 1970s about analogue versus propositional representations that (at least in the domain of language) were won by the propositionalists. Two components of the debate have changed, however. First, there are now powerful new arguments (e.g., the Chinese room argument developed by Searle, 1980) and data (e.g., Barsalou, Solomon, & Wu, 1999) that question the adequacy of propositional theories based on abstract symbols. Second, alternative accounts of language, which are more realistic than those based on static images, are being developed (e.g., Glenberg & Robertson, 2000; Lakoff, 1987).

All current, formal theories of meaning (i.e., those implemented on a computer or whose premises are mathematical) are based on abstract, amodal, arbitrary symbols. These symbols are elements, such as nodes, links, and features encoded as numbers. The symbols are *abstract* in that the same type of node may be used to represent, say, a kitchen chair, whether it is metal or plastic or wood. The symbol is *amodal* in that the same symbol may be used whether the information is conveyed by sight, language, or touch. Most important, the symbol has an *arbitrary* relation to what it is supposed to represent: For example, the theorist may select the feature code *11011101* to represent a kitchen chair, but that set of numbers has no intrinsic relation to actual chairs, and the theorist could have used pretty much any other set of numbers.

This arbitrariness is important for several reasons. First, by using arbitrary numbers, the theorist is ensured that only the information related to the theory is included in the encoding: There is no excess information that could interfere with symbol manipulation or inference. Second, the arbitrariness is an important condition that underlies the information-processing view of thinking, reasoning, and meaning. The condition is that all meaning arises from the relations among the symbols and that all reasoning results from the manipulation of symbols. In fact, thinking is itself symbol manipulation. This is the *physical symbol system hypothesis* of Newell (1980). If thinking is symbol manipulation and symbol manipulation is to be the same in all thinking machines (human and not so), then the symbols cannot depend on the particular physical or perceptual characteristics of the machine. Instead, the symbols must be arbitrary from the point of view of the particular machine. Thus, the thinking program works the same from machine to machine because it depends only on the relations among the abstract symbols, and those relations are the same from machine to machine.

This account of symbols and thinking may not seem to correspond to the rich intuitions about memory (e.g., that it includes images) or rich intuitions about thinking (e.g., that one often thinks in particulars, not in the abstract symbols of logic). These intuitions notwithstanding, formal theories of memory and cognition are formulated using abstract, amodal, arbitrary symbols. For example, Hintzman's (1986) MINERVA II uses a vector of numbers to encode memories. The vector is nothing other than an abstract, amodal, arbitrary symbol. Of course, the same is true for all published global models of memory. Masson's (1995) connectionist theory of semantic memory makes use of an 80-place vector to represent concepts. These vectors are abstract, amodal, arbitrary symbols, as are all the representations in all connectionist networks that model memory. High dimensional space theories of meaning (Burgess & Lund, 1997; Landauer & Dumais, 1997) make use of large vectors of numbers but remain abstract, arbitrary symbols.

Semantic networks may appear different because the nodes (which are prototypical abstract, amodal, arbitrary symbols) are labeled with words. The difference is an illusion. The point of these networks is to provide the meaning of the words, that is, to define them, and that definition is supposed to arise from the system of relations to other nodes. The labels are there only for the convenience of the reader, so that the reader knows what the theorist intends a given node to stand for. But the label allows the reader to impart to the node his or her knowledge of the meaning of the word, and it is this imparting that underlies the illusion that meaning is represented. To appreciate this illusion, imagine a densely and richly connected semantic network. In this network, however, each node is labeled with *10001110*, for example. Could one determine what the network is representing? That is, is there a way to derive meaning from the relations alone? Searle's (1980) Chinese room argument (discussed below) implies that the answer is *no*.

Similarly, theories based on propositions may look different than abstract symbol theory, but they are not. A proposition is like a miniature semantic network. There is a relational term (which is itself an abstract symbol) and several arguments that are being related. Each argument is an abstract, amodal, arbitrary symbol. Hence, a proposition meant to correspond to the idea of "the chair is on the floor" may be presented as "Rel: On (Arg1:chair; Arg2:floor)." In fact, however, the words *(on, chair, floor)* are a convenience and an illusion. Within the theory, the proposition is much closer to "Rel: 001001 (Arg1:100011; Arg2:110000)." Can meaning be derived from such symbols?

Abstract symbol theories of meaning and memory have become so commonplace that people accept them uncritically. What could be wrong with them? The short answer is everything. Here is a small list of problems, many of which have been culled from Barsalou (1993), who discussed them in greater detail. Where could those symbols have come from? There is no evolutionary story that culminates in a brain with abstract, amodal, arbitrary symbols. There are no convincing cognitive development stories that describe how the specific, modal, and analogical sensory representations of the newborn and toddler get transformed into abstract symbols. When one looks into the brain, all one sees are neurons that are modal; that is, the neurons are influenced by the perceptual and motor processes many synapses downstream or upstream. How many dimensions (e.g., elements in the vector) and which dimensions (color? angle?) contribute to the abstract symbol? How are those dimensions learned? Do the dimensions of encoding stay constant (as is required for the mathematics of the theories to work) throughout one's life even though what is important will change as one matures? Abstract symbol theories provide no answers.

Furthermore, the symbol grounding problem (Harnad, 1990; Searle, 1980) is a curse on abstract symbols. The problem is revealed by Harnad's version of Searle's Chinese room argument. Both Searle and Harnad have demonstrated that contrary to the basic claim of the physical symbol system hypothesis, meaning cannot arise from the manipulation of abstract symbols. Harnad suggested that you imagine landing at an airport in a country (perhaps China) whose language you do not speak. You are equipped solely with a dictionary written in that language. You see a sign and wish to translate it. You look up the first word (an abstract, amodal, arbitrary symbol) in your dictionary to find its meaning. The definition of that word is a list of other abstract symbols, that is, more Chinese characters. So you look up the meaning of the first word in the definition to find that it is defined in terms of still other abstract symbols. The point is that you will never be able to discover the meaning of any of the symbols simply from their relations to other abstract symbols. Meaning cannot arise simply from symbol manipulation; instead, the symbols must be grounded; that is, they must make contact with something outside of the system, such as objects in the world.

But how is grounding achieved? Lakoff (1987) reviewed data and arguments about the impossibility of grounding arbitrary symbols. An important component of Lakoff's review is an argument developed by Putnam (1981). Putnam began with a set of abstract symbols that were related to one another. He then demonstrated that the set of relations was insufficient to uniquely identify the set of corresponding objects in the world. That is, any set of relations among symbols, no matter how complex, can be put into correspondence with a variety of objects sharing the same relations. In short, if one thought in terms of abstract symbols, one could never be certain what one was thinking about. At this point, the reader may be snickering: There must be something wrong with Glenberg's (and Lakoff's and Putnam's) reasoning: Clearly, one does know what one is thinking about, so how could the argument be correct? Remember, however, that the argument is meant to demonstrate problems with abstract, amodal, arbitrary symbols—not all symbols and not all thinking.

Consider again the phenomena described earlier: People can easily discriminate between descriptions of novel situations that are nonsense and those that make sense. Why is the discrimination impossible for theories based on abstract, amodal, arbitrary symbols? First, these theories cannot do what people seem to do effortlessly: simulate the combination (often using imagery) of ideas. The reason is that the symbols (e.g., 1000111) are arbitrarily related to their referents. Hence, literally moving symbols close to one another accomplishes little in contrast to moving together an image of a chair and a floor. Second, the only information that the theory has access to is that which is explicitly coded into the symbols and relations or that is logically deducible from the symbols. Thus, consider what is necessary to figure out that a map can be used to fan a fire or, in terms of abstract symbol theory, that the symbol *10011001* can be put into relation *11110001* with symbol *10011010*. The system may have encoded thousands of facts about each of the two symbols, such as "symbol 10011001 (one of the original symbols) can be put into relation 1110010 (a new relation) to symbol 11000000 (a new symbol)."

Attempting to deduce a logical relation between the two original symbols results in a combinatorial explosion that would soon overwhelm even the most powerful computers. More devastatingly, given enough time and enough facts, a logical path can be found to connect almost any two symbols. For example, a rock can be crushed into small pebbles, small pebbles can be glued together into a thin sheet, thin sheets can be waved . . . hence, a rock can be used to fan a fire. But this is just the conclusion that most people fail to derive when reading sentences, such as those used in Glenberg and Robertson (2000); that is, when the symbol system is given enough facts, it derives conclusions that people do not.

In addition to the demonstrations involving novel combinations of ideas, several other forms of empirical evidence question the hegemony of abstract symbol theories. One type of evidence comes from an investigation into the data once used to support a form of abstract symbol theory, namely, propositional theory. Strong support for propositional theory appears to come from the difficulty of processing negated sentences, such as "the star is not above the cross." Many experimenters (e.g., Carpenter & Just, 1975) have demonstrated that the time needed to verify that a negated sentence matches (or mismatches) a picture is much longer than the time needed to verify the corresponding positive sentence "The star is above the cross." According to propositional theory, the positive sentence is represented as a simple proposition, such as "above (star, cross)," whereas the negated sentence requires an embedded proposition, "not (above [star, cross])."[3] The complex embedding is thought to slow encoding of the negated sentence and to slow the comparison of the propositions underlying the sentence to those representing the picture.

There is, of course, something strange about this finding. If negated sentences are so difficult, why are they so common in natural language? Givon (1978) suggested an answer, and Glenberg, Robertson, Jansen, and Johnson-Glenberg (1999) provided the experimental evidence. According to Givon, negatives are used felicitously in particular contexts, namely, when one needs to deny a presupposition. For example, if you were to approach a friend on the street and say "What's new?" it would be odd if the friend replied, "I'm not pregnant." However, suppose that the friend had told you, perhaps many months ago, that she was trying to become pregnant. Then her reply is immediately interpretable, sensible, and felicitous. Glenberg et al. (1999) reported two findings relating to Givon's suggestion. First, the difficulty with negatives is easily replicated when they are presented out of the appropriate pragmatic context. But second, the effect disappears completely when the negated sentences are put into contexts that allow them to deny a presupposition. Thus, one of the major effects supporting propositional theory is nothing but an artifact of taking a linguistic form out of the context in which it works.

The other type of evidence strongly questioning abstract symbol theory comes from experiments conducted in Barsalou's laboratory (reviewed in Barsalou et al., 1999). These simple but powerful experiments are meant to demonstrate that much of semantic knowledge is not abstract but perceptual. In one experiment, participants were asked to list the features of a concept such as "watermelon" or "half watermelon." What would an abstract symbol theory predict? Given that a watermelon and a half watermelon are the same concept except perhaps that one is smaller, the features should be the same. But what if conceptual knowledge is perceptual; that is, one determines the features by consulting an imagelike representation and describing

---

[3] Or more properly Abstract Relation 2 (Abstract Relation 1 [Abstract Symbol 1, Abstract Symbol 2]).

the features perceived rather than consulting a list of features? In this case, the features available from an image of a watermelon and a half watermelon are different. The first is green, the second is red; the first is smooth, the second is grainy and has black seeds. As predicted by the perceptual point of view, people listed many more internal features when asked to list features of a half watermelon than when asked to list the features of a watermelon. It is important to note that this finding held for participants explicitly given imagery instructions and for those given neutral instructions that did not mention imagery.

In another experiment reported by Barsalou et al. (1999), participants verified that concepts (e.g., *monkey*) had particular properties (e.g., tail). On the false trials, the properties (e.g., banana) were associated with the concept. These associated false trials prevented participants from responding on the basis of familiarity and required consideration of the concept itself. The critical dependent variable was reaction time. Barsalou et al. reported that perceptual variables, such as size and salience of the feature in an image, accounted for a statistically significant 18–29% of the variance in reaction times. In contrast, associative variables, such as concept to property strength, did not account for a significant proportion of the variance.

The conclusion from Barsalou et al.'s (1999) experiments is that semantic information, such as features, is derived from perceptual information. On the basis of these and other data, Barsalou (1993, 1999) developed a theory of conceptual knowledge based on perceptual symbols. Perceptual symbols are not (completely) abstract, not amodal, and not arbitrary. Instead, these perceptual symbols correspond to brain states in perceptual systems and hence are often multimodal. According to Barsalou, these symbols are used in cognitive simulations. In fact, competence in using the symbols in simulations (e.g., how competently one can simulate cutting a watermelon, a monkey eating, an airplane flying, or an atom splitting) is what corresponds to knowledge, in contrast to the number of abstract, amodal, arbitrary symbols associated with the concept.

Alternative to Abstract Symbols: Embodied Meaning and the Indexical Hypothesis

Embodied approaches to meaning and cognition are being developed in several fields and multiple laboratories. In computer science, there is the work of Brooks (1991); in linguistics, Lakoff (1987), Langacker (1987), and Tomasello (1998); in philosophy, Newton (1996); in developmental psychology, Mandler (1992), Mac-Whinney (1998), and Thelen and Smith (1994); and in cognitive psychology, Barsalou (1999), Glenberg (1997), Rieser, Garing, and Young (1994), and Schwartz and Black (1999). Although there is much theoretical variability, there are several common themes. First, thinking is more a matter of biology and interaction with the environment than computation. Second and consequently, modes and processes of thinking and cognition must reflect the construction and operation of the bodies (including the perceptual systems) of the thinkers. Barsalou's notion of perceptual symbols is embodied in that those symbols are intimately dependent on how perceptual systems work rather than being divorced from perception as with arbitrary symbols.

My own approach to embodied cognition (Glenberg, 1997; Glenberg & Robertson, 1999, 2000) begins with a broad but uncontroversial speculation: Cognition has evolved. Given that, then cognition must contribute to survival and reproductive success, and that can only be through effective action that takes into account the body. For example, consider an animal (e.g., a bird) faced with a predator (e.g., a snake). Effective action for the bird includes flapping its wings and flying away. If the animal were a mole, then effective action might include diving into a hole. But if the mole tried to flap its wings or the bird tried to dive into a hole, they would be dead and not making contributions to the gene pool. Similarly for humans—one's actions must take into account the capabilities of one's body.

Given that cognition is designed (by evolution) to contribute to action and that cognition is the process by which one generates meaning through one's construal of situations, then it would be odd if action and meaning were unrelated. Instead, consider the following approach to meaning based on Glenberg (1997):

> The meaning of a situation to an individual is the set of actions available to that individual in that situation. The set of actions results from the mesh of affordances, action-based knowledge, and action-based goals.

Affordances (Gibson, 1979) are interactive qualities: how an organism, with its type of body and perceptual apparatus, can interact with an object or environment. For example, what makes an object a chair (to an adult human) is that the object affords sitting. Of course, an ordinary chair also affords many other actions—the adult can stand on it, lift it, or throw it. All of these affordances depend on the type of body the adult has. The chair does not afford sitting for an elephant. Although it does afford sitting for a toddler, it does not afford lifting and throwing for the toddler.

The meaning of a situation also depends on the individual's knowledge about the situation. So if I know that I recently glued the rickety legs in place, I must be able to use that knowledge to block the affordance of sitting or standing on the chair. Or if I know that the person who vacated the chair did so only temporarily, then my knowledge of social norms prevents me from sitting in the chair. Finally, the meaning of a situation depends on one's goal: Does one want to rest, change the bulb in a ceiling fixture, or protect oneself from a snarling dog?

Mesh is the process by which components of action (affordances, knowledge, goals) are combined to produce a coherent meaning, that is, a coherent set of effective actions. Unlike association formation or construction of propositions, mesh is a process that respects intrinsic constraints of physics and biology. That is, not all affordances can be combined to accomplish goals. Thus, I can sit in a chair to accomplish the goal of eating, but I cannot sit in the chair to accomplish the goal of changing a ceiling fixture. I can mesh the affordances of an ordinary chair (I can lift it) with the goal of protecting myself from a snarling dog, but I cannot mesh the affordances of a chair with the goal of protection from a hurricane. When mesh results in a coherent set of actions (i.e., actions that can actually be taken), one has a coherent interpretation or meaning of the situation. The mesh process works because all of the components of meaning (affordances, knowledge, goals) can be framed in terms of actions. Thus, their combination can be accomplished within the same field, namely, the field of human action.[4]

The indexical hypothesis (Glenberg & Robertson, 1999, 2000; Kaschak & Glenberg, 2000) applies the theory of embodied cognition to language. The link is needed because language is a system of abstract, amodal, arbitrary symbols. For example, the word *chair* is used whether I am talking about a big chair or a little chair, whether the chair is seen or felt, and the form of the word is arbitrary (as demonstrated by the change in form but not meaning across languages). If manipulation of abstract, amodal, arbitrary symbols cannot produce meaning, how does one understand language? According to the indexical hypothesis, there are three steps. First, words and phrases are indexed or mapped onto real objects or their perceptual symbols (Glenberg & Robertson, 1999). Second, affordances are derived from the objects or perceptual symbols (Glenberg & Robertson, 2000). Third, the affordances are meshed as directed by syntax but under the intrinsic constraints of physics and biology (Kaschak & Glenberg, 2000). The syntax of the sentence "Art is sitting on the chair" guides the mesh so that the resulting conceptualization has Art on the chair rather than vice versa. In brief, language understanding results from the combination of ideas, not simply the manipulation of abstract symbols.

The indexical hypothesis helps one to understand why some descriptions of novel situations make sense (one can form a coherent mesh of affordances to accomplish goals) and others do not. For example, one can mesh the affordances of a (road) map with the goal of fanning a fire, but one cannot mesh the affordances of a rock and the goal of fanning a fire. Understanding these sentences does not require logical deduction from premises. Instead, for both the sensible and nonsense sentences, one attempts to mesh the affordances derived from the perceptual symbols with the goals. When the mesh process is not successful, comprehension fails. Of course, if one is thinking of a map as something that appears on a computer screen, then it no longer has the affordance needed to fan a fire, and if one is thinking of a rock as a thin piece of slate, then it does have the proper affordances. But that is

---

[4]Mesh is similar to Barsalou's notion of simulation using perceptual symbols. The major difference is that mesh includes the notion of constraints, whereas it is not clear how simulation is constrained (Glenberg, 1999).

the point: The sensible combination of ideas is not simply putting words together; instead it requires indexing the words to objects (or their perceptual symbols) and deriving the affordances of the referents. Similarly, the indexical hypothesis allows one to understand when an innovative denominal verb makes sense. When the affordances of the underlying noun (e.g., a magazine) can be used to accomplish a goal (e.g., swatting a fly), the innovation is understood.

What Language Needs From Memory (and Vice Versa)

The data on understanding novel combinations and the data supporting perceptual symbols seem incontrovertible. One cannot possibly understand on the basis of the manipulation of abstract, amodal, arbitrary symbols. Instead, something like mesh is used. Given that that is the case, researchers in language comprehension need the help of memory theorists. In particular, the language researcher needs ways of investigating and modeling the sorts of representations that could be useful in the mesh process.

Of course, memory researchers have developed ideas about perceptual representations. There are theories of imagery (Paivio, 1971); there are processes that respect perceptual characteristics (e.g., L. R. Brooks, 1968); and researchers have speculated about whole memory systems devoted to perceptual representations (e.g., precategorical acoustic storage of Crowder & Morton, 1969; structural description system of Schacter, Cooper, & Treadwell, 1993). But the representations discussed do not seem to have the right characteristics to engage in mesh. In particular, these sorts of representations do not encode affordances, nor are they sensitive to intrinsic constraints. In fact, in all but their names, these representations are composed of abstract, amodal, arbitrary symbols.

Here are some of the questions about affordances that need to be resolved. First, can one come to an operational definition of an affordance that can be used to determine if a particular object has a particular affordance and if that affordance is encoded in memory? Are all memory representations in terms of affordances, or are other, perhaps abstract, characteristics also encoded? At the least, it makes sense to store something akin to Barsalou's (1999) perceptual symbols because then affordances can be derived from the symbols—one does not have to know which affordances to store for future use. But this leads to two associated problems. First, memory is better for attended features of a situation than nonattended features. If attention is drawn to particular affordances (to guide effective action in the current situation), how does one remember the whole perceptual symbol? Perhaps it is necessary to attend to at least the global features of an object to derive specific affordances, and this attention results in the storage of a perceptual symbol. The second problem is to describe how one goes about deriving affordances from a perceptual symbol (or from a real object, for that matter). Gibson (1979) proposed that affordances are directly perceived from objects in situations. Whereas that might work for real objects, at the least, it seems unsatisfactory for perceptual symbols.

Given that we develop a handle on affordances and perceptual symbols, many of the questions familiar to memory researchers can be addressed: Are affordances forgotten or rendered irretrievable? What are the mechanisms of forgetting? Can one count on proactive interference, encoding specificity, transfer-appropriate processing, priming, and other familiar phenomena to hold in this domain?

A difficult problem is to figure out whether it is possible to formalize the concept of mesh (how affordances fit together with each other and with action-based goals) and whether it is necessary to formalize the concept. As researchers, we like our theories to be as specific as possible to maximize clarity and testability. That desire has driven us toward the belief that the only good theory is a formal one (i.e., mathematical or computer simulation theory). But formalization has costs; namely, for some phenomena, formalization obfuscates rather than enhances understanding. For example, the molecular biologist must determine the shape of a protein chain to determine how an enzyme accomplishes its job: Can this shape succeed in bringing reactant surfaces in contact? It may be relatively easy to see whether the shape will work when looking at an image of the molecule. However, no one has yet determined how to formally model this sort of fit of enzyme to reactant. That is, no one has an algorithm that can determine if two randomly selected shapes fit together. In addition, formalization and abstraction may serve little use. That is, a complex mathematical description of the shape of the enzyme may not apply to other enzymes that accomplish other jobs. The important theoretical statement is nonformal; namely, the shape of the enzyme allows reactant surfaces to be brought together.

Is mesh a process that benefits from the type of formalization common in cognitive theory? Although it is too early to say for certain, I am skeptical for several reasons. First, I chose the molecular biology example for a reason. I envision the mesh process as being a type of fit similar to how folded molecular chains can fit together. If that conceptualization of the process is correct, then formalization may be inappropriate. Second, the concern for formalization of theories has grown with the acceptance of the abstract symbol theory of meaning and the computational metaphor. If thinking is a biological phenomenon, not a computational one, then the effort toward formalization may be misguided.

Do these ideas have any use for the memory theorist? The answer is *absolutely*. A major contribution of these ideas is to replace, or at least to modify, the concept of *association*. As memory researchers, we have always known that an important problem is how ideas combine. Unfortunately, we have been stuck with a weak metaphor for describing that combination, namely, an association. The metaphor is weak because it does not specify what accomplishes the combination, the circumstances under which ideas can be combined, and the constraints on the resulting combination. One way to appreciate the weakness is to note that in essence, an association is nothing more than a conditional probability: *A* is associated with *B* means that $p(A \mid B) > p(A)$. Memory researchers have tried to overcome this limitation in associations by inventing labeled associations. For example, the link between two symbols may be designated as "cause" or "next to." But this solution does not go far. First, the labels are abstract symbols that suffer from the same problems as other abstract symbols. Second, the label does not tell when a cause is inferred, how it is inferred, or what it means to be a causal relation, as opposed to any other relation. I developed these arguments elsewhere in more detail (see Glenberg, 1997).

In contrast, the metaphor of mesh suggests when ideas can be combined (when the underlying actions can be combined to accomplish goals) and that the resulting combination is emergent in the sense that it is not readily predictable from its parts. Consider two examples of emergence. First, maps can be used to locate landmarks; but they can also be used to fan fires, or when a ball is stuck under your car, a map can be spread flat, rolled into a tube, and used to prod the ball loose. Thus, the fundamental properties of a map emerge from the combination of affordances (a map can be rolled into a tube) and goals (can prod the ball). As a second example, consider manufacturing a spinner for a child's board game using an orange, a bowl of water, and a broken pencil. The jagged edge of the pencil can be thrust through the orange, and then the damaged orange can be floated in the bowl of water and spun, so that the pencil points to various game board options. In understanding the previous sentence, one's representations of damaged and unusable objects (a broken pencil, an inedible orange) are meshed to create something new with emergent properties, namely, the representation of a spinner. It is hard to imagine how a system of associations could possibly be used to determine that such a device could be built or even described.

Mesh potentially provides a handle for understanding a variety of memory phenomena. When is a retrieval cue effective? A retrieval cue is successful if the conceptualization underlying the verbal cue meshes with the conceptualization underlying the target. Hence, both conditions of encoding and conditions of retrieval must be considered, as the encoding specificity principle explains. How does organization help memory? Organizational processes generate meshed representations of nominally separate ideas. Why does enactment enhance memory (Cohen, 1981)? Enacting an action (e.g., break a match) requires a more complete specification of the mesh (because the conceptualization must be detailed enough to guide real action) than imaging the actions or talking about them. How can one understand the distinction between data-driven and conceptually driven processing? In both cases, a process of mesh is at work, but the difference is in what is meshing. For conceptually driven processing, the mesh is controlled by the characteristics (i.e., affordances) of the objects named by the verbal items. For data-driven processing, the mesh is controlled by the orthographic or auditory characteristics of the verbal item itself. For example, overt repetition of two words may literally change the musculature, so that one word becomes easier to produce given utterance of the other word. Thus, the literal actions underlying production of the words mesh. A mechanism such as this may underlie the priming of novel verbal associations (Poldrack & Cohen, 1997).

Conclusion

I began with a couple of simple demonstrations of the obvious: People can determine if newly combined ideas are sensible or not. The implications of these demonstrations are not simple, however. First, they imply that we cognitive psychologists have been fooling ourselves with our easy-to-simulate, formal theories of memory and cognition. That ease of simulation has tremendous costs. It requires the use of abstract, amodal, arbitrary symbols that cannot underlie meaning. That, in turn, forces us to generate theories and experiments that focus on structure (e.g., list length, serial position, modality, repetition) rather than what memory is surely for, namely, encoding meaningful information that guides actions. The second implication of the demonstrations is that we need to consider a type of representation that can be used to discriminate between sense and nonsense. One type of representation that has promise is the embodied perceptual symbol from which affordances can be derived. Then the combination of affordances under the constraints of biology, physics, and (when dealing with language) syntax provides a way to discriminate between sensible and nonsense combinations.

These ideas hold out the promise of bringing together a variety of disparate-appearing memory phenomena, such as levels of processing, organization, encoding specificity, priming, and so forth. A key to understanding these phenomena is to replace the tried but not true idea of an association: It is too weak of an idea to do the job. Perhaps even more difficult is that we cognitive psychologists may have to give up on the sine qua non of cognitive psychology, namely, formal theories. If cognition is inherently biological, analogical, and emergent, then we may be missing the point by insisting on computation.

References

Barsalou, L. W. (1993). Flexibility, structure, and linguistic vagary in concepts: Manifestations of a compositional system of perceptual symbols. In A. C. Collins, S. E. Gathercole, & M. A. Conway (Eds.), *Theories of memories* (pp. 29–101). London: Erlbaum.

Barsalou, L. W. (1999). Perceptual symbol systems. *Behavioral and Brain Sciences, 22,* 577–660.

Barsalou, L. W., Solomon, K. O., & Wu, L.-L. (1999). Perceptual simulation in conceptual tasks. In M. K. Hiraga, C. Sinha, & W. Wilcox (Eds.), *Cultural, typological, and psychological perspectives in cognitive linguistics: The proceedings of the 4th Conference of the International Cognitive Linguistics Association* (Vol. 3, pp. 209–228). Amsterdam, The Netherlands: Benjamins.

Brooks, L. R. (1968). Spatial and verbal components in the act of recall. *Canadian Journal of Psychology, 22,* 349–368.

Brooks, R. A. (1991). Intelligence without representation. *Artificial Intelligence Journal, 47,* 139–159.

Burgess, C., & Lund, K. (1997). Modelling parsing constraints with high-dimensional context space. *Language and Cognitive Processes, 12,* 177–210.

Carpenter, P. A., & Just, M. A. (1975). Sentence comprehension: A psycholinguistic processing model of verification. *Psychological Review, 82,* 45–73.

Clark, E., & Clark, H. H. (1979). When nouns surface as verbs. *Language, 55,* 767–811.

Cohen, R. L. (1981). On the generality of some memory laws. *Scandinavian Journal of Psychology, 22,* 267–281.

Crowder, R. G. (1976). *Principles of learning and memory.* Hillsdale, NJ: Erlbaum.

Crowder, R. G., & Morton, J. (1969). Precategorical acoustic storage (PAS). *Perception and Psychophysics, 5,* 365–373.

Crowder, R. G., & Wagner, R. K. (1992). *The psychology of reading: An introduction* (2nd ed.). New York: Oxford University Press.

Gibson, J. J. (1979). *The ecological approach to visual perception.* New York: Houghton-Mifflin.

Givon, T. (1978). Negation in language: Pragmatics, function, ontology. In P. Cole (Ed.), *Syntax and semantics 9: Pragmatics* (pp. 61–112). New York: Academic Press.

Glenberg, A. M. (1997). What memory is for. *Behavioral and Brain Sciences, 20,* 1–55.

Glenberg, A. M. (1999). Perceptual symbols in language comprehension. *Behavioral and Brain Sciences, 22,* 618–619.

Glenberg, A. M., & Robertson, D. A. (1999). Indexical understanding of instructions. *Discourse Processes, 28,* 1–26.

Glenberg, A. M., & Robertson, D. A. (2000). Symbol grounding and meaning: A comparison of high-dimensional and embodied theories of meaning. *Journal of Memory and Language, 43,* 379–401.

Glenberg, A. M., Robertson, D. A., Jansen, J. L, & Johnson-Glenberg, M. C. (1999). Not propositions. *Journal of Cognitive Systems Research, 1,* 19–33.

Harnad, S. (1990). The symbol grounding problem. *Physica D, 42,* 335–346.

Hintzman, D. L. (1986). "Schema abstraction" in a multiple-trace memory model. *Psychological Review, 93,* 411–428.

Kaschak, M. P., & Glenberg, A. M. (2000). Constructing meaning: The role of affordances and grammatical constructions in sentence comprehension. *Journal of Memory and Language, 43,* 508–529.

Lakoff, G. (1987). *Women, fire, and dangerous things: What categories reveal about the mind.* Chicago: University of Chicago Press.

Landauer, T. K., & Dumais, S. T. (1997). A solution to Plato's problem: The latent semantic analysis theory of acquisition, induction, and representation of knowledge. *Psychological Review, 104,* 211–240.

Langacker, R. W. (1987). *Foundation of cognitive grammar. Vol. 1: Theoretical prerequisites.* Stanford, CA: Stanford University Press.

MacWhinney, B. (1998). The emergence of language from embodiment. In B. MacWhinney (Ed.), *The emergence of language* (pp. 213–256). Mahwah, NJ: Erlbaum.

Mandler, J. M. (1992). How to build a baby: II. Conceptual primitives. *Psychological Review, 99,* 587–604.

Masson, M. E. J. (1995). A distributed memory model of semantic priming. *Journal of Experimental Psychology: Learning, Memory, and Cognition, 21,* 3–23.

Newell, A. (1980). Physical symbol systems. *Cognitive Science, 4,* 135–183.

Newton, N. (1996). *Foundations of understanding.* Philadelphia: Benjamins.

Paivio, A. (1971). *Imagery and verbal processes.* New York: Holt, Rinehart & Winston.

Poldrack, R. A., & Cohen, N. J. (1997). Priming of new associations in reading time: What is learned. *Psychonomic Bulletin and Review, 4,* 398–402.

Putnam, H. (1981). *Reason, truth, and history.* Cambridge, England: Cambridge University Press.

Rieser, J. J., Garing, A. E., & Young, M. F. (1994). Imagery, action and young children's spatial orientation: It's not being there that counts, it's what one has in mind. *Child Development, 65,* 1262–1278.

Schacter, D. L., Cooper, L. A., & Treadwell, J. (1993). Preserved priming of novel objects across size transformation in amnesic patients. *Psychological Science, 4,* 331–335.

Schwartz, D., & Black, T. (1999). Inferences through imagined actions: Knowing by simulated doing. *Journal of Experimental Psychology: Learning, Memory, and Cognition, 25,* 116–136.

Searle, J. R. (1980). Minds, brains and programs. *Behavioral and Brain Sciences, 3,* 417–424.

Thelen, E., & Smith, L. B. (1994). *A dynamic systems approach to the development of cognition and action.* Cambridge, MA: MIT Press.

Tomasello, M. (1998). *The new psychology of language.* Mahwah, NJ: Erlbaum.

Vita of Robert G. Crowder
(September 16, 1939–July 27, 2000)

Education

BA, Psychology, University of Michigan, 1960
PhD, Psychology, University of Michigan, 1965

Undergraduate Academic Honors

Oreon E. Scott Freshman Scholarship Award, 1958
Phi Beta Kappa, 1959
Graduated with High Distinction and High Honors in Psychology, 1960
Fulbright Fellowship for study in France, 1960–1961

Employment

Lecturer in Psychology, Yale University, 1965
Assistant Professor of Psychology, Yale University, 1965–1969
Associate Professor of Psychology, Yale University, 1969–1976
Professor of Psychology, Yale University, 1976–2000
Investigator, Haskins Laboratories, 1976–2000

Administration

Director of Graduate Studies, Psychology, 1969–1972
Director of Undergraduate Studies, Psychology, 1973–1976, 1985–1995
Director, Social Sciences Center, Summer Term, 1978
Acting Chair, Psychology, Spring Term, 1982

Professional Societies and Recognitions

Acoustical Society of America (Member)
American Men and Women in Science (Listed)
American Psychological Association (Fellow)
   Division 3 Executive Committee (Member-at-Large), 1981–1983
American Psychological Society (Fellow)
Center for Advanced Study in the Behavioral Sciences (Fellow), 1982–1983
Eastern Psychological Association (Member)

National Institutes of Mental Health: Cognition, Emotion, and Personality Initial
Review Group (Member), 1983–1988; (Chair), 1986–1988
Psychonomic Society
Governing Board (Member), 1981–1986
Publications Committee (Member), 1981–1983
Society of Experimental Psychologists (Member)
University of Bologna, Bologna, Italy, Spring Term (Contract Professor), 1987

Editorships

Acta Psychologica (Consulting Editor), 1976–1991
Journal of Experimental Psychology: Learning, Memory, and Cognition (Consulting Editor), 1982–1999
Journal of Verbal Learning and Verbal Behavior, now *Journal of Memory and Language* (Consulting Editor), 1971–1993
Memory & Cognition (Editor), 1977–1981, (Consulting Editor), 1990–2000
Music Perception (Consulting Editor), 1988–2000
Psychonomic Bulletin and Review (Consulting Editor), 1992–1999

Publications: Books

Crowder, R. G. (1976). *Principles of learning and memory.* Hillsdale, NJ: Erlbaum.
Crowder, R. G. (1982). *The psychology of reading: An introduction.* New York: Oxford
University Press.
(1985). *Psicologia de la lectura.* Madrid, Spain: Alianza Editorial. (Spanish translation)
(1987). *Psicologia della lettura.* Bologna, Italy: Il Mulino. (Italian translation)
Crowder, R. G., & Wagner, R. K. (1992). *The psychology of reading: An introduction,
second edition.* New York: Oxford University Press.
Schab, F. R., & Crowder, R. G. (1995). *Memory for odors.* Mahwah, NJ: Erlbaum.

Publications: Research Articles

Crowder, R. G., & Melton, A. W. (1965). The Ranschburg phenomenon: Failures of
immediate recall correlated with repetition of elements within a series. *Psychonomic
Science, 2,* 295–296.
Carluccio, L., & Crowder, R. G. (1966). Constant order of pairs in the presentation
and testing of paired associates. *Journal of Experimental Psychology, 72,* 614–616.
Crowder, R. G. (1966). Visual presentation of stimuli in immediate memory. *Psychonomic Science, 6,* 449–450.
Crowder, R. G., Chisholm, D. D., & Fell, D. A. (1966). Transfer from serial to
continuous paired-associate learning. *Psychonomic Science, 6,* 455–456.
Crowder, R. G. (1967a). Prefix effects in immediate memory. *Canadian Journal of
Psychology, 21,* 450–461.

Crowder, R. G. (1967b). Proactive and retroactive inhibition in the retention of a T-maze habit in rats. *Journal of Experimental Psychology, 74,* 167–171.

Crowder, R. G. (1967c). Reciprocity of retention and interpolated-task scores in short-term memory. *Perceptual and Motor Skills, 24,* 903–909.

Crowder, R. G. (1967d). Short-term retention for words with a perceptual-motor interpolated task. *Journal of Verbal Learning and Verbal Behavior, 6,* 753–761.

Crowder, R. G. (1968a). Evidence for the chaining hypothesis of serial verbal learning. *Journal of Experimental Psychology, 76,* 497–500.

Crowder, R. G. (1968b). The relation between interpolated-task performance and proactive inhibition in short-term memory. *Journal of Verbal Learning and Verbal Behavior, 7,* 577–583.

Crowder, R. G. (1968c). Repetition effects in immediate memory when there are no repeated elements in the stimuli. *Journal of Experimental Psychology, 78,* 605–609.

Crowder, R. G. (1968d). Intraseriel repetition effects in immediate memory. *Journal of Verbal Learning and Verbal Behavior, 7,* 446–451.

Crowder, R. G., Cole, M., & Boucher, R. (1968). Extinction and response competition in original and interpolated learning of a visual discrimination. *Journal of Experimental Psychology, 77,* 422–428.

Crowder, R. G. (1969a). Behavioral strategies in immediate memory. *Journal of Verbal Learning and Verbal Behavior, 8,* 90–94.

Crowder, R. G. (1969b). Improved recall for digits with delayed recall cues. *Journal of Experimental Psychology, 82,* 258–262.

Crowder, R. G. (1969c). On free recall and free recall scoring in immediate memory. *Psychonomic Science, 14,* 255–256.

Crowder, R. G. (1969d). Phonic interference and the prefix effect. *Journal of Verbal Learning and Verbal Behavior, 8,* 302–304.

Crowder, R. G., & Hoenig, Y. J. (1969). Intertrial competition and prefix effect. *Journal of Experimental Psychology, 79,* 368–370.

Crowder, R. G., & Morton, J. (1969). Precategorical acoustic storage (PAS). *Perception & Psychophysics, 5,* 365–373.

Crowder, R. G. (1970). The role of one's own voice in immediate memory. *Cognitive Psychology, 1,* 157–178.

Crowder. R. G., & Raeburn, V. P. (1970). The stimulus suffix effect with reversed speech. *Journal of Verbal Learning and Verbal Behavior, 9,* 342–345.

Crowder, R. G. (1971a). The sound of vowels and consonants in immediate memory. *Journal of Verbal Learning and Verbal Behavior, 10,* 587–597.

Crowder, R. G. (1971b). Waiting for the stimulus suffix: Decay, delay, rhythm, and readout in immediate memory. *Quarterly Journal of Experimental Psychology, 23,* 324–340.

Morton, J., Crowder, R. G., & Prussin, H. A. (1971). Experiments with the stimulus suffix effect. *Journal of Experimental Psychology, 91,* 169–190.

Wearing, A. J., & Crowder, R. G. (1971). Dividing attention to study sentence processing. *Journal of Verbal Learning and Verbal Behavior, 10,* 254–261.

Darwin, C. J., Turvey, M. T., & Crowder, R. G. (1972). An auditory analogue of the Sperling partial-report procedure. *Cognitive Psychology, 3,* 255–267.

Crowder, R. G., & Davis, K. L. (1972). The relation between lisping and visual recognition memory in children. *Perception & Psychophysics, 11,* 391–396.

Roediger, H. L., & Croweder, R. G. (1972). Instructed forgetting: Rehearsal control or retrieval inhibition? *Cognitive Psychology, 3,* 244–254.

Crowder, R. G. (1973a). The delayed stimulus suffix effect following arrhythmic stimulus presentation. *Quarterly Journal of Experimental Psychology, 25,* 433–439.

Crowder, R. G. (1973b). Precategorical acoustic storage for vowels of short and long duration. *Perception & Psychophysics, 13,* 502–506.

Crowder, R. G. (1973c). Representation of speech sounds in precategorical acoustic storage. *Journal of Experimental Psychology, 93,* 14–24.

Crowder, R. G., & Cheng, C. M. (1973). Phonemic confusability, precategorical acoustic storage, and the suffix effect. *Perception & Psychophysics, 15,* 145–148.

Watkins, M. J., Watkins, O. C., & Crowder, R. G. (1974). The modality effect in free and serial recall as a function of phonological similarity. *Journal of Verbal Learning and Verbal Behavior, 13,* 430–447.

Roediger, H. L., & Crowder, R. G. (1975). The spacing of lists in free recall. *Journal of Verbal Learning and Verbal Behavior, 14,* 590–602.

Crowder, R. G. (1976). The locus of the lexicality effect in short-term memory for phonologically identical lists. *Bulletin of the Psychonomic Society, 7,* 361–363.

Roediger, H. L., & Crowder, R. G. (1976a). Recall instructions and the suffix effect. *American Journal of Psychology, 89,* 115–125.

Roediger, H. L., & Crowder, R. G. (1976b). A serial position effect in recall of United States presidents. *Bulletin of the Psychonomic Society, 8,* 275–278.

Crowder, R. G. (1978a). Mechanisms of backward masking in the stimulus suffix effect. *Psychological Review, 85,* 502–524.

Crowder, R. G. (1978b). Memory for phonologically uniform lists. *Journal of Verbal Learning and Verbal Behavior, 17,* 73–89.

Repp, B., Healy, A. F., & Crowder, R. G. (1979). Categories and context in the perception of isolated, steady-state vowels. *Journal of Experimental Psychology: Human Perception and Performance, 5,* 129–145.

Crowder, R. G. (1982a). A common basis for auditory memory in perception and immediate memory. *Perception & Psychophysics, 31,* 477–483.

Crowder, R. G. (1982b). Decay of auditory information in vowel discrimination. *Journal of Experimental Psychology: Human Learning and Memory, 8,* 153–162.

Crowder, R. G. (1982c). The demise of short-term memory. *Acta Psychologica, 50,* 291–323.

Crowder, R. G. (1982d). Disinhibition of masking in auditory sensory memory. *Memory & Cognition, 10,* 424–433.

Nairne, J. S., & Crowder, R. G. (1982). On the locus of the stimulus suffix effect. *Memory & Cognition, 10,* 350–357.

Crowder, R. G. (1983). The purity of auditory memory. *Philosophical Transactions of the Royal Society of London, B, 382,* 251–265.

Crowder, R. G. (1984). Perception of the major/minor distinction. I. Historical and theoretical foundations. *Psychomusicology, 4,* 1–12.

Crowder, R. G., & Repp, B. H. (1984). Single-format contrast in vowel identification. *Perception & Psychophysics, 35,* 372–378.

Greene, R. L., & Crowder, R. G. (1984a). The effect of semantic similarity on long-term recency. *American Journal of Psychology, 97,* 441–449.

Greene, R. L., & Crowder, R. G. (1984b). Modality and suffix effects in the absence of auditory stimulation. *Journal of Verbal Learning and Verbal Behavior, 23,* 371–382.

Serafine, M L., Crowder, R. G., & Repp, B. H. (1984). Integration of melody and text in memory for song. *Cognition, 16,* 285–303.

Crowder, R. G. (1985a). Perception of the major/minor distinction. II. Experimental investigations. *Psychomusicology, 5,* 3–24.

Crowder, R. G. (1985b). Perception of the major/minor distinction. III. Hedonic, musical, and affective discriminations. *Bulletin of the Psychonomic Society, 23,* 314–316.

Crowder, R. G. (1986). Auditory and temporal factors in the modality effect. *Journal of Experimental Psychology: Learning, Memory, and Cognition, 12,* 268–278.

DeWitt, L., & Crowder, R. G. (1986). Recognition of novel melodies after brief delays. *Music Perception, 3,* 259–274.

Greene, R. L., & Crowder, R. G. (1986). Recency effects in delayed recall of mouthed stimuli. *Memory & Cognition, 14,* 355–360.

Serafine, M. L., Davidson, J., Crowder, R. G., & Repp, B. H. (1986). On the nature of melody-text integration in memory for songs. *Journal of Memory and Language, 25,* 123–135.

Crowder, R. G., & Greene, R. L. (1987). On the remembrance of times past: The irregular list technique. *Journal of Experimental Psychology: General, 116,* 265–278.

DeWitt, L., & Crowder, R. G. (1987). Tonal fusion of consonant musical intervals: The oomph in Stumpf. *Perception & Psychophysics, 41,* 73–84.

Greene, R. L., & Crowder, R. G. (1988). Memory for serial position: Effects of spacing, vocalization, and stimulus suffixes. *Journal of Experimental Psychology: Learning, Memory, and Cognition, 14,* 740–748.

Schab, F. R., & Crowder, R. G. (1988). The role of succession in temporal cognition: Is the time-order error a recency effect in memory? *Perception & Psychophysics, 44,* 233–242.

Banaji, M., & Crowder, R. G. (1989). The bankruptcy of everyday memory. *American Psychologist, 44,* 1185–1193. [Reprinted in J. Rubenstein & B. Slife (Eds.), *Taking sides: Clashing views on controversial psychological issues* (6th ed.). Guilford, CT: Dushkin.]

Crowder, R. G. (1989). Imagery for musical timbre. *Journal of Experimental Psychology: Human Perception and Performance, 15,* 472–478.

Schab, F. R., & Crowder, R. G. (1989). Accuracy of temporal coding: Auditory–visual comparisons. *Memory & Cognition, 17,* 384–397.

Crowder, R. G., Serafine, M. L., & Repp, B. H. (1990). Physical interaction and association by contiguity in memory for the words and melodies of songs. *Memory & Cognition, 18,* 469–476.

Kastner, M. P., & Crowder, R. G. (1990). Perception of the major/minor distinction. IV: Emotional connotations in young children. *Music Perception, 8,* 189–202.

Neath, I., & Crowder, R. G. (1990). Schedules of presentation and temporal distinctiveness in human memory. *Journal of Experimental Psychology: Learning, Memory, and Cognition, 16,* 316–327.

Repp, B. H., & Crowder, R. G. (1990). Stimulus order effects in vowel discrimination. *Journal of Acoustical Society of America, 88,* 2080–2090.

Crowder, R. G., Reznick, J. S., & Rosenkrantz, S. L. (1991). Perception of the major/minor distinction. V: Preferences among infants. *Bulletin of the Psychonomic Society, 29,* 187–188.

Pitt, M. A., & Crowder, R. G. (1992). The role of spectral and dynamic cues in imagery for musical timbre. *Journal of Experimental Psychology: Human Perception and Performance, 18,* 728–738.

Neath, I., Surprenant, A. M., & Crowder, R. G. (1993). The context-dependent stimulus suffix effect. *Journal of Experimental Psychology: Human Perception and Performance, 19,* 698–703.

Speer, S. R., Crowder, R. G., & Thomas, L. M. (1993). Prosodic structure and sentence recognition. *Journal of Memory and Language, 32,* 336–358.

Surprenant, A. M., Pitt, M. A., & Crowder, R. G. (1993). Auditory recency in immediate memory. *Quarterly Journal of Experimental Psychology, 46A,* 193–223.

Crowder, R. G., & Neath, I. (1995). The influence of pitch on time perception in short melodies. *Music Perception, 12,* 379–386.

Neath, I., & Crowder, R. G. (1996). Distinctiveness and very short-term serial position effects. *Memory, 4,* 225–242.

Marks, A. R., & Crowder, R. G. (1997). Temporal distinctiveness and modality. *Journal of Experimental Psychology: Learning, Memory, and Cognition, 23,* 164–180.

Publications: Book Chapters

Crowder, R. G. (1972). Visual and auditory memory. In J. F. Kavanagh & I. G. Mattingly (Eds.), *Language by ear and by eye: The relation between speech and learning to read.* Cambridge, MA: MIT Press.

Crowder, R. G. (1975). Inferential problems in echoic memory. In P. M. A. Rabbit & S. Dornic (Eds.), *Attention and performance V.* London: Academic Press.

Crowder, R. G. (1978a). Audition and speech coding in short-term memory. In J. Requin (Ed.), *Attention and performance VII.* Hillsdale, NJ: Erlbaum.

Crowder, R. G. (1978b). Language and memory. In J. F. Kavanagh & W. N. Strange (Eds.), *Speech and language in the laboratory, school, and clinic.* Cambridge, MA: MIT Press.

Crowder, R. G. (1978c). Sensory memory systems. In E. C. Carterette & M. P. Friedman (Eds.), *Handbook of perception* (Vol. 9). New York: Academic Press.

Crowder, R. G. (1979). Similarity and order in memory. In G. H. Bower (Ed.), *The psychology of learning and memory* (Vol. 13). New York: Academic Press.

Crowder, R. G. (1980). Echoic memory and the study of aging memory systems. In L. W. Poon, J. L. Fozard, L. S. Cermak, D. Arenberg, & L. W. Thompson (Eds.), *New directions in memory and aging.* Hillsdale, NJ: Erlbaum.

Crowder, R. G. (1981). The role of auditory memory in speech perception and discrimination. In T. Meyers, J. Laver, & J. Anderson (Eds.), *The cognitive representation of speech.* Amsterdam, The Netherlands: North-Holland.

Crowder, R. G. (1982). General forgetting theory and the locus of amnesia. In L. S. Cermak (Ed.), *Human memory and amnesia.* Hillsdale, NJ: Erlbaum.

Crowder, R. G. (1984). Current issues in the psychology of reading. In H. Stevenson & C. Q. Jing (Eds.), *Proceedings of the first US–China conference.* Washington, DC: National Academy of Science.

Crowder, R. G. (1985a). Access and the forms of memory. In N. M. Weinberger, J. L. McGaugh, & G. Lynch (Eds.), *Memory systems of the brain: Animal and human cognitive processes.* New York: Guilford Press.

Crowder, R. G. (1985b). Basic theoretical concepts in human learning and cognition. In L. G. Nilsson & T. Archer (Eds.), *Perspectives on animal learning and human memory: The Umeå Conference.* Hillsdale, NJ: Erlbaum.

Crowder, R. G., & Greene, R. L. (1987). The context of remembering: Comments on the chapters by Glenberg, Gorfein, and Wickens. In D. S. Gorfein & R. R. Hoffman (Eds.), *Memory and learning: The Ebbinghaus Centennial Conference.* Hillsdale, NJ: Erlbaum.

Crowder, R. G. (1989). Modularity and dissociations of memory systems. In H. L. Roediger, III, & F. I. M. Craik (Eds.), *Varieties of memory and consciousness: Essays in honour of Endel Tulving.* Hillsdale, NJ: Erlbaum.

Crowder, R. G. (1991a). Imagery and the perception of musical timbre. In G. R. Lockhead & J. R. Pomerantz (Eds.), *The perception of structure: Essays in honor of Wendell R. Garner.* Washington, DC: American Psychological Association.

Crowder, R. G. (1991b). The microscope metaphor in human memory. In W. E. Hockley & S. Lewandowsky (Eds.), *Relating theory and data: Essays on human memory in honor of Bennet B. Murdock.* Hillsdale, NJ: Erlbaum.

Crowder, R. G., & Pitt, M. A. (1992). Research on memory/imagery for musical timbre. In D. Reisberg (Ed.), *Auditory image.* Hillsdale, NJ: Erlbaum.

Crowder, R. G. (1993a). Auditory memory. In S. McAdams & E. Bigand (Eds.), *Thinking in sound: The cognitive psychology of human audition.* Oxford, England: Oxford University Press.

Crowder, R. G. (1993b). Faith and skepticism in memory research. In G. M. Davies & R. H. Logie (Eds.), *Memory in everyday life*. Amsterdam, The Netherlands: North-Holland.

Crowder, R. G. (1993c). Systems and principles in memory theory: Another critique of pure memory. In A. F. Collins, S. E. Gathercole, M. A. Conway, & P. E. Morris (Eds.), *Theories of memory*. East Sussex, England: Erlbaum.

Banaji, M. R., & Crowder, R. G. (1994). Experimentation and its discontents. In P. E. Morris & M. Grunewald (Eds.), *Theoretical aspects of memory, second edition*. London: Routledge.

Crowder, R. G., & Schab, F. R. (1995). Imagery for odors. In F. R. Schab & R. G. Crowder (Eds.), *Memory for odors*. Mahwah, NJ: Erlbaum.

Crowder, R. G., & Surprenant, A. M. (1995). On the linguistic module in auditory memory. In B. de Gelder & J. Morais (Eds.), *Language and literacy: Comparative approaches*. East Sussex, England: Erlbaum.

Schab, F. R., & Crowder, R. G. (1995a). Implicit measures of odor memory. In F. R. Schab & R. G. Crowder (Eds.), *Memory for odors*. Mahwah, NJ: Erlbaum.

Schab, F. R., & Crowder, R. G. (1995b). Odor recognition memory. In F. R. Schab & R. G. Crowder (Eds.), *Memory for odors*. Mahwah, NJ: Erlbaum.

Crowder, R. G. (1996). The trouble with prospective memory: A provocation. In M. Brandimonte, G. O. Einstein, & M. McDaniel (Eds.), *Prospective memory: Theory and applications*. Mahway, NJ: Erlbaum.

Crowder, R. G., & Greene, R. L. (2000). Serial learning: Cognition and behavior. In E. Tulving & F. I. M. Craik (Eds.), *The Oxford handbook of memory*. Oxford, England: Oxford University Press.

Crowder, R. G., & Surprenant, A. M. (2000). Sensory memory. In A. E. Kazdin (Ed.), *Encyclopedia of psychology*. New York: Oxford University Press and American Psychological Association.

Glenberg, A. M., & Crowder, R. G. (2000). Melton, Arthur. In A. E. Kazdin (Ed.), *Encyclopedia of psychology*. New York: Oxford University and American Psychological Association.

Publications: Major Reviews, Comments, and Miscellaneous

Crowder, R. G. (1976a). Learning. In *Collier's encyclopedia* (Vol. 14). New York: Macmillan.

Crowder, R. G. (1976b). Learning and motivation back in the classroom [Review of G. H. Bower (Ed.), *Psychology of learning and motivation: Advances in research and theory* (Vol. 9)]. *Contemporary Psychology, 21*, 688–689.

Crowder, R. G. (1977). A handbook for what purpose? [Review of W. K. Estes (Ed.), *Handbook of learning and cognitive processes. Vol. 4: Attention and memory*]. *Contemporary Psychology, 22*, 368–369.

Crowder, R. G. (1984a). Broadbent's Maltese cross memory model: Wisdom, but not particularly unconventional. *Brain and Behavioral Sciences, 7,* 72.

Crowder, R. G. (1984b). Is it just reading? Comments on the papers of Mann, Morrison, and Wolford and Fowler. *Developmental Review, 4,* 48–61.

Crowder, R. G. (1986a). A history of subliminal perception in autobiography. *Brain and Behavioral Sciences, 9,* 28–29.

Crowder, R. G. (1986b). Remembering experience and the experience of remembering. *Brain and Behavioral Sciences, 9,* 566.

Crowder, R. G. (1989). Categorical perception of speech: A largely dead horse, surpassingly well kicked. *Brain and Behavioral Sciences, 12,* 760.

Banaji, M. R., & Crowder, R. G. (1991). Some everyday thoughts on ecologically valid methods. *American Psychologist, 46,* 78–79.

Crowder, R. G. (1992a). Adaptation and learning as models for learning and memory. *Contemporary Psychology, 37,* 139–142.

Crowder, R. G. (1992b). Review of *Neurological impairments of short-term memory,* by G. Vallar & T. Shallice (Eds.). *American Journal of Psychology, 105,* 136–140.

Crowder, R. G. (1993). Short-term memory: Where do we stand? *Memory & Cognition, 21,* 142–145.

Author Index

Numbers in italics refer to listings in reference sections.

Subject Index

About the Editors

Henry L. Roediger III, PhD, is the James S. McDonnell Distinguished University Professor and department chair at Washington University in St. Louis, MO. He received a BA in psychology from Washington and Lee University and a PhD from Yale University, where he worked with Robert G. Crowder and Endel Tulving. He taught at Purdue University, the University of Toronto, and Rice University before coming to Washington University in 1996. His research interests focus on issues surrounding implicit measures of memory and illusions of memory. He edited the *Journal of Experimental Psychology: Learning, Memory, and Cognition,* was founding editor of *Psychonomic Bulletin and Review,* and currently serves as a consulting editor for four other journals. He is the coauthor of three textbooks that been through a combined 17 editions. He is a member of the Society of Experimental Psychologists and has served as president of the Midwestern Psychological Association, chair of the Governing Board of the Psychonomic Society, and president of Division 3 (Experimental Psychology) of the American Psychological Association. He held a Guggenheim Fellowship in 1994–1995, and he is a Fellow of the American Association for the Advancement of Science, the American Psychological Association, the American Psychological Society, and the Canadian Psychological Association.

James S. Nairne, PhD, is a professor of psychological sciences at Purdue University in West Lafayette, IN. He received his undergraduate training from the University of California at Berkeley and his PhD in psychology from Yale University. His research specialty is human memory, following in the functionalist tradition of his thesis advisor, Robert G. Crowder. He is an associate editor for the *Journal of Memory and Language* and a consulting editor for *Memory,* and he has served on several editorial boards, including the boards of the *Journal of Experimental Psychology: Learning, Memory, and Cognition* and *Memory & Cognition.* His introductory psychology textbook *Psychology: The Adaptive Mind* is now in its second printing. He recently received the Year 2000 Excellence in Education Award from Purdue University and was a G. Stanley Hall invited speaker at the 2000 Annual Convention of the American Psychological Association in Washington, DC.

Ian Neath, PhD, is an associate professor of psychological sciences at Purdue University in West Lafayette, IN. He received his BA from Rice University in 1987 and PhD in cognitive psychology from Yale University in 1991. He recently authored a textbook on human memory and is a member of the Psychonomic Society.

Aimée M. Surprenant, PhD, is an associate professor of psychological sciences at Purdue University in West Lafayette, IN. She received her PhD in cognitive psychology from Yale University in 1992 and spent 2 years as a postdoctoral Fellow in Indiana University's Department of Speech and Hearing Sciences. Her research focuses on the effects of noise on the perception of and memory for auditorily presented information. She a member of the Psychonomic Society, the Acoustical Society, and the American Psychological Association.